MAINE

VERMONT

Augusta ★

Montpelier ★ N.H.

★ Concord

MASS.

Albany ★ Boston ★

NEW YORK ★ Providence

Hartford ★ RHODE ISLAND

CONNECTICUT

NESOTA

St. Paul ★ WISCONSIN

Madison ★

MICHIGAN

Lansing ★

IOWA

Des Moines ★

ILLINOIS INDIANA OHIO

Springfield ★ Indianapolis ★ Columbus ★

PENNSYLVANIA

Harrisburg ★ ★ Trenton

NEW JERSEY

Dover

DELAWARE

WASHINGTON, D.C. ✪ ★ Annapolis

MARYLAND

W. VA. Richmond

Charleston ★ ★ Richmond

ka

Jefferson City ★

MISSOURI

Frankfort ★ VIRGINIA

KENTUCKY

★ Nashville

TENNESSEE Raleigh ★

N. C.

Little Rock ★

ARKANSAS MISS. ALABAMA

Columbia ★

★ Atlanta S. C.

Jackson ★ Montgomery ★ GEORGIA

LOUISIANA

★ Tallahassee

Baton Rouge ★

FLORIDA

STATE AND LOCAL GOVERNMENT

The Essentials

STATE AND LOCAL GOVERNMENT

The Essentials

FOURTH EDITION

Ann O'M. Bowman
University of South Carolina

Richard C. Kearney
North Carolina State University

Houghton Mifflin Harcourt Publishing Company
Boston   New York

The fourth edition of *State and Local Government: The Essentials* is dedicated to states and localities; innovators and change makers.

Publisher: Suzanne Jeans
Senior Sponsoring Editor: Traci Mueller
Marketing Manager: Edwin Hill
Discipline Product Manager: Lynn Baldridge
Senior Development Editor: Jeffrey Greene
Associate Project Editor: Susan Miscio
Senior Media Producer: Lisa Ciccolo
Content Manager: Janet Edmonds
Art and Design Manager: Jill Haber
Cover Design Director: Tony Saizon
Senior Photo Editor: Jennifer Meyer Dare
Senior Composition Buyer: Chuck Dutton
New Title Project Manager: Patricia O'Neill
Editorial Assistant: Sareeka Rai
Marketing Assistant: Samantha Abrams

Cover Photo: © Richard Hamilton Smith/Corbis

Printed in the U.S.A.

Library of Congress Control Number: 2007939712

ISBN-13: 978-0-618-96828-2
ISBN-10: 0-618-96828-8

3456789-EB-12 11 10 09 08

CONTENTS

8 Public Administration: Budgeting and Service Delivery 166

9 The Judiciary 195

10 State–Local Relations 223

11 Local Government: Structure and Leadership 243

12 Taxing and Spending 269

PREFACE

This book is unabashedly pro-government—state and local government, that is. Despite the drumbeat of criticism of government and public officials in the mass media, we like politics and public service. We believe that government can be a force for good in society. We do acknowledge some of the concerns voiced by critics of government. Yes, there continue to be inefficiencies, and sure, there are some politicians who, once elected, seem to forget the interests of the people back home, not to mention what their parents taught them. But by and large, state and local governments work well. On a daily basis, they tackle some of the toughest problems imaginable, designing and implementing creative and successful solutions to problems ranging from crime and corrections to education and the environment.

The full-length edition of State and Local Government will continue to appear at regular intervals. But some instructors prefer to assign a briefer paperback text to accommodate the demands of a quarter system, to leave time for other readings, and for many other reasons. In this fourth abbreviated edition of our text, we again attempt to capture the essentials of state and local government in all their immediacy and vitality. A major goal is to foster continuing student interest and involvement in state and local politics, policy, and public service. Many of the students who read this text will work in state and local government. Some will run successfully for public office. All, no matter where they work, will deal with state and local government throughout their lives. We want our readers to know that state and local government is a place where one person can still make a difference and serve a cause. For students who go on to graduate study in political science, public administration, or related fields, states and localities are fertile fields for research. And for those who are taking this course because they "have to" and who claim to dislike politics and government, we hope they will keep an open mind as they explore the contemporary world of politics at the grass roots.

THE THEME OF *STATE AND LOCAL GOVERNMENT: THE ESSENTIALS*

This book revolves around a central theme: The increased capacity and responsiveness of state and local governments. In a way, this is yesterday's news. It has been decades since these levels of government were routinely dismissed as outmoded and ineffective. But state and local governments continue to be proactive, expanding their capacity to address effectively the myriad problems confronting their citizens. And from Alabama to Wyoming, they are increasingly more responsive to their rapidly changing environment and the demands of the citizens.

Our confidence in these governments does not blind us, however, to the varying capabilities of the 50 states and more than 88,000 units of local government. Some are better equipped to operate effectively than others. Many state and local governments benefit from talented leadership, a problem-solving focus, and an engaged citizenry. Others do not fare so well and their performance disappoints. Still, as a group, states and localities are the driving forces—the prime movers—in the American federal system. Even those jurisdictions perennially clustered at the lower end of various ratings scales have made quantum leaps in their capability and responsiveness.

MAJOR CHANGES IN THE FOURTH EDITION

The political landscape of state and local government is forever changing. As a result, the fourth edition incorporates many new topics and emerging issues, without sacrificing the central theme of increased governmental capacity and responsiveness. Among the fresh items are the growing importance of "culture wars," the most recent data on elections and citizen participation, the changing role of political parties and other organizations in campaigns, the efforts to reform and restrain state legislatures, and the renewed interest in regional governance. Moreover, the fourth edition contains new material on key court decisions and efforts to evaluate systematically judges' performance, and market-based methods for delivering public services. The public administration chapter includes new sections on the surprisingly large unfunded liabilities of retiree pensions and health care. In exploring these topics and issues, we emphasize the differences across states and localities. In the fourth edition, coverage of local governments has been expanded and new examples of policymaking have been added. Finally, we have made numerous updates to the tables and figures in the book, which yield opportunities for students to conduct their own web-based research.

STRUCTURE AND CONTENT UPDATES

This book provides basic and up-to-date coverage of state and local institutions, processes, and policies. It can be used as a "stand-alone" text or in conjunction with supplementary readings.

In Chapter 1, we introduce the functions of nonnational governments and explore the theme of capacity and responsiveness. The central importance of federalism and intergovernmental relations is recognized in Chapter 2, which traces the twists and turns of the federal system from the scribblings of the framers to the Supreme Court's latest pronouncements on the Tenth Amendment. This chapter also includes a section on tribal governments and discussion of the pause in devolution. The evolution and modern reform of the fundamental legal underpinnings of state governments—their constitutions—are discussed in Chapter 3. Chapter 4 explores citizen participation and elections, focusing on the increased access of citizens and the demands they are making on government. Chapter 5, "Political Parties, Interest Groups, and Campaigns," includes essential material on party organization and interparty competition. Types and techniques of interest groups and the "new era" of political campaigns also receive attention.

Coverage of the three branches of government—legislative, executive, and judicial—includes results of the 2007 elections. Legislative dynamics, behavior, processes, and capacity are illustrated in Chapter 6. The roles, responsibilities, and powers of governors are examined in Chapter 7, with illustrations from today's chief executives. Chapter 8 offers coverage of public administration, budgeting, and personnel policy, along with the politics of bureaucracy and the privatization, new public management, and e-government movements. In Chapter 9, judicial selection and decisionmaking are considered within the context of judicial federalism and state court reform. A section on crime and criminal justice illustrates the importance of the state judiciary.

Local governments, although still considered to be creatures of the state, are not treated as afterthoughts in this book. Most of the chapters provide a local dimension, whether political processes or governmental institutions. In addition, two chapters focus explicitly on the localities. Chapter 10 is devoted to state–local relations, including the distribution of authority between the two levels of government, and the all-important issue of urban sprawl and smart growth. Chapter 11 focuses on the multiple types and structures of local government and on leadership and governance in these jurisdictions. Finally, in Chapter 12, the principles and political economy of taxing and spending are explained, along with the gradual recovery of the states and localities from the fiscal crisis that struck most of them in the early 2000s.

Throughout the text, policy examples are used to illustrate key concepts and critical points. Policymaking is, after all, a central function of government, regardless of level. Special attention is given to education, criminal justice, economic development, social welfare, and environmental protection policy.

Those who prefer a more comprehensive and detailed treatment of state and local government, including separate policy chapters, are invited to examine the seventh edition of *State and Local Government* by the same authors (Houghton Mifflin, ©2008, ISBN 978-0-618-77089-2).

Much effort has been invested in making this book accessible to students. Examples throughout the chapters showcase the innovative, the unusual, and the insightful in state and local politics. New photographs provide visual images to bring the current world of state and local government to life for the reader. Maps, tables, and figures provide recent information in an engaging, colorful format. A glossary of key terms is located in the margins of the text. Each chapter opens with a chapter outline and a number of focus questions intended to highlight the chapter's most important issues and to spark discussion about the material. At the end of each chapter, major points are bulleted in a Chapter Recap section. References to websites, which can be accessed through the book's website, **college. hmco.com/pic/bowmanessentials4e**, encourage student curiosity, engagement, and individual research.

TEACHING AND LEARNING AIDS

In addition to the chapter-by-chapter links, the companion website makes a number of other resources available to students and instructors. For instructors, we offer PowerPoint slides of key tables, figures, and illustrations from the text and a computerized test bank. Our "Evolution of Devolution" timeline illustrates how the capacity and responsibilities of state and local governments have fluctuated over time.

A very helpful Instructor's Resource Manual with Test Items, written by Professor Jeffrey Greene of the University of Montana, is available to the instructor.

The manual features learning objectives, chapter overviews, suggested readings and lecture topics, multiple-choice questions, terms for identification, and essays.

On-line ACE practice questions allow students to test their understanding of important concepts. They will also find flashcards to review important terms and definitions. Both sites are accessible at **college.hmco.com/pic/bowmanessentials4e.**

ACKNOWLEDGMENTS

First, we would like to thank our colleagues who reviewed the fourth edition of the Essentials version. They provided us with many thoughtful observations and examples that we have incorporated whenever possible. These include Roy Dawes, Gettysburg College, Steven Schrier, Suffolk County Community College; James E. Tejkowski, Lewis & Clark Community College; and Nelson Wikstrom, Virginia Commonwealth University.

We also extend our appreciation to the good folks at Houghton Mifflin, especially the persistent Jeff Greene, Traci Mueller, and Susan Miscio. Research assistance at the University of South Carolina was provided by Milton Stark. At North Carolina State University, Danielle Seale assisted with various aspects of the book. Kathy Morgan compiled the user-friendly, comprehensive index. Finally, Carson, Blease, Kathy, Joel, and Laura contributed in many special ways to the final product, as usual. We assure them that they are not taken for granted.

A. O'M. B.
R. C. K.

STATE AND LOCAL GOVERNMENT

The Essentials

New Directions for State and Local Government

1

CHAPTER OUTLINE

Studying State and Local Government in the Twenty-First Century

The Capacity of States and Localities

The People: Designers and Consumers of Government

Linking Capacity to Results

FOCUS QUESTIONS

1. In what ways have state and local governments changed over the last two decades?

2. What are some of the challenges facing state and local governments today?

3. What are some of the qualities that characterize state governments today?

With appropriate oratorical flourishes, the New York Governor, Eliot Spitzer, delivered his 2008 State of the State message. Although parts of the speech were specific to the state—such as the references to the Poughkeepsie Rail Bridge over the Hudson River—many of the themes resonated beyond New York's borders. Economic growth, health care, tax reform, and educational improvements were topics in countless gubernatorial addresses throughout the country. Governor Spitzer's themes were universal; his upbeat "we can do this together" exhortations have been echoed in one state capitol after another. Several times during his speech, the Governor alluded to the adventurous and courageous explorers who, 400 years ago, traversed the area that became New York. He ended his speech with these words: "We are dreamers, visionaries, environmentalists, and builders of the first order. If we embrace those traits that have long defined New Yorkers—determination, pragmatism, optimism, compassion and good hard work—we too can make that journey to a better New York."[1] In New York and elsewhere, state and local governments are indeed leading the country into the future.

STUDYING STATE AND LOCAL GOVERNMENT IN THE TWENTY-FIRST CENTURY

The study of state and local government has typically received short shrift in the survey of U.S. politics.[2] Scholars and journalists tend to focus on glamorous imperial presidents, a rancorous and gridlocked Congress, and an independent and powerful Supreme Court. National and international issues capture the lion's share of media attention. Yet state and local politics are fascinating, precisely because they are up close and personal. True, a governor seldom gets involved in an international peace conference; state legislatures rarely debate global economics. But the actors and institutions of states and localities are directly involved in our day-to-day lives. Education, welfare, health care, and crime are among the many concerns of state and local governments. These issues affect all of us. Table 1.1 provides a sample of new state laws that took effect in 2008.

From Sewers to Science: The Functions of State and Local Governments

State and local governments are busy. They exist, in large measure, to make policy for and provide services to the public. This is no easy task. Nonnational governments must operate efficiently, effectively, and equitably, and they must do so with limited financial resources. An efficient government is one that maximizes the output (services) from a given input (resources). A government performs effectively if it accomplishes what it sets out to do. Another expectation is that gov-

TABLE 1.1   A Sample of New State Laws Taking Effect in 2008

STATE	DESCRIPTION OF THE LAW
Arizona	Increases the penalty for businesses that knowingly hire illegal immigrants
California	Prohibits businesses from injecting microchips into employees
Colorado	Gives homeowners more time to pay delinquent mortgage payments
Illinois	Bans photographing people without their permission in restrooms and tanning salons
Minnesota	Outlaws the use of mercury in cosmetics, including mascara and eyeliner
New Hampshire	Offers same-sex couples the state-level rights provided by traditional marriage
New York	Creates a bill of rights for stranded airline passengers
North Carolina	Requires businesses that sell alcohol to recycle beverage containers
Oklahoma	Provides an online site listing state tax breaks given to corporations
Texas	Levies a $5 per customer charge at strip clubs
Washington	Bans the sending of text messages via cell phone while driving

SOURCE: Pauline Vu, "New Year Ushers in New Laws," www.stateline.org (December 28, 2007).

ernment function fairly—that its services be delivered in an equitable manner. It is no wonder, then, that state and local governments constantly experiment with new programs and new systems for delivering services, all the while seeking efficiency, effectiveness, and equity. For instance, the massive restructuring of Wyoming's state government was intended, according to the governor, to produce "a better method of delivering services from the state government to the citizens."[3] Each year, the Ford Foundation sponsors "Innovations in American Government" awards to recognize the creativity that abounds in governments throughout the nation. Five jurisdictions are selected for the prestigious and lucrative prize. The criteria for the awards are that the government's innovation be original, successful, and easily replicated by other jurisdictions. Among the winners of the innovation award in 2007 were:

- Florida's online ACCESS system, which simplifies and streamlines the process of applying for public assistance.
- North Carolina's Community Care network, which provides affordable health care in rural areas of the state.
- Seattle's Climate Protection Initiative, which aims to reduce the emissions of carbon dioxide in the city.
- Genesee County, Michigan's Urban Land Program, which has developed new solutions for problems related to property abandonment.[4]

Although some of the winning innovative projects are internal to government operations and carry the promise of increased efficiency, others have a policy goal, such as education or economic development. The unifying characteristic is governmental willingness to try something new.

Our Approach

The argument of this book is that states and localities have the capacity to play central roles in the U.S. federal system. **Capacity** refers to a government's ability to respond effectively to change, make decisions efficiently and responsively, and manage conflict.[5] Capacity, then, is tied to governmental capability and performance. In short, states and communities with capacity work better than those without it.

But what factors make one government more capable than another? Governmental institutions such as the bureaucracy matter. The fiscal resources of a **jurisdiction** and the quality of its leadership make a difference. Much of the research on capacity has focused on the administrative dimension of government performance, evaluating items such as financial management, information technology, and strategic planning. In a recent study of state government performance, the highest overall scores went to Utah and Virginia (each state received an A–) and Delaware, Kentucky, Michigan, Minnesota, and Washington (with grades of B+).[6] Earlier evaluations of forty large counties had Fairfax, Virginia, and Maricopa, Arizona, earning the best grades. Among the thirty-five cities examined, Austin, Texas, and Phoenix, Arizona, were at the top of the list. Other things being equal, we would expect high-scoring states, counties, and cities to produce "better" government than low-scoring jurisdictions.

capacity

The ability of government to respond effectively to change, make decisions efficiently and responsively, and manage conflict.

jurisdiction

The territorial range of government authority; "jurisdiction" is sometimes used as a synonym for "city" or "town."

A survey in Iowa showed another side to governance. When asked about the characteristics of good government, Iowans put trustworthiness, ethics, financial responsibility, and accountability at the top of the list.[7] Residents of the Hawkeye State are not unusual; all of us want our institutions and leaders to govern honestly and wisely. As political scientist David Hedge reminds us, better government is found in jurisdictions that are responsible and democratic.[8] But states and localities face significant challenges as they govern. Complex, often contradictory forces test the most capable of governments. State and local governments need all the capacity they can muster and maybe even a little bit of luck to meet those challenges.

Federalism

A system of government in which powers are divided between a central (national) government and regional (state) governments.

Federalism, with its overlapping spheres of authority, provides the context for state and local action. Intervention by the national government in the affairs of a state or local government is defensible, even desirable in some cases. For example, the environmental problems of the 1960s and 1970s exceeded state and local governments' ability to handle them, so corrective action by the national government was generally welcomed. However, some federal actions are greeted less enthusiastically. For instance, No Child Left Behind (NCLB), the education law promoted by President George W. Bush in 2002, was considered too intrusive by many state leaders and school districts. Throughout the country, legislators debated resolutions challenging the authority of this federal law; and by the time Congress took up its reauthorization in 2007, state leaders were demanding more flexibility and more funding to implement the law's provisions.[9]

Our approach takes into account intergovernmental relations (that is, the relationships among the three levels of government)—particularly the possibilities for cooperation and conflict. Jurisdictions (national, state, or local) possess policymaking authority over specific, but sometimes overlapping, territory. They confront innumerable situations in which boundaries blur and they must work together to accomplish an objective. This point was brought home most vividly in the wake of the September 11, 2001, terrorist attacks on the United States, and again, four years later, when Hurricane Katrina struck the Gulf Coast. Local governments were the first to respond, but before long, federal and state governments were heavily involved. Each level of government tends to see problems from its own perspective and design solutions accordingly. In sum, both cooperation and conflict define the U.S. federal system.

THE CAPACITY OF STATES AND LOCALITIES

With notable exceptions, states and their local governments in the 1950s and 1960s were havens of traditionalism and inactivity. Many states were characterized by unrepresentative legislatures, glad-handing governors, and a hodge-podge court system. Public policy tended to reflect the interests of the elite; delivery of services was frequently inefficient and ineffective. According to former North Carolina governor Terry Sanford, the states "had lost their confidence, and people their faith in the states."[10] No wonder that, by comparison, the federal government appeared to be the answer, regardless of the question. In fact, political scientist Luther Gulick proclaimed, "It is a matter of brutal record. The American State is finished. I do not predict that the states will go, but affirm that they have gone."[11]

Those days are as outmoded as a black-and-white television set. States and their local governments have proved themselves capable of designing and implementing "an explosion of innovations and initiatives."[12] As a result, even many national leaders have embraced the roles of states and localities as laboratories for policy experimentation. A 2002 *New York Times* story with the headline, "As Congress Stalls, States Pursue Cloning Debate," is indicative of states pushing the policy envelope.[13]

The blossoming of state governments in the 1980s—their transformation from weak links in the federal chain to viable and progressive political units—resulted from several actions and circumstances.[14] In turn, the resurgence of state governments has generated a host of positive outcomes. During the 1990s, states and localities honed their capacity and became **proactive** rather than reactive. They faced hard choices and creatively crafted new directions. A word of caution is necessary, however. Not all states enjoy the same level of capacity, and furthermore, fiscal stresses such as those endured by state governments in the early 2000s sorely test the ability of even the most capable states to function effectively.

proactive

An anticipatory condition, as opposed to a reactive one.

How States and Localities Increased Their Capacity

Several factors contributed to the resurgence of the states. U.S Supreme Court decisions in the 1960s on legislative apportionment made for more equitable representation; the extension of two-party competition in the 1970s to states formerly dominated by one party gave voters more choices. At the same time, states and localities expanded their lobbying presence in the nation's capital, exerting influence on the design and funding of intergovernmental programs.

Most important, state governments quietly and methodically reformed themselves by modernizing their constitutions and restructuring their institutions. During the past three decades, more than three-quarters of the states have ratified new constitutions or substantially amended existing ones. Formerly thought of as the "drag anchors of state programs" and as "protectors of special interests,"[15] these documents have been streamlined and made more workable. Even in states without wide-ranging constitutional reform, tinkering with constitutions is almost endless, thanks to the amendment process. Almost every state general election finds constitutional issues on the ballot.

States have also undertaken various internal adjustments intended to improve the operations of state governments.[16] Modernized constitutions and statutory changes have strengthened the powers of governors by increasing appointment and removal powers and by allowing longer terms, consecutive succession, larger staffs, enhanced budget authority, and the power to reorganize the executive branch. Throughout the country, state agencies are staffed by skilled administrators. The bureaucracy itself is more and more demographically representative of the public. Annual rather than biennial sessions, more efficient rules and procedures, additional staff, and higher salaries have helped make reapportioned state legislatures more professional, capable, and effective. State judicial systems have also been the targets of reform; examples include the establishment of unified court systems, the hiring of court administrators, and the creation of additional layers of courts.

Increased Capacity and Improved Performance

The enhanced capacity enjoyed by state and local governments has generated a range of mostly positive results. The five factors discussed below reinforce the performance of states and localities.

Improved Revenue Systems Economic downturns and limits on taxing and spending have caused states to implement new revenue-raising strategies to maintain acceptable service levels. States also granted local governments more flexibility in their revenue systems. South Carolina, for example, now allows counties the option of providing property-tax relief to residents while increasing the local sales tax.

rainy day funds

Money set aside when a state's finances are healthy, for use when state revenues decline. Formally called "budget stabilization funds."

As a rule, state governments prefer to increase user charges, gasoline taxes, and so-called sin taxes on alcohol and tobacco and only reluctantly raise sales and income taxes. Over time, revenue structures have been redesigned to make them more diversified and more equitable. State **rainy day funds,** legalized gambling through state-run lotteries and pari-mutuels, and extension of the sales tax to services are examples of diversification strategies. Exemptions of food and medicine from consumer sales taxes and the enactment of property-tax breaks for poor and elderly people characterize efforts at tax equity. These revamped revenue structures helped states deal with the budget crises they confronted in the early 2000s.

Funds raised by New Mexico's specialty license plate help to restore and preserve landmarks along the state's portion of historic Route 66.

SOURCE: © AP/New Mexico Department of Revenue

States continue to tinker with their revenue-raising schemes. One successful foray into creative revenue raising has been the specialty license plate. Maryland, for example, has generated hundreds of thousands of dollars with its "Treasure the Chesapeake" plate. Monies generated by the plates are earmarked for special programs—in this case, water-quality monitoring and erosion control in the Chesapeake Bay. Nearly all states now offer specialty plates. In New York for instance, owners can equip their cars, for an extra fee, with license plates honoring their favorite professional sports team or NASCAR driver. A brand new approach to generating cash for states comes from the world of retail stores: the marketing of official gift cards. For example, both Kentucky and Ohio sell gift cards that can be used at state park locations for various park services and merchandise.

Another effort of enterprising localities is to sell merchandise. Los Angeles County has marketed coroner toe tags as key chains; Portland and Tampa rent the entire outside surfaces of their buses to advertisers. New York City, which loses thousands of street signs (Wall Street is especially popular) to souvenir-stealing tourists, now sells replicas. But the revenue generated by those actions is dwarfed by Chicago, which has sold (actually, leased for 99 years) four city-owned parking garages to an investment bank for a tidy sum of $563 million. As these examples show, states and localities are willing to experiment when it comes to revenue enhancement.

Expanding the Scope of State Operations State governments have taken on new roles and added new functions. In some instances, states are filling in the gap left by the national government's de-emphasis of an activity; in other cases, states are venturing into uncharted terrain. It was states that designed the first family leave legislation giving workers time off to care for newborn babies and ailing relatives and the first Amber Alert systems to broadcast information about abducted children. The federal government eventually followed suit with a national family leave act and a national Amber Alert system. In addition, states have taken the initiative in ongoing intergovernmental programs by creatively using programmatic authority and resources. Prior to federal welfare reform in the mid-1990s, several states had established workfare programs and imposed time limits on the receipt of welfare benefits, provisions that were at the center of the subsequent federal legislation.

The innovative behavior continues. Illinois and Wisconsin launched I-SaveRx, the first state-sponsored program to help residents buy cheaper prescription drugs in Ireland and Canada. States persist in expanding their scope of operations, whether it is California's venture into stem-cell research or Florida's strides in bioterror readiness. New York has proposed a new program to fight childhood obesity, Active-8 Kids; Texas has launched a privately funded transportation project to construct thousands of miles of high-speed toll lanes capable of carrying cars, trucks, and trains. In short, states are embracing their role as policy innovators and experimenters in the U.S. federal system.

Faster Diffusion of Innovations Among states, there have always been leaders and followers. The same is true for local governments. Now that states and localities have expanded their scope and are doing more policymaking, they are looking more frequently to their neighbors for advice, information, and models.[17] As a result, successful solutions spread from one jurisdiction to another. For example, Florida was the first state to create a way for consumers to stop telephone solicitations. By 1999, five more states had passed laws letting residents put their names on a "do-not-call" list for telemarketers. Seven additional states adopted similar legislation over the next two years before Congress enacted a national statute.[18] Another fast-moving innovation was a 2004 New York law that required cigarettes that were sold in the state to be self-extinguishing. Concerned over fire safety, California followed suit and by 2007, nineteen other states had adopted the law.[19]

Local-level innovations spread rapidly, too. Education and environmental protection offer many examples of this phenomenon. When Dade County, Florida, hired a private company to run a public elementary school, other school districts hoping to improve quality and cut costs quickly followed suit. Initial experiments with privatization spawned other innovations such as charter schools. The issue of global warming was addressed at the local level in 2005 when the mayor of Seattle became the first local official to commit his city to a plan to reduce the emission of greenhouse gases. By 2007, more than 650 mayors of other U.S. cities had jumped on the global warming bandwagon.[20] It is worth noting, of course, that the diffusion of new ideas depends in large part on their fit and effectiveness.

Obviously, state and local governments learn from one another. Communication links are increasingly varied and frequently used. A state might turn to nearby states when searching for policy solutions. Regional consultation and emulation is logical: Similar problems beset jurisdictions in the same region, a program used in a neighboring state may be politically more acceptable than one from a distant state, and organizational affiliations bring state and local administrators together with their colleagues from nearby areas.

Interjurisdictional Cooperation Accompanying the quickening flow of innovations has been an increase in interjurisdictional cooperation. States are choosing to confront and resolve their immediate problems jointly. A similar phenomenon has occurred at the local level with the creation of regional organizations to tackle areawide problems collectively. Interjurisdictional collaboration takes many forms, including informal consultations and agreements, interstate committees, legal contracts, reciprocal legislation, and interstate compacts. For example, all fifty states and the District of Columbia have a mutual agreement to aid one another when natural disasters such as hurricanes, earthquakes, and forest fires strike. Five states—Mississippi, Minnesota, West Virginia, Florida, and Massachusetts—were among the first to band together to share information and design tactics in their lawsuits against tobacco companies in the mid-1990s; by 1998, thirty-seven other states had joined in the effort to recover the Medicaid costs of treating tobacco-caused diseases.[21] In the same year, twenty states filed an antitrust lawsuit against Microsoft Corporation, claiming that the firm illegally stifled competition, harmed consumers, and undercut innovation in the computer software industry. In another instance, nine eastern states decided that the best way to compel large power plants to reduce their carbon emissions was to band together in a regional effort.[22] By 2007, forty-four states had joined the Streamlined Sales Tax Project, an ongoing effort to craft an interstate agreement on the simplification of sales and use taxes. The intent is to make it easier for states to collect taxes on items purchased online on the Internet. In each of these instances, the states worked together because they could see some benefit from cooperation.

Increased jurisdictional cooperation fosters a healthy climate for joint problem solving. In addition, when state and local governments solve their own problems, they protect their power and authority within the federal system. It appears that states are becoming more comfortable working with one another. The beginning of the twenty-first century was indeed historic. States were engaged in more cooperative interactions than ever before.[23]

Increased National-State Conflict An inevitable by-product of more capable state and local governments is intensified conflict with the national government. One source of this discord has been federal laws and grant requirements that supersede state policy; another is the movement of states onto the national government's turf. National-state conflict is primarily a cyclical phenomenon, but contention has increased in recent years. The issue of unfunded mandates—the costly requirements that federal legislation imposes on states and localities—has been particularly troublesome. In an effort to increase the visibility of the mandates issue, several national organizations of state and local officials sponsored a "National Unfunded Mandate Day" in both 1993 and 1994. Making a strong case against mandates, then-governor George Voinovich of Ohio stated: "Unfunded mandates devastate our budgets, inhibit flexibility and innovation in implementing new programs, preempt important state initiatives, and deprive states of their responsibility to set priorities."[24] Congress responded in 1995 by passing a mandate relief bill that requires cost-benefit analyses of proposed mandates; however, the law contains some loopholes that have weakened its impact.

Conflict between the national government and the states has characterized various policy areas: the removal of the exemption of local governments from federal antitrust laws (laws against business monopolies), disagreement over energy and water resources, the minimum drinking age, the speed limit on interstate highways, air- and water-quality standards, interstate trucking, severance taxes (fees imposed on the extraction of natural resources such as petroleum), registration and taxation of state and municipal bonds, offshore oil drilling, land management and reclamation, and the storage and disposal of hazardous chemical wastes. Some of the disputes pit a single state against the national government, as in Nevada's fight to block the U.S. Energy Department's plan to build a nuclear fuel waste storage facility 100 miles northwest of Las Vegas. In other conflicts, the national government finds itself besieged by a coordinated, multistate effort, for example, when ten states sued the U.S. Environmental Protection Agency over the regulation of greenhouse gases.[25]

National-state conflicts are resolved (and sometimes made worse) by the federal judicial system. Cases dealing with alleged violations of the U.S. Constitution by state and local governments are heard in federal courts and decided by federal judges. Sometimes the rulings take the federal government into spheres long considered the purview of state and local governments.

Challenges Facing State and Local Governments

Increased capacity does not mean that all state and local problems have been solved. Nonnational governments face three tough challenges today: fiscal stress, interjurisdictional conflict, and political corruption.

Fiscal Stress The most intractable problem for states and localities involves money. Given the cyclical peaks and troughs in the national economy as well as the frequent fundamental changes in public finance, state and local finances remain vulnerable. Both the early 1990s and the early 2000s provide evidence of that vulnerability.

As the 1990s dawned, recessionary clouds hovered over the financial horizon. Policymakers in cash-strapped states searched furiously for solutions. New York faced a budget shortfall of close to $1 billion; California, a whopping $9 billion. By the fall of 1991, thirty-one states had raised taxes by a combined $16.2 billion, and twenty-nine states had cut spending by $7.5 billion.[26] Others followed the California approach and tried to stave off fiscal imbalance by **downsizing** state agencies. As those tactics took effect and as the economy rebounded, states were enjoying revenue boomlets by the mid-1990s. By the end of the decade, states had amassed huge surpluses, and in legislature after legislature, cutting taxes, eliminating surcharges, and funding new programs became priorities.

> **downsizing**
> Reducing the size and cost of something, especially government.

However, states cannot afford to become complacent when it comes to revenues, as the events of the early 2000s demonstrated. An economic downturn again created conditions of fiscal stress for states and localities. "Nearly every state faced budget gaps beginning in fiscal year 2002, and those gaps grew in fiscal 2003 and 2004."[27] As expected, states responded by drawing on their rainy day funds, using trust fund surpluses, and seeking special financing mechanisms. But these actions only went so far, and states were still forced to increase taxes (especially on tobacco products and alcohol), impose new fees, and cut spending.[28] By 2007, the economic picture was brighter, but fiscal stress remains a serious threat, even for the most capable of states.

Increased Interjurisdictional Conflict Tension is inherent in a federal system because each of the entities has its own set of interests, as well as a share of the national interest. When one state's pursuit of its interests negatively affects another state, conflict occurs. Such conflict can become destructive, threatening the continuation of state resurgence. In essence, states end up wasting their energies and resources on counterproductive battles among themselves.

Interjurisdictional conflict is particularly common in two policy areas very dear to state and local governments: natural resources and economic development. States rich in natural resources want to use these resources in a manner that will yield the greatest return. Oil-producing states, for instance, levy severance taxes that raise the price of oil. And states with abundant water supplies resist efforts by arid states to tap into the supply. The most serious disputes often occur among neighboring states. One illustration is the protracted dispute between California and six other western states over water allocations from the Colorado River. In short, the essential question revolves around a state's right to control a resource that occurs naturally and that is highly desired by other states. Resource-poor states argue that resources are in fact national and should rightfully be shared among states.

In the area of economic development, conflict is extensive because all jurisdictions want healthy economies. Toward this end, states try to make themselves attractive to business and industry through tax breaks and regulatory relaxation. Conflict arises when states become involved in bidding wars—that is, when an enterprise is so highly valued that actions taken by one state are matched and exceeded by another. Suppose, for example, that an automobile manufacturer is considering shutting down an existing facility and relocating. States hungry for manufacturing activity will assemble a package of incentives such as below-cost land, tax concessions, and subsidized job training in an attempt to attract the manufacturer. The state that wants to keep the manufacturer will try to match these inducements. In the long run, economic activity is simply relocated from one state to another. The big winner is the manufacturer.

A particularly fascinating interjurisdictional contest involves the recurring rounds of U.S. military base closures and consolidations. Military bases are economic plums that no jurisdiction wants to lose. Thus states mount public relations efforts to protect local bases and to grab jobs that will be lost in other states. Politics and lobbying are supposed to play no role in the Pentagon's decisions about which bases will remain open and which ones will close, but states prefer to hedge their bets. In the 2005 round, Texas devoted $250 million to defend its bases, Massachusetts allocated $410 million. As one observer put it, "It is a war of all against all."[29]

Political Corruption Corruption exists in government, which is no great surprise. Most political systems can tolerate the occasional corrupt official, but if corruption becomes commonplace, it undermines governmental capacity and destroys public trust. Public reaction ranges from cynicism and alienation (corruption as "politics as usual") to anger and action (corruption as a spur to reform). A survey found that the more extreme the corrupt act (a city clerk embezzling $100,000 versus a police officer accepting free food at a restaurant), the harsher the public's judgment.[30] Even so, mitigating motives or circumstances tend to reduce the public's outrage (for example, a public official taking a bribe but using the money to pay his sick child's hospital bills). But governmental scandals have been linked tentatively to another negative effect—a slowdown in economic growth. Research on states found that federal corruption convictions are associated with declines in job growth primarily because, from a business perspective, corruption creates uncertainty and inflates costs.[31]

transparency

A characteristic of a government that is open and understandable, one in which officials are accountable to the public.

States and localities have taken great precautions to reduce the amount of wrongdoing occurring in their midst. Government has much more **transparency** than ever before, with more openness and more rules. But the statutes and policies are only as good as the people whose behavior they regulate. There are numerous examples of corrupt behavior. In 2005, Governor Bob Taft and several other state and local officials in Ohio ran afoul of state ethics laws by failing to disclose gifts they had received from lobbyists. (Governor Taft was also embroiled in "coingate," a scandal related to the investment of state funds in rare coins.) Former Illinois governor George Ryan was convicted in 2006 on federal charges of taking payoffs, gifts, and vacations in return for government contracts and leases while he was Illinois secretary of state. In 2007, federal agents charged eleven public officials—mayors, city council members, and school board members—in New Jersey with taking bribes in exchange for help securing public contracts.[32] Clearly, states and localities are not corruption-free. What is reassuring, however, is that the amount of corruption is relatively low, given the vast number of public officials at nonnational levels of government. Still, even in states and communities with relatively clean government, the possibility of scandal is real; thus, it remains a potential drain on governmental capacity.

THE PEOPLE: DESIGNERS AND CONSUMERS OF GOVERNMENT

A book on state and local government is not only about places and governments; it is also about people—the public and assorted officeholders—and the institutions they create, the processes in which they engage, and the policies they adopt. Thus, this volume contains chapters on institutions, such as legislatures, and on processes, such as elections; and it discusses policies, such as those pertaining to education. But in each case, people are the ultimate focus: A legislature is composed of lawmakers and staff members who deal with constituents; elections involve candidates, campaign workers, and voters (as well as nonvoters); and education essentially involves students, teachers, administrators, parents, and taxpayers. In short, the word *people* encompasses an array of individuals and roles in the political system.

Ethnic-Racial Composition

Three hundred million people live in the United States. Some can trace their heritage back to the *Mayflower,* whereas others look back only as far as a recent naturalization ceremony. Very few can claim indigenous (native) American ancestry. Instead, most Americans owe their nationality to some forebear who came here in search of a better life or—in the case of a significant minority, the descendants of slaves—to ancestors who made the journey to this country not out of choice but because of physical coercion. The appeal of the United States to economic and political refugees from other countries continues, with Mexicans, Central Americans, and eastern Africans among the most recent arrivals.

The United States is a nation of immigrants. This gives it ethnic richness and cultural diversity. Current U.S. Census figures put the Anglo population at 75 percent, the African American population and the Latino population each at 12 percent, and the Asian population at 4 percent.[33] (The percentages total more than 100 percent because of some double-counting.) These figures vary, of course, from one jurisdiction to another. Approximately 34 million, or 12 percent, of the nation's population was foreign born as of 2004, with 53 percent of the foreign born from Latin America, and another 25 percent from Asia.[34]

One aspect of immigration—illegal immigration—is putting the words from the sonnet inscribed on the Statue of Liberty (containing the phrase "Give me your tired, your poor, your huddled masses") to a severe test. Controversy has arisen over the costs of providing public services such as health care, education, and welfare to illegal immigrants. Although accurate numbers are hard to come by, one estimate placed the number of illegal immigrants at approximately 10 million.[35] During 2006, more than 450 bills on the topic were introduced in legislatures around the country. Nearly all of the proposals were intended to clamp down on illegal immigration by requiring verification of workers' legal status and restricting the issuance of drivers' licenses to U.S. citizens and legal immigrants. The politics of the issue proved dicey in some states as the proposals faced strong opposition from Latino community groups and civil liberties advocates.

Clearly, ethnicity and culture still matter, despite the image of America as a melting pot. Researchers have found that a state's racial and ethnic diversity goes a long way in explaining its politics and policies.[36] Looking toward the future, census projections for the year 2050 estimate a nation of approximately 420 million people, with the Anglo population dropping to 50 percent of the total, the African American population increasing slightly to 15 percent, the Latino population reaching 25 percent, and an Asian population at 8 percent. If trends hold, state policy in the mid-twenty-first century will be affected.

Population Growth and Migration

As a whole, the United States grew by an estimated 6 percent during the period 2000 to 2006. Disaggregating the data by state reveals several trends. Reflecting the pattern of the previous decade, high rates of growth occurred in the western states; substantially slower growth rates characterized the Northeast and Midwest. (The map in Figure 1.1 displays the estimated percentage change in each state's population from 2000 to 2006.) Nevada and Arizona continued to outpace the growth in other states, with rates of 24.9 percent and 20.2 percent, respectively. A strong labor market and an attractive, inexpensive lifestyle are among those states' features. Only two states—Louisiana and North Dakota—are estimated to have lost population during the period.[37] (Prior to Hurricane Katrina, Louisiana was growing at a rate slightly above the national average.) In percentage terms, Georgia (14.4) and Florida (13.2) retained their roles as the South's growth leaders. California grew by an estimated 7.6 percent, which meant an increase of 2.6 million people in the Golden State.

For cities, the population trends from 2000 to 2006 are equally compelling. Higher rates of growth are much more prevalent in cities in the **Sunbelt** region than in cities of the **Frostbelt.** The growth leaders among large cities (defined as cities of 100,000 population or more) included places that are suburbs such as McKinney (a suburb of Dallas, Texas), Gilbert and Chandler (suburbs of

Sunbelt
An unofficial region of the United States, generally comprising the South and the West.

Frostbelt
An unofficial region of the United States, generally consisting of the Northeast and the Midwest.

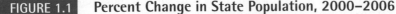

FIGURE 1.1   **Percent Change in State Population, 2000–2006**

SOURCE: www.census.gov/population/cen2006.

Phoenix, Arizona) and North Las Vegas and Henderson (suburbs of Las Vegas, Nevada). Population growth in these cities topped an estimated 35 percent in the six-year time frame. Detroit (–8.4 percent), Cleveland (–6.9 percent), and Pittsburgh (–6.5 percent) led the list of large cities with population losses. The case of New Orleans is one that deserves an asterisk in any discussion of population loss. The city had been losing population prior to Hurricane Katrina, but the aftermath of the 2005 storm accelerated the population exodus dramatically. The change from 2000 to 2006 for the Big Easy was an estimated –53.9 percent, according to the U.S. Census Bureau.[38]

Population changes carry economic and political consequences for state and local governments. As a general rule, power and influence follow population. A state's representation in the U.S. Congress and its votes in the Electoral College are at stake. Speculation about the impact of the 2010 Census on state influence in the U.S. House of Representatives in 2012 has already begun. The smart money is on Texas to pick up four seats, Arizona and Florida each to add two seats, and five states to gain one seat each. At the other end of the spectrum, both New York and Ohio are projected to lose two seats, while nine other states will likely lose one each.[39] Population projections suggest that the electoral influence of Sunbelt states will continue to grow into the foreseeable future. The stakes are high for local governments, too. As a central city's population size is eclipsed by its suburban population, a loss in the city's political clout results. Aware of the importance of "the count," many cities spent thousands of dollars on media advertisements encouraging residents to mail in their 2000 census forms.

Political Culture

political culture

The attitudes, values, and beliefs that people hold toward government.

One of the phrases that a new arrival in town may hear from longtime residents is "We don't do things that way here." **Political culture**—the attitudes, values, and beliefs that people hold toward government—is the conceptual equivalent of simply saying "It's *our* thing."[40] As developed by political scientist Daniel Elazar in the 1960s, the term refers to the way in which people think about their government and the manner in which the political system operates. Political culture is a soft concept—one that is difficult to measure—yet it has remained quite useful in explaining state politics and policy.

According to Elazar, the United States is an amalgam of three major political cultures, each of which has distinctive characteristics. In an *individualistic political culture,* politics is a kind of open marketplace in which people participate because of essentially private motivations. In a *moralistic political culture,* politics is an effort to establish a good and just society. Citizens are expected to be active in public affairs. In a *traditionalistic political culture,* politics functions to maintain the existing order, and political participation is confined to social elites. These differing conceptions about the purpose of government and the role of politics lead to different behaviors.

Political culture is a factor in the differences (and similarities) in state policy. Research has found that moralistic states demonstrate the greatest tendency toward policy innovation, whereas traditionalistic states exhibit the least.[41] In economic development policy, for example, political culture has been shown to influence a state's willingness to offer tax breaks to businesses.[42] Other research has linked political culture to state environmental policy and state expenditures on AIDS programs.[43]

Today, few states are characterized by pure forms of these cultures. The mass media have had a homogenizing effect on cultural differences; migration has diversified cultural enclaves. This process of cultural erosion and synthesis has produced hybrid political cultures. For example, Florida, once considered a traditionalistic state, now has many areas in which an individualistic culture prevails, and even a moralistic community or two. In an effort to extend Elazar's pioneering work, researcher Joel Lieske has used race, ethnicity, and religion to identify contemporary subcultures.[44] With counties as the building blocks and statistical analysis as the method, he identified ten distinctive regional subcultures. A state like Pennsylvania, which Elazar characterized as individualistic, becomes a mix of "heartland," Germanic, ethnic, and rural/urban counties in Lieske's formulation. Very few states are dominated by a single subculture, as are Utah by a Mormon subculture and New Hampshire and Vermont by an Anglo-French subculture.

Political culture is not the only explanation for why states do what they do, of course. Socioeconomic characteristics (income and education levels, for example) and political structural factors (the amount of competition between political parties) also contribute to states' and communities' actions. In fact, sorting out the cause-and-effect relationships among these variables is a daunting job.[45] For example, why do some states pass more laws to regulate handguns than other states do? Emily Van Dunk's study found that several factors were important, although the crime rate and partisanship, surprisingly, were not among them.[46] States with nontraditional political cultures adopt more handgun regulations, as do states with more women in the legislature and those with populations that are more urbanized and nonwhite. In general, political factors, socioeconomic characteristics, and the particulars of a specific problem combine to produce government action.

The variation among states makes for a nation that is highly diverse. However, one recent exercise in identifying the most typical state in the country proved interesting. Based on twelve key statistics—four measuring race and ethnicity, four looking at income and education, and four describing the typical neighborhood in each state—Wisconsin was found to be the microcosm of the nation.[47] Rounding out the top five were Missouri, Kansas, Indiana, and Ohio. The states least like the country as a whole: Mississippi, West Virginia, and New York. Table 1.2 lists the states from most typical to least. The numbers refer to a standardized score with a potential range of zero to fifty.

| TABLE 1.2 | How Typical Is Your State? |

State	Score	State	Score
1. Wisconsin	36.4	19. Pennsylvania	25.0
2. Missouri	35.2	20. Arizona	24.8
3. Kansas	34.4	21. Delaware	24.1
4. Indiana	30.8	22. Tennessee	22.3
5. Ohio	30.1	23. South Dakota	21.4
6. Oklahoma	29.9	24. Kentucky	20.3
7. Oregon	29.3	25. New Mexico	20.3
8. Nebraska	29.0	26. Iowa	19.6
9. Georgia	27.3	27. Texas	19.6
10. Minnesota	26.9	28. Illinois	19.5
11. Michigan	26.8	29. Rhode Island	19.0
12. Washington	26.3	30. Maryland	18.9
13. Wyoming	25.9	31. Colorado	18.8
14. North Carolina	25.8	32. Louisiana	18.3
15. Florida	25.6	33. Idaho	18.1
16. Montana	25.3	34. Vermont	17.9
17. Virginia	25.3	35. Maine	17.4
18. Alaska	25.1	36. New Hampshire	17.4

37. Utah	17.0	44. Nevada	13.5
38. Hawaii	16.3	45. Connecticut	13.1
39. South Carolina	15.8	46. Massachusetts	11.6
40. California	15.3	47. New Jersey	11.4
41. Arkansas	15.0	48. New York	6.5
42. Alabama	14.6	49. West Virginia	4.8
43. North Dakota	13.8	50. Mississippi	2.8

SOURCE: Mark Preston, "The 'Most' Representative State: Wisconsin," CNN, www.cnn.com/2006/POLITICS/07/27/mg.thu/index.html (July 27, 2006).

Culture Wars

culture wars

Political conflicts that emerge from deeply held moral values.

In 2004, when San Francisco's mayor ordered city clerks to remove all references to gender on local marriage license applications, the action opened the door for same-sex marriages to take place in the city. As gay activists and supporters celebrated, many politically conservative groups denounced the action and promised legal challenges and political repercussions for the mayor. This type of social conflict over morality issues is known informally as **culture wars,** or "morality politics." And these culture wars are defining the politics of many communities and states. Besides gay rights, battlegrounds in the culture wars include abortion, pornography, and prayer in schools.

These issues tend to involve deeply held values, sometimes connected to religion, and they are less about economics than are many political issues. According to political scientist Elaine Sharp, culture wars have several distinctive features.[48] The issues are highly salient to people, eliciting passionate reactions; they mobilize people across different neighborhoods and racial and ethnic groups; and the ensuing political activism often takes unconventional forms, such as demonstrations. Throughout the country, battle lines have been drawn over issues such as more restrictive abortion laws and displaying the Ten Commandments in public buildings. But the most volatile culture war of the mid-2000s involved gay marriage.

The Massachusetts Supreme Court ruled in 2003 that, under the state's constitution, same-sex couples were entitled to enter into marriages, a decision that angered the governor and many Bay State lawmakers. Generally, states bar gay and lesbian couples from marrying: Forty-one states have enacted defense of marriage acts (DOMAs) that prohibit same-sex marriage. But in the aftermath of the Massachusetts decision, many of these states wanted to take it one step further and put a gay marriage ban into the state constitution. In the 2004 elections, eleven states did so by approving constitutional amendments codifying marriage as an exclusively heterosexual institution, seven more states did so in 2006. As of 2008, Massachusetts remained the only state issuing marriage licenses to same-sex couples, and its neighbor Rhode Island agreed to recognize same-sex marriages performed elsewhere. Other states taking actions supportive of gay marriage include Connecticut, New Hampshire, New Jersey, and Vermont, which recognize marriage-like civil unions, and California and Oregon, which grant nearly all the same spousal rights to same-sex couples registered as domestic partners.[49] But no matter what decision a state makes, it leaves in its wake people who are extremely dissatisfied. Culture wars have the potential to divide states and localities.

LINKING CAPACITY TO RESULTS

State and local governments have become the new heroes of American federalism. Their ability to solve pressing problems is one of the reasons why. The interaction of three unique characteristics of our fifty-state system—diversity, competitiveness, and resiliency—makes it easier.[50] Consider the *diversity* of the United States. States and their communities have different fiscal capacities and different voter preferences for public services and taxes. As a result, citizens and businesses are offered real choices in taxation and expenditure policies across different jurisdictions.

Diversity is tempered, however, by the natural *competitiveness* of a federal system. No state can afford to be too far out of line with the prevailing thinking on appropriate levels of taxes and expenditures because citizens and business may opt to relocate. In essence, each jurisdiction is competing with every other jurisdiction. Such competition over the price and performance of government stabilizes the federal system.

The third characteristic, *resiliency,* captures the ability of state governments to recover from adversity. States are survivors. As noted earlier in the chapter, to find fresh policy ideas these days, look at the state level, which has witnessed a veritable burst of activism in policy initiatives. Resiliency is the key.

As one astute observer of the U.S. governmental scene has commented, "Over the past decade, without ever quite admitting it, we have ceased to rely on Congress (or the federal government, for that matter) to deal with our most serious public problems. . . . [T]he states have been accepting the challenge of dealing with problems that no other level of gover nment is handling."[51] The recent comments of an Oregon legislator are apropos: "The states have become the petri dishes for new and evolving ideas."[52] Return to the first page of this chapter and reread Governor Spitzer's inspiring words. The twenty-first century began full of challenges, but states and their local governments are taking charge. In the final analysis, that is what increased capacity is all about.

CHAPTER RECAP

- State and local governments are directly involved in our daily lives.
- The story of states and localities over the past two decades has been one of transformation. They have shed their backward ways, reformed their institutions, and emerged as capable and proactive.
- State resurgence is exemplified in improved revenue systems, the expanded scope of state operations, faster diffusion of innovations, more interjurisdictional cooperation, and increased national-state conflict.

- Several persistent challenges dog states and localities: fiscal stress, interjurisdictional competition, and political corruption.
- The United States is becoming more racially and ethnically diverse. The estimated increase in population in Sunbelt states such as Nevada and Arizona outpaces the rest of the nation. Meanwhile, population loss appears to be the case for states like North Dakota and post-Katrina Louisiana.
- An outbreak of culture wars is redefining the politics of some communities and states.
- As a whole, the states are diverse, competitive, and resilient. With increased capacity to govern effectively, they are producing results.

Key Terms

capacity *(p. 3)*

jurisdiction *(p. 3)*

federalism *(p. 4)*

proactive *(p. 5)*

rainy day funds *(p. 6)*

downsizing *(p. 10)*

transparency *(p. 12)*

Sunbelt *(p. 13)*

Frostbelt *(p. 13)*

political culture *(p. 15)*

culture wars *(p. 16)*

Internet Resources

Originally, states were assigned the same (except for the two-letter state abbreviation) type of URL: **www.state.ak.us.** The suffix *gov* was reserved for the federal government. Some states such as Alaska still use this web address. Beginning in 2003, states were authorized to use *gov* and many states have switched to it. Alabama is an example: **www.alabama.gov.** Other states have opted to do something different, such as Florida's portal at **www.myflorida.com,** Montana's at **www.discoveringmontana.com,** or Oklahoma's at **www.youroklahoma.com.**

A website that offers a wealth of policy information about the states, along with links to multistate organizations, national organizations of state officials, and state-based think tanks is **www.stateline.org,** established by the Pew Center on the States.

The website of *Governing* magazine, **www.governing.com,** contains up-to-date, in-depth discussions of issues in states and localities.

For a look at what is going on in state governments around the country, see the Council of State Governments, which can be found at **www.csg.org.**

At **www.census.gov,** the website of the U.S. Bureau of the Census, you can find historical, demographic data on states and localities.

A comprehensive website that will take you to the official websites of states and local governments is **www.usa.gov/.**

The website for *State Politics and Policy Quarterly,* a scholarly journal that publishes research on important state-level questions is **www.press.uillinois.edu/journals/sppq.html.**

2

Federalism and the States

FOCUS QUESTIONS

1. What is the proper balance of power and responsibility between the national government and the states?

2. In what areas has there been a resurgence of state and local governments?

3. What models describe the power relationships among the three levels of government?

4. What is a key ingredient of federalism, particularly in financial interactions?

5. In what areas does the national government impose certain controversial requirements on state governments?

A single broad and enduring issue in American federalism transcends all others: What is the proper balance of power and responsibility between the national government and the states? The debate over this profound question was first joined by the Founders in preconstitutional days and argued between the Federalists and the Anti-Federalists. It continues today in the halls of Congress, the federal courts, and the state and local governments, over issues ranging from the profane to the profound.

The immediate aftermath of the September 11, 2001, terrorist attack on the World Trade Center towers provided stark evidence of the undisputed duties and responsibilities of federal, state, and local governments. As corporate workers fled the towers for their lives, New York City police and firefighters mounted the stairways into the burning buildings. State and local emergency agencies quickly coordinated the on-the-scene response. National political leaders, for their part, focused on international relations, intelligence gathering, and military responses. Today, however, response to the threats of terrorism, as well as to natural disasters such as hurricanes, floods, fires, and earthquakes, is intergovernmentally complex with respective roles and responsibilities still being sorted out.

The arrival of Hurricane Katrina in New Orleans and adjoining portions of the Louisiana and Mississippi Gulf Coast in 2005 was a terrible event for local

New Orleans Mayor Ray Nagin greets a vendor at the reopening of a street market two years after it was destroyed by Hurricane Katrina.
SOURCE: © AP/Wide World Photos

residents and a bad time for federalism. Approximately 1330 lives were lost, and $96 billion in property damage was incurred. Reactions to the disaster by all levels of government were disjointed, uncoordinated, and altogether inept. The response by the Bush White House and leaders of the Department of Homeland Security (which includes the Federal Emergency management Agency) was late and confused. Governor Kathleen Blanco and New Orleans Mayor Ray Nagin were very late ordering a mandatory evacuation before the storm. What resulted was mass fear, chaos, and loss of life.

These two disasters—one caused by humans and the other primarily by nature—have spawned a critical analysis of American federalism that has significant implications for all levels of government.[1] For example, who should control the National Guard? Following 9/11 and Katrina, Congress amended the 200-year old Insurrection Act to empower the president to circumvent the governors to call up the Guard in emergencies. (President Bush had sought to federalize the Louisiana Guard after Katrina, but Governor Blanco refused to permit it.) In addition, more than six years of multiple deployments of state guard units to the Middle East have seriously weakened the capacity of the states to respond effectively to the next disaster, whatever its causes.

These types of conflicts help define U.S. federalism. As a system for organizing government, federalism has important consequences that often affect our political and personal lives in ways both direct and hidden.

THE CONCEPT OF FEDERALISM

In a nation—a large group of people organized under a single, sovereign government and sharing historical, cultural, and other values—powers and responsibilities can be divided among different levels of government in three ways: through a unitary government, a confederacy, or a federal system. To understand our federal system, we must know how it differs from the other forms of government.

Unitary, Confederate, and Federal Systems

unitary system

One in which all authority is derived from a central authority.

The great majority of countries (more than 90 percent) have a **unitary system** in which most, if not all, legal power is located in the central government. The central government may create or abolish regional or local governments as it sees fit. These subgovernments can exercise only those powers and responsibilities granted to them by the central government. In France, the United Kingdom, Argentina, Egypt, and the many other countries with unitary systems, the central government is strong and the regional or local jurisdictions are weak.

confederacy

A league of sovereign states in which a limited central government exercises few independent powers.

A **confederacy** is the opposite of a unitary system. In a confederacy, the central government is weak and regional governments are powerful. The regional jurisdictions establish a central government to deal with areas of mutual concern, such as national defense and a common currency, but they severely restrict the central government's authority in other areas. If they see fit, they may change or even abolish the central government. The United States began as a confederacy, and the southern states formed one following secession in 1861.

federal system

A means of dividing the power and functions of government between a central government and a specified number of geographically defined regional jurisdictions.

A **federal system** falls somewhere between the unitary and confederate forms in the way it divides powers among levels of government. This system has a minimum of two governmental levels, each of which derives its powers directly from the people, and each of which can act directly on the people within its jurisdiction without permission from any other authority. Each level of government is supreme in the powers assigned to it, and each is protected by a constitution from being destroyed by the other.[2] Thus federalism is a means of dividing the power and functions of government between a central government and a specified number of geographically defined regional jurisdictions. In effect, people hold dual citizenship, in the national government and in their regional government.

In the U.S. federal system, they are called states. In other federal systems, such as that of Canada, regional governments are known as provinces. Altogether there are approximately twenty federal systems in the world.

The Advantages and Disadvantages of Federalism

Federalism as it has evolved in the United States is a reasonably effective system of government. But it is not perfect; nor is it well suited to the circumstances of most other nations. Ironically, federalism's weaknesses are closely related to its strengths.

The advantages of federalism are as follows:

1. *A federal system helps manage social and political conflict.* It broadly disperses political power within and among governments. For example, the U.S. Sen-

ate represents the geographical diversity of the states, with two senators for each territorial unit, and the House of Representatives is apportioned on the basis of population. This system enables national as well as subregional concerns to reach the central government. Local interests are expressed in state capitols through state legislatures and, of course, in city and county councils and other local legislative bodies. Many potential places exist for resolving conflicts before they reach the crisis stage. Also, federalism achieves unity through diversity. Ethnicity, color, language, religious preference, and other differences are not distributed randomly in the population; rather, people who share certain traits tend to cluster together spatially. And state and local governments represent such groups. For example, the large and growing Hispanic population of Texas is increasingly gaining representation in the state legislature and in mayoral and city council offices.

2. *Federalism promotes administrative efficiency.* The wide variety of services that citizens demand are delivered more efficiently without a large central bureaucracy. From public elementary education to garbage collection, the government closest to the problem seems to work best in adapting public programs to local needs.

3. *Federalism encourages innovation.* States and localities can customize their policies to accommodate diverse demands and needs—and, indeed, such heterogeneity flourishes. New policies are constantly being tested by the more than 88,000 government "laboratories" that exist throughout the country, thus further encouraging experimentation and flexibility. The term "laboratory" became literal in the past several years as California, Wisconsin, and other states decided to invest state resources in stem-cell research, in stark opposition to continuing federal government research funding restrictions.

4. *A federal system maximizes political participation in government.* Citizens have opportunities to participate at all three levels of government through elections, public hearings, and other means. The local and state governments serve as political training camps for aspiring leaders who can test the waters in a school board or county council election and, if successful, move on to higher electoral prizes in the state or national arena. The great majority of presidents and U.S. senators and representatives got their start in state or local politics. Through almost one million offices regularly filled in elections, citizens can have a meaningful say in decisions that affect their lives. And if one level of government is unable or unwilling to address citizen demands, there are two others available.

5. *A federal system helps protect individual freedom.* Federalism provides numerous potential points of opposition to national government policies and political ideology. James Madison argued that the numerous checks inherent in a federal system would control the effects of **factions,** making "it less probable that a majority of the whole will have a motive to invade the rights of other citizens."[3] Thus the states serve as defenders of democracy by ensuring that no national ideological juggernaut can sweep over the entire nation, menacing the rights of individual citizens.

factions

Any groups of citizens or interests united in a cause or action that can threaten the rights or interests of the larger community.

Now we turn to a list of disadvantages:

1. *Federalism may facilitate the management of conflict in some settings, but in others it makes conflict more dangerous.* Federal experiments in Canada and Nigeria bear out this point. In Canada, the ethnically French province of Quebec fueled a secessionist movement during the 1970s that still simmers. Recurring violent ethnic conflict in Nigeria is another example of the failure of federalism.

2. *Although provision of services through governments that are close to the people can promote effectiveness and efficiency, federalism can also hinder progress.* It is extraordinarily difficult, if not impossible, to coordinate the efforts of all state and local governments. Picture trying to get 88,000 squawking and flapping chickens to move in the same direction at once. Business interests level this criticism today as they increasingly encounter government regulations on products and services that vary widely across the United States.

3. *Not surprisingly, so many governments lead to duplication and confusion.* For example, fifty sets of laws on banking and lending practices can make doing business across state lines tough for a firm.

4. *Federalism may promote state and local innovation, but it can also hinder national programs and priorities.* These many points of involvement can encourage obstruction and delay and result in an ineffective national government. The confusion and ineptitude exhibited in the aftermath of Katrina is an obvious example.

5. *Broad opportunity for political participation is highly desirable in a democracy, but it may encourage local biases that damage the national interest.* For example, hazardous, radioactive, and solid wastes must be disposed of somewhere, but local officials and citizens are quick to protest: "Not in my back yard!"

THE HISTORY OF U.S. FEDERALISM

The men who met in Philadelphia during the hot summer of 1787 to draw up the U.S. Constitution were not wild-eyed optimists, nor were they revolutionaries. In fact, as we'll see in this section, they were consummate pragmatists whose beliefs shaped the new republic and created both the strengths and weaknesses of our federal system.

Early History

The Framers of the Constitution held to the belief of English political philosopher Thomas Hobbes that human beings are contentious and selfish. Some of them openly disdained the masses. Most of the Framers agreed that their goal in Philadelphia was to find a means of controlling lower forms of human behavior while still allowing citizens to have a voice in making the laws they were compelled to obey. As noted earlier, the "philosopher of the Constitution," James Madison, formulated the problem in terms of factions, groups that pursue their own interests without concern for the interests of society as a whole. Political differences and self-interest, Madison felt, led to the formation of factions, and the Framers' duty was to identify "constitutional devices that would force various interests to check and control one another."[4]

Three practical devices to control factions were placed in the U.S. Constitution. The first was a system of representative government in which citizens would elect individuals who would filter and refine the views of the masses. The second was the division of government into three branches: executive, legislative, and judicial. The legislative body was divided into two houses, each with a check on the activities of the other. Equal in power would be a strong chief executive with the authority to veto legislative acts, and an independent judiciary. Finally, the government was structured as a federal system in which the most dangerous faction of all—a majority—would be controlled by the sovereign states. Madison's ultimate hope was that the new Constitution would "check interest with interest, class with class, faction with faction, and one branch of government with another in a harmonious system of mutual frustration."[5]

Sometimes today there appears to be more frustration than harmony, but Madison's dream did come true. The U.S. federal system is the longest-lived constitutional government on earth. Its dimensions and activities are vastly different from what the Framers envisioned, but it remains a dynamic, adaptable, responsive, and usually effective system for conducting the affairs of government.

The Move Toward Federalism

The drive for independence by the thirteen American colonies was, according to the Declaration of Independence, in large measure a reaction to "a history of repeated injuries and usurpations" under a British unitary system of government. The Declaration proudly proclaimed the colonies' liberation from the "absolute tyranny" exercised over them by the English Crown. The struggle for independence dominated political debate in the colonies, and there was little time to develop a consensus on the form of government best suited to the future needs of American society. Hence the move toward federalism was gradual. It is interesting that the first independent government established in America was a confederacy; thus Americans tested two types of government—unitary and confederate—before deciding permanently on the third.

The Articles of Confederation During the War for Independence, the colonies, now called states, agreed to establish a confederation. A unicameral (one-house) Congress was created to exercise the authority of the new national government. Its powers were limited to the authority to wage war, make peace, enter into treaties and alliances, appoint and receive ambassadors, regulate Indian affairs, and create a postal system. The states held all powers not expressly granted to the Congress. The governing document was the Articles of Confederation (effective from 1776 to 1787).

The inherent weaknesses of the confederacy quickly became apparent. The states had significant authority within their individual borders, but the central government was unable to carry out its basic responsibilities because it did not have the power to force the states to pay their share of the bill. Bankruptcy was a chronic concern. Furthermore, the lack of national authority to regulate either domestic or international commerce led to discriminatory trade practices by the states, particularly through the use of protective tariffs. These and many other defects were important concerns. But the key event that brought together representatives of the states to draft a constitution for a new type of government was Shays's Rebellion. In 1787, Daniel Shays, a Revolutionary War officer, led an armed revolt of New England farmers who were fighting mad about debt and taxes. The weak central government had difficulty putting down the rebellion.

The Constitutional Convention How did the Framers create a long-lasting and successful system of government that seems to have the best features of both unitary and confederate forms? Above all they were pragmatists. Informed by their own colonial experiences,[6] they developed a practical compromise on the key issues of the day, including the proper role of the national government and the states. The reconciliation of the interests and powers of the states with the need for a strong national government is the United States' most distinctive political contribution.

Delegates from each of the states assembled at the constitutional convention. Here, the interests of large and small states diverged. The large states supported the Virginia Plan, which proposed a strong central government spearheaded by a powerful bicameral Congress. Because representation in both chambers was to be based on population, larger states would be favored. The smaller states countered with the New Jersey Plan, which put forward a one-house legislature composed of an equal number of representatives from each state.

The New Jersey Plan was defeated by a vote of 7 to 3, but the smaller states refused to give in. Finally, Connecticut moved that the lower house (the House of Representatives) be based on the population of each state and the upper house (the Senate) on equal state membership. This Great Compromise was approved, ensuring that a faction of large states would not dominate the small ones.

The Framers reached another important compromise by specifying the powers of the new central government. Those seventeen powers, to be exercised through Congress, included taxation, regulation of commerce, operation of post offices, establishment of a national court system, declaration of war, conduct of foreign affairs, and administration of military forces.

A third key compromise reached by the Framers concerned the question of who should resolve disputes between the national government and the states: Congress, the state courts, or the Supreme Court? The importance of the decision that the Supreme Court would be the final arbiter was understood only years later, when the Court established the supremacy of the national government over the states through several critical rulings.

State-Centered Federalism

Despite the fact that the new Constitution made the national government much stronger than it had been under the Articles of Confederation, the sovereign power of the states was still important.[7] As James Madison wrote, "The powers delegated by the proposed Constitution to the federal government are few and defined. Those which are to remain in the State governments are numerous and infinite."[8]

The first decades under the new Constitution witnessed a clash between profoundly different views on governing. George Washington, John Adams, Alexander Hamilton, and their fellow "Federalists" favored national supremacy, or **nation-centered federalism.** Opposed to them were Thomas Jefferson and the Republicans, who preferred **state-centered federalism.** Much of the debate then, as today, concerned the meaning of the **reserved powers** clause of the **Tenth Amendment** to the Constitution. Ratified in 1791, the Tenth Amendment gave support to the states by openly acknowledging that "the powers not delegated to the United States by the Constitution, nor prohibited by it to the States, are reserved to the States respectively, or to the people." But, in fact, the Tenth Amendment was an early omen of the eventual triumph of nation-centered federalism. As pointed out by constitutional scholar Walter Berns, if the states were intended to be the dominant federal actors, they would not have needed the Tenth Amendment to remind them.[9]

Those who defended the power of the states under the Constitution—that is, state-centered federalism—saw the Constitution as a *compact,* an agreement, among the sovereign states that maintained their sovereignty, or the right of self-governance. The powers of the national government listed in the Constitution— the **enumerated (delegated) powers**—were to be interpreted narrowly, and the states were obliged to resist any unconstitutional efforts by the national government to extend its authority.[10]

This **compact theory** of federalism became the foundation for states' rights arguments. In particular, it became central to the fight of the southern states against what they considered discrimination by the North. During the 1820s, a national tariff seriously damaged the economy of the southern states. The slave-based agricultural economy of the South had already begun a protracted period of decline while the North prospered. The tariff, which placed high taxes on imported manufactured goods from Europe, hit the South hard, for the South produced few manufactured goods. Rightly or wrongly, southerners blamed the "tariff of abominations" for many of their economic problems.

In 1828, Vice President John C. Calhoun of South Carolina asserted that the United States was composed of sovereign states united in a central government through a compact. The powers of the national government had been entrusted to it by the states, not permanently handed over. Calhoun claimed that the states thus had complete authority to reinterpret or even *nullify* (reject) the compact at any time. Most important, Calhoun declared that if a large majority of the states sided with the national government, the nullifying state had the right to *secede,* or withdraw from the Union.

In 1832, after an additional tariff was enacted by the national government, South Carolina nullified it. President Andrew Jackson and the Congress threatened military action to force the state to comply with the law, and Jackson even threatened to hang Calhoun, who by this time had resigned from the vice presidency.[11]

Ultimately, eleven southern states (led by South Carolina) did secede from the Union, at which point they formed the Confederate States of America. The long conflict between state sovereignty and national supremacy and the slavery

---

nation-centered federalism

A theory holding that the national government is dominant over the states.

state-centered federalism

A theory holding that the national government represents a voluntary compact or agreement between the states, which retain a dominant position.

reserved powers

Those powers residing with the states by virtue of the Tenth Amendment.

Tenth Amendment

The amendment to the Constitution, ratified in 1791, reserving powers to the state.

enumerated (delegated) powers

Those powers expressly given to the national government in Article I, Section 8, of the Constitution.

compact theory

A theory of federalism that became the foundation for states' rights arguments.

question as well were definitively resolved by five years of carnage in such places as Antietam, Shiloh, and Gettysburg, followed by the eventual readmittance of the renegade states to the Union. The Civil War, often referred to in the South as The War Between the States, remains the single most violent episode in American history, resulting in more than 620,000 deaths (more than in all our other wars combined).

The Growth of National Power Through the Constitution and the Judiciary

After the Civil War, a nation-centered concept of federalism evolved. For the most part, the national government became the primary governing force, with the states and localities generally following its lead. Recently the states have been more inclined to act independently, but they are restrained by the history of the Supreme Court's interpretations of key sections of the Constitution that supported the national government.

The National Supremacy Clause Article III of the Constitution created the U.S. Supreme Court. The supremacy of national law and the Constitution is grounded in the **national supremacy clause** (Article VI), which provides that the national laws and the Constitution are the supreme laws of the land. Later decision of the Supreme Court established the Court's role as arbitrator of any legal disputes between the national government and the states.

national supremacy clause

Article VI of the Constitution, which makes national laws superior to state laws.

The Necessary and Proper Clause The fourth chief justice of the United States, John Marshall, was the architect of the federal judiciary during his thirty-four years on the bench. Almost single-handedly, he made it a coequal branch of government. Several of his rulings laid the groundwork for the expansion of national governmental power. In the case of *McCulloch* v. *Maryland* (1819), two issues were before the bench: the right of the national government to establish a national bank, and the right of the state of Maryland to tax that bank, once it was established.[12]

necessary and proper clause

Portion of Article I, Section 8, of the Constitution that authorizes Congress to enact all laws "necessary and proper" to carry out its responsibilities.

The crux of the issue was how to interpret the **necessary and proper clause.** The final power delegated to Congress under Article I, Section 8, is the power "to make all laws which shall be *necessary and proper* for carrying into execution the foregoing powers, and all other powers vested by this Constitution in the Government of the United States" (emphasis added). Thomas Jefferson argued that necessary meant "indispensable," whereas Alexander Hamilton asserted that it meant merely "convenient." Hamilton argued that in addition to the enumerated powers, Congress possessed **implied powers.** In the case of the national bank, valid congressional action was implied through the powers of taxation, borrowing, and currency found in Article I, Section 8.

implied powers

Those powers that are not expressly granted by the Constitution but inferred from the enumerated powers.

The bank dispute was eventually heard by Chief Justice Marshall. Marshall was persuaded by the Hamiltonian point of view. He pointed out that the Constitution nowhere stipulates that the only powers that may be carried out are those expressly described in Article I, Section 8. Thus he ruled that Congress had the implied power to establish the bank and that Maryland had no right to tax it. Significantly, *McCulloch* v. *Maryland* meant that the national government had an almost unlimited right to decide how to exercise its delegated powers. Over the years, Congress has enacted a great many laws that are only vaguely, if at all, associated with the enumerated powers and that stretch the phrase *necessary and proper* beyond its logical limits.

commerce clause

Part of Article I, Section 8, of the U.S. Constitution, which permits Congress to regulate trade with foreign countries and among the states.

The Commerce Clause Another important ruling of the Marshall Court extended national power through an expansive interpretation of the **commerce clause** of Article I, Section 8. The commerce clause gives Congress the power "to regulate commerce with foreign nations, and among the several states, and with the Indian tribes." In *Gibbons* v. *Ogden* (1824),[13] two important questions were addressed by Marshall: What is commerce? And how broadly should Congress's power to regulate commerce be interpreted?

The United States was just developing a national economy as the Industrial Revolution expanded. National oversight was needed, along with regulation of emerging transportation networks and of state activities related to the passage of goods across state lines (interstate commerce). The immediate question was whether New York could grant a monopoly to run a steamship service between New York and New Jersey. Marshall's answer? No, it could not. He defined commerce very broadly and held that Congress's power to regulate commerce applied not only to traffic across state boundaries but, in some cases, also to traffic of goods, merchandise, and people *within* a state. The Court further expanded the meaning of "commerce" in rulings during the twentieth century.

general welfare clause

The portion of Article I, Section 8, of the Constitution that provides for the general welfare of the United States.

The General Welfare Clause The **general welfare clause** of Article I, Section 8, states that "the Congress shall have power to lay and collect taxes, duties, imposts, and excises to pay the debts and provide for the common defense and *general welfare* of the United States" (emphasis added). Before the Great Depression of the 1930s, it was believed that poor people were responsible for their own plight and that it was up to private charity and state and local governments to provide limited assistance. The Great Depression inflicted massive unemployment and poverty throughout the country and made necessary a major change in the national government's attitude. Despite their best efforts, the states and localities were staggered by the tremendous loss of tax revenues and by the need to help poor and displaced persons obtain food and shelter. Franklin D. Roosevelt, who won the presidency in 1932, set in motion numerous "New Deal" programs that completely redefined federal responsibility for the general welfare.

Fourteenth Amendment

Enacted in 1868, this amendment contains citizenship rights, due process, and equal protection provisions that states must apply to all citizens.

The Fourteenth Amendment Ratified by the states in 1868, the **Fourteenth Amendment** had the effect of granting former slaves official status as citizens of the United States and of the state in which they lived. It included two other very important principles as well—*due process* and *equal protection* of the laws. The federal courts have used the Fourteenth Amendment to increase national power over the states in several critical fields, especially with respect to civil rights, criminal law, and election practices.

The Growth of National Power Through Congress

The U.S. Supreme Court has not been the only force behind nation-centered federalism; Congress has worked hand in hand with the judiciary. The interstate commerce clause represents a good example. Given the simple authority to control or eliminate state barriers to trade across state lines, Congress now regulates commercial activities within a state's boundaries as well, as long as these activities purportedly have substantial national consequences (examples include banking and corporate fraud). Congress has also used the authority of the interstate commerce clause to expand national power into fields only vaguely related to commerce, such as protecting endangered species. The states have made hundreds of legal challenges to such exercise of the commerce power, but until very recently almost all of these were resolved by the U.S. Supreme Court in favor of the national government.

Sixteenth Amendment

Enacted in 1913, an amendment that grants the national government the power to levy income taxes.

Taxing and Spending Power Probably the most controversial source of the rise in national power in recent years has been the use of the *taxing and spending power* by Congress to extend its influence over the state and local governments. Under Article I, Section 8, Congress holds the power to tax and spend to provide for the common defense and general welfare. But the **Sixteenth Amendment,** which grants Congress the power to tax the income of individuals and corporations, moved the center of financial power from the states to Washington, D.C. Through the income tax, the national government raises vast sums of money. A portion of this money is sent to the states and localities. Because Congress insists on some sort of accountability in how state and local governments spend these funds, attached to federal grants are a variety of conditions to which the recipients must adhere if they are to receive the money. The federal government also imposes mandates and regulations related to the purposes of the individual grant. For example, in 2000 Congress set a blood-alcohol standard of .08 for drunk driving; noncomplying states faced the loss of significant federal transportation dollars. In 2004, Delaware became the last state to comply.

federal preemption

The principle that national laws take precedence over state laws.

Federal Preemption The national government has also seized power through the process known as **federal preemption.** The legal basis for preemption is Article VI of the Constitution, the national supremacy clause. Whenever a state law conflicts with a national law, the national law is dominant.

Congressional passage of a national law that supersedes existing state legislation directly preempts. One such federal law concerns federal preemption of state authority to regulate tobacco advertising. Another case of preemption is the Real ID Act of 2005, which requires the states to standardize their drivers' licenses and to verify the citizenship status of all applicants for licenses. In 2007, Washington State adopted legislation barring compliance with the dictates of Real ID unless the federal government delivers the $250 million estimated for implementation costs in that state. Montana also refused to cooperate with the federal government on this unfunded mandate, and another 28 states were considering taking the same path.

Smothering (Then Resuscitating) the Tenth Amendment Actions by the Congress and the federal courts have gradually undermined the Tenth Amendment, which reserves to the states all powers not specifically granted to the national government or prohibited to the states. In fact, it is very difficult to identify any field of state activity not intruded on by the national government today.

The Supreme Court has sent mixed signals on the relevance of the Tenth Amendment. A good example of the Court's fickle federalism involves the Fair Labor Standards Act (FLSA). Following forty years of case law that essentially relegated the Tenth Amendment to the basement of federalism, the Court surprisingly ruled in favor of state and local governments in the 1976 case of *National League of Cities* v. *Usery*. At issue was the constitutionality under the interstate commerce clause of the 1974 amendments to the FLSA, which extended federal minimum wage and maximum hour requirements to state and local employees. In this case, the Court said that Congress did not have the constitutional right to impose wage and hour requirements on employees carrying out basic—or integral—functions, such as law enforcement or firefighting.[14]

But just nine years later, the Court reversed itself in *Garcia* v. *San Antonio Metropolitan Transit Authority*. A spate of litigation had not been able to resolve the issue of just which state and local activities are "integral." So the Court expressly overturned its findings in *Usery* and once again applied federal wage and hour laws to nonnational governments—in this specific instance, to a mass transit system run by the city of San Antonio.[15] What really offended the states was the written opinion of the Court, in which it excused itself from such future controversies involving state claims against congressional power exercised under the commerce clause. Now Congress alone, with little or no judicial oversight, would be allowed to determine, through the political process, how extensively it would intrude on what had been state and local prerogatives. One dissenting Supreme Court justice wrote that "all that stands between the remaining essentials of state sovereignty and Congress is the latter's underdeveloped capacity for self-restraint."[16] In the view of some critics, the states were relegated to the status of any other special-interest group and the Tenth Amendment was irrelevant. Other critics more optimistically observed that the narrow 5-to-4 decision could be revisited by a more conservative Supreme Court at a later date.[17]

Sure enough, in 1995 the Court seemingly reaffirmed the Tenth Amendment in *U.S.* v. *Lopez* by recognizing a limit to Congress's power over interstate commerce. Ironically, this case also involved San Antonio, where a high school student, Alfonso Lopez, was arrested for bringing a handgun to school. He was charged with violating the Gun Free School Zones Act of 1990, which banned the possession of a firearm within 1,000 feet of a school. Here, the Court ruled that Congress had unconstitutionally extended its power to regulate interstate commerce because there was no connection between the gun law and interstate commerce.[18] A 2000 Supreme Court ruling further restricted Congress's power to regulate interstate commerce by finding that female rape victims cannot sue their attackers in federal court under the Violence Against Women Act. Instead, they must pursue their claims in state court.[19]

The Court continued to recalibrate the scales of power in favor of the states in a series of rulings beginning in 1997. First, the Court gave states the authority to incarcerate convicted sexual predators in mental institutions once their criminal sentences have ended.[20] Next, the Court ruled that Congress offended "the very principle of separate state sovereignty" by requiring local police to conduct background checks on people who want to purchase handguns (although they may do so voluntarily). Thus, a major section of the so-called Brady Bill was declared unconstitutional.[21] The Court then let stand a lower-court ruling that upheld the constitutionality of California's Proposition 209, which banned race- or sex-based hiring preferences in college admissions, hiring decisions, and government contracting.[22] The Court also upheld Oregon's Death with Dignity Act, which permitted doctor-assisted suicides[23] and granted states the freedom to restrict anti-abortion demonstrations outside health clinics.[24]

Recent rulings based on the Eleventh Amendment have revived the notion of the sovereign immunity of the states. According to this doctrine, which dates back to the Middle Ages, a king (the state) cannot be sued without his (its) consent (the Eleventh Amendment protects states from lawsuits by citizens of other states or foreign nations). Supreme Court decisions have upheld the sovereign immunity of the states from being sued in federal courts in cases involving lawsuits by Indian tribes,[25] patent infringement when a state ventures into commercial activities,[26] and discrimination against older employees.[27] The Court also protected the states against private complaints before federal agencies.[28] But in a 2004 case, the Court restricted the states' Eleventh Amendment immunity under the Americans with Disabilities Act.[29]

The Rehnquist Court positioned itself on the side of the states in most conflicts with the national government. However, the Supreme Court does not decide unilaterally in favor of the states in all cases, notwithstanding one justice's complaint that the majority has become "(a) mindless dragon that indiscriminately chews gaping holes in federal statutes."[30] For example, the Court limited the authority of the states to regulate tobacco advertising.[31] The Court's willingness to overturn the Florida Supreme Court's decisions in issues concerning the ballot counting in the 2000 presidential race indicates that ideology and partisanship sometimes trump federalism.[32] Court watchers await with interest the direction that Chief Justice John Roberts will take on federalism issues.

Federal intrusions into the affairs of state and local governments continue to be burdensome and unwelcome. For now, the Tenth and Eleventh Amendments are useful weapons for fending off federal encroachments on the power of state and local officials, but their power can be shattered by a single justice's change of heart or by the conservative Supreme Court majority today.

MODELS OF FEDERALISM

Perceptions of the role of the states in the federal system have shifted from time to time throughout our history. Those who study the federal system have generally described these perceptions through various models or metaphors that attempt to present federalism's complexity in a readily understandable form. Such models have been used both to enhance understanding and, when opportunities arise, to pursue ideological and partisan objectives.

Dual Federalism (1787–1932)

dual federalism

A model of federalism in which the responsibilities and activities of the national and state governments are separate and distinct.

The model of **dual federalism** holds that the national and state governments are sovereign and equal within their respective spheres of authority as set forth in the Constitution. The national government exercises those powers specifically designated to it, and the remainder are reserved for the states. The metaphor is that of a layer cake, with two separate colored layers one on top of the other.

Dual federalism, which has its roots in the compact theory, was dominant for the first 145 years of U.S. federalism, although the Civil War and other events led to substantial modifications of the model.[33] Until 1860, the functions of the national government remained largely restricted to the delegated powers. Federal financial assistance to the states was very limited. The states had the dominant influence on the everyday lives of their citizens. After the Civil War shattered secession and dealt the compact theory of state-centered federalism a death blow, the nation-centered view became paramount.

Cooperative Federalism (1933–1964)

The selection of a specific date for the demise of dual federalism is rather subjective, but 1933, when Franklin D. Roosevelt became president, is a reasonable estimate. Roosevelt's New Deal buried dual federalism by expanding national authority over commerce, taxation, and the economy.

cooperative federalism

A model of federalism that stresses the linkages and joint arrangements among the three levels of government.

Cooperative federalism recognizes the sharing of responsibilities and financing by all levels of government. Beginning with the Great Depression, the national government increasingly cooperated with states and localities to provide jobs and social welfare, to develop the nation's infrastructure, and to promote economic development.

The cooperative aspects of this era were measured in governmental finances. The national government spent huge amounts of money to alleviate the ravages of the Great Depression and to get the U.S. economic machinery back into gear. Total federal expenditures rose from 2.5 percent of the gross national product (GNP) in 1929 to 18.7 percent just thirty years later, far surpassing the growth in state and local spending during the same period. The number of federal grants-in-aid rose from twelve in 1932, with a value of $193 million, to twenty-six in 1937, with a value of $2.66 billion. A substantial amount of the federal aid was sent directly to local governments, particularly counties and school districts. The variety of grant programs also exploded, with disbursements for maternal and child health care, aid to the blind, treatment of venereal disease, public housing, road and bridge construction, and wildlife conservation.

Contemporary Variations on Cooperative Federalism (Since 1964)

The broad theme of cooperative federalism has many variations. All of them stress intergovernmental sharing. Among these variations are creative federalism and new federalism.

creative federalism

A model of cooperative federalism in which many new grants-in-aid, including direct national-local financial arrangements, were made.

Creative federalism was devised by President Lyndon B. Johnson to promote his dream of a "Great Society." Johnson sought to build the Great Society through a massive, grant-funded attack on the most serious problems facing the nation: poverty, crime, poor health care, and inadequate education, among others. More than two hundred new grants were put into place during the Johnson presidency. Johnson's policy of vast government spending bypassed the states in distributing funds directly to cities and counties for some seventy of the new programs. Understandably, the states did not appreciate losing influence over how localities could spend their national dollars.

new federalism

A model that represents a return of powers and responsibilities to the states.

New federalism is a model that has been employed with distinct but related meanings in different presidencies. The new federalism initiated by Richard Nixon was intended to restore power to the states and localities and to improve intergovernmental arrangements for delivering services. Among the major policy changes were the establishment of ten regional councils to coordinate national program administration across the country and the implementation of revenue sharing to give states and localities greater flexibility in program spending and decision making.

Ronald Reagan's brand of new federalism, like Nixon's version, sought to give more power and program authority to states and localities, at least in theory. However, Reagan's main goal—to shrink the size of the national government—soon became obvious. Reagan's new-federalism initiative won congressional approval to merge fifty-seven categorical grants into nine new block grants and to eliminate another sixty categorical grants. The states got more authority, but the funding for the new block grants decreased almost 25 percent from the previous year's allocation for the separate categorical grants.[34]

Reagan and his congressional allies chipped away at other grant programs in an effort to reduce the size of government, and also terminated revenue sharing in 1986. Called *general revenue sharing* (GRS) when enacted during the Nixon administration, this program was highly popular with state and local officials. GRS provided funds to state and general-purpose local governments with no strings attached. It was discontinued largely because of the mounting national budget deficit; another factor was Congress's desire to exert greater control over, and take more credit for, how federal monies were spent.

The Reagan legacy lived on when George H.W. Bush (senior) entered the White House in 1988. Although the style was different—in the view of many state and local officials, the Bush administration was more sympathetic—the substance remained the same.[35] The Bush administration continued emphasizing the sorting out of national, state, and local responsibilities in such areas as transportation and education.

By 1994, with the election of Republican majorities in the U.S. House and Senate as well as the election of many new Republican governors, new federalism came back in style with impressive force. The New Federalists, whose ranks included many Democrats, sought once again to sort out intergovernmental responsibilities. For the first time in recent memory, the states and localities were basically united and working together through a coalition of government interest groups, including the National Governors' Association and the National

League of Cities, to design smaller, more efficient government with greater program and policy flexibility for the states and localities.

devolution

The delegating of power and programs from the federal to state and local governments.

This planned delegating of power from the federal to state and local governments is termed **devolution.** The constellation of supporters for devolution was impressive. The governors, acting as individuals and through the National Governors' Association, found a sympathetic President Clinton and congressional majority, and a Supreme Court increasingly likely to rule in favor of state authority. Moreover, public opinion is consistently in favor of greater state and local government authority. Public opinion polls show that citizens believe state and local governments do a better job than the national government in spending money and delivering services.[36] Together, these powerful forces for devolution gradually reversed more than a century of centralizing tendencies in U.S. federalism. This trend was so striking that it has been called the "devolution revolution."

Although such steps are encouraging to states and localities, the federal government seems always to be standing by to jerk the rug out from under their feet. As observed by former Tennessee governor Lamar Alexander, "Conservatives are as bad as liberals about imposing mandates once they come to Washington."[37] Serious discussion about additional turnbacks and innovations lost steam in 1998 as conservative moralistic forces in Congress sought to usurp state authority over property rights and blood-alcohol limits, among other issues.

The views of the second president Bush were poorly articulated, but legislative initiatives of his administration and of Republican supporters in Congress sought to preempt state authority over school testing systems and the right-to-die decisions, override state laws that guarantee patient rights, obstruct state laws that permit the medical use of marijuana, and impose new homeland security requirements on the states. The predominance of business interests in Washington, D.C., appeared to have stanched devolution through what one writer calls "the law of political physics—that for every flurry of state and local business regulations, there is an equal and opposite" effort by business to counter it in the nation's capitol.[38] The centralizing policies of the Bush administration were most apparent in homeland security and the "War on Terror," which served as a convenient justification for many centralizing actions by the president and Congress. Surveillance provisions, federalization of the state Guards, and various mandates had a combined effect of pulling power back into Washington, D.C.

INTERGOVERNMENTAL RELATIONS

Cooperative federalism demands positive interactions among governments at all levels. Whatever the short-term trend of federal-state-local relations, cooperative activities are constantly growing among the three levels of government. For that matter, so are relationships between the states and Indian tribes.

Tribal Governments

With the arrival of the Europeans, the number of the estimated 7 to 10 million people who lived in what is now the continental United States was soon severely depleted by warfare, disease, and famine. Hundreds of treaties, statutes, and other agreements notwithstanding, the Native Americans were eventually deprived of their traditional lands and isolated on reservations. Today, some 2.5 million people identify themselves as Native American, belonging to 557 recognized tribes. About one-third of them continue to live on tribal reservations, mostly in the western portion of the United States. The Navajo Nation, for instance, has a population of more than 250,000 and covers some 17 million acres, extending from northwest New Mexico to northeast Arizona and southeast Utah.

Tribes are semi-sovereign nations exercising self-government on their reservations. They are under the authority and supervision of Congress, and are subject to the authority of federal courts, but their legal relationship with the states is complex. Tribal governments are permitted to regulate their internal affairs, hold elections, and enforce their own laws under congressional supervision. States are prevented from taxing or regulating tribes, or extending judicial power over them. Off the reservation, however, Native Americans are subject to the same legalities as any other state residents. They enjoy voting rights in both federal and state elections.

Recently, the tribes and the states have adopted a more consultative relationship to pursue common interests, such as fishing and hunting rights, and regulation of gambling on reservations. Occasionally, however, interactions between tribal governments, the state, and nearby local governments are testy. Actions concerning tribal land use may conflict with local zoning or state environmental policy. The tax-free sale of gasoline and alcohol and tobacco products on the reservation diminishes sales tax revenues. Tribes seek to recover ancestral lands from present occupants. And tribal casinos sometimes offer games that are prohibited under state law. When conflicts arise, states and tribal governments may sort out their differences through compacts. Otherwise, Congress may be asked to enter the fray.

Interstate Cooperation

Cooperation Under the Constitution There are four formal provisions for cooperation among the states.

1. The *full faith and credit clause* of the Constitution binds every citizen of every state to the laws and policies of other states. Crossing a state boundary does not alter a legal obligation. The courts have interpreted full faith and credit to apply to contracts, wills, divorces, and many other legalities. The clause does not, however, extend to criminal judgments. Yet to be determined is whether gay marriages or civil unions granted by one state must be recognized by other states.
2. The *interstate rendition clause* begins where full faith and credit leaves off, covering persons convicted of criminal violations. Governors are required to extradite (return) fugitives to the state in which they were found guilty or are under indictment (although in certain cases they may refuse).
3. The *privileges and immunities clause* states that "the citizens of each state shall be entitled to all privileges and immunities of citizens in the several states." This clause was intended by the Framers to prevent any state from discriminating against citizens of another state who happen to be traveling or

temporarily dwelling outside their own state's borders. Of course, states do discriminate against nonresidents in such matters as out-of-state tuition, hunting and fishing license fees, and residency requirements for voting. The Supreme Court has upheld these and other minor discrepancies, so long as the "fundamental rights" of nonresidents are not violated.

4. Finally, the *interstate compact clause* authorizes the states to negotiate compacts. Early interstate compacts were used to settle boundary disputes. About 150 are in effect today in a variety of areas, including shared water resources, pest control, riverboat gambling, and education.

Informal Cooperation Among the States Interstate cooperation can be facilitated through a variety of informal methods. One example is the establishment of regional interstate commissions, such as the Appalachian Regional Commission (ARC), which was created by national legislation in 1965 to attack poverty in the states of Appalachia.

In addition, states have developed uniform laws to help manage common problems ranging from child support to welfare cheating. Interstate cooperation also occurs through information sharing among elected and appointed officials and the organizations to which they belong, such as the National Governors Association and the National Conference of State Legislatures. It may take place in legal actions, as demonstrated by the state attorneys general who united to sue the tobacco companies for driving up medical costs. Or, one state may contract with another for a service, as Hawaii does with Arizona for a medical management information system.

Of course, interstate relations do not always go smoothly; occasionally, the states get into serious (and not so serious) conflicts and disagreements. Those that the states cannot settle themselves are taken directly to the U.S. Supreme Court for resolution. One conflict recently resolved by the Court involves which state owns Ellis Island, where millions of immigrants landed just offshore from New York City between 1892 and 1954, and where thousands of tourists visit today. Originally the Island comprised only three acres, but landfill projects expanded it to 27.5 acres. In 1998, after some two hundred years of dispute, the Court decided that New York retained sovereignty over the original three acres, while New Jersey gained control of the landfill area. With a nod to the biblical king Solomon, the Court divided the Great Hall, where some 12 million immigrants were processed, equally between the two states.[39]

Intergovernmental Financial Relations

Revenues are the funds that governments have at their disposal. They are derived from taxes, fees and charges, and transfers from other levels of government. Expenditures are the ways in which the governmental revenues are disbursed. Governments spend money to operate programs, to build public facilities, and to pay off debts.

grant-in-aid
An intergovernmental transfer of funds or other assets, subject to conditions.

The **grant-in-aid** is the primary mechanism for transferring money from the national to the state and local governments. The national government makes grants available for a number of reasons: to redistribute wealth, to establish minimum policy standards, and to achieve national goals. But grants are primarily designed to help meet the needs of state and local governments, including environmental protection, transportation, community and regional development, education, and health care. Federal grant outlays total more than $400 billion a year.

Discretion of Recipients There are two major variations in grants: the amount of discretion (independence) the recipient has in determining how to spend the money, and the conditions under which the grant is awarded. Imagine a spectrum running from maximum discretion to minimum discretion. The grant labels that correspond to these endpoints are **revenue sharing** and **categorical grants,** respectively. Under revenue sharing, states and communities are allocated funds that they may use for any purpose. A categorical grant, in contrast, can be used by the recipient government only for a narrowly defined purpose, such as removing asbestos from school buildings or acquiring land for public use.

Located between revenue sharing and categorical grants on the discretion spectrum are block grants. **Block grants** are *broad-based grants;* that is, they can be used anywhere within a functional area such as transportation or health care. The difference between categorical and block grants is that the recipient government decides how block grants will be spent. For instance, a local school system can decide whether the purchase of personal computers is more important than buying microscopes for the science laboratory. Today there are about 625 grants in existence, including 17 block grants. Block grants give nonnational governments considerable flexibility in responding to pressing needs and preferred goals. These grant mechanisms assume that state and local governments can make rational choices among competing claims.

Conditions for Grants Grants also vary in the manner in which they are awarded. A **formula grant** makes funding available automatically, based on state and local conditions such as poverty level or unemployment rate. A **project grant** is awarded to selected applicants, based on administrative assessments of the strength of competing proposals. Block grants are distributed on a formula basis; categorical grants can be either formula- or project-based.

Recognition of these two characteristics—the amount of discretion enjoyed by the recipient jurisdiction and the manner in which the grant is awarded—is important for understanding the grant system. Another, less prominent factor also affects intergovernmental financial relations: the existence of *matching requirements*. Most federal grants require that the recipient government use its own resources to pay a certain percentage of program costs. This arrangement is designed to stimulate state and local spending on programs deemed to be in the national interest and to discourage nonnational governments from participating in a program simply because money is available.

FEDERAL PURSE STRINGS

Federalism today turns less on theory and more on money. The distribution of intergovernmental monies and the conditions attached to them define the

revenue sharing

A "no-strings" form of financial aid from one level of government to another.

categorical grant

A form of financial aid from one level of government to another to be used for a narrowly defined purpose.

block grant

A form of financial aid from one level of government to another for use in a broad area.

formula grant

A funding mechanism that automatically allocates monies based on conditions in the recipient government.

project grant

A funding mechanism that awards monies based on the strength of an applicant government's proposal.

distribution of governmental power and authority. Federalism is a matter not only of which level of government will do what, but of which level will pay for it. Some have called this a period of "fend-for-yourself federalism," with each jurisdiction essentially on its own in a Darwinian struggle for financial survival.

The Importance of Federal Funds

Figure 2.1 provides a historical look at national grant-in-aid expenditures. The second set of bars in Figure 2.1 documents the growing proportion of national dollars in the expenditures of state and local governments, but reflecting the fact that aid to states and localities still consumes a relatively small share of the federal government's budget.

FIGURE 2.1	**Historical Trends in Federal Grant-in-Aid Outlays**

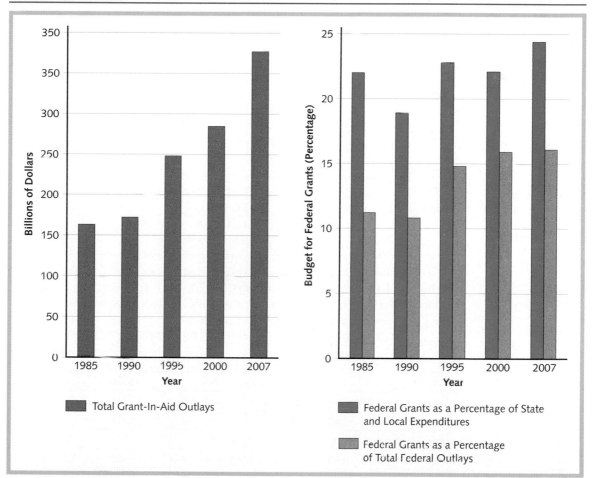

NOTE: Figures for 2007 are estimates.

SOURCE: U.S. Office of Management and Budget, Trends in Federal Grant to State and Local Governments, Fiscal Year 2007, www.cbo.gov/ftpdoc.cfm?index.

Although the Washington-funded portion of state and local government expenditures is only around 32 percent, it represents an important source of revenue for nonnational governments. However, the funds were not spread evenly across the country (see Table 2.1). Alaska and Wyoming received the most per capita. Federal grants poured into these states at the rate of $4,908 and $3,230, respectively. In last place is Nevada, where federal grant monies averaged just $995 per person.

TABLE 2.1   **Federal Grants to State and Local Governments, 2004, in Rank Order**

STATE	GRANTS PER CAPITA	STATE	GRANTS PER CAPITA
Alaska	$4,908	Delaware	1,495
Wyoming	3,230	North Carolina	1,472
New York	2,601	Washington	1,464
New Mexico	2,450	South Carolina	1,464
North Dakota	2,388	Arizona	1,456
Vermont	2,290	Nebraska	1,449
Massachusetts	2,163	New Hampshire	1,446
Rhode Island	2,155	Oregon	1,442
Montana	2,155	Ohio	1,441
South Dakota	2,101	Idaho	1,432
Maine	2,094	Minnesota	1,413
West Virginia	2,039	Iowa	1,367
Mississippi	1,853	Wisconsin	1,358
Louisiana	1,724	Georgia	1,332
Hawaii	1,709	Michigan	1,308
Arkansas	1,701	New Jersey	1,303
Tennessee	1,671	Illinois	1,300
Kentucky	1,626	Kansas	1,268
Maryland	1,590	Texas	1,236
Connecticut	1,586	Utah	1,234
Alabama	1,547	Colorado	1,226
California	1,519	Indiana	1,192
Missouri	1,518	Florida	1,127
Pennsylvania	1,605	Virginia	1,071
Oklahoma	1,496	Nevada	995

SOURCE: Kendra A. Hovey and Harold A. Hovey State Fact Finder 2006 (Washington, DC: Congressional Quarterly Press, 2006), p. 128.

States battle in Congress over their share of grant allocations, which are affected by such factors as the poverty level and existence of military installations in the state. The states attempt to influence competitive project grant awards and lobby Congress to adjust the weighing of certain factors in formula grants in their favor. State and local influence is wielded by the representatives sitting in Congress and through various actions by elected state and local officials and their Washington lobbyists.

National expenditures in nongrant forms also affect state and local economies substantially. In the nongrant category are payments to individuals (representing 65 percent of total federal grants in 2007, up from 36 percent in the 1980s), notably through the Social Security system; Medicaid payments; purchases by the national government; and wages and salaries of federal workers, most of whom work outside of Washington, D.C. In this sense, federal expenditures emphasize people more than places.

Here's the Check and Here's What to Do with It: Mandates, Preemptions, Set-asides, and Cost Ceilings

Although many voices are crying, "Let the states and localities do it," Congress continues to impose mandates and preempt the states. In addition, Congress includes set-asides and cost ceilings in block grants. Old habits die hard, and one of Congress's oldest habits is to place requirements and conditions on the states. Washington-based politicians of both major political parties may claim to support state power in principle, but when it conflicts with other priorities, devolution takes a back seat.

federal mandate
A requirement that a state or local government undertake a specific activity or provide a particular service as a condition of funding.

Federal mandates are especially burdensome when they are unfunded—that is, when the national government requires the states and localities to take action but does not pay for it. Who does pay? The states and localities do. Recent federal mandates require the states to establish elaborate school testing programs, staff homeland security operations, make Viagra available to Medicare recipients, and instruct them to standardize their drivers' licenses. The total cost of these "mandate millstones" hanging round the necks of states and localities runs up to $29 billion annually.[40] Mounting opposition to mandates without money finally convinced Congress to enact the Unfunded Mandate Reform Act of 1995, which provides that any bill imposing a mandate of more than $50 million on a state or local government must include a cost estimate. If passed, the legislation must include sufficient funds to pay for the mandate. Indications are that proposed laws containing unfunded mandates are facing tougher scrutiny in Congress than before and that Congress is taking a more consultative approach with state and local officials. However, members of Congress are always threatening to revert to their mandating ways.

As noted earlier, *preemption* represents another intrusion of the national government into the state sphere. It takes two forms: *total* preemption, whereby the national government seizes all regulatory authority for a given function from states and localities; and *partial* preemption, whereby the national government establishes minimum national standards for state-implemented programs. Both forms prevent states from doing what they want. One example of a totally preemptive action is the Americans with Disabilities Act, which requires states and localities to make physical and occupational accommodation for disabled persons. Many partial preemptions involve environmental protection, whereby states may regulate pollution emissions so long as state standards are at least as stringent as those of the federal government. A new concern of global preemption is raised by the 1994 General Agreement on Tariffs and Trade (GATT), which permits foreign corporations to challenge in the World Trade Organization state laws that may unfairly discriminate against them.

Thus, when mandates and preemptions are taken into consideration, a less optimistic picture of intergovernmental relations emerges. To the states and localities it seems that the country has shifted from cooperative federalism to coercive federalism or, in the words of Governor Ben Nelson of Nebraska, demoted states from significant policymakers to branch managers "of a behemoth central government."[41]

set-asides

Requirements in block grants that assign a certain percentage expenditure for a particular activity.

Set-asides offer an alternative mechanism through which policymakers in Washington, D.C., can influence the behavior of distant governments. Set-asides are provisions in block grants that designate a certain minimum percentage expenditure on a particular activity. For example, the Alcohol, Drug Abuse, and Mental Health Block Grant contains requirements that states spend at least 50 percent of the funds on services to intravenous (IV) drug users. The Congress reasoned that the sharing of hypodermic needles among addicts was contributing to the spread of the AIDS virus and that states were not doing enough to address the problem. But state leaders, though they admitted AIDS was a national priority, argued that the problem was not uniformly spread around the country. Why should Montana spend the same proportion of its funds on IV drug users as New York? Perhaps Montana should spend its drug abuse funds on adolescent alcohol abusers. In any case, the issue is clear: Who should decide how federal funds are to be spent—the government allocating the funds or the one implementing the program?

THE FUTURE OF FEDERALISM

For the states and localities, a decade of national policy gridlock has meant a golden opportunity to reverse more than a century of centralizing forces. They have taken up the slack in the federal system and are busily innovating, developing and implementing policies in a great variety of fields, from social welfare and health care to education and economic development. As laboratories of democracy, states have experimented with and designed numerous policies that later have served as models for other states and for Congress. For instance, states have recently pioneered policy initiatives on cost savings on prescription drugs, health insurance for children and the poor, a patients' bill of rights, campaign finance reform, stem cell research, nanotechnology, and global warming, among many other fields. Hordes of lobbyists representing the health care industry, insurance, and other interests have been attracted to state capitals like bees to honey.

Some states, including California, Massachusetts, Oregon, and Wisconsin, consistently rank high as policy initiators. But others predictably bring up the rear. Counting as policy laggards are Alabama, Mississippi, and South Carolina.[42] Why are some states more innovative than others? A host of factors come into play, including political culture, the presence of policy entrepreneurs, levels of population and population growth, urbanization, and state wealth. And while all states achieve positive policy breakthroughs at one time or another, most are also guilty of occasional boneheaded decisions. Policy diversity flourishes. Take immigration policy, for example. While Congress flailed about to no useful effect in 2007, thirty-three states enacted immigration law reform. Some, including Arizona, Colorado, and Georgia, passed tough, anti-immigrant measures. Others, including Nebraska, gave illegals in-state college tuition rates and other resident benefits.

As the population and economic activities of the nation expand, sentiment is building that Washington is not the best location for addressing all the nation's complex policy problems. Whereas centrally designing and implementing policies and programs once was believed to be the best approach, today it implies wasteful and ineffective one-size-fits-all government. The trend in government, as well as in business, is, where feasible, to decentralize decision making to the lowest feasible level of the organization. For the U.S. federal system, that means sending decision making to the states and localities and even, in some instances, to nonprofit organizations and citizens' groups.

In fairness to the national government, remember that much federal intervention has been in response to state failures to govern effectively and fairly. Corruption, racial prejudice and exclusion, and rampant parochialism, among other shortcomings, have prompted presidential, congressional, and judicial interventions that have, on the whole, helped the states move to the much higher plane they inhabit today.

Unfortunately, at the very time that state and local governments are most needed as policy leaders and problem solvers, certain social and economic forces seriously threaten state and local government capability. Globalization of business, unfavorable federal tax changes, and economic recessions have reduced state and local revenues. Millions of children remain in poverty. The ranks of the medically uninsured are rising. Illegal drugs and gang activity, homelessness, and a flood of immigrants present seemingly impossible challenges. Finally, the growing disparity of wealth and income threatens our great reservoir of political and social stability, the middle class.

For its part, the federal government is provoking growing criticism for tying the hands of the states and localities with mandates, preemptions, and confused and conflicting policy directives. Most state and local governments *want* to become more creative, but they are also being *forced* to do so to figure out how to implement and pay for federally mandated requirements. This conflicted, ambiguous federalism is something less than empowerment.[43] When the president, federal agencies, or members of Congress take actions to squash innovative programs such as legalization of medical marijuana or assisted suicide, they profess to do so for purposes of the national interest or high moral principles. But some think the issue is also about money and power and, perhaps at the most basic level, about the need for Congress to justify its existence in an increasingly state and local political world.

The states are determined to oppose further federal preemptions of their powers and responsibilities. They have fought to protect the health, safety, and physical environment of their citizens, often with standards and a level of commitment that far exceed those of the federal government. They have continued to serve as political laboratories for experiments in service delivery, health care, and other fields, despite severe reductions in federal financial support and expensive government-spending requirements. As the burdens of governing 300 million Americans have grown, the limitations of the national government have become evident. Effective federalism in the United States today demands a cooperative partnership among nation, states, and localities.

Even homeland security, usually considered to be primarily a national government responsibility, actually calls for more—not less—intergovernmental cooperation.[44] State and local governments play critical roles in all four key functions of homeland security: prevention, preparedness, response, and recovery. Local governments are first responders to any sort of disaster, natural or human-caused, while states provide crisis management, emergency services, and coordination, and steer recovery efforts.

The question of the balance of power and responsibility in U.S. federalism is no less important now than it was two hundred years ago. The focus of the debate has shifted, however, to a pragmatic interest in how the responsibility of governing should be sorted out among the three levels of government. As pointed out by an insightful observer of U.S. government, "The American federal system has never been static. It has changed radically over the years, as tides of centralization and decentralization have altered the balance of power and the allocation of functions among the different levels of "government."[45] The pendulum marking the balance has swung to and fro over the two centuries of U.S. federalism. Today it swings in the direction of the state and local governments.

CHAPTER RECAP

- U.S. federalism is an ongoing experiment in governance.
- A fundamental question is: What is the proper balance of power and responsibility between the national government and the states?
- Until recently, the trend has been generally in the direction of a stronger national government. But there has been a resurgence of the state and local governments as political and policy actors.
- The power relationships among the three levels of government are described by various models, including dual and cooperative federalism. The operative model is cooperative federalism, under the variant known as new federalism.
- A key ingredient of federalism is intergovernmental relations, particularly in financial interactions.
- The national government imposes certain controversial requirements on grants-in-aid, including mandates, preemptions, and set-asides.

Key Terms

unitary system *(p. 22)*
confederacy *(p. 22)*
federal system *(p. 22)*
factions *(p. 23)*
nation-centered federalism *(p. 27)*
state-centered federalism *(p. 27)*
reserved powers *(p. 27)*
Tenth Amendment *(p. 27)*
enumerated (delegated) powers *(p. 27)*
compact theory *(p. 27)*
national supremacy clause *(p. 28)*
necessary and proper clause *(p. 28)*
implied powers *(p. 28)*
commerce clause *(p. 29)*
general welfare clause *(p. 29)*
Fourteenth Amendment *(p. 29)*

Sixteenth Amendment *(p. 30)*
federal preemption *(p. 30)*
dual federalism *(p. 33)*
cooperative federalism *(p. 33)*
creative federalism *(p. 34)*
new federalism *(p. 34)*
devolution *(p. 35)*
grant-in-aid *(p. 37)*
revenue sharing *(p. 38)*
categorical grant *(p. 38)*
block grant *(p. 38)*
formula grant *(p. 38)*
project grant *(p. 38)*
federal mandate *(p. 40)*
set-asides *(p. 42)*

Internet Resources

Examples of unfunded mandates are found on a Heritage Foundation webpage at **www.regulation.org/states.html**. Costs of unfunded mandates are tracked by NCSL in their mandate monitor at: **www.ncsl.org/standcomm/scbudg/ manmon.htm.**

Federalism decisions of the U.S. Supreme Court and other federalism topics may be reviewed at the Council of State Governments' website at **www.statesnews .org** or **www.csg.org.** Other websites that often feature federalism news and issues are **www.governing.com** and **www.stateline.org.**

For current information on relationships among the three levels of government see **www.governing.com.**

The website **www.census.gov** has comparative data on the states and localities, particularly on state and local finances.

Information on tribal governments and politics may be acquired at **www .tribal-institute.org** and **www.narf.org.**

3 State Constitutions

FOCUS QUESTIONS

1. What is the purpose of a state constitution?

2. How have state constitutions evolved?

3. How have state constitutions evolved to meet the challenges of modern governance?

4. What are the methods for changing state constitutions?

*S*tate constitutions are alike in many important respects, but they are decidedly different in others. Consider the recent public votes on state constitutional changes. Alabama voters refused to strike segregationist language from their state's constitution, preferring to keep provisions (now unenforceable under federal law) mandating racially segregated schools and imposing poll taxes. After vitriolic debate, South Carolina voters agreed to replace liquor mini-bottles with "free pour" in bars and restaurants. California voters approved $3 billion in public funding for embryonic stem-cell research. And New Mexico became the twelfth state to allow the medical use of marijuana. So long as these and countless other state constitutional amendments do not intrude on federal law, they stand. This demonstrates that constitutions are, in their essence, *political* documents—products of state history, culture, events, economy, and above all, the clash of interests.

All state constitutions both distribute and constrain political power among groups and regions. They set forth the basic framework and operating rules for government, allocate power to the three branches, establish the scope of state and local governmental authority, and protect individual rights.[1] Constitutions represent the **fundamental law** of a state, superior to statutory law. They provide a set of rules for the game of state government, and those who master the regulations and procedures have a distinct advantage over novices. Everything that a state government does and represents is rooted in its constitution. Constitutions do not describe the full reality of a political system, but they do

fundamental law

The basic legal and political document of a state; it prescribes the rules through which government operates.

46

provide a window through which to perceive its reality. Only the federal Constitution and federal statutes take priority over state constitutions. This is why the constitution is called the fundamental law.

To most people, however, constitutional law still means the federal document. State constitutions are often neglected in secondary school and college courses in history and political science. Astonishingly, one national survey discovered that 51 percent of Americans were not aware that their state had its own constitution.[2]

In the U.S. system of *dual constitutionalism,* in which there are both national and state constitutions, the national government is supreme within the spheres of authority specifically delegated to it in the U.S. Constitution. Powers granted to the national government are denied to the states. But the national Constitution is incomplete. It leaves many key constitutional issues to the states, including those pertaining to local finance, public education, and the organization of state and local government.[3] In theory, state constitutions are supreme for all matters not expressly within the national government's jurisdiction or preempted by federal constitutional or statutory law. In practice, however, congressional actions and federal court interpretations have expanded the powers of the national government and, in some cases, eroded the powers of the states. And, in reality, many concurrent powers, such as taxing, spending, and protecting citizens' health and safety, are shared by all levels of government.

The earliest state constitutions were simple documents reflecting an agrarian economy, single-owner businesses, and horse-and-buggy transportation. As American society and the economy changed, the rules of state government also required transformation. Some reforms have reflected changing political fortunes: Newly powerful groups have pressed to revise the state constitution to reflect their interests, or one or another political party has gained control of state government and sought to solidify its power. Constitutional reforms have promoted different views of politics and the public interest, as when Progressive reformers rallied for honest and efficient government in the late nineteenth and early twentieth centuries.[4] For the past 50 years, constitutional revisions have concentrated power in the governor's office, unified court systems, and generally sought to make state government more efficient, effective, and responsive to shifting social and economic forces. The fact that constitutions are subject to change also recognizes that human judgment is not infallible, nor human understanding perfect.[5] Through constitutional reform, states can elevate their role as democratic laboratories by responding to the changing needs and opinions of citizens. This is in sharp contrast to the seldom-amended federal Constitution.

THE EVOLUTION OF STATE CONSTITUTIONS

When the states won their independence from Great Britain more than two hundred years ago, there was no precedent for writing constitutions. A constitution of the Five Nations of the Iroquois called the Great Binding Law existed, but it was oral and not particularly relevant to the people in the colonies.[6] The thirteen colonial charters provided the foundation for the new state constitutions. These were brief documents (around five pages each) that the Crown had granted to trading companies and individuals to govern settlements in the new territories. As the settlements became full colonies, the charters were expanded to incorporate the "rights of Englishmen"—political and civil rights first enumerated by the Magna Carta in 1215. For distant territories too remote from their native country to be governed by its laws, these charters also laid down some basic principles of colonial government.[7]

In a sense, the existence of these documents helped fuel the fires of independence. In what was to become Connecticut, early settlers escaping the oppressive rule of the Massachusetts Bay Colony took matters of governance into their own hands. Under the leadership of Thomas Hooker, these ambitious farmers established an independent government free from references to the British Crown. The Fundamental Orders of 1639 contended that "the choice of the public magistrates belongs unto the people by God's own allowance. The privilege of election belongs to the people . . . it is in their power, also, to set the bounds and limitations of the power [of elected officials]."[8] Years later, a representative of King James II was sent to take possession of the Fundamental Orders and unite the New England colonies under the Crown. In a night meeting, as the Orders were laid out on a table before the king's men, the candles suddenly were extinguished. When they were rekindled, the document had disappeared. According to legend, a patriot had hidden it in a nearby hollow tree, later to be known as the Charter Oak. Infuriated, the king's men dissolved the colony's government and imposed autocratic rule that lasted many years. But they never found the Fundamental Orders, which essentially governed Connecticut until the Constitution of 1818 was adopted.[9]

The First State Constitutions

Following the War of Independence, the former colonies drafted their first constitutions in special revolutionary conventions or in legislative assemblies. With the exception of Massachusetts, the new states put their constitutions into effect immediately, without popular ratification. The making of the first state constitutions was not a casual or simple affair. Critical questions had to be answered in constitutional conventions, including those concerning how the new government would be structured, how and when elections would be held, and how land once owned by the Crown would be distributed. Territorial integrity was not well defined. For example, in what is now known as Kentucky, people frustrated with Virginia's rule met in 1784 and petitioned the Congress for statehood. It took six years and nine constitutional conventions before Kentucky became a state. Complicating factors causing delay involved the "necessity of communicating across the mountains, the change from the Articles of Confederation to the Constitution of the United States, Indian attacks, [and] the revelation of a plot to have Kentucky secure independence and join Spain."[10]

In content, most of these documents simply extended the colonial charters, removing references to the king and inserting a bill of rights. All incorporated the principles of limited government: a weak executive branch, the separation of

Connecticut's Charter Oak as depicted on the U.S. quarter.
SOURCE: United States Mint image.

powers, checks and balances, a bill of rights to protect the people and their property from arbitrary government actions, and (except for Pennsylvania) a bicameral legislature.[11] The earliest constitutions were not truly democratic. Essentially, they called for government by an aristocracy. Officeholding and voting, for instance, were restricted to white males of wealth and property.[12]

Only one of the thirteen original state constitutions, that of Massachusetts, survives (although it has been amended 120 times). It is the oldest functional constitution in the world. Its longevity can be attributed in large part to the foresight of its drafter, John Adams, who grounded the document in extensive research of governments that took him all the way back to the ancients. Even after many amendments, the Massachusetts constitution reflects a composite of the wisdom of the foremost political philosophers of the eighteenth century: John Locke, Jean-Jacques Rousseau, and the Baron de Montesquieu.[13] In this enduring document, Massachusetts establishes itself as a commonwealth (from the words *common weal*, meaning "general well-being"), on the principle that its citizens have a right to protect and manage their collective interests. (Kentucky, Pennsylvania, and Virginia are also commonwealths.)[14]

Legislative Supremacy

The first state constitutions reflected their framers' fear and distrust of the executive—a result of their experiences with the colonial governors. The governors were not all tyrants; but because they represented the British Crown and Parliament, they became a symbol of oppression to the colonists. As a result, the guiding principle of the new constitutional governments was **legislative supremacy,** and the legislatures were given overwhelming power at the expense of governors. Most governors were to be elected by the legislature, not the people, and were restricted to a single term of office. State judiciaries also were limited in authorized powers; and judges, like governors, were to be elected by the legislature.

legislative supremacy

The legislature's dominance of the other two branches of government.

The Growth of Executive Power

Disillusionment with the legislatures soon developed, spreading rapidly through the states during the early 1800s. There were many reasons for disenchantment, including the legislatures' failure to address problems caused by rapid population growth and the Industrial Revolution; the growing amount of legislation that favored private interests; and a mounting load of state indebtedness, which led nine states to default on their bonds in a single two-year period.

Gradually the executive branch began to accumulate more power and stature through constitutional amendments that provided for popular election of governors, who were also given longer terms and the authority to veto legislative bills. As executive power grew, public confidence in state legislatures continued to erode. This circumstance was reflected in the process of constitutional revision. One delegate at Kentucky's 1890 constitutional convention proclaimed that "the principal, if not the sole purpose of this constitution which we are here to frame, is to restrain the legislature's will and restrict its authority."[15] Also affecting constitutional change were broader social and economic forces in the United States, such as the extension of suffrage and popular participation in government, the rise of a corporate economy, the Civil War and Reconstruction, the growth of industry and commerce, the process of urbanization, and a growing movement for government reform. States rapidly replaced and amended their constitutions from the early 1800s to 1920 in response to these and other forces. The decade of the Civil War saw the highest level of constitutional activity in U.S. history, much of it in the southern states; between 1860 and 1870, twenty-seven constitutions were replaced or thoroughly revised as Confederate states ratified new documents after secession, then redrew the documents after Union victory to incorporate certain conditions of readmission to the United States.

Constitutional change after Reconstruction was driven by the Populist and Progressive reform movements. During the late 1800s, the Populists championed the causes of the "little man," including farmers and laborers. They sought to open the political process to the people through such constitutional devices as the initiative, the referendum, and the recall (see Chapter 4). The Progressives, who made their mark during the 1890–1920 period, were kindred spirits whose favorite targets were concentrated wealth, inefficiencies in government, machine politics, corruption, and boss rule in the cities. Reformers in both groups successfully promoted constitutional reforms such as regulation of campaign spending and party activities, replacement of party conventions with direct primary elections, and selection of judges through nonpartisan elections.

WEAKNESSES OF CONSTITUTIONS

Despite the numerous constitutional amendments and replacements enacted during the nineteenth and early twentieth centuries, by 1950 the states were buffeted by a rising chorus criticizing their fundamental laws. Ironically, many states were victims of past constitutional change, which left them with documents that were extravagantly long, frustratingly inflexible, and distressingly detailed. In general, state constitutions still provided for a feeble executive branch, granting limited administrative authority to the governor, permitting the popular election of numerous other executive branch officials, and organizing the executive into a hodgepodge of semiautonomous agencies, boards, and commissions. State judiciaries remained uncoordinated and overly complex, whereas legislatures suffered from archaic structures and procedures. Statutory detail, out-of-date language, local amendments (those that apply only to designated local governments), and other problems contaminated the documents and straitjacketed state government.

Excessive Length

From the first constitutions, which averaged 5,000 words, state documents had expanded into enormous tracts of verbiage averaging 27,000 words by 1967. (The U.S. Constitution contains 8,700 words.) Some of this growth resulted from increasing social and economic complexity, as well as from a perceived need to be very specific about what the legislatures could and could not do. The states did have to delineate their residual powers (those powers not delegated to the national government), identify the scope of their responsibility, and define the powers of local governments. In addition, state constitutions are much easier to amend than the federal Constitution. However, some constitutions went too far. Louisiana's exceeded 253,000 words. If local provisions were counted, Georgia's contained around 583,500 words, surpassing Tolstoy's *War and Peace* in length. Even today, the constitution of South Carolina limits local government indebtedness but then lists seventeen pages of exceptions. Maryland's constitution devotes an article to off-street parking in Baltimore. Oklahoma's sets the flash point for kerosene at 115 degrees for purposes of illumination,[16] and California's addresses a compelling issue of our time—the length of wrestling matches. A 2002 constitutional amendment in Florida prohibits "cruel and unusual confinement of pigs during pregnancy." The dubious prize for most verbose constitution today (Georgia's was replaced with a much briefer version) goes to Alabama's 340,136-word document. Table 3.1 provides an overview of the fifty state constitutions, including each one's length.

Not surprisingly, lengthy state constitutions tend to be plagued by contradictions and meaningless clauses. Some even address problems that are no longer with us, such as the regulation of steamboats[17] or the need to teach livestock feeding in Oklahoma public schools.

Verbose constitutions, such as those of Alabama, Oklahoma, and Colorado, fail to distinguish between fundamental law and issues that properly should be

| TABLE 3.1 | State Constitutions |

STATE	NUMBER OF CONSTITUTIONS	EFFECTIVE DATE OF PRESENT CONSTITUTION	ESTIMATED NUMBER OF WORDS	NUMBER OF AMENDMENTS	
				SUBMITTED TO VOTERS	ADOPTED
Alabama	6	1901	340,136	1088	794
Alaska	1	1959	15,988	41	29
Arizona	1	1912	28,876	254	141
Arkansas	5	1874	59,500	190	92
California	2	1879	54,645	870	514
Colorado	1	1876	74,522	315	150
Connecticut	4	1965	17,256	30	29
Delaware	4	1897	19,000	*	138
Florida	6	1969	51,456	141	110
Georgia	10	1983	39,526	86	66
Hawaii	1	1959	20,774	128	108
Idaho	1	1890	24,232	206	119
Illinois	4	1971	16,510	17	11
Indiana	2	1851	10,379	78	46
Iowa	2	1857	12,616	57	52
Kansas	1	1861	12,296	123	93
Kentucky	4	1891	23,911	75	41
Louisiana	11	1975	54,112	210	150
Maine	1	1820	16,276	203	171
Maryland	4	1867	46,600	257	221
Massachusetts	1	1780	36,700	148	120
Michigan	4	1964	34,659	66	28
Minnesota	1	1858	11,547	214	119
Mississippi	4	1890	24,323	158	123
Missouri	4	1945	42,600	170	109
Montana	2	1973	13,145	54	30
Nebraska	2	1875	20,048	344	224
Nevada	1	1864	31,377	226	134
New Hampshire	2	1784	9,200	287	145
New Jersey	3	1948	22,956	74	41
New Mexico	1	1912	27,200	284	155
New York	4	1895	51,700	291	216

(cont. on next page)

TABLE 3.1					
				NUMBER OF AMENDMENTS	
STATE	NUMBER OF CONSTITUTIONS	EFFECTIVE DATE OF PRESENT CONSTITUTION	ESTIMATED NUMBER OF WORDS	SUBMITTED TO VOTERS	ADOPTED
North Carolina	3	1971	16,532	42	34
North Dakota	1	1889	19,130	262	149
Ohio	2	1851	48,521	275	163
Oklahoma	1	1907	74,025	340	175
Oregon	1	1859	54,083	477	238
Pennsylvania	5	1968	27,711	36	30
Rhode Island	3	1986	10,908	11	10
South Carolina	7	1896	22,300	679	492
South Dakota	1	1889	27,675	223	213
Tennessee	3	1870	13,300	61	38
Texas	5	1876	80,000	614	439
Utah	1	1896	11,000	158	107
Vermont	3	1793	10,286	211	53
Virginia	6	1971	21,319	51	43
Washington	1	1889	33,354	170	97
West Virginia	2	1872	26,000	121	71
Wisconsin	1	1848	14,392	193	144
Wyoming	1	1890	31,800	123	97

*Proposed amendments are not submitted to the voters in Delaware.
NOTE: The information in this table is current through January 1, 2007. The constitutions referred to include those Civil War documents customarily listed by the individual states.
SOURCE: Copyright 2007, vol. 38, The Council of State Governments. Reprinted by permission of The Council of State Governments.

decided by the state legislature.[18] Excessive detail leads to litigation, as the courts must rule on conflicting provisions and challenges to constitutionality; hence the courts are often unnecessarily burdened with decisions that should be made by the legislature. Once incorporated into a constitution, a decision becomes as close to permanent as anything can be in politics. In contrast to a statute, which can be changed by a simple legislative majority, constitutional change requires an extraordinary majority, usually two-thirds or three-fourths of the legislature. This requirement hampers the legislature's ability to confront problems quickly and makes policy change more difficult. Of course, enshrining a principle in the constitution can be a deliberate strategy to protect special interests. Too many amendments may also deprive local governments of needed flexibility to cope with their own problems. Indeed, too much detail generates confusion, not only for legislatures and courts but also for the general public. It encourages political subterfuge to get around archaic or irrelevant provisions and breeds disrespect or even contempt for government.

State constitutions are political documents and, contrary to the admonitions of reformers, may sometimes be used to address some of the most controversial issues in politics, such as abortion rights, gay marriage, and sex education. Many detailed provisions explicitly favor or protect special interests, including public utilities, farmers, timber companies, religious fundamentalists, and many others. There is enormous variance in the length of state constitutions (see Table 3.1). What accounts for such disparity? Studies by political scientists find, not surprisingly, that interest groups play an important role. In states with only one strong political party, where legislative outcomes tend to be unpredictable because of dissension among members of the majority party, interest groups try to insulate their "pet" agencies and programs from uncertainty by seeking protective provisions for them in the constitution.[19] Also, research indicates that long, detailed documents tend to become even longer because their very complexity encourages further amendment, until they finally grow so cumbersome that political support develops for a simpler version. Finally, the easier it is to amend a constitution, the higher the amendment rate.[20]

Problems of Substance

In addition to the contradictions, anachronisms, wordiness, and grants of special privilege found in state constitutions, their *substance* has drawn criticism. Specific concerns voiced by reformers include the following:

- *The long ballot.* As elected executive branch officials are not beholden to the governor for their jobs, the governor has little or no formal influence on their decisions and activities. Reformers who seek to maximize the governor's powers would restrict the executive branch to only two elected leaders: the governor and the lieutenant governor.
- *A glut of executive boards and commissions.* This Jacksonian-era reform product was intended to expand opportunities for public participation in state government and to limit the powers of the governor. Today, it leads to fragmentation and a lack of policy coordination in the executive branch.
- *A swamp of local governments.* There are some 88,000 municipalities, counties, and special-purpose districts in the states. Sometimes they work at cross-purposes, and nearly always they suffer from overlapping responsibilities and an absence of coordination.
- *Restrictions on local government authority.* Localities in some states have to obtain explicit permission from the state legislature before providing a new service, tapping a new source of revenue, or exercising any other authority not specifically granted them by the state.
- *Unequal treatment of racial minorities and women.* Even today, constitutional language sometimes discriminates against African Americans, Latinos, women, and other groups by denying them certain rights guaranteed to white males.

CONSTITUTIONAL REFORM

Shortly after World War II, problems of constitutional substance began to generate increasing commentary on the sorry condition of state constitutions. One of the most influential voices came in 1955 from the U.S. Advisory Commission on Intergovernmental Relations, popularly known as the Kestnbaum Commission. In its final report to the president, the Commission stated that

> the Constitution prepared by the Founding Fathers, with its broad grants of authority and avoidance of legislative detail, has withstood the test of time far better than the constitutions later adopted by the States. The Commission believes that most states would benefit from a fundamental review of their constitution to make sure that they provide for vigorous and responsible government, not forbid it.[21]

Model State Constitution

An ideal of the structure and contents of a state constitution, emphasizing brevity and broad functions and responsibilities of government.

Another important voice for constitutional reform was the National Municipal League, which developed a **Model State Constitution** in 1921 that is now in its sixth version.[22]

Thomas Jefferson believed that each generation has the right to choose for itself its own form of government. He suggested that a new constitution every nineteen or twenty years would be appropriate. Between 1960 and 1980, it would appear that the states took his remarks to heart. Every state altered its fundamental law in some respect during this period, and new or substantially revised constitutions were put into operation in more than half the states. During the 1970s alone, ten states held conventions to consider changing or replacing their constitution. One of these was Louisiana, which set a record by adopting its eleventh constitution; Georgia is in second place with ten.

positive-law tradition

A state constitutional tradition based on detailed provisions and procedures.

higher-law tradition

A state constitutional tradition based on basic and enduring principles that reach beyond statutory law.

Two state constitutional traditions are evident today.[23] The **positive-law tradition** is represented by the detailed and lengthy documents of states such as Alabama, New York, and Texas. Detailed provisions tend to usurp the law-making powers of state legislatures by locking in rigid procedures and policies that typically favor strong political or economic interests. The original **higher-law tradition** is represented by the U.S. Constitution and the National Municipal League's Model State Constitution. It is embodied in brief documents that put forward basic, enduring principles and processes of government, and that view public policy choices as the proper responsibility of legislatures. Of course, no constitutional formula can be suitable for all the states because they differ too much in history, society, economics, and political culture. The best constitutions strike a balance between the need for stability and the requirement for enough flexibility to deal with emerging problems. Today, the higher-law tradition is once again in favor in those states whose constitutions have become briefer, more readable, and simple enough for the average citizen to understand. In others, however, conflicts between special interests are often resolved through constitutional change.

The Essential State Constitution

The Model State Constitution has twelve basic articles that are embodied to a greater or lesser extent in the various state constitutions in existence today. The following list provides a brief description of each article and the ways in which its contents are changing.

Bill of Rights Individual rights and liberties were first protected in state constitutions. They closely resemble, and in some cases are identical to, those delineated in the first eight amendments to the U.S. Constitution. State constitutions and courts were the principal guardians of civil liberties until the U.S. Supreme Court's interpretation of the Fourteenth Amendment extended the protective umbrella of the national courts over the states in 1925.[24] U.S. Supreme Court rulings also applied the U.S. Bill of Rights to the states, especially during the Warren Court beginning in 1953. Some states had failed to uphold their trust, particularly those that perpetuated the unequal treatment of women and minorities.

In the 1980s, however, activist states began to reassert guarantees of individual rights under state constitutions. At a minimum, all state constitutions must protect and guarantee those rights found in the U.S. Bill of Rights. But state constitutional provisions may guarantee additional or more extensive rights to citizens. Seventeen states now have equal rights amendments that guarantee sexual equality and prohibit sex-based discrimination. The U.S. Constitution does not guarantee a right to privacy, but ten states do so. And thirteen states give constitutional rights to crime victims. Some constitutional provisions border on the exotic. Californians possess the right to fish, residents of New Hampshire hold the right to revolution, and all Massachusetts citizens enjoy freedom from excessive noise. (See Table 3.2 for other rights provisions.)

The major reason for the rebirth of state activism in protecting civil liberties and rights has been the conservatism of the U.S. Supreme Court. One commentator accused the Supreme Court of having abdicated its role as "keeper of the nation's 'conscience.'"[25] The states' power to write and interpret their constitutions differently from the U.S. Constitution's provisions in the area of protecting civil rights and liberties has been upheld by the Supreme Court, as long as the state provisions have "adequate and independent" grounds.[26] Increasingly, civil rights and liberties cases are being filed by plaintiffs in state rather than federal courts, based on state bill of rights protections.

Power of the State This very brief article states simply that the enumerated powers are not the only ones held by the state—that, indeed, the state has all powers not denied to it by the state or national constitutions.

Suffrage and Election This article provides for the legal registration of voters and for election procedures. Recent extensions of voting rights and alterations in election procedures have been made in response to U.S. Supreme Court decisions and to national constitutional and statutory changes. Generally, states

TABLE 3.2	Excerpts from State Bills of Rights

Alabama: "The legislature may hereafter, by general law, provide for an indemnification program to peanut farmers for losses incurred as a result of Aspergillus flavus and freeze damage in peanuts."

Alaska: "Public schooling shall always be conducted in English."

Illinois: "The equal protection of the laws shall not be denied or abridged on account of sex by the State or its units of local government."

Montana: "Human dignity is inviolable."

New York: "Every citizen may freely speak, write, and publish his sentiments on all subjects. . . ."

North Carolina: "Secret political societies shall not be tolerated."

Pennsylvania: "The people have a right to clean air, pure water, and to the preservation of the natural, scenic, historic, and esthetic values of the environment. Pennsylvania's public natural resources are the common history of all the people, including generations yet to come. . . ."

Rhode Island: "The power of the state and its municipalities to regulate and control the use of land and waters in the furtherance of the preservation, regeneration, and restoration of the natural environment, and . . . of the rights of the people to enjoy and freely exercise the rights of fishery and the privileges of the shore . . . shall be liberally construed, and shall not be deemed a public use of private property."

have improved election administration; liberalized registration, voting, and officeholding requirements; and shortened residency requirements. Some states have amended this article to provide for public financing of election campaigns; others have adopted provisions designed to count ballots more accurately.

The Legislative Branch This article sets forth the powers, procedures, and organizing principles of the legislature, including the apportionment of state legislatures on the basis of one person, one vote. District lines must be redrawn every ten years, after the national census has revealed population changes. Nineteen states have placed term limits on their elected officials in this article.

On the basis of this article, states have taken numerous actions to approach greater conformity with the Model State Constitution, including increasing the length and frequency of legislative sessions and streamlining rules and procedures. Instead of stipulating specific dollar amounts for legislators' pay and fringe benefits (which are soon rendered inappropriate by inflation), most state constitutions now establish a procedure to determine and occasionally adjust the compensation of legislators.

Interestingly, the model constitution for many years recommended a unicameral legislature as a means to overcome complexity, delay, and confusion. In its most recent revision, the National Municipal League tacitly recognized the refusal of the states to follow this suggestion (only Nebraska has a single-house general assembly) by providing recommendations appropriate for a bicameral body.

The Executive Branch The powers and organization of the executive branch, which are outlined in this article, have seen many notable modifications.

Essentially, executive power continues to be centralized in the office of the governor. Governors have won longer terms and the right to run for re-election. Line-item vetoes, shorter ballots, the authority to make appointments within the executive branch, and the ability to reorganize the state bureaucracy have also increased gubernatorial powers. A number of states have opted for team election of the governor and lieutenant governor.

The Judicial Branch All states have substantially revised not only their courts' organization and procedures but also the election of judges. Moreover, a large majority have unified their court systems under a single authority, usually the state supreme court. Many states now select judges through a merit plan rather than by gubernatorial appointment, legislative election, or popular election (see Chapter 9). The states have also established commissions to investigate charges against judges and to recommend discipline or removal from the bench when necessary.

Finance This article consists of provisions relating to taxation, debt, and expenditures for state and local government. In many states, tax relief has been granted to senior citizens, veterans, and disabled people.

Local Government Here, the authority of municipalities, counties, and other local governments is recognized. Most states have increased local authority through home rule provisions, which give localities more discretion in providing services. Local taxing authority has been extended. In addition, mechanisms for improved intergovernmental cooperation, such as consolidated city and county governments and regional districts to provide services, have been created.

Public Education On the basis of this article, the states establish and maintain free public schools for all children. Higher-education institutions, including technical schools, colleges, and universities, are commonly established in this section.

Civil Service The Model State Constitution sets forth a *merit system* of personnel administration for state government under which civil servants are to be hired, promoted, paid, evaluated, and retained on the basis of competence, fitness, and performance instead of political party affiliation or other such criteria.

Intergovernmental Relations As recommended by the Model State Constitution, some states stipulate specific devices for cooperation among various state entities, among local jurisdictions, or between a state and its localities. They may detail methods for sharing in the provision of certain services, or they may list cost-sharing mechanisms such as local option sales taxes.

Constitutional Revision In this article the methods for revising, amending, and replacing the constitution are described. Generally, the trend has been to make it easier for the voters, the legislature, or both to change the constitution.

Constitutions Today

In general, state constitutions today conform more closely to the higher-law tradition and the Model State Constitution than did those of the past. They are shorter, more concise, and simpler, and they contain fewer errors, anachronisms, and contradictions. They give the state legislatures more responsibility for determining public policy through statute rather than through constitutional amendment. The two newest states, Alaska and Hawaii, have constitutional documents that follow the model constitution quite closely.

However, much work remains to be done. Some state constitutions are still riddled with unnecessary detail because new amendments have continually been added to the old documents, and obsolete provisions and other relics can still be found. But there are more important deficiencies as well—deficiencies that demand the attention of legislators and citizens in states whose constitutions inhibit the operations of state government and obstruct the ability to adapt to change. In some jurisdictions, the governor's formal powers remain weak; a plethora of boards and commissions makes any thought of executive management and coordination a pipe dream; local governments chafe under the tight leash of state authority; and many other problems persist. Constitutional revision must be an ongoing process if the states are to cope with the changing contours of American society and stay in the vanguard of innovation and change.

METHODS FOR CONSTITUTIONAL CHANGE

There are only two methods for altering the U.S. Constitution. The first is the constitutional convention, wherein delegates representing the states assemble to consider modifying or replacing the Constitution. Despite periodic calls for a national constitutional convention, only one has taken place—in Philadelphia, more than two hundred years ago. Two-thirds of the states must agree to call a convention; three-fourths are required to ratify any changes in the Constitution.

The second means of amending the U.S. Constitution is through congressional initiative, wherein Congress, by a two-thirds vote of both houses, agrees to send one or more proposed changes to the states. Again, three-fourths of the states must ratify the proposals.

Since 1787, more than one thousand amendments have been submitted to the states by Congress. Only twenty-seven have been approved (the most recent one, in 1992, limits the ability of members of Congress to increase their pay), and the first ten of these were appended to the Constitution as a condition by several states for ratification. Note that neither method for amending the U.S. Constitution provides for popular participation by voters, in sharp contrast to the citizen-participation requirements for state constitutional change, as we shall see in the next section.

interpretation
An informal means of revising constitutions whereby members of the executive, legislative, or judicial branch apply constitutional principles and law to the everyday affairs of governing.

Informal Constitutional Change

One informal and four formal methods for amending state constitutions exist. The informal route is **interpretation** of constitutional meaning by the state legislature, executive branch, courts, or attorneys general, or through usage and custom. Governors issue executive orders; courts and attorneys general issue advisory opinions on meanings of specific provisions; state agencies make decisions and implement policy. The force of habit can be a powerful influence, specific constitutional provisions notwithstanding. It is a good bet that one or more antiquated or unrealistic constitutional provisions are ignored in every state. A common example is the requirement that all bills be read, in their entirety, three times in each house for enactment. Another is the list of conditions for holding political office, such as a belief in God.

State supreme courts play the most direct role in changing constitutions through interpretation. In large measure, a constitution is what the judges say it is in their decisions from the bench. Judicial interpretation of constitutions may be based on a variety of standards, including strict attention to the express language of the document and to the original intent of the framers or authors of amendments, deference to legislative enactments or executive actions, precedent, policy considerations, and individual rights. The power of the state supreme courts to review executive actions, legislative actions, and decisions of lower courts is known as **judicial review.** This power evolved in the states much as it did on the national level—through the courts' own insistence that they hold this authority. During recent years, as the U.S. Supreme Court has become more conservative and less activist in its interpretations of the law, some state courts have moved in the opposite direction and earned reputations as progressive judicial activists.

Formal Constitutional Change

The four formal procedures for constitutional change are legislative proposal, initiative, constitutional convention, and constitutional commission. All of them involve two basic steps: initiation and **ratification.** The state legislature, or in some cases the voters, propose (initiate) a constitutional change. Then the proposed amendment is submitted to the voters for approval (ratification).

Legislative Proposal Historically, **legislative proposal** is the most common road taken to revision; more than 90 percent of all changes in state constitutions have come through this method, which is permitted in all fifty states. The specifics of legislative proposal techniques vary, but most states require either two-thirds or three-fifths of the members of each house to approve a proposal before it is sent to the voters for ratification. Twelve states require two consecutive legislative sessions to consider and pass a proposed amendment. The procedure can become quite complicated. For instance, South Carolina's legislative proposal must be passed by two-thirds of the members of each house; it is then sent to the people during the next general election. If a majority of voters show approval, the proposal returns to the next legislative session, in which a majority of legislators have to concur.

Almost all states accept a simple majority for voter ratification of a proposed revision. In New Hampshire, however, two-thirds of the voters must approve of the proposal. And Tennessee requires approval by a majority of the number of citizens who cast a vote for governor.

judicial review

The power of the U.S. Supreme Court or state supreme courts to declare unconstitutional not only actions of the executive and legislative branches but also decisions of lower courts.

ratification

The formal approval of a constitution or constitutional amendment by a majority of the voters of a state.

legislative proposal

The most common means of amending a state constitution, wherein the legislature proposes a revision, usually by a two-thirds majority.

Legislative proposal is probably best suited to revisions that are relatively narrow in scope. However, some legislatures, such as South Carolina's, have presented a series of proposals to the voters over a period of years and thereby have significantly revised the constitution. The disadvantage to such a strategy is that it tends to result in a patchwork of amendments that can conflict or overlap with other constitutional provisions.

Initiative Eighteen states permit their citizens to initiate and ratify changes in the constitution on their own, bypassing the legislature (see Table 3.3). Only five of these initiative states are east of the Mississippi River, reflecting the fact that the initiative was a product of the Progressive reform movement of the early 1900s. Most of the territories admitted as states during this period chose to permit the **initiative** (known as constitutional initiative in some states). Twenty-three states also authorize the initiative for enacting statutory change. The initiative is used much less often than legislative proposal in amending constitutions.

The number of signatures needed for the initiative petition to be valid varies widely: Arizona requires 15 percent of total votes cast in the last gubernatorial election, whereas Massachusetts requires merely 3 percent.[27] Moreover, to ensure that an initiative favoring one region does not become embodied in the constitution, eight states specify that the petition signatures must be collected widely throughout the state.

In general, a petition for constitutional amendment is sent to the office of the secretary of state for verification that the required number of registered voters have signed their names. Then the question is placed on a statewide ballot in the next general election. Ratification requires a majority vote of the people in most states.

It is usually easy enough to collect the required number of signatures to place a proposed amendment on a statewide ballot. But actual passage of the initiative is much more difficult once it receives a close public examination and opposing interests are activated. If the legislature is circumvented altogether and propositions are placed directly on the general-election ballot by citizens, the procedure is called a **direct initiative.** If a legislature participates by voting on the citizen proposal, as in Massachusetts and Mississippi, the procedure is known as an **indirect initiative.**

The initiative is useful in making limited changes to the state constitution and, in recent years, has addressed some controversial issues that state legislatures have been loath to confront. Voters in several states have recently addressed same-sex marriage, abortion rights, property rights, legalized gambling, and school vouchers.

A major advantage of the initiative is that it permits the people's will to counter a despotic or inertia-ridden legislature. For instance, Illinois voters in 1978 reduced the size of the House of Representatives from 177 to 118 after the legislature voted itself a huge pay raise during a period of economic hardship. Another advantage is that this method appears to enhance citizen interest and participation in government.

However, the initiative can also be abused by special-interest groups with selfish motives who seek to gain privileges, and under crisis conditions it can result in ill-conceived, radical changes to the constitution. Indeed, the initiative can

initiative

A proposed law or constitutional amendment that is placed on the ballot by citizen petition.

direct initiative

A procedure by which the voters of a jurisdiction propose the passage of constitutional amendments, state laws, or local ordinances, bypassing the legislative body.

indirect initiative

Similar to the direct initiative, except that the voter-initiated proposal must be submitted to the legislature before going on the ballot for voter approval.

TABLE 3.3		States Authorizing Constitutional Amendment by Citizen Initiative
STATE	YEAR	NUMBER OF SIGNATURES REQUIRED ON INITIATIVE PETITION
Arizona	1910	15% of total votes cast for all candidates for governor at last election.
Arkansas	1909	10% of voters for governor at last election.
California	1911	8% of total voters for all candidates for governor at last election.
Colorado	1910	5% of total legal votes for all candidates for secretary of state at last general election.
Florida	1972	8% of total votes cast in the state in the last election for presidential electors.
Illinois[a]	1970	8% of total votes cast for candidates for governor at last election.
Massachusetts[b]	1918	3% of total votes cast for governor at preceding biennial state election (not fewer than 25,000 qualified voters).
Michigan	1908	10% of total voters for all candidates at the gubernatorial election.
Mississippi	1992	12% of total votes for all candidates for governor at last election.
Missouri	1906	8% of legal voters for all candidates for governor at last election.
Montana	1904	10% of qualified electors, the number of qualified electors to be determined by number of votes cast for governor in preceding general election.
Nebraska	1912	10% of total voters for governor at last election.
Nevada	1904	10% of voters who voted in entire state in last general election.
North Dakota	1914	4% of population of the state.
Ohio	1912	10% of total number of electors who voted for governor in last election.
Oklahoma	1907	15% of legal voters for state office receiving highest number of voters at last general state election.
Oregon	1902	8% of total votes for all candidates for governor at last election of which governor was elected for four-year term.
South Dakota	1898	10% of total votes for governor in last election.

[a] Only Article IV, the Legislature, may be amended by initiative petition.
[b] Before being submitted to the electorate for ratification, initiative measures must be approved at two sessions of a successively elected legislature by not less than one-fourth of all members elected, sitting in joint session.
SOURCE: "Separately Elected State Officials" adapted from *The Book of States*, 2007, p. 173, Vol. 39. Reprinted by permission of The Council of State Governments.

constitutional convention

An assembly of delegates chosen by popular election or appointed by the legislature or the governor to revise an existing constitution or to create a new one.

result in just the kind of excessive detail and poorly drafted verbiage that is so widely condemned by constitutional scholars and reformers. It can also make doing routine business extremely difficult. In California, for example, an initiative prevents local governments from hiking taxes without two-thirds approval of the electorate.

Constitutional Convention Legislative proposals and initiatives are quite specific about the type of constitutional change that is sought. Only those questions that actually appear on the ballot are considered. In contrast, a **constitutional convention** assembles delegates who suggest revisions or even an entirely new document; the proposed changes are then submitted to the voters for ratification. The convention is especially well suited for considering far-reaching constitutional changes or a new fundamental law.

The convention is the oldest method for constitutional change in the states and is available in all fifty of them. The process begins when the electorate or the legislature decides to call for a constitutional convention. In fourteen states, the question of calling a convention must be regularly voted on by the electorate, but most convention calls have been routinely rejected. Alaskans and Iowans hold an "automatic convention call" every ten years; in New York and Maryland, the convention issue is submitted to the voters every twenty years. Except in Delaware, where the legislature can take direct action, proposals emerging from the convention must be ratified by the voters before they become part of the constitution.

Delegates to a convention are usually elected on a nonpartisan ballot by the voters from state house or senate districts. Conventions are usually dominated by professionals, lawyers, educators, and business people. This delegate composition is not surprising because convention calls are strongly supported by higher socioeconomic groups in urban areas.

The characteristics of a delegate pool are important for several reasons. First, the delegates need knowledge of and experience in state government and politics if they are to contribute meaningfully to the debate and drafting of proposed amendments. It is usually not too difficult to attract qualified people for service; the experience is important and unique, and many consider it a privilege. Second, the delegates should represent a cross-section of the state's population insofar as possible. If the delegate pool does not reflect gender, racial, regional, ethnic, and other salient characteristics of the population, the fruit of its labor may lack legitimacy in the eyes of substantial numbers of voters. Finally, partisanship should be avoided where possible. Partisan differences can wreck consensus on major issues and destroy the prospects for voter ratification of suggested amendments that emerge from the convention.

Voter approval of convention proposals is problematic. If partisan, racial, regional, religious, or other disagreements dominate media reports on the convention, voter approval is difficult to obtain. People naturally tend to be skeptical of suggestions for sweeping changes in the basic structures and procedures of government. Furthermore, if they have not been regularly involved with and informed of the progress of the convention, they may be reluctant to give their approval to the recommendations.

Delegates usually understand these dynamics and are sensitive to how their proposed changes may affect the general public. They must, for example, carefully consider how to present the proposed amendments for ratification. There are two choices: the all-or-nothing strategy of consolidating all changes in a single vote, and the piecemeal strategy of offering each proposal as a separate ballot decision. In recent years, voters have tended to reject inclusive packages. Each suggested change is certain to offend some minority, and when all the offended minorities coalesce, they may well constitute a majority of voters.

**constitutional
commission**

A meeting of delegates
appointed by the governor
or legislature to study
constitutional problems
and propose solutions.

Constitutional Commission Often called a *study commission,* the **constitutional commission** is usually established to study the existing document and to recommend changes to the legislature or to the voters. Depending on the mandate, the constitutional commission may examine the entire constitution with a view toward replacement or change, focus on one or more specific articles or provisions, or be given the freedom to decide its own scope of activity. Commission recommendations to the legislature and/or governor are only advisory, thus helping to account for this method's popularity with elected officials, who sometimes prefer to study a problem to death rather than engage it head on. Some or all of the recommendations may be submitted to the voters; others may be completely ignored. Only in Florida can a commission send its proposals directly to voters.

Constitutional commissions operated in 2003 in Alabama, and Utah's revision commission functions permanently. Service on a constitutional commission can be a thankless task, as legislators sometimes ignore the commission's recommendations or employ them as a symbolic device for relieving political pressure. For example, Kentucky's 1987–1988 Revision Commission recommended seventy-seven changes to the constitution, but only one was referred by the legislature to the voters as a proposed amendment.[28] When used properly, however, commissions can furnish high-quality research both inexpensively and relatively quickly.

STATE RESPONSIVENESS AND CONSTITUTIONAL REFORM

Each state's constitution is designed specifically to meet the needs of that state. The rich political culture, history, economics, values, and ideals of the state's community are reflected in state constitutional language. Through their constitutions, the states experiment with different governmental institutions and processes. As avid patriot Thomas Paine observed more than two hundred years ago, "It is in the interest of all the states, that the constitution of each should be somewhat diversified from each other. We are a people founded upon experiments, and have the happy opportunity of trying variety in order to discover the 'best.'"[29]

State constitutions were the original guardians of individual rights and liberties, with their own bills of rights preceding that of the U.S. Constitution by many years. They are reassuming their rightful position in American government today as independent state constitutional law develops further. Yet few tasks in government are more difficult than modernizing a constitution. The process requires "sustained, dedicated, organized effort; vigorous, aggressive and imaginative leadership; bipartisan political support; education of the electorate on the issues; judicious selection of the means; and seemingly endless 'patience.'"[30] In the words of constitutional scholar W. Brooke Graves, "The advocate of constitutional reform in an American state should be endowed with the patience of Job and the sense of time of a geologist."[31] The solemn duty of framing the original state constitutions, so effectively discharged by our predecessors, must be matched by the continuous oversight of present and future generations. Changes are necessary to adjust state governments to the vagaries of the future.

The constitutional changes enacted in the states since the Kestnbaum Commission report have generally resulted in documents in the higher-law tradition, documents that "are shorter, more clearly written, modernized, less encumbered with restrictions, more basic in content and have more reasonable amending processes. They also establish improved governmental structures and contain substantive provisions assuring greater openness, accountability and equity."[32]

The states have made a great deal of progress in modernizing their governments. As state constitutional scholar Richard Leach has put it, "There are not many constitutional horrors left."[33]

Recent constitutional amendments have responded to, and indeed caused, profound changes in state government and politics. Since the genesis of modern reform in the mid-1960s, some forty states have adopted new constitutions or substantially amended existing ones. Problems persist, and future constitutional tinkering and replacements will be necessary. But in most states, the constitutional landscape is much cleaner and more functional than it was a generation ago.

CHAPTER RECAP

- The constitution is the fundamental law of a state, superior to statutory law.
- State constitutions evolved from the original colonial charters. Shifting from an original basis of legislative supremacy, they have gradually increased executive power.
- Some constitutions continue to suffer from excessive length and substantive problems.
- Constitutional reform has modernized the documents and made them conform more closely to present challenges of governance.
- Methods for changing constitutions include interpretation, judicial review, legislative proposal, initiative, constitutional convention, and constitutional commission.

Key Terms

fundamental law *(p. 46)*
legislative supremacy *(p. 50)*
Model State Constitution *(p. 55)*
positive-law tradition *(p. 55)*
higher-law tradition *(p. 55)*
interpretation *(p. 59)*
judicial review *(p. 60)*

ratification *(p. 60)*
legislative proposal *(p. 60)*
initiative *(p. 61)*
direct initiative *(p. 61)*
indirect initiative *(p. 61)*
constitutional convention *(p. 62)*
constitutional commission *(p. 64)*

Internet Resources

For full texts of state statutes and constitutions, see individual state websites (for example, **www.state.fl.us.** State constitutions can also be accessed through **www.law.cornell.edu/statutes.html, www.findlaw.com/11statgov/ indexconst.html,** or **www.constitution.org.** The Alaska constitution draws heavily on the Model State Constitution. It is located in the state of Alaska Documents Library at **www.law.state.ak.us.**

For everything you would care to know about Nebraska's UNICAM go to **www.unicam.state.ne.us.**

A helpful site is the center for State Constitutional Studies at **www.camlaw .rutgers.edu/statecon.**

Citizen Participation and Elections

4

CHAPTER OUTLINE

Participation

Elections

Direct Democracy

Citizen Access to Government

The Effects of Citizen Participation

FOCUS QUESTIONS

1. What are some of the reasons that voter participation varies from state to state?

2. Which ballot-based process, available to voters in many states, has emerged as an important policymaking tool?

3. In addition to voting, what are some ways in which citizens can participate in their state and local government?

4. What are some innovations and programs states can use to increase civic participation in government?

---

*T*ired of low voter turnout in election after election in his home state, an Arizonan came up with a clever idea: offer voters a chance to win one million dollars. From that idea came a 2006 ballot proposal—the Arizona Voter Reward Act. Supporters argued that providing a financial incentive would motivate more people to vote. After all, the odds of winning the election lottery would be far better than the Powerball jackpot. Opponents contended that the million dollar prize was, in effect, bribing people to vote and furthermore, higher turnout would not necessarily mean a better outcome.[1] One thing the proposal did was to focus attention on a serious issue: the relatively low rates of voter turnout in the United States. But is a voter lottery a credible way to address the issue? Arizonans thought not and defeated the ballot measure by a two to one margin. And the turnout rate among the voting age population in the 2006 election in the Grand Canyon state? 46 percent.

PARTICIPATION

participation

Actions through which ordinary members of a political system attempt to influence outcomes.

Democracy assumes citizen **participation**—acting to influence government. In contemporary America, there is persistent evidence that citizens are not much interested in participation. We have grown accustomed to reports of low voter turnout and public hearings that few attend. In his influential book, *Bowling*

Alone, political scientist Robert Putnam documented this gradual disengagement of people from all sorts of community activities and organizations.[2]

On the surface, government works just fine with limited participation: The interests of the active become translated into public policy, and those who are inactive can be safely ignored because they do not vote.[3] If, however, some traditional nonvoters (such as low-income, less-educated citizens) went to the polls, then vote-seeking candidates would be forced to pay more attention to their interests, and public policy might be nudged in a different direction. In this light, it is important to understand both why many people do participate and why others do not. This chapter addresses individual citizen involvement in government; Chapter 5 takes up collective participation (that is, participation by political parties and interest groups).

Participatory Options

In a representative democracy, voting is the most common form of participation. For many citizens, it is a matter of civic responsibility. It is a fundamental facet of citizenship—after all, it is called "the right to vote." Citizens go to the polls to elect the officials who will govern them. But there are other methods of participation. Consider the citizen who is unhappy because the property taxes on her home have increased substantially from one year to the next. What options are available to her besides voting against incumbent officeholders at the next election? As shown in Figure 4.1, she can be either active or passive; and her actions, either constructive or destructive. Basically, she has four potential responses: loyalty, voice, exit, and neglect.[4]

According to this formulation, voting is an example of *loyalty,* a passive but constructive response to government action. Specifically, this response reflects the irate taxpayer's underlying support for her community despite her displeasure with particular tax policies. An active constructive response is *voice*: The aggrieved property owner could contact officials, work in the campaign of a candidate who promises to lower tax assessments, or (assuming that others in the community share her sentiments) participate in anti-tax groups and organize demonstrations.

Destructive responses (those that undermine the citizen–government relationship) are similarly passive or active. If the citizen simply shrugs and concludes that "you can't fight city hall," she is exhibiting a response termed *neglect*. She has nearly given up on the community and does not participate. A more active version of giving up is to *exit*—that is, to leave the community altogether (a response often referred to as "voting with your feet"). The unhappy citizen will relocate in a community that is more in line with her tax preferences.

Every citizen confronts these participatory options. It is much healthier for the political system if citizens engage in the constructive responses, but some individuals are likely to conclude that constructive participation is of little value to them and opt for neglect or, in more extreme cases, exit.

Nonparticipation

What motivates the citizens who choose neglect as their best option? One explanation for nonparticipation in politics is socioeconomic status. Individuals with lower levels of income and education tend to participate less than wealth-

| FIGURE 4.1 | **Possible Responses to Dissatisfaction in the Community** |

Each of these participatory options affects public policy decisions in a community. Citizens who choose the voice option frequently find themselves in the thick of things.

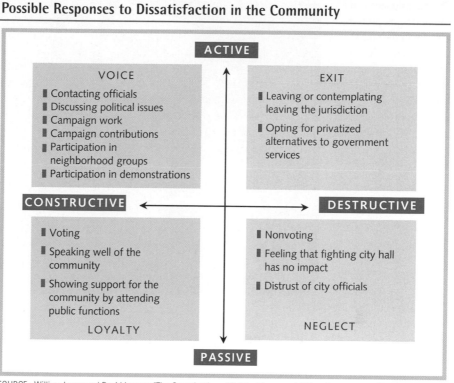

ier, more educated individuals do.[5] Tied closely to income and education levels is occupational status. Unskilled workers and hourly wage earners do not participate in politics to the same degree that white-collar workers and professionals do. Individuals of lower socioeconomic status may not have the time, resources, or civic skills required to become actively involved in politics.

Other explanations for nonparticipation have included age (younger people have participated less than middle-aged individuals), race (blacks have participated less than whites), and gender (women have participated less than men). However, of these factors, only age has continued to affect political activity levels. African American political participation actually surpasses that of whites when socioeconomic status is taken into consideration,[6] and the gender gap in the types and levels of political participation has disappeared.[7] America's youth, however, remain less likely to frequent polling places, although the recent up-surge in voting among the eighteen- to twenty-nine–year-old group may signal a new trend in youthful participation. Groups such as Kids Voting USA have developed programs to socialize children about political affairs, assuming that children who get into the habit of citizen participation at an early age will be more politically active as adults.[8] For older youth, websites such as the MTV-sponsored Rock

Chanting slogans and carrying signs, protesters take to the streets of Atlanta to voice their opposition to proposed changes in immigration laws.
SOURCE: ©AP/Wide World Photos.

the Vote encourage active participation in politics and government. Another factor that exerts an independent effect on participation is where one lives. Big-city dwellers (those who live in places with a population of 1 million or more) are less likely than people in small communities (less than 5,000 inhabitants) to participate in various civic activities, including contacting local officials, attending community meetings, and voting in local elections.[9]

The explanation for nonparticipation does not rest solely with the individual. Institutional features—the way the political system is designed—may suppress participation. For example, local governments that have instituted nonpartisan elections, in which candidates run without party affiliation, have removed an important mobilizing factor for voters. Voter turnout tends to be lower in these elections than in partisan contests. City council meetings scheduled at 10:00 A.M. put a tremendous strain on workers who must take time off from their jobs if they want to attend; consequently, attendance is low. And localities in which it is difficult for citizens to contact the appropriate official with a service request or complaint are not doing much to facilitate participation. Features like these play an often unrecognized role in dampening participation.

The Struggle for the Right to Vote

State constitutions in the eighteenth and early nineteenth centuries entrusted only propertied white males with the vote. They did not encourage public involvement in government, and the eventual softening of restrictions on suffrage did not occur without a struggle. Restrictions based on property ownership and wealth were eventually dropped, but women, blacks, and Native Americans were still denied the right to vote.

In an effort to attract women to its rugged territory, Wyoming enfranchised women in 1869. The suffragists—women who were actively fighting for the right to vote—scored a victory when Colorado extended the vote to women in 1893. Gradually, other states began enfranchising women, and in 1920 the Nineteenth Amendment to the U.S. Constitution, forbidding states to deny the right to vote "on account of sex," was ratified.

Even after the Fifteenth Amendment (1870) extended the vote to blacks, some southern states clung defiantly to traditional ways that denied blacks and poor people their rights. Poll taxes, literacy tests, and white primaries were among the barriers erected by segregationists. U.S. Supreme Court decisions such as *Smith* v. *Allwright* (1944), which outlawed white primaries, and federal actions such as the Civil Rights Act of 1964 and the Twenty-Fourth Amendment (1964), which made poll taxes unconstitutional, helped blacks gain access to the polls. But in some jurisdictions, informal methods designed to discourage participation by African Americans continued.

Voting Rights Act of 1965

The law that effectively enfranchised racial minorities by giving the national government the power to decide whether individuals are qualified to vote and to intercede in state and local electoral operations when necessary.

The **Voting Rights Act of 1965** finally broke the back of the segregationists' efforts. Under its provisions, federal poll watchers and registrars were dispatched to particular counties to investigate voter discrimination. To this day, counties covered under the Voting Rights Act (all of nine southern states and parts of seven other states) must submit to the U.S. Department of Justice any changes in election laws, such as new precinct lines or new polling places. Over time, judicial interpretations, congressional actions, and Justice Department rules have modified the Voting Rights Act. One of the most important modifications has been to substitute an effects test for the original intent test. In other words, if a governmental action has the effect of discouraging minority voting, whether intentionally or not, the action must be rejected. Civil rights activists welcomed this change because proving the intent of an action is much more difficult than demonstrating its effect.

Voting Patterns

Voter turnout is affected by several factors. First, it varies according to the type of election. A presidential race usually attracts a higher proportion of eligible voters than a state or local election does. In 2004, with a presidential race underway, voter turnout was approximately 59 percent of the voting-age population; in 2006, when there was no presidential election on the ballot—but many governors' races—turnout was only 40 percent. Second, popular candidates running a close race seem to increase voter interest. When each candidate has a chance to win, voters sense that their vote will matter more than in a race with a sure winner. Third, not only partisan competition but party ideology affects voter turnout.[10] When candidates take distinctive ideological stances in competitive elections, the incentive for party-identifiers to vote increases.

There are noteworthy differences among states in terms of the proportions of both voting-age population registered and voter turnout. Nationally, voter registration stands at approximately 76 percent of the voting-age population. But when we look at the figures for individual states, wide variations appear. Compare two states with similar voting-age populations: Nebraska, with 1.23 million, and Nevada, with 1.39 million. Eighty-eight percent of the voting-age population in Nebraska was registered; in Nevada, the comparable figure was 64.6 percent.[11] Registration matters because people who are registered tend to vote, and votes translate into political power.

States can also be differentiated according to voter turnout rates (see Figure 4.2). In 2004, the highest turnout rates were recorded in Minnesota, where 76.2 percent of the voting-age population voted, and Oregon, where 74 percent voted. Arizona, with 42.3 percent voting, garnered the dubious distinction of being the state with the lowest voter turnout in 2004.[12] States with moralistic political cultures typically experience higher voter turnout than do states with traditionalistic political cultures. States with competitive political parties (as opposed to states where one party dominates) tend to have elections with a higher proportion of voters participating; each party needs to mobilize individuals who identify with it in order to win. Finally, states can affect turnout by the way in which they administer the elections: Is voting a convenient exercise, or is it an arduous task marked by long lines at the polling places and confusing ballots once inside the voting booth?

Registering to vote is getting easier. Passage of the National Voter Registration Act in 1993 means that individuals can register to vote when they apply for a driver's license, welfare benefits, or unemployment compensation, or when they register their automobile. States allow voters to register by mail and some states, such as Florida, have taken another step by allowing on-line voter registration; any computer terminal with an Internet connection can be a registration site. And many states have moved the closing date for registration nearer to the actual date of the election, giving potential voters more time to register. This factor is important because campaigns tend to heighten the public's interest in the election. Most states now close their registration books fewer than thirty days before an election, and Maine, Minnesota, New Hampshire, Wisconsin, and Wyoming allow registration on election day.[13] North Dakota is the only state in the nation that does not require voter registration.

The voting experience is changing too, with many states giving their citizens the choice to cast their votes before the day of the election. The list below outlines the options:

- fifteen states allow "no-excuse" early voting (for example, California and Texas)
- sixteen states allow "no-excuse" in-person absentee voting (for example, Idaho and Indiana) before the election
- four states require an excuse (e.g., will be out of town on Election Day, disabled, etc.) for early in-person absentee voting (for example, Kentucky and Missouri)
- one state has set up a vote-by-mail system (Oregon)[14]

Fourteen states (for example, Alabama and New York) do not allow early voting or in-person absentee voting. In other words, a voter must go to the polls on Election Day or provide an acceptable reason for requesting an absentee ballot. Does making voting easier matter? Analysis of Oregon's vote-by-mail system showed that the turnout rate increased, especially among groups such as home-

FIGURE 4.2   **State Voter Turnout, 2004**

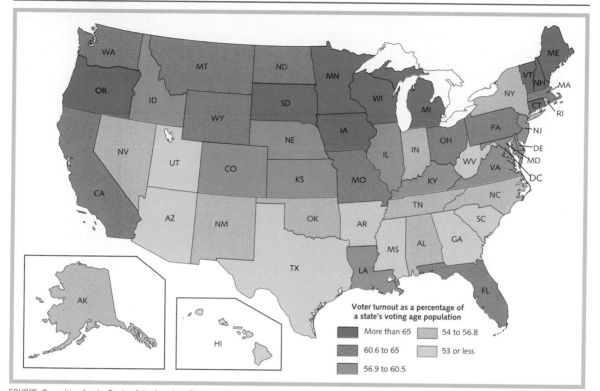

SOURCE: Committee for the Study of the American Electorate, *2004 CSAE Election Report,* www.fairvote.org/reports/CSAE2004electionreport.pdf (December 10, 2004).

makers, the disabled, and people in the twenty-six to thirty-eight-year old range.[15] In 2006, approximately 20 percent of voters cast their ballots before election day; the numbers in Florida and Washington exceeded 40 percent.[16] As more states loosen the restrictions on early voting, the notion of election *day* is gradually giving way.

ELECTIONS

Elections are central to a representative democracy. Voters choose governors and legislators, and in most states, lieutenant governors, attorneys general, secretaries of state, and state treasurers; in some, they also choose the heads of the agriculture and education departments, judges, and the public utility commissioners. At the local level, the list of elected officials includes mayors and council members, county commissioners, county judges, sheriffs, tax assessors, and school board members. If state and local governments are to function effectively, elections must provide talented, capable leaders. But elections are not just about outcomes; they are also about the process itself. Florida's troubles with

| TABLE 4.1 | **Voting Equipment in Use** |

TYPE OF EQUIPMENT	PERCENTAGE OF ELECTORATE USING THE EQUIPMENT
Optical Scan	41.2
Electronic	38.2
Lever Machines	11.2
Punch Cards	4.8
Mixed	4.0
Paper Ballots	0.6

SOURCE: "Election Reform: What's Changed, What Hasn't, and Why, 2000–2006," www.electononline.org (May 25, 2006), p. 11.

ballot design, voting machines, and recount rules in the 2000 presidential election underscored the need for elections to be administered fairly and transparently.

Significant changes in election management and especially in voting technology have occurred during the past few years. Table 4.1 lists the different kinds of voting equipment available and the percentage of the electorate using it, as of 2006. Although electronic voting machines (akin to automatic teller machines) are becoming more popular, concerns over their accuracy and security remain. At issue is whether these systems should provide a VVPAT, or voter-verified paper audit trail, to supplement the record of the count in the electronic machine's memory.

Primaries

For a party to choose a nominee for the general-election ballot, potential candidates must be winnowed. In the pre-Jacksonian era, party nominees were chosen by a legislative caucus—that is, a conference of the party's legislators. Caucuses gave way to the mechanism of state party conventions, which were similar to national presidential nomination conventions but without most of the spectacle; popularly elected delegates from across a state convened to select the party's nominees. Then the Progressive movement sought to open up the nomination process and make it more democratic. Political parties adopted the **primary system,** whereby voters directly choose from among several candidates to select the party's nominees for the general election. The use of primaries has effectively diminished the organizational power of political parties.

Thirteen states still allow for party conventions in particular instances, such as nominations for lieutenant governor and attorney general (Michigan) and selection of a slate of nominees by third parties (Kansas). Connecticut, the last state to adopt primaries, operates a challenge system whereby party nominees for various state offices are selected at a convention; but if a contest develops at the convention and a second candidate receives as much as 15 percent of the votes, the convention's nominee and the challenger square off in a primary.[17]

primary system

The electoral mechanism for selecting party nominees to compete in the general election.

closed primary

A primary in which only voters registered in the party are allowed to participate.

open primary

Voters decide which party's primary they will participate in.

Primary Types Primaries can be divided into two types: closed and open. The only voters who can participate in a **closed primary** for a particular party are those who are registered in that party; an **open primary** does not require party membership. However, even this basic distinction lends itself to some variation. States differ, for example, in terms of the ease with which voters can change party affiliation and participate in the closed primary of the other party. In eleven states, a voter is an enrolled member of one party (or is an Independent and may or may not be eligible to vote in either party's primary) and can change that affiliation only well in advance of the primary election.[18] New Mexico and Pennsylvania are two of the states that conduct completely closed primaries. Fifteen other closed-primary states (Iowa and Wyoming are examples) allow voters to change their party registration on election day, thus accommodating shifts in voters' loyalties.

Open primaries account for (and perhaps contribute to) fleeting partisan loyalties among the public. The key difference among states with open primaries is whether a voter is required to state publicly which party's primary he is participating in. Ten states, including Alabama and Indiana, require voters to request a specific party's ballot at the polling place. Eleven other open-primary states make no such demand; voters secretly select the ballot of the party in which they wish to participate. Idaho and Wisconsin are examples of states in which primaries are truly open.

blanket primary

A primary in which a voter can choose from among candidates of both parties on a single ballot.

For many years, California and Washington operated a **blanket primary,** which allowed voters to cross over from one party's primary ballot to the other's primary ballot in a single election. A voter could select from among Democratic candidates for governor and among Republican candidates for the legislature, in effect participating in both primaries. Federal court rulings in 2000 (California) and 2003 (Washington) put an end to blanket primaries; California joined the ranks of the closed primary states, and Washington opted for an open primary system.

runoff election

A second election pitting the top two vote-getters from a first election in which no candidate received a majority of the votes cast.

Louisiana does something completely different: The Pelican State uses a single nonpartisan primary for its statewide and congressional races. Voters can choose from among any of the candidates, regardless of party affiliation. If a candidate receives a majority of votes in the first round of voting, she is elected to office; if she does not, the top two vote-getters face each other in a **runoff election.** The nonpartisan, or "unitary," primary is particularly disruptive to political party power. In New York City, Mayor Michael Bloomberg, arguing that local party machines had "a chokehold on ballot access," fought unsuccessfully to change the city's charter to allow nonpartisan primaries.[19] Not surprisingly, the chief opposition to his proposal came from the Big Apple's Democratic and Republican parties.

Primary Runoff Elections A runoff election is held in some states if no one candidate for an office receives a majority of votes in the primary. Primary runoff elections are used by parties in nine states: Alabama, Arkansas, Florida, Georgia, Mississippi, North Carolina, Oklahoma, South Carolina, and Texas. (Kentucky and South Dakota use primary runoffs but only in certain instances.) In the past, these states were one-party (Democratic) states, so the greatest amount of competition for an office occurred in the Democratic Party's primaries, in which as many as ten candidates might enter a race. When many candidates compete, it is quite probable that no one will receive a majority of the votes, so the top two vote-getters face each other in a runoff. This process ensures that the party's nominee is preferred by a majority of the primary voters.

Theoretically, the rationale for the runoff primary is majority rule. But political circumstances have changed since several southern states adopted the runoff primary system in the 1920s, and the Democratic Party no longer dominates the region. In many southern states the two parties are competitive, and in some, the Republican Party has overtaken the Democrats. This raises an important question: Has the runoff primary outlived its usefulness? It is often difficult for a party to mobilize its voters for the primary runoff election, and voter participation in the runoff drops, on average, by one-third.[20] Moreover, runoffs are costly for states and localities that have to administer them and for candidates who have to campaign again. One solution to this problem for parties might be the ranked choice or **instant runoff** that San Francisco, Burlington, Vermont, and a few other cities have begun using in their municipal elections.[21] In an instant runoff, voters rank the primary candidates in their order of preference. If no candidate receives a majority of first choices, the candidate with the fewest of them is eliminated, and voters who ranked the eliminated candidate first now have their ballots counted for their second choice. The process continues until one candidate has a majority; a runoff primary election is avoided.

instant runoff
Voters use preference rankings to select candidates at a single election.

General Elections

Primaries culminate in the general election through which winning candidates become officeholders. When the general election pits candidates of the two major parties against one another, the winner is the candidate who receives a majority of the votes cast. In a race where more than two candidates compete (which occurs when an Independent or a third-party candidate enters a race), the leading vote-getter may not receive a majority of the votes cast, but instead receives a **plurality.** A few states allow candidates to run under the label of more than one party, which is called **fusion.** In New York in 2006, for example, Eliot Spitzer was the candidate for governor of the Democratic, Independence, and Working Families parties.

Political parties have traditionally been active in general elections, mobilizing voters in support of their candidates. Their role has diminished over time, however, because general-election campaigns have become more candidate-centered and geared to the candidate's own organization.[22] One new twist in the past two decades has been the emergence of legislative party caucuses as major factors in general elections. In large states with professionalized legislatures, the funds distributed to their party's nominees by legislative party caucuses run into the millions of dollars. In addition to funding, legislative party caucuses provide other types of election assistance, such as seminars on issues and on campaign management, making these organizations powerful players in some states' politics.

plurality
The number of votes (though not necessarily a majority) cast for the winning candidate in an election with more than two candidates.

fusion
A state-election provision that allows candidates to run on more than one party ticket.

Most states schedule their gubernatorial elections in "off-years"—that is, in years in which no presidential election is held. Only eleven states elected governors during the presidential election year of 2008; forty-one held their statewide races in other years. (The number sums to fifty-two because New Hampshire and Vermont limit their governors to two-year terms, thereby holding gubernatorial elections in both off- and on-years.) Among those forty-one off-year states, five—Kentucky, Louisiana, Mississippi, New Jersey, and Virginia—have elections that take place in odd-numbered years. Off-year elections prevent the presidential race from diverting attention from state races and also minimize the possible **coattail effect,** by which a presidential candidate can affect the fortunes of state candidates of the same party. By holding elections in off-years, races for governor may serve as referenda on the sitting president's performance in office. Generally, however, the health of a state's economy is a critical issue in gubernatorial elections.[23]

coattail effect

The tendency of a winning (or losing) presidential candidate to carry state candidates of the same party into (or out of) office.

Recent State Elections

The stakes were high for the 2006 state elections, with thirty-six governors' seats and 84 percent of state legislative seats up for election. Republicans held twenty-two of thirty-six contested gubernatorial seats, including the governorships in the four largest states. Democrats, buoyed by their victories in the only two governors' races held in 2005 (New Jersey and Virginia), wanted to extend their winning streak. It had been more than a decade since Democrats had held a majority of the governors' offices, and they had been stung in 2003 when the Democratic governor of California, Gray Davis, had been recalled from office and replaced by Republican Arnold Schwarzenegger. Three-fourths of the thirty-six contests in 2006 involved incumbent governors trying to win re-election; nine of the races were for open seats. Schools and taxes topped the list of issues in most of the 2006 gubernatorial campaigns, followed by the economy, immigration, and ethics.[24]

When the dust settled after the 2006 elections, it was Democrats who were smiling. For the first time since 1994, Democrats could claim a majority of the nation's governorships. By picking up open seats in five states (Arkansas, Colorado, Massachusetts, New York, and Ohio) and ousting one Republican incumbent (Maryland), Democrats increased their gubernatorial numbers to twenty-eight. Twenty-two seats were in Republican hands, including California and Texas, where GOP incumbents were re-elected, and Florida. In legislative races, Democrats experienced a net gain of more than 300 seats, which was sufficient to shift partisan control of the lawmaking branch in several states.

Only three gubernatorial elections took place in 2007; four states held legislative elections. In Louisiana, the announcement by the incumbent Democratic governor that she would not seek re-election led 12 candidates to throw their hats into the ring; in this case, the state's unique nonpartisan primary. In a heated—and expensive—campaign, Republican Congressman Bobby Jindal emerged the victor, with 53 percent of the vote. In Kentucky, the incumbent GOP governor was ousted by a Democratic challenger with extensive prior experience in state government as a legislator, attorney general, and lieutenant governor. In the Bluegrass state, accusations of ethics violations contributed to voter dissatisfaction with the sitting governor. No partisan shifts occurred in Mississippi, however, where the incumbent Republican governor easily won a second term in office. Thus gubernatorial partisanship, in the aggregate, did not change for 2008: 28 Democrats and 22 Republicans. In legislative races, the trend toward increased Democratic strength continued. Democrats gained control of the state senates in both Mississippi and Virginia, while partisan control was stable in Louisiana and New Jersey.[25]

Nonpartisan Elections

A **nonpartisan election** removes the political party identification from candidates in an effort to depoliticize the electoral campaign. Elections that have been made nonpartisan include those for many judicial offices and local-level positions. The special task of judges—adjudicating guilt or innocence, determining right and wrong—does not lend itself to partisan interpretation. The job of local governments—delivering public services—has also traditionally been considered nonideological. Nonpartisan local elections are likely to be found in municipalities, as well as in school districts and special districts.

nonpartisan election

An election without party labels.

Under a nonpartisan election system, all candidates for an office compete in a first election and, if there's no majority winner, the top two vote-getters run in a second election (runoff). Although approximately three-quarters of cities use nonpartisan elections, some regional variation exists in their usage. The prevalence of nonpartisanship is somewhat lower in the Northeast and Midwest than it is in western cities.[26]

Most studies have concluded that nonpartisanship depresses turnout in municipal elections that are held independent of state and national elections. The figures are not dramatic, but in what are already low-turnout elections, the difference can run as high as 10 percent of municipal voters.[27] Studies have shown that lower turnout results in lessened representation of Latinos and Asian Americans on city councils and in the mayor's office.[28] Nonpartisan elections seem to produce a city council that is somewhat elite by socioeconomic standards and a greater number of officeholders who consider themselves Republicans.

What does it take to get elected? In the absence of political parties, candidates are forced to create their own organizations in order to run for office. They raise and spend money (much of it their own), and they seek the support of business and citizen groups. Money matters; and according to studies of city elections in Atlanta and St. Louis, so do incumbency and newspaper endorsements.[29] In some communities, **slating groups** function as unofficial parties by recruiting candidates and financing their campaigns; citizens' groups can also be an important factor in local elections.[30]

slating groups

Nonpartisan political organizations that endorse and promote a slate of candidates.

DIRECT DEMOCRACY

What happens when the government does not respond to the messages that the people are sending? More and more frequently, the answer is to transform the messages into ballot propositions and let the citizens make their own laws. As explained in Chapter 3, *initiatives* are proposed laws or constitutional amend-

popular referendum

A special type of referendum whereby citizens can petition to vote on actions taken by legislative bodies.

referendum

A procedure whereby a governing body submits proposed laws, constitutional amendments, or bond issues to the voters for ratification.

recall

A procedure that allows citizens to vote elected officials out of office before their term has expired.

ments that are placed on the ballot by citizen petition, to be approved or rejected by popular vote. An initiative lets citizens enact their own laws, bypassing the state legislature. This mechanism for legislation by popular vote was one of several reforms of the Progressive era, which lasted roughly from 1890 to 1920. Other Progressive reforms included the popular referendum and the recall. The **popular referendum** allows citizens to petition to vote on actions taken by legislative bodies. It provides a means by which the public can overturn a legislative enactment. (A popular referendum is different from a general **referendum**—a proposition put on the ballot by the legislature that requires voter approval before it can take effect. Constitutional amendments and bond issues are examples of general referenda.) The **recall** election, another citizen-initiated process, requires elected officials to stand for a vote on their removal before their term has expired. Recall provides the public with an opportunity to force an official out of office.

The key characteristic shared by initiative, popular referendum, and recall is that they are actions begun by citizens. The Progressives advocated these mechanisms to expand the role of citizens and to restrict the power of intermediary institutions such as legislatures, political parties, and elected officials.[31] Their efforts were particularly successful in the western part of the United States, probably owing to the difficulty of amending existing state constitutions in the East and to an elitist fear of the working class (namely, the industrialized immigrants in the Northeast and the rural black sharecroppers in the South). The newer western states, in contrast, were quite open, both procedurally and socially. In 1898, South Dakota became the first state to adopt the initiative process. And the initiative was actually used for the first time in Oregon in 1902, when citizens successfully petitioned for ballot questions on mandatory political party primaries and local-option liquor sales. Both of the initiatives were approved.

Today, twenty-four states allow the initiative for constitutional amendments, statutes, or both; Mississippi is the most recent addition, having adopted it in 1992. Popular referendum is provided for in twenty-five states, and recall of state officials in eighteen. These figures understate the use of such mechanisms throughout the country, however, because many states without statewide initiative, popular referendum, and recall allow their use at the local government level. Table 4.2 lists some of the states that give citizens all three of the direct democracy options and some of the states with none of them.

| TABLE 4.2 | **Five States That Do, Five States That Don't** |

ALL THREE DIRECT DEMOCRACY OPTIONS	NONE OF THE DIRECT DEMOCRACY OPTIONS
Arizona	Georgia
California	Iowa
Colorado	North Carolina
North Dakota	Vermont
Wyoming	Virginia

SOURCE: Initiative and Referendum Institute, www.iandrinstitute.org/statewide_i%26r.htm (September 16, 2007).

The Initiative

The first step in the initiative process is the petition. A draft of the proposed law (or constitutional amendment) is circulated along with a petition for citizens to sign. The petition signature requirement varies by state but usually falls between 5 and 10 percent of the number of votes cast in the preceding statewide election. To ensure that a matter is of statewide concern and that signatures have been gathered beyond a single area, some states set geographic distributional requirements. In Montana, for example, signature requirements must be met in at least one-third of the legislative districts; in Nebraska, in two-fifths of the counties.[32] Signatures can be gathered by door-to-door canvassing, buttonholing people at shopping malls and sporting events, posting downloadable petition forms on the Internet, and sending forms to a pre-selected list of likely signers.

The Popularity of Initiatives One of the most influential modern initiatives was California's Proposition 13 (1978), which rolled back property taxes in the state and spawned an immediate wave of tax-reduction propositions across the land. The increased popularity of initiatives has at least two explanations: (1) Some observers believe that wavering public confidence in government has led citizens to take matters into their own hands. The attitude seems to be "if government can't be trusted to do the right thing, we'll do it ourselves." (2) New methods of signature collection have brought the initiative process within the reach of virtually any well-financed group with a grievance or concern. An example from Massachusetts makes the point. When then-governor Paul Cellucci could not get the legislature to pass his tax-cut proposals, he took the issue straight to the voters. Using donations from supporters, he paid a company to collect sufficient signatures on petitions, and he got his issue on the ballot.[33] Massachusetts voters approved it.

Recent Initiatives If ballot questions are any indication of the public's mood, then the public has had quite an attitude lately. Here is a sampling of initiatives on 2006 ballots, and the outcomes.

- Arizona, a measure that defines marriage as solely between a man and a woman (failed).
- California, a proposal to increase the penalties for sex crimes (passed).
- Idaho, a measure that restricts the use of eminent domain for private projects (failed).
- Michigan, a proposal to prohibit state universities from discriminating for/against individuals on the basis of race (passed).
- Oregon, a measure that restores voter-approved term limits struck down by the courts (failed).
- South Dakota, a proposal that prohibits the school year from beginning before September (failed).[34]

Questions About the Initiative Is the initiative process appropriate for resolving tough public problems? Seldom are issues so simple that a yes-or-no ballot question can adequately reflect appropriate options and alternatives. A legislative setting, in contrast, fosters the negotiation and compromise that produce workable solutions. Legislatures are deliberative bodies, not instant problem solvers. Legislators are of two minds when it comes to direct citizen involvement in policymaking. On the one hand, having the public decide a controversial issue such as abortion or school prayer helps legislators out of tight spots. On the other hand, increased citizen law-making intrudes on the central function of the legislature and usurps legislative power. Given the popularity of initiatives, legislators must proceed cautiously with actions that would make them more difficult to use. So far, efforts to increase the signature requirements or to limit the kinds of topics an initiative may address have been unsuccessful. A citizenry accustomed to the initiative process does not look kindly on its dismantling. A survey of Oregon citizens found 81 percent agreeing with this statement: "Ballot initiatives enhance the democratic process in Oregon by allowing voters to decide important policy issues."[35]

Still, direct democracy enthusiasts should heed the words of political scientist Valentina Bali who studied local compliance with a California initiative intended to dismantle bilingual education programs: ". . . the large number of constraints suggests that the final policy outcome of an initiative can be quite limited after the initiative's implementation."[36] Initiative sponsors have learned that if they want their initiative to have the desired impact, they have to keep the pressure on, even after the measure has been approved.

The Recall

Recalls, too, were once a little-used mechanism in state and local governments. Only eighteen states provide for recall of state officials; and in seven of them, judicial officers are exempt. City and county government charters, even in states without recall provisions, often include mechanisms for recall of local elected officials. In fact, the first known recall was aimed at a Los Angeles city council member in 1904. Recalls have a much higher petition signature requirement than initiatives do; it is common to require a signature minimum of 25 percent of the votes cast in the last election for the office of the official sought to be recalled. (Kansas, for example, requires a 40 percent minimum.)

Recall efforts usually involve a public perception of official misconduct. On occasion, however, simply running afoul of citizen preferences is enough to trigger a recall, as former California governor Gray Davis discovered in 2003. Californians unhappy with Davis's leadership in resolving the state's budget crunch and its problems with energy deregulation, collected sufficient signatures (a total of 986,874) to force a recall election. The ballot contained two sections: the recall question (a yes-or-no choice) and a list of candidates vying to replace the incumbent if the yeses prevail. After a seventy-seven-day campaign, 61.2 percent of the Golden State's registered voters turned out to recall Davis by a 55 to 45 percent margin.[37] The winning candidate, a body-builder turned movie star, Arnold Schwarzenegger, captured 49 percent of the vote in a 135-candidate race.

The rationale for the recall process is straightforward: Public officials should be subject to continuous voter control. As the organizer of the successful campaign to recall a mayor stated, "We've shown you can fight city hall."[38] Whether it is used or not, the power to recall public officials is valued by the public. A national survey indicated that two-thirds of those polled favored amending the U.S. Constitution to permit the recall of members of Congress.[39]

Initiatives and recalls have helped open up state and local government to the public. Yet ironically, increased citizen participation can also jam up the machinery of government, thus making its operation more cumbersome. Advocates of greater citizen activism, however, would gladly trade a little efficiency to achieve their goal.

CITIZEN ACCESS TO GOVERNMENT

As we saw in Figure 4.1, citizens have opportunities to participate in government in many nonelectoral ways. Because state and local governments have undertaken extensive measures to open themselves to public scrutiny and stimulate public input, citizen access to government has been increased. Many of these measures are directly connected with the policymaking process. At minimum, they enable government and the citizenry to exchange information, and thus they contribute to the growing capacity of state and local governments. At most, they may alter political power patterns and resource allocations.

Opening Up Government

Many of the accessibility measures adopted by state and local governments are the direct result of public demands that government be more accountable. Others have resulted from an official effort to involve the public in the ongoing work of government.

open meeting laws

Statutes that open the meetings of government bodies to the public.

Open Meeting Laws Florida's 1967 "sunshine law" is credited with sparking a surge of interest in openness in government, and today **open meeting laws** are on the books in all fifty states. These laws do just what the name implies: They open meetings of government bodies to the public, or, in Florida's terminology, they bring government "into the sunshine." Open meeting laws apply to both the state and local levels and affect the executive branch as well as the legislative branch. Basic open meeting laws have been supplemented by additional requirements in many states. Advance public notice of meetings is required in all states; most insist that minutes be kept, levy penalties against officials who violate the law, and void actions taken in meetings held contrary to sunshine provisions. New technology is playing a role; for example in New York, state agencies have developed plans to broadcast their meetings via the Internet.

Some states remain relatively resistant to the sun's rays. In the late 1990s, Rhode Island failed to adopt a package of tougher open meeting laws despite extensive media attention and public pressure. At the same time, North Dakota legislators strengthened the state's open meeting law but exempted themselves from most of the provisions.[40] In general, however, the trend is toward more openness. For example, the advent of electronic mail—making cyberspace meetings possible—led Colorado, and many other states, to expand their open records laws. Now, the stored e-mail files of the state's politicians are open to the public.

Administrative Procedure Acts After state legislation is passed or a local ordinance is adopted, an administrative agency typically is responsible for implementation. This process involves the establishment of rules and regulations and, hence, constitutes powerful responsibility. In practice, agencies often have wide latitude in translating legislative intent into action. For example, if a new state law creates annual automobile safety inspections, it is the responsibility of the state's Department of Motor Vehicles to make it work. Unless the law specifies the details, bureaucrats will determine the items to be covered in the safety inspection, the number and location of inspection stations, and the fee to be charged. These decisions are just as important as the original enactment.

To ensure public access to this critical rule-making process, states have adopted **administrative procedure acts,** which usually require public notice of the proposed rule and an opportunity for citizen comment. All states provide for this "notification and comment" process, as it is known. In addition, some states give citizens the right to petition an administrative agency for an adjustment in the rules.

administrative procedure acts

Acts that standardize administrative agency operations as a means of safeguarding clients and the general public.

Advisory Committees Another arena for citizen participation that is popular in state and especially local governments is the **advisory committee,** in the form of citizen task forces, commissions, and panels. Regardless of name, these organizations are designed to study a problem and to offer advice, usually in the form of recommendations. People chosen to serve on an advisory committee tend to have expertise as well as interest in the issue and, in most cases, political connections. But not always. Back when Barbara Roberts was Oregon's governor, she invited a random cross-section of Oregonians to attend interactive, televised meetings at one of thirty locations. The governor went live (on cable television) to each of the sites to ask citizens to assess the performance of their governments. She got an earful. But she also received invaluable input.[41] These days, the **focus group** plays a similar role by providing a small group setting for intense discussion and debate about public issues.[42]

advisory committee

An organization created by government to involve members of the public in studying and recommending solutions to public problems.

Citizen advisory committees provide a formal structure for citizen input. If officials heed public preferences, citizen advice can become the basis for public policy. Citizen advisory organizations also provide elected officials with a "safe" course of action. In a politically explosive situation, a governor can say, "I've appointed a citizen task force to study the issue and report back to me with recommendations for action." The governor thus buys time, with the hope that the issue will gradually cool down. Another benefit of these organizations is that they ease citizen acceptance of subsequent policy decisions, since the governor can note that an action "was recommended by an impartial panel of citizens." This is not to suggest that citizen advisory committees are merely tools for manipulation by politicians, but they do have uses beyond citizen participation.

focus group

A small group of individuals assembled to provide opinion and feedback about specific issues in government. Participants are often paid for their time.

Engagement via Technology and Volunteerism

States and localities have changed their procedures to make government more accessible. Technology plays a role in engaging citizens with their government; so does volunteerism.

E-Government The Internet has brought state and local government into citizens' homes in a way earlier technology could not. States and localities have already incorporated electronic communications into their daily operations. Websites abound; e-mails proliferate. People can click on a city's homepage and find an array of useful information, such as the agenda for the next city council meeting, the minutes of previous council sessions, the city budget, the comprehensive plan, and the like. Some mayors, such as R. T. Rybak of Minneapolis use Weblogs or "blogs" as a way to stay in touch with their constituents—and bypass conventional media. States have created elaborate websites that link the user to vast databases and information resources.

Now states and localities are expanding their use of the Internet in dealing with the public. It started with the downloading of public reports and generic forms and has moved into more highly individualized interaction such as filing of taxes, applying for licenses and permits, and accessing personal information. Although some have touted the use of the Internet in voting, worries over security and accuracy have slowed the move to the Internet as a virtual polling place. The Internet also offers an efficient way for government to gauge public opinion and preferences. This aspect of e-government was put to good use in 2003, when Maine's new governor confronted a $1 billion deficit. Clearly, cuts would have to be made, but in which programs? Governor John Baldacci came up with a novel idea: create a budget-balancing game that Pine Tree state residents could play on the state's website.[43] The simulation required players to choose which programs to cut and which taxes to increase as they tried to whittle away at the deficit and achieve a balanced budget. Players were encouraged to e-mail the governor with their suggestions once they made their way through the thicket of competing programs.

One of the major concerns as the push toward e-government grows is that the so-called technology have-nots will be left behind. Low-income Americans lag far behind middle- and upper-income groups in their access to the Internet. This digital divide has led many communities to install personal computers in libraries, as well as in government information kiosks located in shopping malls and transit stations. In an effort to get its rural communities wired, North Dakota spent more than $3 million to connect some sixty communities to a broadband network.[44] Other concerns involve security and privacy. Fear that hackers might break into government computers or that personal information might be misused tempers some public enthusiasm for e-government.

volunteerism

A form of participation in which individuals or groups donate time or money to a public purpose.

Volunteerism Voluntary action is another constructive participatory activity unrelated to the ballot box. People and organizations donate their time and talents to supplement or even replace government activity. **Volunteerism** is a means of bringing fresh ideas and energy, whether physical or financial, into government while relieving some of the service burden. One highly visible example of volunteerism is the "Adopt a Highway" program. Over the past ten years, the number of local businesses and civic clubs willing to pick up litter along designated stretches of state highways has skyrocketed. You have probably noticed the "Adopt a Highway" signs with the names of volunteering groups listed underneath. The state saves money, the roadsides stay cleaner, and the volunteering groups have good feelings and free advertising to go along with their sore backs. Washington created the first statewide volunteerism office in 1969, and within twenty years all states had volunteer programs in place. One of the most ambitious efforts has been "Volunteer for Minnesota," which assists local communities in the design of a program, including the actual recruitment, training, and placement of volunteers.

Local governments use volunteers in various ways. Generally, volunteerism is most successful when citizens can develop the required job skills quickly or participate in activities they enjoy, such as library work, recreation programs, or fire protection.[45] In addition to providing services to others, volunteers can be utilized for self-help; that is, they can engage in activities in which they are the primary beneficiaries. For example, some New York City neighborhoods take responsibility for the safety and maintenance of nearby parks. Residential crime-watch programs are another variety of self-help. In both of these instances, the volunteers and their neighborhoods benefit. Overall, studies show, volunteerism is especially successful in rural areas and small towns.

Important supplements to government volunteer programs are those of the nonprofit sector. Members of local faith-based groups and civic organizations, for example, often volunteer their time in support of community improvement projects such as Habitat for Humanity, Meals on Wheels, and Sistercare. Sometimes volunteerism has a political agenda, as does the group of nearly 1,000 volunteers who call themselves "The Minutemen." Periodically, they mass along stretches of the border with Mexico to monitor illegal entry into the United States. Their actions have added fuel to the firestorm of debate over illegal immigration.

THE EFFECTS OF CITIZEN PARTICIPATION

Consider again the four quadrants of Figure 4.1. Constructive participatory behaviors, whether active or passive, invigorate government. The capacity of state and local governments depends on a number of factors, one of which is citizen participation. Underlying this argument is the implicit but strongly held belief shared by most observers of democracies that an accessible, responsive government is a legitimate government. Some commentators held out hope that new media technologies such as cable television and the Internet would stimulate interest in politics and move more people into the constructive quadrants. However, recent research indicates that this has not happened. Instead, politically-interested individuals use these technologies to become better informed while the politically-uninterested opt for entertainment programming.[46]

An active public, one that chooses the *voice* option in Figure 4.1, has the potential to generate widespread change in a community. Public policy tends to reflect the interests of active citizens. The mobilization of lower-class voters, for instance, is linked to more generous state welfare policies.[47] From the perspective of government officials and institutions, citizen participation can be a nuisance because it may disrupt established routines. The challenge is to incorporate citizen participation into ongoing operations. A noteworthy example is Dayton, Ohio, where neighborhood-based "priority boards" shape city services and policies. As a Dayton official noted, "Citizen participation in this city is just a way of life."[48] Citizen involvement may not be easy or efficient, but, in a democracy, it is the ultimate test of the legitimacy of that government.

The stakes for citizen participation are potentially high. Political scientists Tom Rice and Alexander Sumberg developed measures to reflect the civic culture of each state, looking at, among other things, the level of citizen involvement and the amount of political equality.[49] Vermont and Massachusetts were found to be the most civic states, Mississippi and Louisiana the least civic. More important, however, is the impact of a state's civic culture on the performance of its government. According to Rice and Sumberg, a state's civic culture is "a powerful predictor of government performance."[50] Statistical analysis shows that the more civic the state, the more innovative and effective its government. Figure 4.3 displays the states' positions when civic culture and government performance are considered simultaneously. The closer a state is to the upper right corner, the better it is on both indicators. Conversely, states landing near the lower left corner score poorly on both factors. The lesson? Citizen participation matters, not only for the individual but also for the government.

, FIGURE 4.3 **Civic Culture and Government Performance**

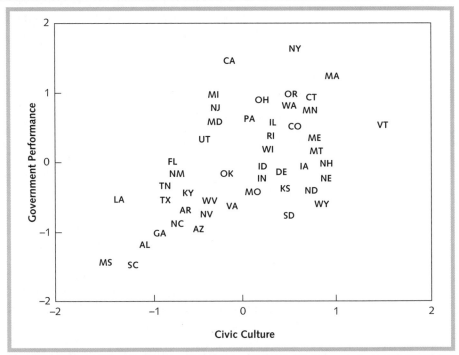

SOURCE: Tom W. Rice and Alexander F. Sumberg, "Civic Culture and Government Performance in the American States," *Publius: The Journal of Federalism* 27, no. 1 (Winter 1997): 110. Reprinted by permission of Oxford University Press.

CHAPTER RECAP

- Citizen participation in the community can be active or passive, constructive or destructive. Local governments have devoted much time and energy to encouraging active, constructive participation among the citizenry.
- Voter turnout rates vary dramatically from one state to another and the reasons have to do with the political culture of the state, the competitiveness of the political parties, and the way elections are administered.
- As a result of the 2007 elections, Democrats control more governorships (28) than Republicans (22) do.
- Almost half of the states have an initiative process, and in those that do, it has become an important tool for policymaking.
- Although it is difficult to mobilize the public in support of a statewide recall of an elected official, it happened in California in 2003 when Governor Gray Davis was recalled from office.
- E-government is on the rise, with states and localities adopting more and more high-tech ways of interacting with citizens. This trend holds tremendous potential for increasing citizen participation in government.
- Volunteerism is a way of bringing fresh ideas and energy into government and helps connect citizens to their community.

Key Terms

participation *(p. 67)*
Voting Rights Act of 1965 *(p. 71)*
primary system *(p. 74)*
closed primary *(p. 75)*
open primary *(p. 75)*
blanket primary *(p. 75)*
runoff election *(p. 75)*
instant runoff *(p.76)*
plurality *(p. 76)*
fusion *(p. 76)*
coattail effect *(p. 77)*

nonpartisan election *(p. 78)*
slating groups *(p. 78)*
referendum *(p. 79)*
popular referendum *(p. 79)*
recall *(p. 79)*
open meeting laws *(p. 82)*
administrative procedure acts *(p. 83)*
advisory committee *(p. 83)*
focus group *(p.83)*
volunteerism *(p. 84)*

Internet Resources

The website of the Federal Election Commission, **www.fec.gov,** contains information about U.S. elections, including laws, voter turnout, and results.

The League of Women Voters, a well-respected organization that encourages informed and active participation of citizens in government, maintains a website at **www.lwv.org.**

A nonpartisan, nonadvocacy website providing up-to-the-minute news and analysis on election reform can be found at **electionline.org.**

MTV's Rock the Vote, an effort to boost political participation among young voters, is at **www.rockthevote.com.**

The organization found at **www.americaspromise.org** encourages volunteers to create "communities of promise" in their hometowns.

www.iandrinstitute.org and **www.ballot.org** provide a wealth of historical data and current information on ballot measures.

To learn more about various state laws on elections, visit each state's home page or see the website of the National Association of Secretaries of State at **www.nass.org.**

Political Parties, Interest Groups, and Campaigns

5

CHAPTER OUTLINE

Political Parties

Interest Groups

Political Campaigns

FOCUS QUESTIONS

1. How have political parties evolved in the face of weakened voter loyalty?

2. What are some of the consequences of increased interparty competition?

3. With interest groups continuing to exert powerful influence on state governments, what is their major focus, and how have they changed recently?

4. What new methods are being employed in political campaigns and how are states dealing with campaign financing?

---

hree Republican state legislators in Iowa found themselves challenged in their bids for re-election in 2006—not by Democrats but by fellow Republicans. It turns out that the policy positions taken by the incumbent GOP legislators were a tad too moderate for some of their brethren in the party. A powerful group called Iowans for Tax Relief (ITR), a coalition of anti-tax folks, Christian right activists, and gun owners, targeted the incumbents for defeat. With the active support of ITR and its political arm, Taxpayers United, the conservative challengers were victorious in the party primary. This illustrates a truth about contemporary partisan politics: Sometimes party loyalty is in short supply.[1]

POLITICAL PARTIES

political parties

Organizations that nominate candidates to compete in elections, and promote policy ideas.

The two major **political parties**—the Democratic Party and the Republican Party—offer slates of candidates to lead us. Candidates campaign hard for the high-profile jobs of governor, state legislator, mayor, and various other state and local positions. In some states, even candidates for judicial positions compete in partisan races. But party involvement in our system of government does not end on election day—the institutions of government themselves have a partisan tone. Legislatures are organized along party lines; governors offer Republican or Democratic agendas for their states; county commissioners of different ideo-logical stripes fight over the best way to provide services to local residents. Through the actions of their elected officials, political parties play a major role in the operation of government.

The Condition of Political Parties

The condition of contemporary American political parties has been described with words such as *decline, decay,* and *demise.* In some ways, the description is accurate, but in other ways, it is overstated. True, the number of people who identify themselves as members of one of the two major parties is only about 60 percent of the electorate, while the number of people calling themselves independents is nearly 40 percent.[2] Furthermore, campaigns are increasingly candidate-centered rather than party-centered, and they rely on personal organizations and political consultants. But at the same time, the party organization has become more professionalized, taking on new tasks and playing new roles in politics and governance. Parties have more financial and technological resources at their disposal.[3] Thus, to some observers, political parties are enjoying a period of *revitalization* and *rejuvenation.* While the debate over political parties continues, it seems clear that they have undergone a *transformation* during the past twenty-five years and that they have proven to be quite adaptable.

American political parties are composed of three interacting parts: the party organization (party committees, party leaders and activists), the party in government (candidates and officeholders), and the party in the electorate (citizens who identify with the party).[4] These parts interact to do many things, but among their central tasks are nominating and electing candidates, educating (some might say, propagandizing) citizens, and once in office, governing.

ideology

Core beliefs about the form and role of the political system.

Parties in the United States function as umbrella organizations that shelter loose coalitions of relatively like-minded individuals. In terms of **ideology,** Republicans tend to be more conservative, favoring a limited role for government; Democrats tend to be more liberal, preferring a more activist government. A general image for each party is discernible: The Republicans typically have been considered the party of big business, the Democrats the party of workers. On many of the social issues of the day—gay rights, abortion, pornography, and prayer in schools—the two parties tend to take different positions. In foreign affairs, Republicans favor a much more assertive U.S. policy than Democrats do. By 2007, the Democratic party could claim about 33 percent of the voting-age public for itself. (See Figure 5.1, which tracks party identification during the recent past.) The Republican Party, however, was experiencing a decline in party identification among the electorate, dropping from 31 percent in 2003 to 25 percent. Many observers link the GOP's downturn to growing public dissatisfaction with the war in Iraq.[5]

The geographical distribution of partisan loyalties has produced some interesting patterns. The South, where conservative political attitudes predominate, is no longer the Democratic stronghold it was forty years ago. In fact, it has become a region of so-called red states, that is, states that vote Republican in presidential elections. Other red states are found in the plains region and the Rocky

| FIGURE 5.1 | **Party Identification in the United States, 1994–2007** |

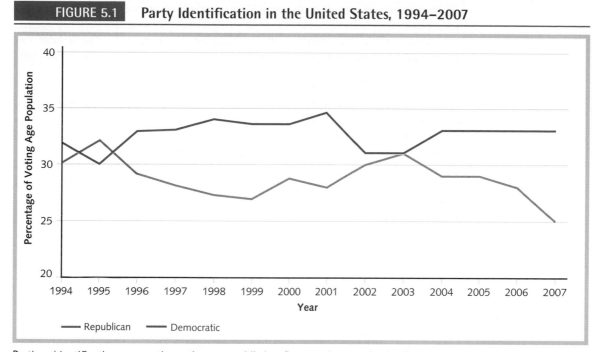

Partisan identification among the voting-age public has fluctuated somewhat in the recent past.
SOURCE: The Pew Research Center for the People and the Press, "Political Landscape More Favorable to Democrats," p. 7, people-press.org/reports/pdf/312.pdf (September 22, 2007).

Mountain west. States that are more reliably Democratic in presidential elections— usually the Northeastern region, the Pacific Coast, and the upper Midwest—are designated "blue" states. (The labels "red" and "blue" refer to the color coded maps that television broadcasters use to show election returns.) States with greater partisan diversity have been called "purple" by some pollsters.[6] It is important not to over-generalize from these colorful, but simple, descriptors of state-level partisanship. Within an individual state, various partisan configurations exist, as research on presidential voting at the county level has shown.[7]

ticket splitting

Voting for candidates of different political parties in a general election.

Voters display a remarkable penchant for **ticket splitting**—that is, voting for a Democrat for one office and a Republican for another in the same election. Many voters are fond of saying that they "vote for the person, not the party." Montanans demonstrated this tendency in 2004 with their strong support for President Bush's re-election . . . and their election of a Democratic governor.

Party Organization

Political parties are decentralized organizations, with fifty state Republican parties and fifty state Democratic parties. Each state also has local party organizations, most typically at the county level. Although they interact, each of these units is autonomous—a situation that promotes independence but is not so helpful to party discipline. Specialized partisan groups, including the College

Democrats, the Young Republicans, Democratic Women's Clubs, Black Republican Councils, and so on, have been accorded official recognition. Party organizations are further decentralized into precinct-level clusters, which bear the ultimate responsibility for turning out the party's voters on election day. Figure 5.2 shows a typical state party organization.

State Parties State governments vary in how closely and vigorously they regulate political parties. In states with few laws, parties have more discretion in their organization and functions.[8] Each state party has a charter or bylaws to govern its operation. The decision-making body is the state committee, sometimes called a central committee, which is headed by a chairperson and composed of members elected in party primaries or at state party conventions. State parties, officially at least, lead their party's push to capture statewide elected offices. Although they may formulate platforms and launch party-centered fundraising appeals, their value to candidates is in the services they provide.[9] In many states, parties host seminars for party nominees on how to campaign effectively; the parties also conduct research into the public's mood and advertise on behalf of their candidates.

FIGURE 5.2	**Typical State Party Organization**

Most political party organizations look something like this. Party workers at the bottom of the chart are direct links to voters.

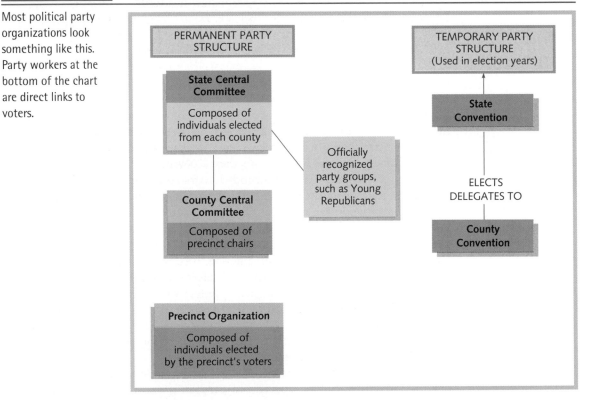

State party organizations differ in their organizational vitality and resources. In nonelection years, the parties operate with limited staff and revenue; in election years, however, they employ on average, nine full-time staffers and seven part-timers, and their funds increase dramatically.[10] Republican organizations generally outstrip Democratic ones in these measures of organizational strength. Although partisan volunteers still canvass neighborhoods, knocking on doors and talking to would-be voters, these activities are increasingly supplemented by Web-based and e-mail appeals for funds and votes. To a candidate, one of the most valuable services the state party can provide is access to its database of party voters.[11]

Local Parties County party organizations are composed of committee members chosen at the precinct level. These workers are volunteers whose primary reward is the satisfaction of being involved in politics. But the work is rarely glamorous. Party workers are the people who conduct voter registration drives, drop off the lawn signs for residents' front yards, and organize candidate forums. On behalf of the party's candidates, they distribute campaign literature, contribute money, make calls to voters, and run newspaper advertisements. Because so many local elected offices are nonpartisan, as noted in Chapter 4, local party organizations focus primarily on state (and national) campaigns.

Local parties are less professionally organized than state parties. Although many local organizations maintain campaign headquarters during an election period, few operate year-round offices. County chairpersons report devoting a lot of time to the party during election periods, but otherwise the post does not take much of their time. Most chairpersons lead organizations without any full-time staff, and vacancies in precinct offices are common.

Factions As the vignette opening this chapter illustrated, political parties frequently develop *factions*— that is, identifiable subsets. These may be ideologically based, as exemplified by the struggle between moderates and liberals for control of state Democratic parties. They may be organized around particular political leaders, or they may reflect sectional divisions within a state. When factions endure, they make it difficult for a party to come together on behalf of candidates and in support of policy. Persistent intraparty factions create opportunities for the opposing party.

Ohio offers a relevant example. Claiming that the leadership of the state's GOP was "out of touch with its base," conservative Christians launched the Ohio Restoration Project in 2005, an effort "to register half a million new voters, enlist activists, train candidates and endorse conservative causes."[12] The group's "patriot pastors" develop voter guides, hold rallies, set up e-prayer networks on the Internet, and raise funds to donate to selected candidates. Leaders of the Ohio Republican Party have cast a wary eye on the project, contending that if the party moves too far to the right on the ideological spectrum, its electoral success could be jeopardized.

For the Democrats, the public's increasing conservatism has forced the party to move toward the center of the ideological spectrum. The emergence of

pragmatism

A practical approach to problem solving; a search for "what works."

candidates who refer to themselves as "New Democrats" and speak the language of **pragmatism** is evidence of that movement.

The Two-Party System

General elections in the United States are typically contests between candidates representing the two major political parties. Such has been the case for the past century and a half. The Democratic Party has been in existence since the 1830s, when it emerged from the Jacksonian wing of the Jeffersonian Party. The Republican Party, despite its label as the "Grand Old Party," is newer; it developed out of the sectional conflict over slavery of the 1850s.

Why Just Two There are numerous reasons for the institutionalization of two-party politics. Explanations that emphasize sectional dualism, such as East versus West or North versus South, have given way to those that focus on the structure of the electoral system. Parties compete in elections in which there can be only one winner. Most legislative races, for example, take place in single-member districts in which only the candidate with the most votes wins; there is no reward for finishing second or third. Hence the development of radical or noncentrist parties is discouraged. In addition, laws regulating access to the ballot and receipt of public funds contribute to two-partyism by creating high start-up costs for third parties. Another plausible explanation has to do with tradition. Americans are accustomed to a political system composed of two parties, and that is how we understand politics.

Third Parties The assessment of former Alabama governor George Wallace that "there ain't a dime's worth of difference between Democrats and Republicans" raises questions about the need for alternative parties. Third parties (also called nonmajor or minor parties) are a persistent phenomenon in U.S. politics. The two major parties may not differ substantially, but for the most part their positions reflect the public mood. Third parties suffer because the two established parties have vast reserves of money and resources at their disposal; new parties can rarely amass the finances or assemble the organization necessary to make significant inroads into the system. Further, third parties typically receive scant attention from the news media, and without it, credibility wanes.[13]

Public interest in partisan alternatives may be increasing. One national survey reported that 53 percent of the electorate believed that there should be a third major political party; scholarly research has found among self-described Independents support for the creation of more parties.[14] Many indicated that their estrangement from the Democratic and Republican parties made them willing to affiliate with a third party that reflected their interests. This sentiment makes it easier to understand why, in 1998, the Reform Party was successful in its quest for the governorship of Minnesota. Two third parties that have enjoyed some success in local races in recent times are the Libertarian Party which seeks to reduce the government's size, and the Green Party, which grew out of the environmental movement. By 2007, Libertarians had been elected to 600 local offices in thirty-seven states, with their impact greatest in California, New

Hampshire, and Pennsylvania. That same year, there were 226 Greens holding local offices in twenty-eight states, including city council positions in cities such as San Francisco, Boston, and Minneapolis.

Interparty Competition These days, most states exhibit meaningful two-party electoral competition. In other words, when you look at a general-election ballot, you will find both the Democrats and the Republicans offering credible candidates for state offices. The extension of interparty competition to states that lacked it in the past is a healthy development in American politics. Heated partisan competition turns a dull campaign into a lively contest. Citizen interest picks up, and voter turnout increases. Citizens who are dissatisfied with the performance of the party in power have another choice.

Beyond electoral competition, an important consideration is which party controls the major policymaking institutions in the state—the governor's office and the state legislature. Generally, there is a link between the partisan composition of the electorate and partisan control of a state's institutions. For instance, in Utah the Republican Party typically has a voter registration advantage over the Democratic Party of more than 2 to 1. Not surprisingly, in the Utah legislature, Republicans outnumber Democrats by a nearly 3 to 1 margin, and a Republican occupies the governor's office. But the electorate–institution relationship is not a simple one. Consider Maryland and Massachusetts, two of the states in which voter registration patterns give the Democratic Party a strong advantage. Both states elected Republicans to the governor's office in 2002 but sustained the Democratic dominance in the legislature. In Maryland and Massachusetts, and in many other states, voting produced an institutional outcome called **divided government.**

In 2007, the Republican Party controlled the governor's office and both houses of the legislature in ten states; the Democratic Party had institutional control of sixteen states. (Among the sixteen states were Maryland and Massachusetts, both of which elected Democratic governors in 2006.) Although these states had **unified government,** in twenty-three states, divided government prevailed. It is important to remember that even with unified partisan control of state institutions, the governor and the legislature may still be at odds, as both Illinois (unified Democratic control) and Georgia (unified Republican control) found in 2007.[15]

Two-party competition has spread at a time when states are becoming the battleground for the resolution of difficult policy issues. Undoubtedly, as governors set their agendas and legislatures outline their preferences, cries of "partisan politics" will be heard. But in a positive sense, such cries symbolize the maturation of state institutions. Partisan politics will likely encourage a wider search for policy alternatives and result in innovative solutions.

Is the Party Over?

Have political parties, as we know them, outlived their usefulness? Should they be cast aside as new forms of political organization and communication emerge? As some have argued, a more educated populace that can readily acquire political information via the Internet is likely to be less reliant on party cues.[16]

divided government

A situation in which one party controls the governor's office and the other party controls the legislature.

unified government

A situation in which both the governor's office and the legislature are controlled by the same party.

dealignment

The weakening of an individual's attachment to political parties.

Today's generation is less loyal to political parties than its grandparents were and is not so likely to vote along party lines. The trend toward **dealignment,** or weakening of individual partisan attachments, slowed for a period but has begun to pick up again. For example, in New York, one-third of the 3 million new registered voters from 1992 to 2004 rejected the major parties and registered as unaffiliated or as Independence Party members.[17] According to one political consultant, "A large group of the electorate tends to be socially tolerant and more receptive to fiscally conservative methods. They don't have a home in either party."[18] This trend is not good news for the two major parties.

Political parties are not sitting idly by as their function in the political system is challenged. Party organizations are making their operations more professional and have more money to spend and more staff to spend it. The past several years have seen the development of party-centered advertising campaigns and a renewed commitment to get-out-the-vote drives. In a few states with publicly funded campaigns, parties as well as candidates have been designated as recipients of funds. All in all, it appears that parties are doing their best to adapt to the changing environment.

INTEREST GROUPS

interest groups

Organizations of like-minded individuals who desire to influence government.

Interest groups have become powerful players in our democratic system. Joining a group is a way for individuals to communicate their preferences—their interests—to government. Interest groups attempt to influence governmental decisions and actions by pressuring decision-making bodies to, for example, put more guidance counselors in public schools, restrict coastal development, keep a proposed new prison out of a neighborhood, or strengthen state licensing of family therapists. Success is defined in terms of getting the group's preferences enacted. In certain states, interest groups actually dominate the policy-making process.

In considering the role of groups in the political system, we must remember that people join groups for reasons other than politics. For instance, a teacher may be a member of a politically active state education association because the group offers a tangible benefit such as low-cost life insurance, but he may disagree with some of the political positions taken by the organization. In general, then, motivations for group membership are individually determined.

Types of Interest Groups

Interest groups come in all types and sizes. If you were to visit the lobby of the state capitol when the legislature was in session, you might find the director of the state school boards association conversing with the chairperson of the education committee, or the lobbyist hired by the state hotel-motel association exchanging notes with the representative of the state's restauranteurs. If a legislator were to venture into the lobby, she would probably receive at least a friendly greeting from the lobbyists and at most a serious heart-to-heart talk about the merits of a bill. You would be witnessing efforts to influence public policy. Interest groups want state government to enact policies that are in their interest or, conversely, not to enact policies at odds with their intent.

The interests represented in the capitol lobby are as varied as the states themselves. One that is well represented and powerful is business. Whether a lobbyist represents a single large corporation or a consortium of businesses, when he talks, state legislators listen. From the perspective of business groups (and other economically oriented groups), legislative actions can cost or save their members money. Therefore, the Chamber of Commerce, industry groups, trade associations, financial institutions, and regulated utilities maintain a visible presence in the state capitol during the legislative session. Table 5.1 documents the influential nature of business interests at the state level. It is important to remember however, that business interests are not monolithic; occasionally they may find themselves on opposite sides of a bill.

Other interests converge on the capitol. Representatives of labor, both established AFL-CIO unions and professional associations such as the state optometrists' group or sheriffs' association, frequent the hallways and committee meeting rooms to see that the legislature makes the "right" decision on the bills before it. For example, if a legislature were considering a bill to change the licensing procedures for optometrists, you could expect to find the optometrists' interest group immersed in the debate. Another workers' group, schoolteachers, has banded together to form one of the most effective state-level groups. In fact, as Table 5.1 indicates, schoolteachers' organizations are ranked among the most influential interest groups in thirty-seven states.[19]

Many other interest groups are active (but not necessarily influential) in state government, and a large number of them are ideological in nature. In other words, their political activity is oriented toward some higher good, such as clean air or fairer tax systems or consumer protection. Members of these groups do not have a direct economic or professional interest in the outcome of a legislative decision. Instead, their lobbyists argue that the public as a whole benefits from their involvement in the legislative process. Penn PIRG, for instance, describes itself as a nonprofit, nonpartisan watchdog group working on behalf of consumers, the environment, and good government in Pennsylvania. The group's motto, and that of other PIRGs (public interest research groups), is "Get active, speak out, make a difference."

Looking at a specific state reveals a mix of active, effective interest groups. For example, the list of effective interest groups in Rhode Island includes the standard set of economic interests such as business groups, labor unions, banks, and utilities. Other groups vying for legislative attention reflect diverse interests such as governmental reform groups, environmental groups, the media (especially the *Providence Journal-Bulletin* and radio talk shows), senior citizens, and the liquor lobby.[20] In fact, a look across the states shows some fairly state-specific interests; some examples are the gaming industry in Nevada, the poultry federation in Arkansas, the stock-growers' association in Montana, and the Ojibwa and Sioux tribes in Minnesota.

TABLE 5.1	The Twenty Most Influential Interests in the States

RANK	INTEREST	NUMBER OF STATES IN WHICH THE INTEREST WAS SEEN AS VERY EFFECTIVE
1	General business organizations (chambers of commerce, etc.)	40
2	Schoolteachers' organizations (NEA and AFT)	37
3	Utility companies and associations (electric, gas, water, telephone/telecommunications)	24
4	Insurance: general and medical (companies and associations)	21
5	Hospital/nursing home associations	21
6	Lawyers (predominately trial attorneys and state bar associations)	22
7	Manufacturers (companies and associations)	18
8	General local government organizations (municipal leagues, county organizations, etc.)	18
9	Physicians/state medical associations	17
10	General farm organizations (state farm bureaus, etc.)	16
11	Bankers' associations	15
12	Traditional labor associations (predominantly the AFL-CIO)	13
13	Universities and colleges (institutions and employees)	13
14	State and local government employees (other than teachers)	11
15	Contractors/builders/developers	13
16	Realtors' associations	13
17	K–12 education interests (other than teachers)	9
18	Individual labor unions (Teamsters, UAW, etc.)	8
19	Truckers and private transport interests (excluding railroads)	9
20	Hunting and fishing groups (includes anti–gun control groups)	9

NOTE: The ranking is determined by more than the "very effective" score.

SOURCE: Adapted from Clive S. Thomas and Ronald J. Hrebenar, "Interest Groups in the States," in Virginia Gray and Russell L. Hanson, eds. *Politics in the American States: A Comparative Approach* (Washington, D.C.: Congressional Quarterly Press, 2004), pp. 119-20. Reprinted by permission.

Interest Groups in the States

Although states share some similarities, the actual interest-group environment differs from one state to another. Variation exists not only in the composition of the involved groups but also in the degree of influence they exert. Research by political scientists Clive Thomas and Ronald Hrebenar, along with a team of researchers throughout the country, provides fresh insights into the interest-group scene. One of the important characteristics is the power of groups vis-à-vis the policymaking institutions in a state. States cluster into one of four different categories. In five states—Alabama, Florida, Montana, Nevada, and West Virginia—interest groups dominate state political institutions such as political parties; that is, groups wield an overwhelming and consistent influence on policymaking.[21] On the other hand, interest groups are comparatively weak in Michigan, Minnesota, and South Dakota. In sixteen states, interest groups enjoy complementary, somewhat balanced relationships with other political institutions. The pattern is less stable in the remaining twenty-six states. Interest group power tends to ebb and flow in these states, with groups playing a dominant role in some instances, but not in others.

For the most part, interest-group politics is defined by its state context. First of all, interest groups and political parties have evolving, multidimensional relationships. Typically, in states where political parties are weak, interest groups are strong; where political parties are strong, interest groups tend to be weaker.[22] Strong parties provide leadership in the policymaking process, and interest groups function through them. In the absence of party leadership and organization, interest groups fill the void, becoming important recruiters of candidates and financiers of campaigns; accordingly, they exert tremendous influence in policymaking.

A second, related truth adds a developmental angle to interest-group politics. As states diversify economically, their politics are less likely to be dominated by a single interest.[23] Thus, we find that the interest-group environment is becoming more crowded, resulting in *hyperpluralism*, or a multiplicity of groups. As states increasingly become the arena in which important social and economic policy decisions are made, more and more groups will go to statehouses, hoping to find a receptive audience.

Local-Level Interest Groups

Interest groups also function at the local level. Because so much of local government involves the delivery of services, local interest groups devote a great deal of their attention to administrative agencies and departments. Groups are involved in local elections and in community issues, to be sure, but their major focus is on the *actions* of government: policy implementation and service delivery.

As in states, business groups are influential in local government. Business-related interests, such as the local chamber of commerce or a downtown merchants' association, usually wield power in the community. An increasingly important group at the local level is the neighborhood-based organization, which in some communities rivals the business interests in influence. Other groups active at the local level include faith-based organizations, public employee unions, and ethnic minority groups.[24] Thus far, however, these groups have not achieved the degree of influence accorded business and neighborhood groups.

Neighborhood organizations deserve a closer look. Some have arisen out of issues that directly affect neighborhood residents—a local school that is scheduled to close, a wave of violent crime, a proposed freeway route that will destroy homes and businesses. Others have been formed by government itself as a way of channeling citizen participation. Neighborhood groups, as well as others lacking a bankroll but possessing enthusiasm and dedication, may resort to tactics such as **direct action,** which might involve protest marches at the county courthouse or human blockades of bulldozers clearing land for a new highway. Direct action is usually designed to attract attention to a cause; it tends to be a last resort, a tactic employed when other efforts at influencing government policy have failed. A study of citizen groups in seven large cities found that 34 percent of the groups engaged in protests or demonstrations at least occasionally.[25]

direct action
A form of participation designed to draw attention to a cause.

Techniques Used by Interest Groups

Interest groups want to have a good public image. It helps a group when its preferences can be equated with what is "good for the state" (or the community). Organizations use slogans like "The timber industry benefits Oregon" or "Schoolteachers have the interests of New York City at heart." Some groups have taken on the label "public interest groups" to designate their main interest as that of the public at large. Groups, then, invest resources in creating a positive image.

Being successful in the state capitol or at city hall involves more than a good public image, however. For example, interest groups have become effective at organizing networks that exert pressure on legislators. If a teacher pay-raise bill is in jeopardy in the senate, for instance, schoolteachers throughout the state may be asked by the education association to contact their senators to urge them to vote favorably on the legislation. To maximize their strength, groups with common interests often establish coalitions.

Sometimes, related groups carve out their own niches to avoid direct competition for members and support.[26] For example, gay and lesbian groups, relatively new to state politics, focus on narrow issues such as ending prohibitions against same-sex marriages rather than on broad concerns.[27] This targeting strategy allows more groups to flourish. Interest groups also hire representatives who can effectively promote their cause. To ensure that legislators will be receptive to their pressures, groups try to influence the outcome of elections by supporting candidates who reflect their interests.

Several factors affect the relative power of an interest group. In their work, Thomas and Hrebenar have identified ten characteristics that give some groups more political clout than others:

- the degree of necessity of group services and resources to public officials;
- whether the group's lobbying focus is primarily defensive or offensive;
- the extent and strength of group opposition;
- potential for the group to enter into coalitions;

- group financial resources;
- size and geographical distribution of group membership;
- political cohesiveness of the membership;
- political, organizational, and managerial skills of group leaders;
- timing and the political climate; and
- lobbyist-policymaker relations [28]

No single interest group is at the high end of all ten of these characteristics all of the time. But many of the groups listed in Table 5.1 possess quite a few of these factors. An indispensable group armed with ample resources, a cohesive membership, and skilled leaders, when the timing is right, can wield enormous influence in the state capitol. This is especially true when the group has taken a defensive posture—that is, when it wants to block proposed legislation. On the other hand, victory comes less easily to a group lacking these characteristics.

lobbying

The process by which groups and individuals attempt to influence policymakers.

Lobbying Lobbying is the attempt to influence government decision makers. States have developed official definitions to determine who is a lobbyist and who is not. A common definition is "anyone receiving compensation to influence legislative action." A few states, such as Nevada, North Dakota, and Washington, require everyone who attempts to influence legislation to register as a lobbyist (even those who are not being paid), but most states exclude from this definition public officials, members of the media, and people who speak only before committees or boards. Because of definitional differences, comparing the number of lobbyists across states raises the proverbial apples-and-oranges problem. But with that in mind, some cautious comparisons can be made. As of 2005, Florida, Illinois, and New York had more than 2,100 registered lobbyists. Smaller interest-group universes were found in Alaska and Maine, each with fewer than 300 registered lobbyists [29]

In most states, lobbyists are required to file reports indicating how and on whom they spent money. Concern that lobbyists would exert undue influence on the legislative process spurred states to enact new reporting requirements and to impose tougher penalties for their violation. Maine and New Jersey, for instance, require lobbyists to report their sources of income, total and categorized expenditures, the names of the individual officials who received their monies or gifts, and the legislation they supported or opposed. Despite stringent disclosure laws, legislator–lobbyist scandals have caused many states to clamp down even harder. In Iowa, for instance, each registered lobbyist is prohibited from spending more than $3.00 per day on a legislator; in Florida, lobbyists cannot give any gifts, regardless of value, to legislators. [30]

As state government has expanded and taken on more functions, the number of interests represented at the statehouse has exploded. [31] The increase in the number of lobbyists has a very simple, but important, cause: Interests that are affected by state government cannot afford to be without representation. An anecdote from Florida makes the point. A few years ago, legislators supported a new urban development program that Florida cities had lobbied for but about which they could not agree on a funding source. After much debate, they found one: a sales tax on dry cleaning. Because the dry-cleaning industry did not have a lobbyist in Tallahassee, there was no one to speak out on its behalf. Indeed, since their views were not represented in the debate over funding sources, dry cleaners were an easy target.[32] (The dry-cleaning industry learned its lesson and hired a lobbyist a few days after the tax was enacted.)

To win over legislators in their decision-making, lobbyists need access, so they cultivate good relationships with lawmakers. In other words, they want connections; they want an "in." There are many ways of establishing connections, such as entertaining, gift giving, and contributing to campaigns. Also, lawmakers want to know how a proposed bill might affect the different interests throughout the state and especially in their legislative districts, and what it is expected to achieve. And lobbyists are only too happy to provide that information. Social lobbying—wining and dining legislators—still goes on in many states, but it is being supplemented by another technique: the provision of information. A new breed of lobbyists has emerged, trained as attorneys and public relations specialists, skilled in media presentation and information packaging. Lobbying in all of its manifestations is an expensive proposition. In the 42 states that report lobbying expenditures, the total for 2005 reached $1.16 billion, an increase of 22 percent over the preceding year.[33]

An analysis of the lobbying environment in three states—California, South Carolina, and Wisconsin—identified the kinds of techniques that lobbyists rely on. Table 5.2 lists the techniques that more than 80 percent of the 595 lobbyists surveyed said they used. Providing information is clearly a large part of a

TABLE 5.2 | **The Most Popular Techniques Used by Lobbyists**

1. Testifying at legislative hearings.
2. Contacting government officials directly to present point of view.
3. Helping to draft legislation.
4. Alerting state legislators to the effects of a bill on their districts.
5. Having influential constituents contact legislator's office.
6. Consulting with government officials to plan legislative strategy.
7. Attempting to shape implementation of policies.
8. Mounting grassroots lobbying efforts.
9. Helping to draft regulations, rules, or guidelines.
10. Shaping government's agenda by raising new issues and calling attention to previously ignored problems.
11. Engaging in informal contacts with officials.
12. Inspiring letter-writing or telegram campaigns.

SOURCE: Anthony Nownes and Patricia Freemann, "Interest Group Activity in the States," *Journal of Politics* 60 (February 1998), p. 92. Copyright © Southern Political Science Association. Reprinted by permission of Blackwell Publishing Ltd.

lobbyist's role, but a few of the techniques, such as having influential constituents contact a legislator's office, tend toward more of a "leaning on" approach. Notice, too, that lobbying is not confined to the legislative process. Lobbyists regularly attempt to shape the implementation of policies after they are enacted.

grassroots lobbying

Group mobilization of citizens to contact public officials on behalf of shared public policy views.

A not-so-new tactic that is enjoying a resurgence is **grassroots lobbying**— "the planned and orchestrated demonstration of public support through the mobilization of constituent action."[34] Since lobbying reforms have changed the political landscape, groups increasingly rely on their members to communicate with legislators (translation: bombard with mail, faxes, and telephone calls) on behalf of the group's issue. Grassroots lobbying is not just a technique for outsiders. Research has found that citizen groups, unions, religious groups, charities, corporations, and trade and professional associations all use grassroots techniques.[35] This has given rise to the term *astroturfing,* or bogus grassroots lobbying.

political action committee (PAC)

An organization that raises and distributes campaign funds to candidates for elective office.

Political Action Committees Political action committees (PACs) have become a regular feature of state politics since the 1980s. Narrowly focused subsets of interest groups, PACs are political organizations that collect funds and distribute them to candidates. PACs serve as the campaign-financing arm of corporations, labor unions, trade associations, and even political parties. They grew out of long-standing laws that made it illegal for corporations and labor unions to contribute directly to a candidate. Barred from direct contributions, these organizations set up "political action" subsidiaries to allow them legal entry into campaign finance.

The impact of PACs on state politics is potentially far-reaching. Some Michigan legislators, for example, consider PACs a potentially dangerous influence on state politics because their money "buys a lot of access that others can't get."[36] And access usually means influence. Analysis of tobacco-industry PACs suggests that their campaign contributions affect legislative behavior: "As legislators [in California, Colorado, Massachusetts, Pennsylvania, and Washington] received more tobacco industry campaign contributions . . . legislators were more likely to be pro–tobacco industry."[37] Similarly, in Florida, campaign contributions from teacher union PACs were shown to have influenced legislators' votes on a school vouchers bill.[38]

States have responded to the proliferation of PACs by increasing their regulation. In New Jersey, for instance, PACs are required to register and to provide information regarding their controlling interests. One likely possibility is that an independent interstate network of groups with money to spend could emerge as a real threat to political parties as a recruiter of candidates and financier of campaigns. As a harbinger of tighter regulation of PACs, Washington enacted a law that restricts contributions from out-of-state PACs. Although most states have acted to limit the amount of PAC contributions, sixteen states allow unlimited contributions. Table 5.3 classifies states according to the stringency of their PAC contribution laws.

| TABLE 5.3 | Variation in PAC Contribution Limitations in the States |

CODE	PAC LIMITATIONS	STATES	
0	*Unlimited Contributions*	Alabama	North Dakota
		California	Oregon
		Illinois	Pennsylvania
		Indiana	South Dakota
		Iowa	Texas
		Mississippi	Utah
		Nebraska	Virginia
		New Mexico	Wyoming
1	*Moderate Contribution Limits* Greater than $5,000 per election year.	Maryland	
		Nevada	
		New Jersey	
		New York	
		North Carolina	
		Tennessee	
2	*Low Contribution Limits* Greater than $1,000, but no more than $5,000 per election year.	Arkansas	Michigan
		Delaware	New Hampshire
		Georgia	Ohio
		Hawaii	Oklahoma
		Idaho	South Carolina
		Kentucky	Washington
		Louisiana	West Virginia
3	*Very Low Contribution Limits* $1,000 or less per election year.	Alaska	Massachusetts
		Arizona	Minnesota
		Colorado	Missouri
		Connecticut	Montana
		Florida	Rhode Island
		Kansas	Vermont
		Maine	Wisconsin

SOURCE: Robert Hogan, "State Campaign Finance Laws and Interest Group Electioneering Activities," *Journal of Politics* 67 (August 2005): 891, Table 1. Reprinted by permission of Blackwell Publishing.

POLITICAL CAMPAIGNS

Political parties and interest groups bump into each other all the time, especially in political campaigns. Like so many things these days, political campaigns aren't what they used to be. But despite changes in campaign styles and technologies,

| FIGURE 5.3 | **The Voting Configuration of a Hypothetical Election District** |

SOURCE: Daniel M. Shea and Michael John Burton, *Campaign Craft: The Strategies, Tactics, and Art of Political Campaign Management.* Copyright © 2001 by Daniel M. Shea and Michael John Burton. Reprinted with permission of Greenwood Publishing Group, Inc., Westport, CT.

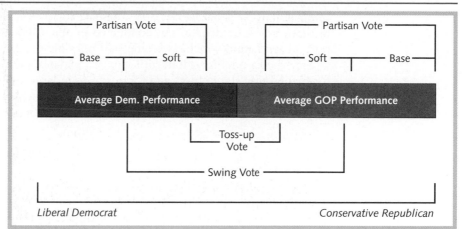

the goal remains the same: attracting enough voters to win the election. Figure 5.3 diagrams the voting configuration in a hypothetical election district. This district typically splits its vote evenly between Democrats and Republicans. Thus, in any given election, each party can count on about 25 percent of the vote (labeled the "base" in the diagram), with another 17 percent that is fairly likely to vote for the party's candidate (the "soft" partisan vote). That leaves about 16 percent of the vote up for grabs (the toss-up vote).[39] The toss-up vote and the soft partisan vote comprise what is typically referred to as the swing vote. Candidates target their energies on the swing vote, the size of which varies with the distribution of the partisan base vote. It is important to remember that most districts are not so evenly divided in their partisan loyalties.

A New Era of Campaigns

In the new era of campaigns, direct contact with potential voters still matters, of course. Candidates for state legislative seats, for example, devote time to door-to-door canvassing, neighborhood drop-ins, and public forums. Yet more and more, they rely on direct mail and electronic media to deliver their messages to voters and on political consultants to help them craft the message.

Mass Media   The mass media, especially television, are intrinsic aspects of modern statewide campaigns. Even candidates for local offices are increasingly using the mass media to transmit their messages. Campaigners can either buy their air time and newspaper space for advertising or get it free by arranging events that reporters are likely to cover. These events range from serious (a candidate's major policy statement) to gimmicky (a candidate climbing into the ring with a professional wrestler to demonstrate his "toughness"); either way, they are cleverly planned to capture media attention.

A candidate seeking free media attention needs to create visual events, be quotable, and relentlessly attack opponents or targeted problems. Televised debates offer another opportunity for free media time. In 2002, the Democratic candidates for governor in Texas debated twice during the primary election campaign. Their debating twice was not particularly unusual; the distinction lay in that one of the debates was conducted in Spanish, an indicator of how important the Latino vote has become, and not only in Texas.

Free media time is seldom sufficient. Candidates, particularly those running for higher-level state offices and for positions in large cities, rely on paid advertisements to reach the public. Paid media advertisements these days seem to be of two distinct varieties: generic and negative. Generic advertisements include

1. the *sainthood spot,* which glorifies the candidate and her accomplishments;
2. the *testimonial spot,* in which other people (celebrities, average citizens) attest to the candidate's abilities;
3. the *bumper-sticker policy spot,* which emphasizes the campaign's popular and noncontroversial themes (good schools, lower taxes, more jobs); and
4. the *feel-good spot,* which identifies and capitalizes on the spirit of a place and its people (for example, "Vermont's a special place" or "Nobody can do it better than Pennsylvania").[40]

Media advertising is important because it is frequently the only contact a potential voter has with a candidate. A candidate's personal characteristics and style—important considerations to an evaluating public—are easily transmitted via the airwaves. And, indeed, advances in communications technology offer new options to enterprising candidates. To many observers, the Internet has the potential to transform campaigning just as television did fifty years ago. Nearly all major candidates for state and local offices routinely maintain campaign websites, some rudimentary, others much more elaborate. Several statewide candidates pioneered the use of campaign e-cards (the electronic equivalent of chain letters) so that supporters could contact people in their e-mail address books about the candidate. One of the keys for the future is the creation of interactive websites that engage Web surfers and keep them coming back. The advent of YouTube provided opportunities for candidates and for their opponents as videos of campaign high points—and low moments—made their way to the website.

Political Consultants Along with increased use of the media, a new occupational specialty sprang up during the 1970s and 1980s: political consulting. Individuals with expertise in polling, direct mail, fundraising, advertising, and campaign management sign on to work for political campaigns. The occupation is undoubtedly here to stay, and several colleges and universities now offer degree programs in practical politics and campaign management.

Consultants form the core of the professional campaign management team assembled by candidates for state offices. They identify and target likely voters, both those who are already in the candidate's camp but need to be reminded to vote and those who can be persuaded to vote for the candidate. Consultants use survey research and focus groups to find out what the public is thinking. They carefully craft messages to appeal to specific subsets of voters, such as the elderly, homeowners, and environmentalists. Advertising on radio and through direct mail are two popular means of getting a candidate's message to targeted segments of the voting public. In fact, recent research has found that much of the public actually prefers narrowcast messages, tailored to their interests.[41]

Any number of factors can influence the result of an election, such as the presence of an incumbent in a race and the amount of funds a challenger has accumulated, but one significant factor is the ability to frame or define the issues during the campaign. Even in a quietly contested state legislative race, district residents are likely to receive mailings that outline the candidate's issue positions, solicit funds, and perhaps comment unfavorably on the opposition. The candidate who has an effective political consultant to help set the campaign agenda and thereby put her opponent on the defensive is that much closer to victory. A study of legislative elections indicates that the use of campaign professionals is especially valuable to challengers who are hoping to unseat incumbents[42]

Negative Campaigning The level of negativism in political campaigns, especially in advertising, has increased, even as the public registers its disapproval of mudslinging, take-no-prisoners campaigns. The strident tone projected in campaigns seems to have fueled cynicism about government and politics, and may have the effect of reducing voter turnout. Tired of the unrelenting nastiness, states are exploring different ways of controlling negative campaigning.

Negative campaign advertising comes in three flavors: fair, false, and deceptive. A fair ad might emphasize some embarrassing aspect of an opponent's voting record or some long-forgotten indiscretion. A false ad, as the label implies, contains untrue statements. More problematic are deceptive advertisements, which distort the truth about an opponent. The task for states is to regulate negative campaign advertising without violating the free-speech guarantees of the U.S. Constitution. False advertising that is done with actual malice can be prohibited by a state, but deceptive ads, replete with accusation and innuendo, are more difficult to regulate[43]

States have enacted laws prohibiting false campaign statements; candidates who use false ads against their opponents can be fined. One of the problems with these laws is that the damage is done long before the remedy can be applied. Fining a candidate after the election is akin to latching the barn door after the horse has fled. Several states have adopted a fair campaign practices code. These codes typically contain broad guidelines such as "Do not misrepresent the facts" or "Do not make appeals to prejudice based on race or sex." The limitation of the codes is that compliance is voluntary rather than mandatory.

In addition to government action, many newspapers have begun to report regularly on the content, presentation, and relative accuracy of campaign advertising. "Ad watches" or "truth boxes," as they are often called, occasionally have led to the retraction or redesign of ads. Despite the efforts of government and the media, however, negative campaign advertising persists because many candidates believe that if done cleverly, it can benefit their campaigns. After all, people may not like negative ads, but they certainly seem to remember them.

Campaign Finance

To campaign for public office is to spend money—a lot of money. In 2005, the race for Virginia governor set a new spending record: $42 million. A little farther north in New Jersey, Jon Corzine spent $40 million to win the governorship; his opponent spent $30 million.[44] In 2007, Congressman Bobby Jindal raised more than $11 million for his campaign and defeated 11 other candidates, winning Louisiana's nonpartisan gubernatorial primary outright with 53 percent of the vote.[45] And big spending is not confined to gubernatorial contests. Even statewide judicial elections (in the states that have them) are becoming costly propositions. Spending in state legislative races was higher than ever in 2006, topping the half-million dollar mark in a few hotly contested races, setting new records around the nation. Winning an election takes money, either the candidate's or someone else's. If the latter, it may come with a string or two attached. And as noted earlier, that is the real concern: To what extent do campaign contributions buy access and influence for the contributor?

Recent research has confirmed several long-standing truths about the costs of campaigning.[46] For instance, close elections cost more than elections in which one candidate is sure to win, since uncertainty regarding the outcome is a spur to spending. A candidate quickly learns that it is easier to get money from potential contributors when the polls show that she has a chance of winning. Also, elections that produce change—that is, in which an incumbent is unseated or the out-party gains the office—typically cost more. Taking on an existing officeholder is a risky strategy that drives up election costs. And an open race in

Campaigning for the Louisiana governorship in 2007, Congressman Bobby Jindal addresses a crowd of supporters. *SOURCE:* ©AP/Wide World Photos.

which there is no incumbent represents an opportunity for the party out of office to capture the seat, thus triggering similar spending by the in-party in an effort to protect the seat. It is no wonder that campaign costs continue to rise.

In addition to PACs, another type of political organization has sprung up: **527 groups.** These groups are not connected to candidates but spend money to influence the outcome of elections. For instance, in West Virginia in 2004, a 527 group called "For the Sake of the Kids" spent $3.6 million in a massive advertising campaign to defeat an incumbent state Supreme Court justice. West Virginia's limits on campaign contributions did not apply because it was a 527 group that was spending the money on an issue (ostensibly, the future for the Mountain State's children), not a candidate. That same year in Washington, a 527 called the Voters Education Committee spent nearly $1.5 million to defeat a candidate for state attorney general. As it turned out, in both West Virginia and Washington, the 527 groups were funded by the U.S. Chamber of Commerce, which disagreed with the candidates' positions on issues related to the regulation of business.[47] The actions of 527's wreak havoc with a state's campaign finance laws.

State Efforts at Campaign Reform Concern over escalating costs and the influence of wealthy special interests in campaigns has led reform groups such as Common Cause to call for improved state laws to provide comprehensive and timely disclosure of campaign finances; impose limitations on contributions by individuals and groups; create a combined public–private financing mechanism for primaries and general elections; and establish an independent commission to enforce tough sanctions on violators of campaign finance laws.

States have performed impressively on the first of these recommendations; in fact, all states have some sort of campaign-financing reporting procedure. Thirty-six states make information on campaign contributions available online in a searchable database; 24 states provide similar access to campaign expenditure data.[48] In response to the fourth recommendation, twenty-six states have established independent commissions to oversee the conduct of campaigns, although they have found it somewhat difficult to enforce the law and punish violators.

The other recommendations have proved more troublesome. States have grappled with the issue of costly campaigns but have made only modest progress in controlling costs. A 1976 decision by the U.S. Supreme Court in *Buckley* v. *Valeo* made these efforts more difficult: The Court ruled that governments cannot limit a person's right to spend money in order to spread his views on particular issues and candidates. In essence, then, a candidate has unlimited power to spend his own money on his own behalf, and other individuals may spend to their hearts' content to promote their own opinions on election-related issues. In 1996, in a lawsuit from Colorado, the Court decided that independent spending by political parties, so-called **soft money,** could not be limited, either. The 2002 federal Bipartisan Campaign Reform Act aims at controlling the flow of soft money, but reports from the 2004 election cycle suggest that loopholes remain.[49] What the Court let stand, however, were state limits on an individual's

527 groups

Named after a section in the U.S. tax code, these groups spend money to influence the outcome of elections, but they do not contribute directly to candidates.

soft money

Unregulated funds contributed to national political parties and non-party political groups.

contributions to candidates and parties; it also ruled that if a candidate accepts public funds, he is then bound by whatever limitations the state may impose.

Some states have established specific limits on the amount of money that organizations and individuals can contribute to a political race. In New York, for example, corporations are limited to a contribution maximum of $5,000 per calendar year, and individuals (other than official candidates) are restricted to $150,000. Florida allows corporations, labor unions, and PACs to contribute a maximum of $500 per candidate. The same limits apply to individuals, excluding the candidate's own contributions. Some states, such as Arizona, Connecticut, North Dakota, Pennsylvania, and Rhode Island, have gone even further by prohibiting contributions from corporations and labor unions.[50] But a totally different philosophy pervades the politics of several states that continue to operate their election systems without any limitations on contributions. In Illinois, Missouri, and Virginia, to name just a few, organizations and individuals can contribute as much as they wish.

States have also considered the other side of the campaign-financing equation: expenditures. All states require candidates and political committees to file reports documenting the expenditure of campaign funds. A few states impose limits on a candidate's total expenditures, but a 2006 U.S. Supreme Court ruling that Vermont's spending limits were too low to allow candidates to compete effectively has complicated that approach. Many have followed Hawaii's lead and set voluntary spending limits. Colorado, for example, has adopted a nonbinding $2 million spending cap for gubernatorial candidates. Michigan takes a different approach: Candidates who accept public funds (governor and lieutenant governor) are restricted to $2 million per election, with additional spending allowable in certain circumstances. Florida and Kentucky have similar systems in place for candidates receiving public funds. In just over half of the states, however, candidates campaign without any spending limits.

Public Funding as a Solution Almost half the states have adopted some sort of public funding of campaigns. (Portland, Oregon, is the only city to embrace public financing for municipal elections.) Individuals voluntarily contribute to a central fund, which is divided among candidates or political parties. The system is fairly easy to administer and is relatively transparent for citizens. In most of the public-funding states, citizens can use their state income tax form to earmark a portion (a dollar or two) of their tax liability for the fund. A checkoff system of this sort does not directly increase taxpayers' tax burden. In a few states, the public fund is amassed through a voluntary surcharge or an additional tax (usually $1, although California allows surcharges of $5, $10, and $25). Indiana has opted for a different approach: Revenues from the sale of personalized motor vehicle license plates support the fund.

In addition to checkoffs and surcharges, some of the public-funding states, including Minnesota and Ohio, offer taxpayers a tax credit (usually 50 percent of the contribution, up to a specific maximum) when they contribute to political campaigns. A more popular supplement to public funding is a state-tax deduction for campaign contributions, an approach used in Hawaii, Oklahoma, and North Carolina. A final though not widely explored approach is direct state appropriation of funds. Maryland, for instance, does not use checkoffs or surcharges but relies instead on a direct state appropriation to candidates for governor and lieutenant governor[51]

Public campaign financing is supposed to rid the election process of some of its evils. Proponents argue that it will democratize the contribution process by freeing candidates from excessive reliance on special-interest money. Other possible advantages include expanding the pool of potential candidates, allowing candidates to compete on a more equal basis, and reducing the cost of campaigning. In Arizona in 2002, nearly 50 percent of the eligible candidates selected the public financing option. That same year, Governor Janet Napolitano became the first governor to be elected with full public financing of her campaign. She won re-election in 2006.

By contributing to the fund, average citizens may feel that they have a greater stake in state elections. Although more research needs to be done, studies suggest that public financing produces as least some of the benefits its supporters claim. For instance, an analysis of gubernatorial campaigns indicated that the use of public funds by incumbents and challengers holds down overall spending. It also narrows the expenditure gap between them. Public financing continues to be an important weapon in the state struggle to reform and control the influence of money in campaigns.[52]

CHAPTER RECAP

- Even though voter loyalties have weakened, political parties have proved remarkably resilient and have taken on new roles in politics and governance.
- The Democratic Party can claim just over 30 percent of the voting-age public for itself; the Republican Party around 25 percent. The rest of the electorate considers itself independents, with a small fraction affiliated with third parties.
- Interparty competition has increased over time. One result has been a rise in divided government.
- Interest groups exert a powerful force in state government, with business lobbyists and teachers' groups the most influential in the majority of states.
- The state interest group system is changing: A more diverse set of interests lobbies at the statehouse; meanwhile, state governments have tightened their regulation of lobbyists.
- Groups are involved in local elections and in community issues, but their major focus is on the actions of government: policy implementation and service delivery.
- Campaigns for state office still involve door-to-door canvassing, neighborhood drop-ins, and public forums, but they increasingly use direct mail, electronic media, and political consultants.
- Running for public office can be an expensive proposition. To try to level the playing field and diminish the role of private money, most states limit contributions and many provide public financing.

Key Terms

political parties *(p. 89)*	interest groups *(p. 96)*
ideology *(p. 90)*	direct action *(p. 100)*
ticket splitting *(p. 91)*	lobbying *(p. 101)*
pragmatism *(p. 94)*	grassroots lobbying *(p. 103)*
divided government *(p. 95)*	political action committee (PAC) *(p. 103)*
unified government *(p. 95)*	527 groups *(p. 109)*
dealignment *(p. 96)*	soft money *(p. 109)*

Internet Resources

The major political parties have official websites: **www.democrats.org** and **www.rnc.org.**

At the state level, illustrative websites are Hawaii's at **www.hawaiidemocrats.org** and Ohio's at **www.ohiogop.org.**

An interesting state-level, third-party website, **www.cagreens.org,** is the site for the Green Party of California.

On its website, **www.commoncause.org,** the reform group Common Cause tracks the activities of its thirty-six state offices.

Another group devoted to cleaning up elections is Public Campaign. Their web site is **www.publicampaign.org.** Another group with a reform focus is the Center for Public Integrity at **www.publicintegrity.org.**

To learn more about 527 groups, see **www.opensecrets.org/527s/.**

Different perspectives are reflected in the websites of the American Civil Liberties Union, **www.aclu.org,** and the Christian Coalition, **www.cc.org.**

www.flchamber.com and **www.ilchamber.org** are the websites for the chambers of commerce for Florida and Illinois, respectively. Other state chambers use similar URLs.

The Texas State Teachers' Association at **www.tsta.org** is an example of a state schoolteachers organization. A different but related perspective is provided by the Oregon Congress of Parents and Teachers Associations at **www.oregonpta.org.**

Other examples of state-level interest groups include The West Virginia Association of Realtors at **www.wvrealtors.com** and the Arizona Hospital and Health-care Association at **www.azhha.org.**

State Legislatures

FOCUS QUESTIONS

1. What are the three principal functions of legislatures?

2. How would you characterize the lawmaking process?

3. In making policy for the state, what powers can legislatures exercise in their competition with governors?

4. The initiative and terms limits confer what benefits and risks on legislatures?

Georgia Democrats used to joke that it would be a cold day in hell before a Republican would be sworn in as speaker of the House of Representatives in the Peach State. As the new speaker put it in 2005, "It was actually a cold day in early January."[1] That year, for the first time in 134 years, both houses of the General Assembly and the governor's office were under GOP control. As soon as the speaker's gavel signaled the opening of the legislative session, the newly-in-charge Republicans got to work making some changes they had sought during their years as a vastly outnumbered minority party. Democrats, new to the role as opposition party, did their best to stop them. Partisan fireworks ensued, but then again, that's what legislatures are all about.

THE ESSENCE OF LEGISLATURES

The New Year dawns quietly in Boise, Idaho; Jefferson City, Missouri; and Harrisburg, Pennsylvania. But it does not remain quiet for long: State legislators are ready to converge on their state capitols. Every January (or February or March in a few states; every other January in some others), state legislatures reconvene in session to do the public's business. More than 7,000 legislators hammer out solutions to intricate and often intransigent public problems. They do so in an institution that is steeped in tradition and governed by layers of formal rules and informal norms.

Legislatures engage in three principal functions: *policymaking, representation,* and *oversight*. The first, policymaking, includes enacting laws and allocating funds. The start of the twenty-first century found legislators debating such issues as election reform, biotechnology, and urban sprawl. These deliberations resulted in the revision of old laws, the passage of new laws, and changes in spending, which is what policymaking is all about. Legislatures do not have sole control of the state policymaking function; governors, courts, and agencies also determine policy, through executive orders, judicial decisions, and administrative regulations, respectively. But, legislatures are the dominant policymaking institutions in state government. Table 6.1 lists issues that attracted legislative attention in 2008. High on the agenda in most states were two awesome tasks: stabilizing state budgets and dealing with issues related to immigration.

In their second function, legislators are expected to represent their constituents—the people who live in their district—in two ways. At least in theory,

TABLE 6.1   Popular Legislative Issues in 2008

ISSUE	WHAT IT'S ALL ABOUT
State budgets	A weakening housing market slowed state revenue growth, causing legislatures to consider spending limits.
Immigration reform	As in 2007, issues of education and health care for immigrants took center stage.
Federal Real ID Act	Several states resisted the costly federal mandate that imposed new standards for state-issued driver's licenses.
Infrastructure finance	How to pay for maintenance and construction of roads and bridges was a hot topic in many states.
Health insurance	Legislatures throughout the country grappled with the problem of making health insurance more affordable.
Education improvement	Two issues predominated: reducing the drop out rate and recruiting high-quality teachers and principals.
Homeowner assistance	As the mortgage crisis continued, more states debated proposals to assist low- and moderate-income families.
Environmental protection	Water conservation and climate change were the topics getting the most legislative attention.
Consumer protection	Spurred by high-profile events, legislatures tackled the issues of food and product safety.
Pension plans	Retirees' pensions and health care coverage received attention from legislatures concerned with costs.

SOURCE: National Conference of State Legislatures, "State Legislatures Face Unsettled Conditions in 2008," www.ncsl.org/programs/press/2007/pr121407.htm (December 22, 2007).

they are expected to speak for their constituents in the legislative chamber—to do the will of the public in designing policy solutions. This is not easy. On quiet issues, a legislator seldom has much of a clue about public opinion. Moreover, on noisy issues, constituents' will is rarely unanimous. Individuals and organized groups with different perspectives may write to or visit their legislator to urge her to vote a certain way on a pending bill. In another representative function, legislators act as their constituents' facilitators in state government. For example, they may help a citizen deal with an unresponsive state agency. This kind of constituency service, or **casework,** as it is often called, may pay dividends at re-election time because voters tend to look favorably on a legislator who has helped them.[2]

casework
Legislative assistance on behalf of a constituent, usually with the bureaucracy.

The oversight function is different from the policymaking and representation functions. Concerned that the laws they passed and the funds they allocated frequently did not produce the intended effect, lawmakers began to pay more attention to the performance of the state bureaucracy. Legislatures have adopted a number of methods for checking up on agency implementation and spending. Their oversight role takes legislatures into the administrative realm. Not surprisingly, agencies rarely welcome this role, although legislatures see it as a logical extension of their policymaking function.

LEGISLATIVE DYNAMICS

State legislative bodies are typically referred to as the legislature, but their formal titles vary. In Colorado, the General Assembly meets every year; in Massachusetts, the General Court; and in Oregon, the Legislative Assembly. The legislatures of forty-four states meet annually; in six (Arkansas, Montana, Nevada, North Dakota, Oregon, and Texas), they meet every two years. (Kentucky had been among the biennial session group until 2000, when voters approved a switch to annual legislative sessions.) The length of the legislative session varies widely. For example, the Utah General Assembly convened in Salt Lake City on January 21, 2008, and adjourned on March 5, 2008, for a total of 45 calendar days in session. In contrast, in states like Michigan and New Jersey, legislative sessions run nearly year-round.

The length of a state's legislative session can be a sensitive issue. In 1997, the Nevada legislature met for 169 days—the longest, most expensive session in its history.[3] Nevadans showed their displeasure the following year when they passed a measure limiting future legislative sessions to 120 days. Voters in the Silver State apparently believe that it should not take more than four months—every two years—to conduct their state's business.

The Senate and the House

State legislatures have two houses or chambers, similar to those of the U.S. Congress. Forty-nine states are bicameral. (As noted in Chapter 3, the exception is Nebraska, which in 1934 established a unicameral legislature.) Bicameralism is a legacy of the postcolonial era, when an upper house represented the interests of the propertied class, and a lower house represented everyone else. Even after this distinction was eliminated, states stuck with the bicameral structure, ostensibly because of its contribution to the concept of checks and balances. It is much tougher to pass bills when they have to survive the scrutiny of two legislative houses. Having a bicameral structure, then, reinforces the status quo. Unicameralism might improve the efficiency of the legislature, but efficiency has never been a primary goal of the consensus-building deliberative process.

In the forty-nine bicameral states, the upper house is called the senate; the lower house is usually called the house of representatives. The average size of a state senate is 40 members; houses typically average about 100 members. As with many aspects of state legislatures, chamber size varies substantially—from the Alaska Senate with 20 members to the New Hampshire house with 400 representatives. Chamber size seldom changes, but in 2003, a voter mandate forced Rhode Island to reduce the size of its 150-member legislature by one-fourth.

For senators, the term of office is usually four years; approximately one-quarter of the states use a two-year senate term. In many states, the election of senators is staggered. House members serve two-year terms, except in Alabama, Louisiana, Maryland, Mississippi, and North Dakota, where four-year terms prevail. The 2008 state legislative sessions found Republicans in control of both chambers in 14 states, the Democratic Party controlling both houses in 23 states, and 12 states in which legislative power was split: Each party controlled one chamber, or the chamber was evenly divided between the two parties.

There are 7,382 state legislators in this country: 1,971 senators and 5,411 representatives. There are more Democrats than Republicans, 54 percent and 45 percent, respectively; men outnumber women 77.4 to 22.6 percent. Legislatures are becoming more racially and ethnically diverse. African Americans oc-

Interested onlookers pack a committee hearing room when the Kansas legislature wrestles with the issue of health care reform. SOURCE: AP/Wide World Photos

cupy 8.1 percent of all legislative seats, Latinos 2.9 percent, Asian Americans 1 percent, and Native Americans 0.5 percent. Yet even these small proportions of women and racial-ethnic minorities represent a substantial increase, relative to their near absence from most legislatures before the 1970s. In terms of occupations, attorneys remain the single largest occupational category (15 percent), which is considerably lower than it was in years past, and the number of business owners is on the rise.[4]

Legislative Districts

Legislators are elected from geographically based districts, with each district in a state containing approximately the same number of inhabitants. Most legislative districts are single-member districts, that is, one legislator represents the district. In Nebraska, for instance, each member of the unicameral legislature represents 32,210 people, more or less. Dividing or apportioning a state into districts is an intensely political process that affects the balance of power in a state. In the 1960s, for example, the less populated panhandle area of Florida was over-represented in the legislature at the expense of the heavily populated southern areas of the state. The balance of power lay with the northern rural regions. Therefore, despite Florida's rapid urbanization during that period, public policy continued to reflect the interests of a rurally based minority.

multimember district

A legislative district that contains more than one seat.

Eight states, including Minnesota and the Dakotas, continue to use **multimember districts** containing more than one lower house seat. In multimember districts, candidates compete for specific seats, and voters in the district vote in as many races as there are seats in the district. Once elected, the legislators represent the entire area. Is there any difference between legislators elected in multimember districts and those in single-member districts? The answer is a cautious "yes" if research on the Arizona legislature can be extended to other states. Researchers found that multimember district lawmakers in the house of representatives tended to be more ideologically extreme than their single-member district counterparts.[5]

malapportionment

Skewed allocation of legislative districts that violate the "one person, one vote" ideal.

Malapportionment **Malapportionment,** or unequal representation, has characterized many legislative bodies. In the past, for example, some states allocated an equal number of senators to each county. (This system calls to mind the U.S. Senate, which has two senators per state.) Because counties vary in population size, some senators were representing ten or twenty times as many constituents as their colleagues were. New Jersey offered one of the most extreme cases. In 1962, one county contained 49,000 residents and another had 924,000; yet each county was allotted one senator, and each senator had one vote in the senate. This kind of imbalance meant that a small group of people had the same institutional power as a group that was nineteen times larger. Such disproportionate power is inherently at odds with representative democracy, in which each person's vote carries the same weight.

Until the 1960s, the federal courts ignored the issue of legislative malapportionment. It was not until 1962, in a Tennessee case in which the malapportionment was especially egregious (house district populations ranged from 2,340 to 42,298), that the courts stepped in. In that case, *Baker* v. *Carr*, the U.S. Supreme Court ruled that the Fourteenth Amendment guarantee of equal protection applies to state legislative apportionment. With this decision as a wedge, the Court ruled that state legislatures should be apportioned on the basis of population. Two years later, in *Reynolds* v. *Sims* (1964), which extended the principle of equal representation to state senates, Chief Justice Earl Warren summed up the apportionment ideal by saying, "Legislators represent people, not trees or acres."[6] Accordingly, districts should reflect population equality: one person, one vote. In the aftermath of this decision, which overturned the apportionment practices of six states, a **reapportionment** fever swept the country, and district lines were redrawn in every state.

reapportionment

The reallocation of seats in a legislative assembly.

Reapportionment provided an immediate benefit to previously underrepresented urban areas, and increased urban representation led to a growing responsiveness in state legislatures to the problems and interests of cities and suburbs. Where reapportionment had a partisan effect, it generally benefited Republicans in the South and Democrats in the North. Other impacts of reapportionment have included the election of younger, better-educated legislators and, especially in southern states, better representation of African Americans. All in all, reapportionment is widely credited with improving the representativeness of American state legislatures.

Redrawing District Lines State legislatures are reapportioned following the U.S. census, which is taken every ten years. Reapportionment allows population fluctuations—growth in some areas, decline in others—to be reflected in redrawn district lines. Twenty-six legislatures **redistrict** themselves; by contrast, twelve states attempt to depoliticize the process by using impartial commissions to develop their redistricting plans.[7] In the remaining states, the redistricting task involves the legislature and either a commission or another political institution such as the governor (Maryland) or the state Supreme Court (Florida).

redistrict

The redrawing of legislative district lines to conform to the one person, one vote ideal.

In states where the legislature redistricts itself (and the state's congressional districts), the party controlling the legislature controls the redistricting process. District lines have traditionally been redrawn to maximize the strength of the party in power. The art of drawing district lines creatively was popularized in Massachusetts in 1812, when a political cartoonist for the *Boston Gazette* dubbed one of Governor Elbridge Gerry's district creations a **gerrymander** because the district, carefully configured to reflect partisan objectives, was shaped like a salamander. Gerrymandering has not disappeared. Political parties poured record sums of money into the 2000 state legislative elections, in large part because of looming reapportionment.

gerrymander

The process of creatively designing a legislative district to enhance the electoral fortunes of the party in power.

Redistricting has become a sophisticated operation in which statisticians and geographers use computer mapping to assist the legislature in designing an optimal districting scheme. Although "one person, one vote" is the official standard, some unofficial guidelines are also taken into consideration. Ideally, districts should be geographically compact and unbroken. Those who draw the lines pay close attention to traditional political boundaries such as counties and, as noted, to the fortunes of political parties and incumbents. As long as districts adhere fairly closely to the population-equality standard (if a multimember district contains three seats, it must have three times the population of a single-member district), federal courts tolerate the achievement of unofficial objectives. But redistricting can produce some oddly shaped districts resembling lobsters, spiders, and earmuffs. Dividing Montgomery County, Maryland, into legislative districts after the 2000 census produced the shapes displayed in Figure 6.1.

Legislatures have to pay attention to the effects of their redistricting schemes on the voting strength of racial minorities. In fact, amendments to the Voting Rights Act and subsequent court rulings instructed affected states to create some districts in which racial minorities would have majority status. The intentional creation of majority-minority districts more favorable to the election of African Americans had a partisan consequence. African Americans are more likely to be Democrats than Republicans; therefore clustering black voters into specific districts diluted the potential Democratic vote of adjacent districts. This increased the likelihood that Republican candidates would win in those nearby districts. For instance, Florida drew thirteen heavily African American state house districts, leaving the other 107 districts with fewer black voters. Some

| FIGURE 6.1 | **State Legislative Districts in Montgomery County, Maryland** |

Although the districts have similar population sizes, their shapes and territorial sizes vary.

SOURCE: http://www
.montgomerycountymd.gov//
Content/gis/images/gallery/
legis02.gif

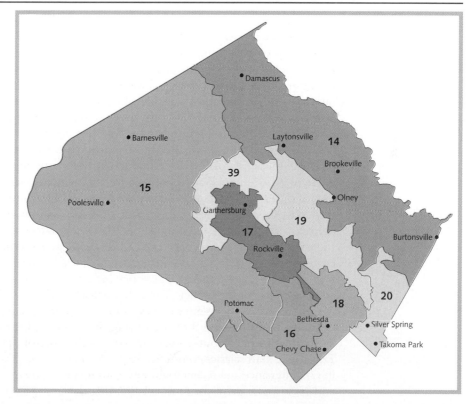

observers contended that this situation made it easier for Republicans to win sixty-five of those seats and thus control the house.[8]

The courts have not spoken with crystal clarity on the question of reapportionment. Yes, the racial composition of districts should be taken into account, but no, racial considerations should not be the sole criterion. In *Vieth* v. *Jubelirer* (2004), the U.S. Supreme Court ruled that reliance on partisan considerations remains an appropriate redistricting option. In *LULAC* v. *Davis* (2006), a newly-drawn congressional district in Texas was found to violate the Voting Rights Act, but the rest of the state's plan, which benefited Republicans, was acceptable to the Court. As one expert, political scientist Ronald Weber, put it, the strategy for line-drawers is "to determine the best way to waste the vote of the partisans of the other party."[9] Thus the practice of redrawing district lines in response to population shifts is an intensely political process, as was demonstrated dramatically in 2003 when Texas Democratic senators left the state thus preventing a **quorum** from being present in the chamber to take up a Republican-sponsored redistricting bill. The redistricting plan was passed eventually, but not before a law enforcement unit, the Texas Rangers, had been dispatched by the Republican governor to track down the absent senators.

quorum

the minimum number of legislators who must be present to transact business.

Legislative Compensation

Legislative compensation has increased handsomely in the past two decades, again with some notable exceptions. Before the modernization of legislatures, salary and per diem (money for daily expenses) levels were set in the state constitution and, thus were impossible to adjust without a constitutional amendment. The lifting of these limits put legislatures, as the policymaking branch of state government, in the curious position of setting their own compensation levels. Recognizing that this power is a double-edged sword (legislators can vote themselves pay raises while the public can turn around and vote them out of office for doing so), almost half of the states have established compensation commissions or advisory groups to make recommendations on legislative remuneration. Arizona carries it one step further by requiring that a commission-recommended pay raise for legislators be submitted to the voters for approval—or rejection.

As of 2007, annual salaries of legislators (excluding per diem) ranged from a low of $200 in New Hampshire to a high of $116,208 in California.[10] Seventeen states paid their legislators more than $30,000 annually. Compare these figures with the more modest pay levels of legislators in Georgia ($16,524), Idaho ($15,646), and Nebraska ($12,000). As a general rule, states paying generous compensation typically demand more of a legislator's time than do low-paying states. New Mexico legislators certainly cannot be accused of seeking elective office for the money. There, legislators receive no salary. What is their financial reward for legislative service? One hundred forty-one dollars per day for living expenses while in Santa Fe during the session, plus a travel allowance.

Legislative pay is but a small fraction of the cost of operating a legislature. Legislative staff salaries consume a large chunk of the expenditures, as do building maintenance and technological improvements. Large states such as California and New York spend the most on their legislatures. However, when legislative costs are calculated on a per capita basis, Alaska is at the top, followed by Hawaii and Rhode Island.[11]

Legislative Leadership

Legislatures need leaders, both formal and informal. Each chamber usually has four formal leadership positions. In the senate, a president and a president pro tempore (who presides in the absence of the president) are in charge of the chamber; in the house, the comparable leaders are the speaker and the speaker pro tempore. These legislative officials are chosen by the members, with voting following party lines. (In some states, the post of senate president is occupied by the lieutenant governor.) Both houses have two political party leadership positions: a majority leader and a minority leader.

The leaders are responsible for making the legislature, which is a relatively de-centralized system, run smoothly and for seeing that it accomplishes its tasks. In a typical chamber, the presiding officer appoints committee members, names committee chairs, controls the activity on the floor, allocates office space and committee budgets, and, in some states, selects the majority leader and the holders of other majority-party posts.[12] The actual influence of the leadership varies from one chamber to another. One factor that affects leaders' power is whether the positions are rotated or retained. Leaders who have the option of retaining their position can build power bases. In the case of rotation, however, one set of leaders is replaced with another on a regular basis, so the leaders are **lame ducks** when they assume the posts. On average, today's leaders are different from the caricatured wheeler-dealers of the past. Successful leaders are those who adapt as the membership changes and the institution evolves.[13]

A good illustration of adaptation was found in the Washington House of Representatives a few years ago. The chamber was evenly split between the two parties, so to avoid deadlock, a power-sharing arrangement was created. Lawmakers decided to use co-speakers and co-committee chairs. The speakership rotated daily between the Republican leader and the Democratic leader; the committee chairs did likewise.

As political parties become more competitive in the states, legislative behavior and decisions take on a more partisan cast. There are Democratic and Republican sides of the chamber, and Democratic and Republican positions on bills. Each party meets in a caucus to design its legislative strategy and generate camaraderie. In states where one political party continues to dominate, partisanship is less important; however, in one-party settings, the dominant party typically develops splits or factions at the expense of party unity. But when the vastly outnumbered minority party begins to gain strength, the majority party usually becomes more cohesive.

In many states, legislative leaders have embraced a new function: fundraising. Leaders tap interest groups and lobbyists for money and divide it among their party's candidates for legislative seats. California has led the way with multimillion-dollar **war chests.** The amount of money raised is not as great in other states, of course, but it has become a significant source of campaign funding. Lobbyists find it difficult to say "no" to a request for funds from the

lame duck

an elected official who cannot serve beyond the current term of office.

war chest

a stash of funds accumulated in advance of a campaign.

leadership. The leaders then allocate the funds to the neediest candidates—those in close races. If those candidates are victorious, their loyalty to party leaders pays legislative dividends.

The Committee System

The workhorse of the legislature is the committee. Under normal circumstances, a committee's primary function is to consider bills—that is, to hear testimony, perhaps amend the bills, and ultimately approve or reject them. Committee action on a bill precedes debate in the house or senate.

All legislative chambers are divided into committees, and most committees have created subcommittees. Committees can be of several types. A *standing committee* regularly considers legislation during the session. A *joint committee* is made up of members of both houses. Some joint committees are standing; others are temporary (sometimes called ad hoc or select committees) and are convened for a specific purpose, such as investigating a troubled agency or solving a particularly challenging public-policy problem. A *conference committee* is a special type of joint committee that is assembled to iron out differences between house- and senate-passed versions of a bill. To get a head start on an upcoming session, most states use *interim committees* during the period when the legislature is not in session. The number of committees varies, but most senates and houses have standing committees on the issues listed in Table 6.2. Most of these committees, in turn, have professional staffs assigned to them.

TABLE 6.2	Standing Committees of the Legislature

Both houses of state legislatures typically have standing committees dealing with these substantive issues:	
Agriculture	Government operations
Banking/financial institutions	Health
Business and commerce	Insurance
Communications	Judiciary and criminal justice
Education	Local affairs
Elections	Public employees
Energy	Rules
Environment and natural resources	Social/human services
Ethics	Transportation

In addition, both houses have standing committees that address the raising and allocating of state funds. These committees may have different names in different chambers:
Appropriations
Finance and Taxation
Ways and Means

A substantive standing committee tends to be made up of legislators who have expertise and interest in that committee's subject matter.[14] Thus farmers would be assigned to the agriculture committee, teachers to the education committee, small business owners to the commerce committee, lawyers to the judiciary committee, and so on. These legislators bring knowledge and commitment to their committees; they also bring a certain bias because they tend to function as advocates for their career interests. Note, too, that every chamber has at least one undesirable committee (usually defined as one whose substance is boring) to which few legislators want to be assigned.[15]

The central concern of a standing committee is its floor success—getting the full chamber to accede to its recommendations on a bill. Several plausible explanations exist for a committee's floor success.[16] A committee whose ideological composition is similar to that of the whole chamber is likely to be more successful than one whose members are at odds with the chamber. The leadership takes this situation into account when it makes committee assignments; thus, very few committees are ideological outliers.[17] Also, committees full of legislatively experienced members generally have more floor success than committees composed of legislative novices. And committees that have a reputation for being tough have more floor success with their bills than committees that pass everything that comes before them.

LEGISLATIVE BEHAVIOR

Legislatures have their own dynamics, their own way of doing things. Senate and house rule books spell out what can and cannot be done, in the same way that an organization's bylaws do. Legislatures are self-regulating institutions, for the most part; it is especially important, therefore, that participants know what is expected of them. To make certain that the chamber's rules are understood, most legislatures conduct orientation sessions for new members.

Legislative Norms

An understanding of the legislature involves not only knowledge of formal structures and written rules but also awareness of informal norms and unwritten policies. For example, nowhere in a state's legislative rules does it say that a freshman legislator is prohibited from playing a leadership role, but the unwritten rules of most legislatures place a premium on seniority. A primary rule of legislative bodies is that "you gotta go along to get along," a phrase that emphasizes teamwork and paying your dues. Legislators who are on opposite sides of a bill to regulate horse racing might find themselves on the same side of a bill to lower the cost of prescription drugs. Yesterday's opponent is today's partner. For this reason, no one can afford to make bitter enemies in the legislature and expect to flourish.

Those who aspire to rise from rank-and-file legislator to committee chairperson and perhaps to party leader or presiding officer find consensus-building skills quite useful. These skills come in handy because many norms are intended to reduce the potential for conflict in what is inherently a setting full of conflict. For instance, a freshman legislator is expected to defer to a senior colleague. Although an energetic new legislator might chafe under such a restriction, one day he will have gained seniority and will take comfort in the rule. Moreover, legislators are expected to honor commitments made to each other, thus encouraging reciprocity: "If you support me on my favorite bill, I will be with you on yours." A legislator cannot be too unyielding. Compromises, which are sometimes principled but more often political, are the backbone of the legislative process. Few bills are passed by both houses and sent to the governor in exactly the same form as when they were introduced.

Informal rules are designed to make the legislative process flow more smoothly. Legislators who cannot abide by the rules, those who refuse to go along, find it difficult to get along. They are subjected to not-so-subtle efforts at behavior modification, such as powerful social sanctions (ostracism and ridicule) and legislative punishment (the bottling up of their bill in committee or their assignment to an unpopular committee), that promote adherence to norms.

Legislative Cue-Taking

Much has been written about how legislators make public-policy decisions, and a number of explanations are plausible. Legislators may adopt the policy positions espoused by their political party. They may follow the dictates of their conscience—that is, do what they think is right. They may yield to the pressures of organized interest groups. They may be persuaded by the arguments of other legislators, such as a committee chairperson who is knowledgeable about the policy area, or a trusted colleague who is considered to be savvy; or they may succumb to the entreaties of the governor, who has made a particular piece of legislation the focus of her administration. Of course, legislators may also attempt to respond to the wishes of their constituents. On a significant issue—one that has received substantial media attention—they are likely to be subjected to tremendous cross-pressures.

Assuming that legislators are concerned about how a vote will be received back home, it seems logical that they would be particularly solicitous of public opinion. State legislators frequently hold opinions at odds with those of their constituents. They occasionally misperceive what the public is thinking; at such times it is difficult for them to act as mere **delegates** and simply fulfill the public's will. To improve the communications link, some legislators use questionnaires to poll constituents about their views; others hold town meetings at various places in the district to assess the public's mood.

It is quite probable that first-term legislators feel more vulnerable to the whims of the public than legislative veterans do. Hence the new legislator devotes more time to determining what the people want, whereas the experienced legislator "knows" what they want (or perhaps knows what they need) and thus functions as a **trustee**—someone who follows his or her own best judgment. Since the vast majority of legislators are returned to office elec-

delegate
A legislator who functions as a conduit for constituency opinion.

trustee
A legislator who votes according to his or her conscience and best judgment.

tion after election, it appears that there is some validity to this argument. A study of Oklahoma and Kansas legislators, for example, found that the members' personal values played a consistently important role in their decision choices.[18]

In the final analysis, the determining factor in how legislators make decisions depends on the issue itself. On the one hand, "when legislators are deeply involved with an issue, they appear to be more concerned with policy consequences" than with constituency preferences.[19] In this situation, the legislators are focused on a goal other than re-election. On the other hand, if legislators are not particularly engaged in an issue and it is important to their constituents, they will follow their constituents' preference. In that sense, they act as **politicos,** adjusting as the issues and cues change.

politico

A legislator who functions as either a delegate or a trustee, depending on the circumstances.

HOW A BILL BECOMES LAW (OR NOT)

A legislative bill starts as an idea and travels a long, complex path before it emerges as law. It is no wonder that of the 6,217 bills introduced in the Illinois legislature in 2005, only 683 had become law by the end of the session.[20] A legislative session has a rhythm to it. Minor bills and symbolic issues tend to be resolved early, whereas major, potentially divisive issues take a much longer time to wend their way through the legislative labyrinth. The budget or appropriations bill typically generates several rounds of contentious debate among legislators.

The lawmaking process has been described in many ways: a zoo, a circus, a marketplace. Perhaps the most apt description is "casino," because there are winners and losers, the outcome is never final, and there is always a new game ahead.[21] Figure 6.2 illustrates a typical lawmaking process, showing at just how many points a bill can be sidetracked.

The diagram of the legislative process shown in this figure cannot convey the dynamism and excitement of lawmaking. (Again, the casino analogy is appropriate.) Ideas for bills are everywhere: with constituents, interest groups, and state agencies. Legislators may turn to their staffs for ideas or to other states. **Policy entrepreneurs,** people who are knowledgeable about certain issues and are willing to promote them, abound. Introducing a bill—"putting it in the hopper," in legislative parlance—is just the beginning.

policy entrepreneur

A person who brings new ideas to a policymaking body.

A bill does not make it through the legislative process without a lot of effort and even a little luck. A bill's chances of passage rise as more legislators sign on as cosponsors, and if the cosponsors are legislative leaders, even better. Assignment of the bill to a favorable committee improves the likelihood that the bill will be scheduled for a hearing in a timely manner. (Many bills get bottled up in committee and never receive a hearing.) Strong support from key interest groups is a powerful advantage, as is the emergence of only weak opposition to the bill. Sometimes, bill passage is a matter of fortuitous timing. For example, a spectacular prison break from an overcrowded state penitentiary might garner support for passage of a prison construction bill.

| FIGURE 6.2 | How a Bill Becomes Law |

At each of the stages in the process, supporters and opponents of a bill clash. Most bills stall at some point and fail to make it to the end.

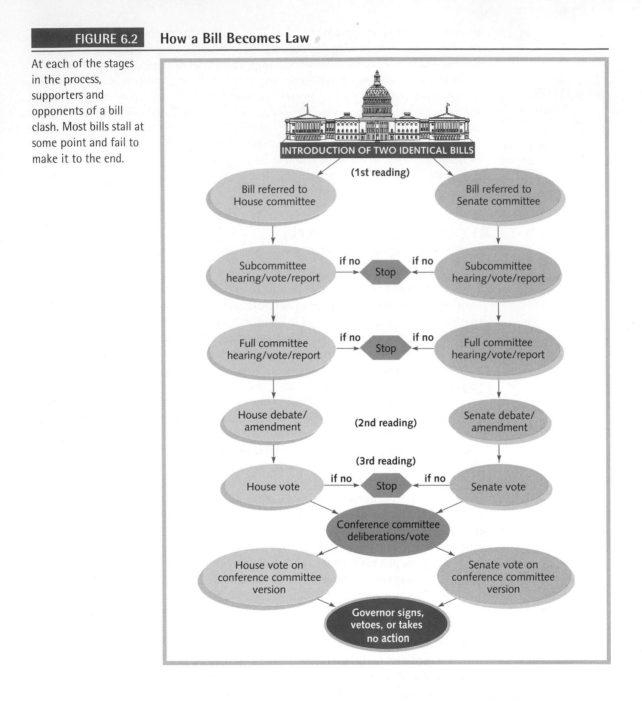

Controversial issues such as abortion raise the stakes. The former speaker of the Wisconsin Assembly, Tom Loftus, described abortion politics in his state as trench warfare in which compromise was virtually impossible. Leadership on the issue came from legislators who felt strongly about the matter and who held safe seats. (In this instance, "safe" meant that taking a position was not likely to cost them too many votes or generate too many serious challengers when they ran for re-election.) As anti-abortion bills were introduced, battle lines were drawn. According to the speaker:

> The pro-choice side, which included the Democratic leadership, tried to keep the bill bottled up in committee, and the pro-life side, through political pressure on the Republicans and conservative Democrats, tried to pull it out so the whole Assembly could vote on it on the floor of the chamber. If the pro-life people could get the bill to the floor for a vote, they would win. To accomplish this end, they needed to gain supporters from the pivotal middle group of legislators, usually moderates of both parties from marginal districts.[22]

The powerful anti-abortion group, Wisconsin Citizens Concerned for Life, pressured vulnerable legislators. These legislators were in a tough position because they knew that "regardless of how you voted, you were going to make a slew of single-issue voters mad."[23] Their strategy became one of parliamentary maneuvering and delay.

Even if a bill is successful in one chamber, potential hurdles await in the other chamber. Representatives and senators may see the same issue in very different terms. In Ohio in 1997, everyone agreed that the state's system for funding public education needed reform. (The Ohio Supreme Court had found the state's school-funding system unconstitutional and had given the legislature one year to devise a new system.) But initial efforts derailed when the house and senate could not agree on a plan. The senate approved a funding package that would have increased the sales tax, provided debt financing, and allowed local school boards to propose property tax increases.[24] The house, dominated by Republicans who had signed an anti-tax pledge the preceding year, approved a bill that did not include tax hikes. Each chamber rejected the other's plan. Hammering out a compromise agreeable to both chambers took a long time, even with the court's order as a spur to action.

Once conference or concurrence committees resolve differences and agreement is secured in both chambers, then the bill is enrolled (certified and signed) and sent to the governor. The governor may do one of three things: (1) sign the act (once passed, a bill is called an act) into law, (2) veto it (in which case the legislature has a chance to have the last word by overriding the veto), or (3) take no action. If the governor does not take action and the session has ended, then in most states the act will become law without the governor's signature. Why not simply sign it if it is going to become law anyway? Sometimes, it is a matter of political symbolism for the governor. In approximately one-third of the states, if the governor does not sign or veto the act and the legislature has adjourned, the act dies, an outcome known as a pocket veto.

During its 2005 session, the Illinois legislature passed only 11 percent of the bills that were introduced. Is this a sign of success or failure? Illinois's figures are lower than those of most states—20 to 25 percent is a common passage rate—but not necessarily a cause for alarm. Not all bills are good ones, and the inability to generate sufficient consensus among legislators may reflect that condition.

LEGISLATIVE REFORM AND CAPACITY

It was not easy to get state legislatures where they are today. During the 1970s, fundamental reforms occurred throughout the country as legislatures sought to increase their capacity and to become more professional. The modernization process never really ends, however.

The Ideal Legislature

In the late 1960s, the Citizens' Conference on State Legislatures (CCSL) studied legislative performance and identified five characteristics critical to legislative improvement.[25] Ideally, a legislature should be functional, accountable, informed, independent, and representative; the acronym is FAIIR.

The *functional* legislature has almost unrestricted time to conduct its business. It is assisted by adequate staff and facilities, and has effective rules and procedures that facilitate the flow of legislation. The *accountable* legislature's operations are open and comprehensible to the public. The *informed* legislature manages its workload through an effective committee structure, legislative activities between sessions, and a professional staff; it also conducts regular budgetary review of executive branch activities. The *independent* legislature runs its own affairs separate from the executive branch. It exercises oversight of agencies, regulates lobbyists, manages conflicts of interest, and provides adequate compensation for its members. Finally, the *representative* legislature has a diverse membership that effectively represents the social, economic, ethnic, and other characteristics of the constituencies.

The fifty state legislatures were evaluated and scored by CCSL according to the FAIIR criteria. For the first time ever, the rankings offered a relatively scientific means of comparing one state legislature with another. Overall, the "best" state legislatures were found in California, New York, Illinois, Florida, and Wisconsin. The "worst," in the assessment of CCSL, were those in Alabama, Wyoming, Delaware, North Carolina, and Arkansas.

The CCSL report triggered extensive self-evaluation by legislatures around the country. Most states launched ambitious efforts to reform their legislatures. The results are readily apparent. In terms of the CCSL criteria, states have made tremendous strides in legislative institution building. The evidence of increased professionalism includes more staff support, higher legislative compensation, longer sessions, and better facilities. Many legislatures revamped their committee systems, altered their rules and procedures, and tightened their ethics regulations. The consequences of these actions are state legislatures that are far more FAIIR now than they were thirty years ago.

The Effects of Reform

Today's legislative institutions are different, but are they better? Although many observers would answer in the affirmative, the legislative reform picture is not unequivocally rosy. Political scientist Alan Rosenthal, who has closely observed legislative reform, warns that "the legislature's recent success in enhancing its capacity and improving its performance may place it in greater jeopardy than before."[26] This prospect certainly was not an intended effect of the reform efforts. Rosenthal's argument is that a constellation of demands pulls legislators away from the legislative core. That is, the new breed of legislator gets caught up in the demands of re-election, constituent service, interest groups, and political careerism, and thus neglects institutional matters such as structure, procedure, staff, image, and community. The legislature as an institution suffers because it is not receiving the necessary care and attention from its members. For example, Minnesota's highly reformed legislature performed poorly in the mid-1990s, mired in a period of bitter partisanship and personal scandal. Some observers blame reform.[27]

Consider the idea of a citizen-legislator, someone for whom service in the legislature is a part-time endeavor. Since the onset of reform, the proportion of legislators who are lawyers, business owners, or insurance or real estate executives has dropped, and the number of full-time legislators has risen. In states such as Michigan, Pennsylvania, and Wisconsin, roughly two-thirds of the lawmakers identify themselves as legislators with no other occupation. The critical issue is whether the decline of the citizen-legislator is a desirable aspect of modernization. Should a state legislature represent a broad spectrum of vocations, or should it be composed of career politicians? One perspective is this: "If I'm sick, I want professional help. I feel the same way about public affairs. I want legislators who are knowledgeable and professional."[28] Another view is represented by a Michigan legislator who believes that his careerist colleagues have lost touch with their constituents: "When you spend all your time in Lansing, you're more influenced by the lobbyists than by your constituents."[29]

In effect, state legislatures are becoming more like the U.S. Congress. Legislators are staying in the legislature in record numbers. Modernization has made the institution more attractive to its members, so turnover rates are declining. But do we really want fifty mini-Congresses scattered across the land? Today's legislatures are more FAIIR than in the past, but reform has also brought greater professionalization of the legislative career, increased polarization of the legislative process, and more fragmentation of the legislative institution.[30] Figure 6.3 shows the pattern of citizen, professional, and "hybrid" state legislatures. The categories are derived from an index developed by political scientist Peverill Squire that reflects legislator salary and benefits, the time demands of legislative service, and the staff resources available to the legislature.[31]

To some analysts, the reforms of the past decades have produced a legislative monster. Richard Nathan, a veteran observer of the states, argues that the key to increased government productivity is the empowerment of the governor.[32] Therefore, the legislative Godzilla must be contained. Nathan advocates term limits, unicameral legislative bodies, rotation of committee memberships, and reduction of legislative staff and sessions as a means of reining in the legislature vis-à-vis the governor. If adopted, Nathan's recommendations would undo thirty-five years of legislative reform. And the governor's political power would be significantly strengthened. This helps explain why, in 2007, Pennsylvania's governor Ed Rendell proposed a far-reaching plan to trim the size of the Keystone State's General Assembly, limit legislative terms, and change the redistricting process.[33] As you might imagine, Governor Rendell's plan fell on deaf ears in the

| FIGURE 6.3 | Legislative Professionalism |

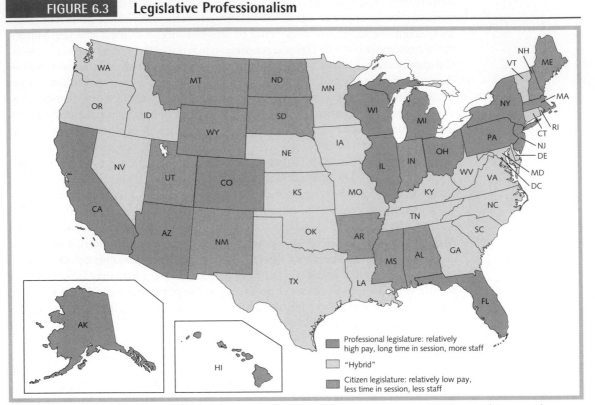

Professional legislature: relatively high pay, long time in session, more staff

"Hybrid"

Citizen legislature: relatively low pay, less time in session, less staff

SOURCE: Pervill Squire, "Measuring State Legislative Professionalism: The Squire Index Revisited," *State Politics and Policy Quaterly* 7 (Summer 2007): pp 220-21.

legislative branch. The legislative-gubernatorial nexus receives further analysis in a later section of this chapter.

Term Limits

In September 1990, Oklahoma voters sent state legislatures reeling. Oklahomans overwhelmingly approved a ballot measure limiting the tenure of state legislators and statewide officers. As it turned out, limiting terms was not just a Sooner thing. Within two months, voters in California and Colorado had followed suit. With a close defeat in Washington slowing it only slightly, the term-limits movement swept the country. In Oregon, a group called LIMITS (Let Incumbents Mosey into the Sunset) grew out of a tax-limitation organization. In Wisconsin, a coalition known as "Badgers Back in Charge" took up the cause of term limitation. And political activists of many stripes—populists, conservatives, and libertarians—found a home in the term-limitation movements in Florida, Michigan, and Texas.[34] In time, twenty-one states slapped limits on legislative terms. The term-limits laws eventually bore the intended fruit: By 2006, more than 850 legislators had been barred from seeking re-election. Particularly hard hit in 2006 was Nebraska where 41 percent of the unicameral legislature was put out of office by term limits.[35] Table 6.3 compares the term-limits provisions of the states where legislative term limits remained in force in 2006. Note that Nebraska voters had approved term limits three times prior to the 2000 initiative, but the courts had invalidated the measures.

In most states, the measure limits service in each chamber separately. In Maine, for example, a legislator is limited to eight years in the house and eight years in the senate. It is quite possible, then, that an individual could serve a total of sixteen years in the legislature under this plan. In a few states, the restriction is on total legislative service. In Oklahoma, for instance, the limitation is twelve years, whether in the house, in the senate, or in a combination of the two. Some term limits are for a lifetime (as in Arkansas and Nevada); others simply limit the number of consecutive terms (as in Ohio and South Dakota).

Limiting legislative terms captured the fancy of a public angry with entrenched politicians. The measure offers voters a chance to strike back at an institution perceived as self-serving and out of touch. But not everyone favors limiting legislative terms. Opponents offer several arguments against them. On a theoretical level, they argue that term limits rob voters of their fundamental right to choose their representatives. In a related vein, they contend that these measures unfairly disqualify a subset of the population—legislators—from

TABLE 6.3	Term Limits in the States

STATE	YEAR ADOPTED	SENATE	HOUSE	YEAR LAW TOOK EFFECT	REFERENDUM VOTE	BALLOT STATUS
Arizona	1992	8	8	2000	74 to 26	Initiative
Arkansas	1992	8	6	2000/1998	60 to 40	Initiative
California	1990	8	6	1998/1996	52 to 48	Initiative
Colorado	1990	8	8	1998	71 to 29	Initiative
Florida	1992	8	8	2000	77 to 23	Initiative
Louisiana	1995	12	12	2007	76 to 24	Referendum
Maine	1993	8	8	1996	67 to 33	Indirect Initiative
Michigan	1992	8	6	2002/1998	59 to 41	Initiative
Missouri	1992	8	8	2002	74 to 26	Initiative
Montana	1992	8	8	2000	67 to 33	Initiative
Nebraska	2000	8	—	2006	56 to 44	Initiative
Nevada	1994	12	12	2006	70 to 30	Initiative
Ohio	1992	8	8	2000	66 to 34	Initiative
Oklahoma	1990	12	12	2002	67 to 33	Initiative
South Dakota	1992	8	8	2000	63 to 37	Initiative

SOURCE: State Legislative Term Limits (2004), www.termlimits.org and the Council of State Governments, *The Book of the States 2003* (2003); updated by the authors.

seeking office. And, finally, they claim that term limits are unnecessary, sufficient legislative turnover occurs without them.

Term limits were expected to produce several consequences:

- Ending the domination of a chamber by powerful, entrenched veteran legislators;
- Increasing the proportion of first-term legislators in any given session;
- Increasing representation by groups underrepresented in the legislature, especially women and minorities, because of the guarantee of open seats;[36]
- Shifting power from the legislature to the governor and to lobbyists.

Three of the four expected consequences have indeed come to pass. The exodus of veteran legislators and the influx of inexperienced members have some observers shaking their heads in dismay. Data from term-limit states like Maine, Oregon, and California reflect procedural difficulties, a slower-working institution, less deliberation in committees, and less complex legislation.[37] As for shifting power to other actors, consensus seems to exist among researchers that governors, agency heads, legislative staff, and interest groups have benefited at the expense of the term-limited legislature.[38] The expectation that terms limits would produce greater representation of underrepresented groups has not been borne out—at least not yet. The number of women in term-limited legislatures has actually decreased slightly, and the increase in racial and ethnic minorities may be due more to their increased voting strength rather than to term limits.[39] Moreover, term limit devotees who wanted to strike back at an out-of-touch institution would be surprised to learn that term-limited legislators actually become less beholden to their constituents.[40] In sum, limiting the terms of legislators has consequences beyond simply forcing incumbents out of office.

Popular as they may be with the public, term limits may have already reached their zenith. Citizen initiatives are the primary vehicle through which the term-limits question has been placed before the voters. And the issue has just about run the gamut of states that allow initiatives. (The Utah legislature imposed term limits on itself in 1994, but it had a change of heart and repealed the law in 2003.) Court challenges have undone legislative term limits in Massachusetts, Oregon, Washington, and Wyoming. And in a surprising move, the Idaho legislature, bowing to an array of political pressures, repealed the term-limits law that was adopted via the initiative process in 1994.[41] Angry Idahoans gathered a sufficient number of signatures to place a question on the 2002 ballot asking whether the legislature's action should be upheld. After a heated campaign, the Repeal the Repeal question was defeated, thus ending term limits in Idaho before they took effect.

RELATIONSHIP WITH THE EXECUTIVE BRANCH

In Chapter 7, you will read about strong governors leading American states boldly in the twenty-first century. In this chapter, you have read about strong legislatures charting a course for that same century. Do these institutions ever collide in their policymaking? Is there conflict between the legislature and the governor in a state? Oh yes. In the words of one observer, "Conflict is the chief manifestation of a new calculus of political and institutional power in state government today."[42]

Tension between the executive and legislative branches is inevitable, but it is not necessarily destructive. It is inevitable because both governors and legislators think that they know what is best for the state. It is not necessarily destructive because the posturing, bargaining, and negotiating may actually produce an optimal solution.

Dealing with the Governor

The increased institutional strength of the legislature and its accompanying assertiveness have made for strained relations with a governor accustomed to being the political star. Institutional conflict is exacerbated under conditions of divided government, that is, when a legislature is controlled by one party and the governor is of the other party. The result of divided government is often gridlock, accompanied by finger pointing and blame-gaming. As the Republican governor of Mississippi, Haley Barbour, said to the Democratic-controlled legislature in his first State of the State address, "As Governor of Mississippi you have two choices . . . you can work with the Legislature, or you can fail. Well, I'm not into failure, so I look forward to working with each of you to make sure we all succeed."[43] As Governor Barbour quickly learned, that is much easier said than done.

A governor and a legislature of the same party do not necessarily make for easy interbranch relations, either. Especially in states where the two parties are competitive, legislators are expected to support the policy initiatives of their party's governor. Yet the governor's proposals may not mesh with individual legislators' attitudes, ambitions, or agendas.

Governors have a media advantage over deliberative bodies such as a legislature. The governor is the visible symbol of state government and, as a single individual, fits into a media world of thirty-second sound bites. In contrast, media images of the legislature often portray deal making, pork barrel politics, and general silliness. To be sure, those images can be quite accurate at times. In an effort to project a more positive image of the legislature in action, the leadership of the California Assembly in 2004 pledged to bring "a new decorum to the often-rowdy lower house."[44] "Gotcha" journalism, the term for media efforts to catch public officials in seemingly questionable situations, certainly complicates legislative life.

Sometimes, governors who have previously served as legislators seem to have an easier time dealing with the lawmaking institution. For example, former Vermont governor Madeleine Kunin, a Democrat, assumed the office after three terms in the legislature and one term as lieutenant governor, "knowing the needs of legislators, the workings of the legislative process, the sensitivities of that process."[45] Usually, about two-thirds of the governors have had legislative experience, although the proportion has recently declined. In 2006, for example, just over half of the fifty governors had put in time in the legislative ranks.

The legislature is not without its weapons. If the legislature can muster the votes, it can override a gubernatorial veto. Legislatures have also enacted other measures designed to enhance their control and to reduce the governor's flexibility in budgetary matters. For example, some states now require the governor to get legislative approval of budget cutbacks in the event of a revenue shortfall. Others have limited the governor's power to initiate transfers of funds among executive branch agencies. These actions reflect the continuing evolution of legislative–executive relations.

Overseeing the Bureaucracy

Legislative involvement with the executive branch does not end with the governor. State legislatures are increasingly venturing into the world of state agencies and bureaucrats, with the attitude that after authorizing a program and allocating funds for it, they should check on what's happened to it. Legislative oversight involves four activities: policy and program evaluation, legislative review of administrative rules and regulations, sunset legislation, and review and control of federal funds received by the state.

Policy and Program Evaluation Legislatures select auditors to keep an eye on state agencies and departments. (In a few states, auditors are independently elected officials.) Auditors are more than super-accountants; their job is to evaluate the performance of state programs as to their efficiency and effectiveness, a task sometimes known as the postaudit function. Specifically, they conduct periodic performance audits to measure goal achievement and other indicators of progress in satisfying legislative intent, a process that has been credited with both saving money and improving program performance. Virginia's Joint Legislative Audit and Review Commission (JLARC), is regarded as a model for the rest of the country.[46] Throughout its thirty-five year history, JLARC has conducted hundreds of evaluations of state programs and saved the state millions of dollars. The key to a useful auditing function is strong legislative support (even in the face of audits that turn up controversial findings) and, at the same time, a guarantee of a certain degree of independence from legislative interference.

Legislative Review of Administrative Rules Forty-seven state legislatures conduct reviews of administrative rules and regulations, but they vary in their methods. They may assign the review function to a special committee (such as a rule review committee) or to a specific legislative agency, or they may incorporate the review function in the budgetary process. In this role, the legislature acts as a gatekeeper, striving to keep agency rules in line with legislative preferences.[47]

Legislative review is a mechanism through which administrative abuses of discretion can be corrected. Legislative bills frequently contain language to the effect that "the Department of Youth Services shall develop the necessary rules and regulations to implement the provisions of this act." Such language gives the agency wide latitude in establishing procedures and policies. The legislature wants to be certain that in the process, the agency does not overstep its bounds or violate legislative intent. If it is found to have done so, then the legislature can overturn the offending rules and regulations through modification, suspension, or veto—depending on the state.

legislative veto

An action whereby the legislature overturns a state agency's rules or regulations.

This issue is a true gray area of legislative–executive relations, and court rulings at both the national and state levels have found the most powerful of these actions, the **legislative veto,** to be an unconstitutional violation of the separation of powers. For example, in 1997 the Missouri Supreme Court declared that the legislature's rule-review process was an unconstitutional intrusion into the executive branch's functions.[48] Legislatures continue to use the budgetary process to review (and sanction) agency behavior. Increasingly, legislatures are requiring state agencies to furnish extensive data to justify their budget requests, and they can use their financial power to indicate their displeasure with agency rules and regulations.

sunset laws

Statutes that set automatic expiration dates for specified agencies and other organizations.

Sunset Legislation Half the states have established **sunset laws** that set automatic expiration dates for specified agencies and other organizational structures in the executive branch. An agency can be saved from termination only through an overt renewal action in the legislature. Review occurs anywhere from every four years to every twelve years, depending on individual state statute, and is conducted by the standing committee that authorized the agency or by a committee established for sunset-review purposes (such as a government operations committee). The reviews evaluate the agency's performance and its progress toward achieving its goals.

During the 1970s, sunset legislation was widely hailed as an effective tool for asserting legislative dominion over the executive branch; but more than thirty years' experience with the technique has produced mixed results, and some states have repealed their sunset laws. Agency reviews tend to be time consuming and costly. And the process has become highly politicized in many states, involving not only agencies and legislators but lobbyists as well. One Texas representative commented that she "never saw so many alligator shoes and $600 suits as when some agency is up for sunset review."[49] On the positive side, sunset reviews are said to increase agency compliance with legislative intent. Statistics show that nationwide, only about 13 percent of the agencies reviewed are eventually terminated, thus making termination more of a threat than an objective reality.[50]

Review and Control of Federal Funds Since the early 1980s, legislatures have played a more active role in directing the flow of federal funds once they have reached the state. Before this time, the sheer magnitude of federal funds and their potential to upset legislatively established priorities caused great consternation among legislators. The executive branch controlled the disposition of these grant funds by designating the recipient agency and program. In some cases, federal money was used to fund programs that the state legislature did not support. Federal dollars were simply absorbed into the budget without debate and discussion, and legislators were cut out of the loop. By making federal fund disbursement part of the formal appropriations process, however, legislators have redesigned the loop.

If legislatures are to do a decent job in forecasting state priorities, some control of federal funds is necessary. In the face of reduced federal aid to states, it is critical for legislators to understand the role that federal dollars have played in program operation. When funding for a specific program dries up, it is the legislature's responsibility to decide whether to replace it with state money.

How effectively are legislatures overseeing state bureaucracies? As with so many questions, the answer depends on who is asked. From the perspective of legislators, their controls increase administrative accountability. A survey of legislators in eight states found legislative oversight committees, the postaudit function, and sunset laws to be among the most effective bureaucratic controls available.[51] Another effective device, and one that legislatures use in special circumstances, is legislative investigation of an agency, an administrator, or a program. But from the perspective of the governor, many forms of legislative oversight are simply meddling and, as such, they undermine the separation of powers.[52]

LEGISLATURES AND CAPACITY

State legislatures are fascinating institutions. Although they share numerous traits, each maintains some uniqueness. Houses and senates have different traditions and styles, even in the same state. And across states, the variation in legislative systems is notable. As Alan Rosenthal writes, "Legislatures are interwoven in the fabric of their states."[53] As institutions, legislatures are dynamic; amid layers of traditions and rules, they change and evolve.

The demands placed on state legislatures are unrelenting. Challenges abound. In these times, the ability of legislatures to function effectively depends on institutional capacity. The extensive modernization that almost all legislatures underwent in the 1970s is evidence of institutional renewal. Structural reforms and a new breed of legislator have altered state legislatures and are sending them in the direction of increased capacity. How ironic then, that with all their institutional success, reformed legislatures continue to struggle with their public image.[54]

One real concern is that the legislatures of some states are being marginalized through a citizen-empowering mechanism, the initiative, and an institution-weakening mechanism, term limits. It is no wonder, then, that in several states, legislators have mounted efforts to increase public knowledge of and respect for the legislative process.

CHAPTER RECAP

- The three principal functions of legislatures are policymaking, representation, and oversight.
- Reapportionment is a battleground for state legislatures because drawing district lines is a partisan process.
- Legislatures operate with their own formal and informal rules. Violations of institutional norms result in sanctions.
- The lawmaking process is a complex one with multiple opportunities for delay and obstruction. Most bills never make it through, and those that do seldom look as they did when they were introduced.

- Although legislatures perform more effectively than they used to, in 2008, fifteen states had legislative term limits in effect. Term limits create open seats and thus, increase competition for legislative seats. But when legislative terms are limited, other institutional actors such as the governor gain power.
- Legislators vie with governors in the policymaking process. Governors have the power to veto, but legislators have the power to override a gubernatorial veto. In addition, the legislature plays several oversight roles with regard to the bureaucracy.
- Legislative capacity has increased but, at the same time, legislatures risk becoming marginalized in states with the initiative process and term limits.

Key Terms:

casework *(p. 115)*

multimember district *(p. 117)*

malapportionment *(p. 117)*

reapportionment *(p. 118)*

redistrict *(p. 118)*

gerrymander *(p. 118)*

quorum *(p. 120)*

lame duck *(p. 121)*

war chest *(p. 121)*

delegate *(p. 124)*

trustee *(p. 124)*

politico *(p. 125)*

policy entrepreneur *(p. 125)*

legislative veto *(p. 135)*

sunset laws *(p. 135)*

Internet Resources

To find out what's up in state legislatures, visit the website of the National Conference of State Legislatures at **www.ncsl.org.**

Most states have websites that allow citizens to follow the progress of legislation during the session. See, for example, the legislative sites for Iowa and West Virginia at **www.legis.state.ia.us** and **www.legis.state.wv.us,** respectively.

The website **www.vote-smart.org** tracks the performance of political leaders, including state legislators.

To learn about model state laws, see the National Conference of Commissioners on Uniform State Laws at **www.nccusl.org.**

An advocacy website, **www.ustl.org** provides up-to-date coverage of the term-limits issue.

An avowedly conservative organization that drafts model legislation on various topics and reviews legislative activities across the states maintains a website at **www.alec.org.**

7

Governors

FOCUS QUESTIONS

1. How has the institution of governor changed from the early days of state governments to contemporary times?

2. What are some of the common duties and powers (formal and informal) that governors exercise?

3. What are some of the other offices typically found in the executive branch?

Should California Governor Arnold Schwarzenegger declare his state a nation and secede from the union? It won't happen, but an interesting case could be made for independence. The California nation would have 37 million people, the eighth-largest economy in the world, and one of the largest land masses and sea shores. California already has established advanced vehicle gas mileage and emission standards, air pollution standards, and climate change policies that go well beyond those of the U.S. government. It is a global leader in stem cell and technology research. California is actively engaged in international relations and negotiations. Any California governor enjoys "global swagger" and national policy and media prominence.[1]

Today, the governors speak with voices of authority on important national and even international policy issues. Although they do not always agree on what they want, the governors are influencing the Congress and president as never before in our history.

Asserting themselves as a righteous third force and speaking through the National Governors Association (NGA), the governors have helped shape federal welfare reform, education reform, and health care reform. And while Congress continually feuds along partisan lines over virtually all significant issues, the governors preach—and often practice—partisan peacemaking to reach common policy ground with their legislatures and to promote positive national policy changes. The challenges of conciliation are complicated by a voting public with no stomach for raising taxes and constricted state budgets, in which some three-quarters of expenditures are earmarked to education, Medicaid, and local government. The governors must make tough choices. Some bravely advance tax hikes despite the possible electoral consequences. Others impose brutal spending cuts on prisons, Medicaid, and higher education.

The governors' enhanced visibility in and contributions to national policy and politics are a tribute to their policymaking capacity and responsiveness to common—and uncommon—problems affecting the citizens of their respective states. It also reflects the policy leadership of the states in the U.S. federal system.

THE OFFICE OF GOVERNOR

It has been said that the American governorship was "conceived in mistrust and born in a straitjacket." Indeed, because the excesses of some colonial governors appointed by the English Crown created strong dislike and distrust of executive power by the early American settlers, the first state constitutions concentrated political power in the legislative branch.

History of the Office

Early governors were typically elected by the legislature rather than by the voters, were restricted to a single one-year term of office, and had little authority. Two states, Pennsylvania and Georgia, even established a plural (multimember) executive. Slowly, the governorships became stronger through longer terms, popular election, and use of the veto; but power did not come easily. The movement for popular democracy during the Jacksonian era led to the election of other executive branch officials, and reaction to the excesses of Jacksonian democracy resulted in numerous independent boards and commissions in the executive branch. Although governors did gain some power, they could not exercise independent authority over these executive boards and commissions.

In the early 1900s, along with their efforts to democratize national politics and clean up the corrupt city political machines, Progressive reformers launched a campaign to reform state government. Their principal target was the weak executive branch. Efforts to improve the state executive branch continued throughout the twentieth century. The essential goal has been to increase the governors' powers to make them more commensurate with the office's increased duties and responsibilities. As a result, constitutional and statutory changes have strengthened the office of the chief executive, reorganized the executive branch, and streamlined the structure and processes of the bureaucracy. The capacity of governors and the executive branch to apply state resources to the solution of emerging problems has thus been greatly enhanced.[2] And, as observed at the beginning of this chapter, the governors have become prominent players in national policymaking.

Today's Governors

Today, being governor is a high-pressure, physically demanding, emotionally draining job. As political scientist Larry Sabato states, "Governors must possess many skills to be successful. They are expected to be adroit administrators, dexterous executives, expert judges of people, combative yet sensitive and inspiring politicians, decorous chiefs of state, shrewd party tacticians, and polished public relations managers."[3] The job is also hard on the governor's private life. It consumes an enormous amount of waking hours at the expense of family activities, hobbies, and, in some cases, more significant money-making opportunities in law, consulting, or business.

Fortunately, governorships are attracting well-qualified chief executives, most of whom are a far cry from the figureheads of the eighteenth and nineteenth centuries and the stereotypical back-slapping, cigar-smoking wheeler-dealers of the first half of the twentieth century. Today's governors are better educated, and better prepared for the job than their predecessors. A large proportion of the recent governors hold law or other graduate degrees. Most of today's governors paid their political dues in state legislatures, gaining an understanding of important issues confronting the state, a working familiarity with influential figures in government and the private sector, and a practical knowledge of the legislative process and other inner secrets of state government. About one-third served previously as elected state executive branch officials, including lieutenant governor and attorney general. Seven are former mayors. Although previous

Massachusetts Governor Deval Patrick testifies before the U.S. Congress on the problems of morgage forclosure.
SOURCE: © AP/Wide World Photos.

elected experience is a great advantage in winning a governorship, a growing number have come straight from the private sector. The attractiveness of the governorship is evident in the fact that ten current chief executives left a congressional seat to take office. Why would someone desert the glamour of the nation's capital for the statehouse in Trenton, Augusta, or Columbia? For political power and the opportunity to make a difference in one's own state. Simply put, being a state chief executive is just more fun. As John Ashcroft, a former two-term Missouri governor, U.S. senator, and U.S. Attorney General, put it, "Anyone who tells you that being senator is as much fun as being governor will lie to you about other things, too."[4] Former West Virginia Governor Bob Wise observed, "Do not go to Congress if you can't handle deferred gratification."[5]

Although still predominantly white males, today's governors are more representative of population characteristics than former chief executives were. Several Latinos have served as governors in recent years, including Bill Richardson of New Mexico and Bob Martinez of Florida. In 1989, the first African American was elected governor—L. Douglas Wilder of Virginia.; the second, Deval Patrick of Massachusetts, took office in 2007. The first Asian American governor not from Hawaii, Gary Locke, was elected in Washington in 1996. Bobby Jindal was elected first Indian-American governor in Louisiana in 2007. In earlier years, several women succeeded their husbands as governor, but recently a growing number have won governorships on their own, including a record number of sitting governors (see Table 7.1).

Getting There: Gubernatorial Campaigns

The lure of the governorship must be weighed against the financial costs. Campaigning for the office has become hugely expensive. Because candidates no longer rely on their political party to support them, they must continuously solicit great sums of money from donors to pay for the campaigning costs—political consultants, opinion polls, air travel, media advertisements, telephone banks, direct mailings, websites, and interactive video links.

TABLE 7.1 **Women Governors, 2008**

NAME	STATE	PARTY	YEAR ELECTED	AGE FIRST ELECTED	PREVIOUS PUBLIC SERVICE
Christine Gregoire	WA	Democrat	2004	57	State attorney general
Janet Napolitano	AZ	Democrat	2002	45	State attorney general
Sarah Palin	AK	Republican	2006	42	City council member, mayor
Jodi Rell	CT	Republican	2006*	58	State legislature, lieutenant governor
Linda Lingle	HI	Republican	2002	49	Mayor
Jennifer Granholm	MI	Democrat	2002	44	Federal prosecutor, attorney general

*Rell was sworn in on July 1, 2004 following Governor John Rowland's resignation, then won her own term in 2006.

To date, the most expensive governor's race was the 2002 election in New York, in which loser Thomas Golisano invested $76.3 million; the winner, George Pataki, spent "only" $44.2 million. The official figures do not include in-kind donations such as free transportation, telephones, door-to-door canvassing, and other contributions from supporters. Generally, elections tend to cost more when they are close, held in a nonpresidential election year, involve a partisan shift (that is, when a Democrat succeeds a Republican, or vice versa), and are held in highly populated and geographically large states (for example, Florida, Texas, California, and New York).[6] On a cost-per-vote basis, races in states with a widely scattered population or hard-to-reach media markets, such as Alaska or Nevada, tend to be the most expensive. Cost per vote in recent gubernatorial elections ranged from $37.13 in New Jersey to only $2.88 in Minnesota.[7] In the 2005 elections, the average amount spent per vote was about $65 million.[8]

Money has a profound influence on gubernatorial election results, but it isn't the only important factor. As one veteran of political campaigns has reflected, "Everyone knows that half the money spent in a political campaign is wasted. The trouble is that nobody knows which half."[9] Other factors are also important in candidate success, such as incumbency and the strength of the candidate's political party in the state electorate.[10] High-profile candidates stand a solid chance of being elected because they possess campaign skills, political experience, and other characteristics that help them raise the campaign funds needed to get their message and persona across to the electorate.[11] Of course, being independently wealthy doesn't hurt either.

Incumbency is a particularly important aspect of a candidate's profile. An incumbent governor running for re-election stands an excellent chance of victory; about three-quarters of incumbents have retained their seats since 1970. Incumbents enjoy a number of important advantages, including the opportunity while in office to cultivate both popularity with the voters and campaign donations from interest groups. However, re-election is no sure thing. Budget and tax woes can lead voters to toss chief executives out of office, particularly those who as candidates pledge not to raise taxes but then do so after election.[12]

THE ROLES OF THE GOVERNOR: DUTIES AND RESPONSIBILITIES

In performing the duties of the office, the governor wears the hats of top policymaker, chief legislator, chief administrator, ceremonial leader, intergovernmental coordinator, economic development promoter, and political party leader. Sometimes several of these hats must be balanced atop the governor's head at once. All things considered, these roles make the governorship one of the most difficult and challenging, yet potentially most rewarding, jobs in the world.

Developing and Making Public Policy

A governor is the leading formulator and initiator of public policy in his state, from his first pronouncements as a gubernatorial candidate until his final days in office. The governor's role as chief policymaker involves many other players, including actors in the legislature, bureaucracy, courts, interest groups, and voting public. Most major policies that are enacted are initiated by the governor, and success or failure depends largely on how competently the governor designs and frames policy proposals and develops public support for them. The governor must also follow through to see that adopted policies are put into effect as originally intended.

Some issues are by nature transitory, appearing on the agenda of state government and disappearing after appropriate actions are taken. These issues are often created by external events, such as a federal court decision that mandates a reduction in prison overcrowding, a new national law requiring a state response, or an act of nature or man such as a tornado, flood, forest fire, or terrorist attack.

Most policy issues, however, do not emerge suddenly out of the mists. Perennial concerns face the governor each year: education, corrections, social welfare, the environment, and economic development. Cyclical issues also appear, periodically increasing in intensity and then slowly fading away. Examples of the latter are consumer protection, ethics in government, reapportionment, and budget imbalances. Of course, national policy issues sometimes absorb the governor's time as well, such as preparing for and responding to acts of terrorism, providing health care insurance to children and the working poor, and dealing with proposals to drill for oil and gas in national parks or just off state shorelines.

Several factors have contributed to stronger policy leadership from the chief executives in recent years, including larger and more able staffs that are knowledgeable in important policy fields; a more integrated executive branch with department heads appointed by the governor; strengthened formal powers of the office, such as longer terms and the veto and budget powers; and the assistance of the National Governors Association, which offers ideas for policy and program development. Of no small importance is the high caliber of individuals who have won the office in recent years.

Marshaling Legislative Action

The gubernatorial role of marshaling action is closely related to that of policymaker because legislative action is required for most of the chief executive's policies to be put into effect. In fact, the governor cannot directly introduce bills; party leaders and policy supporters in the house and senate must actually put the bills in the hopper. Dealing with legislators is a demanding role for a governor, consuming more time than any other role, and representing for many the single most difficult aspect of the job.

Executive–Legislative Tensions Developing a positive relationship with the legislature requires great expenditures of a governor's time, energy, and resources. Several factors hinder smooth relations between the chief executive and the legislature, including partisanship and personality clashes. Even the different natures of the two branches can cause conflict. Governors are elected by a statewide constituency and therefore tend to take a broad, comprehensive, long-range view of issues, whereas legislators, who represent relatively small geographical areas and groups of voters, are more likely to take a piecemeal, parochial approach to policymaking.

According to one study, the amount of strife between the two branches is influenced by three factors: the size of the majority and minority parties, the personalities of the governor and legislative leaders, and the nearness of an election year.[13] Following the 2007 elections, there were 28 Democratic governors, and 22 Republican governors. In a majority of the states today, however, the governor has to deal with a one- or two-house majority from the opposing political party. When the opposition party is strong, the governor must seek bipartisan support to get favored legislation passed. Often, a governor facing a large legislative majority from the opposing party has only the veto and the possibility of mobilizing public support as weapons against the legislature. Independent governors don't even have a minority party to count on, but this does not preclude success. Former Maine Independent governor King observed that "I have no automatic friends in the legislature, but I have no automatic enemies. I have 186 skeptics."[14]

A governor who ignores or alienates members of the opposing political party can quickly find himself in the desert without a drink of water. Republican governor Gary Johnson of New Mexico took office proudly proclaiming his intention not to compromise his lofty principles with "a bunch of careerist Democratic officeholders who had brought the curse of bloated government upon the Land of Enchantment."[15] The comment led to overridden vetoes, an ineffective administration, and an exhausting shouting contest between Johnson and the legislature. Arizona Governor Janet Napolitano, a Democrat, assumed a combative posture with her majority Republican legislature. She vetoed more than 100 bills during her first term (2002–2006) but won favor with the voters and was re-elected to a second term in 2006.[16] Arnold Schwarzenegger, who famously referred to opposing California legislators as "girlie men" and "stooges," experienced contrition late in his first term (2002–2006) when four ballot initiatives he had staked his governorship on went down to resounding defeat by the voters. He changed his approach on both the Democrats and on the issues in time to win re-election in 2006 and achieve policy victories in 2007.[17]

Even in states where the governor's own party enjoys a large majority in both houses of the legislature, factions are certain to develop along ideological, rural-urban, geographical, institutional, or other divisions. Ironically, a very large legislative majority can create the greatest problems with factionalism, primarily because there is no sizable opposition to unite the majority party. The stronger the numbers of the majority party, the more likely it is to degenerate into intraparty rivalries beyond the governor's control. As one Democratic governor lamented in the face of a 4-to-1 majority of his own party in the legislature, "You've got Democrats, you've got moderate Democrats, you've got suburban Democrats, you've got urban Democrats, you've got rural Democrats."[18]

Executive Influence on the Legislative Agenda Despite the difficulties in dealing with the legislature, most governors dominate the policy agenda, usually by working hand in hand with legislative leaders. The governor's influence begins with the State of the State address, which kicks off each new legislative session, and in most states continues with the annual budget message. In 2006, the governors stressed jobs, fiscal problems, health care, and improvements in education.

During the session, the governor might publicly threaten to veto a proposed bill or appeal directly to a particular legislator's constituency. Most of the drama, however, takes place behind the scenes. The governor might promise high-level executive branch jobs or judgeships (either for certain legislators or for their friends) to influence legislative votes. Or, she might offer some sort of **pork barrel** reward, such as funding a highway project in a legislator's district or approving an appropriation for the local Strawberry Festival. Private meetings or breakfasts in the governor's mansion flatter and enlist support from small groups or individual legislators. Successful governors are usually able to relate to representatives and senators on a personal level. Many are former members of the state legislature, so they can rely on their personal connections and experiences to win over key supporters.

In addition, all governors have legislative liaisons who are assigned to lobby for the administration's program. Members of the governor's staff testify at legislative hearings, consult with committees and individuals on proposed bills, and even write floor speeches for friends in the legislature. Some governors designate a floor leader to steer their priorities through the legislature.

Most governors, however, are careful not to be perceived as unduly interfering in the internal affairs of the legislature. Too much meddling in legislative affairs can bring a political backlash that undermines a governor's policy program. The role of chief legislator, then, requires a balancing act that ultimately determines the success or failure of the governor's agenda.

Administering the Executive Branch

As chief executive of the state, the governor is (in name, at least) in charge of the operations of numerous agencies, departments, boards, and commissions. In the view of many voters, the governor is directly responsible not only for pivotal matters such as the condition of the state's economy but also for mundane concerns such as the number and depth of potholes on state highways. Most governors are sensitive to their chief administrative responsibilities and spend a great amount of time and energy attending to them. Constitutional and statutory reforms, including the concentration of executive power in the office of the governor and the consolidation of numerous state agencies, have considerably strengthened the governor's capacity to manage the state. (See Chapter 8 for further discussion of public administration.) If governors are diligent in expeditiously appointing talented and responsive people to policymaking posts, they should feel no compulsion to micromanage the state's day-to-day affairs. Instead, they can focus their energies on leadership activities such as identifying goals, marshaling resources, and achieving results.

In many respects, the governor's job is comparable to that of the chief executive officer of a large corporation. Governors must manage tens of thousands of workers, staggering sums of money, and complex organizational systems. They

pork barrel
Favoritism, by a governor or other elected official, in distributing government monies or other resources to a particular program, jurisdiction, or individual.

must establish priorities, manage crises, and balance contending interests. But there are important differences as well. For one, governors are not paid comparably for their responsibilities. In terms of expenditures and employees, most states are as big or bigger than *Fortune* 500 companies, whose chief executive officers typically earn tens of millions of dollars a year in salary and other forms of remuneration. Yet the 50 governors averaged only $131,600 annually, and Maine's makes but $70,000.[19] Moreover, governors confront several unique factors that constrain their ability to manage.

Restraints on Management Reforms of the executive branch have allowed for more active and influential management, but significant restraints still exist. For example, the separation-of-powers principle dictates that the governor share his authority with the legislature and the courts, either or both of which may be politically or philosophically opposed to any given action. Changes in state agency programs, priorities, or organization typically require legislative approval, and the legality of such changes may be tested in the courts.

The governor's ability to hire, fire, motivate, and punish is severely restricted by the courts, merit-system rules and regulations, collective bargaining contracts, independent boards and commissions with their own personnel systems, and other elected executive branch officials pursuing their own administrative and political agendas. Thus, most employees in the executive branch are outside the governor's formal sphere of authority and may challenge that authority almost at will. Career bureaucrats—who have established their own policy direction and momentum over many years, and who see governors come and go—usually march to their own tune. In sum, governors must manage through third parties and networks in the three branches of government as well as in the private and nonprofit sectors. They have very little unilateral authority.

Governors as Managers Some governors minimize their managerial responsibilities, preferring to delegate them to trusted staff persons and agency heads. Others provide strong administrative and policy leadership in state government. Former Virginia Governor Mark Warner (2001–2005) enjoyed unusual success by using a collaborative decision-making style, thereby earning a national award for Virginia as "Best Managed State."

But the constraints on the governor's managerial activities are not likely to lessen, nor are the potential political liabilities. The governors who courageously wade into the bureaucratic fray must invest a great deal of time and scarce political resources, yet they risk embarrassing defeats that can drag their administrations into debilitation and disrepute. After all, "Reorganized the State Bureaucracy" hardly resonates as a campaign slogan. Meanwhile, in the face of social and economic changes, the management of state government has become increasingly complex and the need for active managerial governors more critical than ever before.

Master of Ceremonies

Some governors thrive on ceremony, and others detest it, but all spend a large portion of their time on it because it helps garner re-election votes. Former governors remember ceremonial duties as the second-most-demanding of the gubernatorial roles, just behind working with the legislature.[20] Cutting the ribbon for a new highway, celebrating the arrival of a new business, welcoming potential foreign business investors, receiving the queen of the Collard Green Festival, announcing "Respect your Parents Week," opening the state fair, and handing out diplomas are the kind of ceremonial duties that take a governor all over the state and often consume a larger portion of the workweek than any other role. Even a seemingly pleasant task can have its personal horrors. George A. Aiken, the late governor of Vermont, dreaded having to pin the ribbon on the winner of the Miss Vermont contest because he couldn't figure out how to put the pin in without getting under the bathing suit.

Coordinating Intergovernmental Relations

Governors serve as the major points of contact between their states and the president, Congress, and national agencies. Everything from emergency response to settling disputes over cross-boundary water pollution and other environmental concerns are carried out through the governor's office. At the local level, governors are involved in allocating grants-in-aid, promoting cooperation and coordination in economic development activities, and various other matters. Governors also provide leadership in resolving disputes with Native American tribes involving casino gambling and related issues.

The role of intergovernmental coordinator is most visible at the national level, where governors are aided by the National Governors Association and the state's Washington office. The NGA meets two times a year in full session to adopt policy positions, and to discuss governors' problems and "best practice" policy solutions. (C-SPAN covers national meetings of the governors.) The NGA's staff analyzes important issues, distributes its analyses to the states, offers practical and technical assistance to governors, and holds a valuable seminar for new governors. The NGA, however, has recently come under fire from conservative Republicans, who object to the organization's perceived "tax and spend" agenda even if it benefits their own states. In fact, in 2003, Republican governors of Hawaii and Texas withdrew from the NGA over this and related issues.

Some thirty-five states have established Washington offices to fight for their interests in Congress, the White House, and, perhaps most important, the many federal agencies that interact with states on a daily basis. A governor's official inquiry can help speed up the progress of federal grant-in-aid funds or gain special consideration for a new federal facility. Washington offices are often assisted by major law and lobbying firms under contract to individual states.

The governor's role as intergovernmental coordinator is becoming more important with each passing year. It reflects the elevated position of the states in the scheme of American federalism and their increasing importance in national and international affairs. It also is a reaction to provocations and intrusions from the national government. Acting together and as individuals, the governors have exercised national policy leadership on critical issues such as taxation of Internet sales, climate change, health care reform, and economic development. Increasingly often, when the national government confronts a policy problem, it turns to the states for solutions.

Promoting Economic Development

As promoter of economic development, a governor works to recruit business and tourists from out of state and to encourage economic growth from sources within the state (see Chapter 12). Governors attend trade fairs, visit headquarters of firms interested in locating in the state, telephone and e-mail promising business contacts, and welcome business leaders. The role may take the governor and the state economic development team to Mexico, China, Germany, or other countries, as well as to other states. Governors also work hard to promote tourism and the arts. But mostly, development entails making the state's climate "good for business" by improving infrastructure, arranging tax and service incentive deals, and engaging in other strategies to entice out-of-state firms into relocating and to encourage in-state businesses to expand or at least stay put.

When a state enjoys success in economic development, the governor usually receives (or at least claims) a major portion of the credit. Sometimes, the personal touch of a governor can mean the difference between an industrial plum and economic stagnation. Success stories are proudly heralded. The economic development policies of Michigan's Governor Engler helped turn a "listing industrial behemoth into a technically sophisticated . . . competitor."[21] West Virginia's governor promised "In five years, West Virginia will be the Silicon Valley of biometrics."[22] Washington Governor Christine Gregoire promoted development of "two 21st Century technologies: life sciences and alternative fuels."[23] Are incumbent governors punished in a re-election attempt when economic growth lags? Research findings on this question are mixed.[24]

Leading the Political Party

By claiming the top elected post in the state, the governor becomes the highest-ranking member of her political party. This role is not as significant as it was several decades ago, when the governor controlled the state's party apparatus and legislative leadership, and had strong influence over party nominations for seats in the state legislature and executive branch offices. The widespread adoption of primaries, which have replaced party conventions, has put nominations largely in the hands of the voters. And legislative leaders are a much more independent breed than before. Still, some governors get involved in legislative elections through campaign aid, endorsements, or other actions. If the governor's choice wins, he or she may feel a special debt to the governor and support him on important legislation.

The political party remains at least marginally useful to the governor for three principal reasons.[25] Legislators from the governor's own party are more likely to support the chief executive's programs. Communication lines to the president and national cabinet members are more likely to be open when the president and the governor are members of the same party. And, finally, the party remains the most convenient means through which to win nomination to the governor's office.

As a growing number of states have highly competitive political parties, governors find that they must work with the opposition if their legislative programs are to pass. For Independent governors, a special challenge exists: how to govern without a party behind them to organize votes and otherwise push proposed laws through the convoluted legislative process. The recent record has been mixed. Maine's Independent governor, Angus King, demonstrated a talent for working successfully with shifting legislative coalitions on a variety of issues. Reform Party governor Jesse Ventura did not experience the same level of success with the Minnesota legislature.

FORMAL POWERS OF THE GOVERNOR

formal powers

Powers of the governor derived from the state constitution or statute.

A variety of powers are attached to the governor's office. A governor's **formal powers** include the tenure of the office, the power of appointment, the power to veto legislation, the responsibility for preparing the budget, the authority to reorganize the executive branch, and the right to use professional staff in the governor's office. These powers give governors the *potential* to carry out the duties of office as they see fit. However, the formal powers vary considerably from state to state. Some governors' offices (Illinois, New York) are considered strong and others (Alabama, Georgia) weak. Also, the fact that these powers are available does not mean that they are used effectively. Equally important are the **informal powers** that governors have at their disposal. These are potentially

informal powers

Powers of the governor not derived from constitutional or statutory law.

empowering features of the job or the person that are not expressly provided for in law. Many of the informal powers are associated with personal traits on which the chief executive relies to carry out the duties and responsibilities of the office. They are especially helpful in relations with the legislature.

Both sets of powers have increased over the past several decades. But governors are more influential than ever before, primarily because of their enhanced formal powers; charisma, however, remains as important as ever. The most successful governors are those who employ their informal powers to maximize the formal powers. The term for this concept is *synergism,* a condition in which the total effect of two distinct sets of attributes working together is greater than the sum of their effects when acting independently. An influential governor, then, is one who skillfully combines formal and informal powers to maximum effectiveness.

Tenure

The governor's tenure power has two characteristics: the duration (number of years) of a term of office and the number of terms that an individual may serve as governor. Both have slowly but steadily expanded over the past two centuries. From the onerous restriction of a single one-year term of office placed on ten of the first thirteen governors, the duration has evolved to today's standard of two or more four-year terms (only New Hampshire and Vermont restrict their governors to two-year terms). In addition, gubernatorial elections have become distinct from national elections now that thirty-nine states hold them in nonpresidential election years. This system encourages the voters to focus their attention on issues important to the state instead of allowing national politics to contaminate state election outcomes.

The importance of longer consecutive terms of office is readily apparent. A two-year governorship condemns the incumbent to a perpetual re-election campaign. As soon as the winner takes office, planning and fundraising must begin for the next election. For any new governor, the initial year in office is typically spent settling into the job. In addition, the first-term, first-year chief executive must live with the budget priorities adopted by his predecessor. A two-year governorship, therefore, does not encourage success in matters of legislation or policy. Nor does it enable the governor to have much effect on the bureaucracy, whose old hands are likely to treat the governor as a mere bird of passage, making her virtually a lame duck when her term begins.

In truth, two four-year terms are needed for a governor to design new programs properly, acquire the necessary legislative support to put them into place, and get a handle on the bureaucracy by appointing competent political supporters to top posts. A duration of eight years in office also enhances the governor's intergovernmental role, particularly by giving him sufficient time to develop and nurture relationships with other governors and to win leadership positions in organizations such as the National Governors' Association. The record of an eight-year chief executive stands on its own, untainted by the successes or failures of the office's previous inhabitant.

The average time actually served by governors has grown with fewer restrictions on tenure. The gubernatorial graybeard is Illinois Governor Jim Thompson, who stepped down after serving his fourth consecutive term in 1990—a twentieth-century record. (North Carolina's Jim Hunt served four nonconsecutive four-year terms (1977–1985 and 1993–2001)). Long periods in office strengthen the governor's position as policy leader, chief legislator, chief administrator, and intergovernmental coordinator, as shown by the policy legacy left in Illinois by Thompson and in North Carolina by Hunt.[26] Another sort of gubernatorial record was set by Cecil H. Underwood, who in 1956 became West Virginia's youngest governor at the age of thirty-four. He was re-elected for a second term in 1996 as the state's *oldest* governor at seventy-four years of age.

There is still some resistance to unlimited tenure. More than one re-election creates fears of political machines and possible abuses of office. And, pragmatically speaking, a long period of "safe governorship" can result in stagnation and loss of vigor in the office. Even in states that do not restrict governors to two consecutive terms, the informal custom is to refrain from seeking a third term.

Appointment Power

Surveys of past governors indicate that they consider appointment power to be the most important weapon in their arsenal for managing the state bureaucracy. The ability to appoint one's own people to top positions in the executive branch also enhances the policy management role. When individuals who share the governor's basic philosophy and feel loyal to the chief executive and her programs direct the operations of state government, the governor's policies are more likely to be successful. Strong appointment authority can even help the governor's legislative role. The actual or implicit promise of important administrative and especially judicial positions can generate a surprising amount of support from ambitious lawmakers.

plural executive

A system in which more than one member of the executive branch is popularly elected on a statewide ballot.

Unfortunately for today's governors, Jacksonian democracy lives on in the **plural executive.** Most states continue to provide for popular election of numerous officials in the executive branch, including insurance commissioners, public utility commissioners, and secretaries of agriculture. Proponents of popular election claim that these officials make political decisions and therefore should be directly responsible to the electorate. Opponents contend that governors and legislators can make appointment decisions more effectively, based on the recommendations of appointed executive branch professionals who are not beholden to special interests.

Should appointment authority depend on the office under consideration? Those offices that tend to cater to special interests, such as agriculture, insurance, and education, probably should be appointive. Less substantive offices such as secretary of state or treasurer probably should perhaps be appointive as well. However, it makes sense to *elect* an auditor and an attorney general because they require some independence in carrying out their responsibilities. (The auditor oversees the management and spending of state monies; the attorney general is concerned with the legality of executive and legislative branch activities.)

Many governors are weakened by their inability to appoint directly the heads of major state agencies, boards, and commissions. These high-ranking officials make policy decisions in the executive branch, but if they owe their jobs in whole or in part to popular election or legislative appointment, the governor's authority as chief executive is diminished significantly. Although nominally in charge of these executive branch agencies, the governor is severely constrained in her ability to manage. Such an arrangement would be unthinkable in a corporation.

The fragmented nature of power in the executive branch diminishes accountability and frustrates governors. Former Oregon Governor Tom McCall once lamented that "we have run our state like a pick-up orchestra, where the members meet at a dance, shake hands with each other, and start to play."[27] When the assorted performers are not selected by the chief conductor, their performance may lack harmony, to say the least. And elected statewide offices provide convenient platforms for aspiring governors to criticize the incumbent.

Most reformers interested in "good government" agree on the need to consolidate power in the governor's office by reducing the number of statewide elected officials and increasing the power of appointment to policy-related posts in the executive branch. Most states have expanded the number of policymaking, or "unclassified," positions in the governor's staff and in top agency line and staff positions. But the number of elected branch officials has remained virtually the same for forty years. Table 7.2 shows the range and number of separately elected officials. North Dakota has the largest number, where twelve statewide offices are filled through elections. At the bottom of the list are the reformer's ideal states, Maine, New Hampshire, and New Jersey, which elect only the governor. The average number of elected officials is about eight.

Why has it been so difficult to abolish multiple statewide offices? The primary answer is that incumbent education superintendents, agricultural commissioners, and others have strong supporters in the electorate. Special-interest groups, such as the insurance industry, benefit from having an elected official—the insurance commissioner—representing their concerns at the highest level of state

TABLE 7.2	Separately Elected State Officials	

OFFICE	NUMBER OF STATES ELECTING
Governor	50
Lieutenant governor	42
Attorney general	43
Treasurer	37
Secretary of state	35
Auditor	24
Education superintendent	13
Secretary of agriculture	13
Insurance commissioner	11
Controller	14

SOURCE: Adapted from *The Book of the States 2007*, vol. 39 (Lexington, Ky.: Council of State Governments, 2007), pg. 179–185 Reprinted by permission of The Council of State Governments.

government. Such groups fiercely resist proposals to make the office appointive. Additional resistance may be credited to the fact that many citizens simply like having an opportunity to vote on a large number of executive branch officials.

Professional Jobs in State Government The vast majority of jobs in the states are filled through objective civil service (merit-system) rules and processes. Governors are generally quite content to avoid meddling with civil service positions, and a few have actually sought to transfer many **patronage** appointments—those based on personal or party loyalty—to an independent, merit-based civil service. (See Chapter 8.) Gubernatorial sacrifice of patronage power is comprehensible in view of the time and headaches associated with naming political supporters to jobs in the bureaucracy. There is always the possibility of embarrassment or scandal if the governor accidentally appoints a person with a criminal record, a clear conflict of interest, or a propensity for sexual harassment or other inappropriate behavior; or someone who causes harm through simple incompetence. Moreover, those who are denied coveted appointments may become angry. One governor, just as he was about to name a new member of a state commission, is quoted as saying, "I now have twenty-three good friends who want on the Racing Commission. [Soon] I'll have twenty-two enemies and one ingrate."[28] A governor benefits from a stable, competent civil service that hires, pays, and promotes on the basis of knowledge, job-related skills, and abilities rather than party affiliation or friendship with a legislator or other politician.

The Power to Fire The power of the governor to hire is not necessarily accompanied by the power to fire. Except in cases of extreme misbehavior or cor-

patronage

The informal power of a governor (or other officeholder) to make appointments on the basis of party membership and to dispense contracts or other favors to political supporters.

ruption, it is very difficult to remove a subordinate from office, even if such action is constitutionally permitted. For instance, if a governor attempts to dismiss the secretary of agriculture, he can anticipate an orchestrated roar of outrage from legislators, bureaucrats, and farm groups. The upshot is that the political costs of dismissing an appointee can be greater than the pain of simply living with the problem.

Several U.S. Supreme Court rulings have greatly restricted the governor's power to dismiss or remove from office the political appointees of previous governors. In the most recent case, *Rutan et al.* v. *Republican Party of Illinois* (1990), the Court found that failure to hire, retain, or promote an individual because of his or her political or party affiliation violates that person's First Amendment rights.[29]

A good appointment to a top agency post is the best way for a governor to influence the bureaucracy. By carefully choosing a competent and loyal agency head, the governor can more readily bring about significant changes in the programs and operations of that agency. Where appointment powers are circumscribed, the chief executive must muster his or her informal powers to influence activities of the state bureaucracy or rely on the seasoned judgment of professional civil servants.

Veto Power

As we noted in Chapter 6, the power to veto bills passed by the legislature bolsters the governor as chief policymaker and chief administrator. A veto also can punish an offending state agency by eliminating a favorite program or cutting the budget. Often the mere threat of a veto is enough to persuade a recalcitrant legislature to see the governor's point of view and compromise on the language of a bill. Vetoes are not easy to override. Most states require a majority of three-fifths or two-thirds of the legislature.

package veto

The governor's formal power to veto a bill in its entirety.

line-item veto

The governor's formal power to veto separate items in a bill instead of the entire piece of proposed legislation.

pocket veto

The governor's power to withhold approval or disapproval of a bill after the legislature has adjourned for the session, thus vetoing the measure.

executive amendment

A type of veto used by the governor to reject a bill and also to recommend changes that would cause the governor to reconsider the bill's approval.

Types of Vetoes The veto can take several forms. The **package veto,** for instance, is the governor's rejection of a bill in its entirety. All governors hold package veto authority. The **line-item veto** allows the governor to strike out one or more objectionable sections of a bill, permitting the remaining provisions to become law. Only Nevada, Maine, and six other states forbid this gubernatorial power. Several states permit a hybrid form of line-item veto in which the governor may choose to reduce the dollar amount of a proposed item for purposes of holding down state expenditures or cutting back support for a particular program. In some states, the line-item veto is permitted only in appropriation bills.

The **pocket veto,** which is available in fourteen states, allows the governor to reject a bill by refusing to sign it after the legislature has adjourned. In two states (Hawaii and Utah) the legislature can re-convene to vote on a pocket veto; otherwise, the bill dies. A governor might use the pocket veto to avoid giving the legislature a chance to override a formal veto or to abstain from going on record against a proposed piece of controversial legislation.

A fourth type of veto is the **executive amendment,** formally provided for in fifteen states and informally used in several others. With this amendatory power, a governor may veto a bill, recommend changes that would make the bill acceptable, and then send it back to the legislature for reconsideration. If the legislature concurs with the suggestions, the governor signs the bill into law.

Use of the Veto The actual use of the veto varies by time, state, and issue. Some states, such as California and New York, often record high numbers of vetoes, whereas others, like Virginia, report few. On average, governors veto around 4 percent of the bills that reach their desks.[30] The variation among states reflects the tensions and conflicts that exist between the governor and the legislature. The largest number of vetoes typically occurs in states with divided party control of the executive and legislative branches.

Governors cast vetoes for many different reasons, including philosophical opposition to policies and budget items, or to make a powerful symbolic statement about an issue. Occasionally, the governor stands as the last line of defense against a flawed bill backed by the legislature because of powerful interest groups. It is not unknown for legislators to secretly ask the governor to veto a questionable bill they have just passed because the bill's contents, although undesirable, are politically popular.

Although the overall rate of veto utilization has remained steady, the proportion of successful legislative overrides has increased in the past two decades. This is an indication of the growing strength and assertiveness of state legislatures, the increase in conflict between the executive and legislative branches, and the prevalence of split-party government. Differences in party affiliation between the governor and the legislative majority probably provoke more vetoes than any other situation, especially when party ideology and platforms openly clash.

Conversely, when mutual respect and cooperation prevail between the two branches, the governor rarely needs to threaten or actually use the veto. Most governors interact with the legislature throughout the bill-adoption process. Before rejecting a bill, the governor will request comments from key legislators, affected state agencies, and concerned interest groups. She may ask the attorney general for a legal opinion. And before actually vetoing proposed legislation, the governor usually provides advance notification to legislative leaders, along with a final opportunity to make amendments.

The veto can be a powerful offensive weapon to obtain a legislator's support for a different bill dear to the governor's heart, particularly near the end of the legislative session. The governor may, for instance, hold one bill hostage to a veto until the legislature enacts another bill that he favors. Former Arizona governor Bruce Babbitt once threatened to veto a popular highway bill unless a teacher salary increase was passed—"No kids, no concrete." The legislature capitulated in the end.[31] In another instance, Wisconsin governor Jim Doyle used a "Frankenstein Veto" to delete 752 words from a bill; the effect was to shift $427 million from transportation to education.[32]

Budgetary Power

The governor's budget effectively sets the legislative agenda at the beginning of each session. By framing the important policy issues and attaching price tags to them, the governor can determine the scope and direction of budgetary debates in the legislature and ensure that they reflect his overall philosophy on taxing and spending. All but a handful of governors have the authority to appoint (and remove) the budget director and to formulate and submit the executive budget to the legislature. In Mississippi and Texas, budget authority is shared with the legislature or with other elected executive branch officials. And in these two states, two budgets are prepared each year: one by the governor and one by a legislative budget board.

Because full budgetary authority is normally housed in the office of the chief executive, the governor not only drives the budgetary process in the legislature but also enjoys a source of important leverage in the bureaucracy. The executive budget can be used to influence programs, spending, and other activities of state agencies. For example, uncooperative administrators may discover that their agency's slice of the budget pie is smaller than expected, whereas those who are attentive to the concerns of the governor may receive strong financial support. Rational, objective criteria may determine departmental budget allocations, but a subtle threat from the governor's office does wonders to instill a cooperative agency attitude.

The governor's budget requests are rarely, if ever, enacted exactly as put forward. Rather, they are usually argued and debated thoroughly in both houses of the legislature. A legislature dominated by the opposing political party is nearly certain to scorn and disparage the governor's budget. Ultimately, "the governor proposes, but the legislature disposes." In fact, no monies may be appropriated without formal action by the legislature. (The budget process is discussed further in Chapter 8.)

During a state budget crisis, governors find themselves in an extremely vulnerable political position, particularly if they promised "no new taxes" when running for office. To balance the budget, a governor may cut spending, seek higher taxes, or both. None of these actions is likely to please many voters.

Reorganization Power

The phrase *reorganization power* refers to the governor's ability to create and abolish state agencies, departments, and other offices and to reallocate administrative responsibilities among them. Reorganizations are usually aimed at the upper levels of the bureaucracy to streamline the executive branch and thereby make it work more efficiently and effectively. The basic premise is that the governor, as chief manager of the bureaucracy, needs the authority to alter administrative structures and processes to meet changing political, economic, and citizen demands. For instance, serious and recurring problems in coordinating the delivery of social services among several existing state agencies may call for a consolidated human services department with expanded powers. A governor with strong reorganization power can bring about such a department without approval of the legislature.

Traditionally, legislatures have been responsible for organization of state government; and in the absence of a constitutional amendment to the contrary or a statutory grant of reorganization power to the governor, they still are. But

executive order

A rule, regulation, or policy issued unilaterally by the governor to affect executive branch operations or activities.

today, more than twenty states specifically authorize their chief executive to reorganize the bureaucracy through **executive order.** By this means, the governor can make needed administrative changes when she deems it necessary. All governors are permitted through constitution, statute, or custom to issue directives to the executive branch in times of emergency, such as during natural disasters or civil unrest.

Administrative reorganization today takes place under the assumption that streamlined government improves bureaucratic performance and saves money by cutting down on duplication, waste, and inefficiency. Achieving a more efficient and user-friendly government is a top priority of governors. Initiatives to reinvent and reinvigorate government aim to make the bureaucracy more flexible and responsive by changing incentive systems for state employees, privatizing certain operations, reducing layers of bureaucracy, implementing e-government, and decentralizing human resource management agency activities. Governor Rod Blagojevich of Illinois counted savings of $3 billion from agency and process consolidations.

Executive branch reorganization is widely practiced, but its actual benefits may be ephemeral. Illinois' recent success is an exception to the rule. Reorganization typically achieves modest financial savings, if any at all.[33] Such actions are not a cure for state fiscal ills. However, executive branch reorganization may help to provide a clearer focus on a particular problem, such as the needs of children, or help to contain administrative costs, and it may serve a variety of political purposes, such as rationalizing the pain of employee layoffs.[34]

The Politics of Reorganization Reorganization is a politically charged process. Mere talk of it sounds alarms in the halls of the legislature, in the honeycombs of state office buildings, and in the offices of interest groups. Reorganization attempts usually spawn bitter controversy and conflict, both inside and outside state government, as assorted vested interests fight for favorite programs and organizational turf. Accordingly, reorganization proposals are frequently defeated or amended in the legislature, or even abandoned by discouraged chief executives. One study of proposed state reorganizations discovered that almost 70 percent resulted in rejection of the plan either in part or in entirety.[35] Even when enacted, reorganizations may generate extreme opposition from entrenched interests in the bureaucracy and, in the final analysis, be judged a failure. In the memorable words of former Kansas governor Robert F. Bennett:

> In the abstract, [reorganization] is, without a doubt, one of the finest and one of the most palatable theories ever espoused by a modern-day politician. But in practice it becomes the loss of a job for your brother or your sister, your uncle or your aunt. It becomes the closing of an office on which you have learned to depend. So there in many instances may be more agony than anything else in this reorganization process.[36]

Most governors who have fought the battle for reorganization would concur. Perhaps this fierce opposition helps explain the rarity of far-reaching executive branch restructuring in the past several years and the preferences for small, incremental steps to reorganize and streamline state agencies.[37]

Staffing Power

The governor relies on staff to provide policy analyses and advice, serve as liaisons with the legislature, and assist in managing the bureaucracy. Professional staff members are a significant component of the governor's team, composing a corps of political loyalists who help the governor cope with the multiple roles of the office. From the handful of political cronies and secretaries of several decades ago, the staff of the governor's office has grown in number, quality, and diversity.[38] The average number of professional and clerical staff members is fifty-seven today. In the larger, more highly populated states staff members number well over one hundred (Florida counts 310).[39] The principal staff positions of the governor's office may include those of chief of staff, legislative liaison, budget director, policy director, public relations director, legal counsel, press secretary, and intergovernmental coordinator.

A question of serious concern, especially in the states whose governors have large staffs, is whether too much power and influence are being placed in the hands of nonelected officials. Clearly, professional staff members have been highly influential in developing and promoting policies for the governor in some states, particularly in states where the governor lacks a coherent set of priorities and lets the staff have free rein. In other states, the chief executive is very much in charge, relying on staff primarily for drafting bills and providing technical information. Given their physical and intellectual proximity to the governor, staff members are in a highly advantageous position to influence their boss. In their role as the major funnel for policy information and advice, they can affect the governor's decisions by controlling the flow of information and individuals into his office.

The Relevance of the Formal Powers

In Table 7.3, the states are scored as to the strength of the governor's formal powers of office. As noted, governors have won stronger powers during the past three decades. But how helpful are the formal powers? Despite the major transformation of the governor's office, governors remain relatively weak because of the setting of state government. They must function in a highly complex and politically charged environment with formal authority that is quite circumscribed by the legislature, the courts, and constitutional and statutory law. Owing to the nature of our federal system, the national government effectively strips them of control over many policy and administrative concerns. Moreover, the business of state government is carried out in a fishbowl, open to regular scrutiny by the media, interest groups, talk-show hosts, and other interested parties. Notwithstanding the continued constraints on the exercise of their authority, however, today's governors as a group are more effective than their predecessors were in carrying out their varied responsibilities. Today, the formal powers of the office are substantially strengthened, and highly qualified people are serving as chief executives.

In theory, governors with strong formal powers, such as the governors in Alaska, New Jersey, and New York, should be more effective than their counterparts in Vermont and Rhode Island. In practice, that tends to be true—but not

TABLE 7.3 Relative Power of the Offices of Governor

	WEAK						MODERATE					STRONG				
2.5	2.6	2.7	2.8	2.9	3.0	3.1	3.2	3.3	3.4	3.5	3.6	3.7	3.8	3.9	4.0	4.1
VT	RI		NH	AL	MS	NV	AR	CA	KS	AZ	DE	CO	IA	IL	ND	UT
			OK	NC	SC	IN	GA	OR	HI	ID	CT	NM	MD	OH		AK
						WY	TX	WI	LA	KY	FL	PA	MN			NJ
							VA				ME		NE			NY
											MA		SD			WV
											MI		TN			
											MO					
											MT					
U.S. average 3.5											WA					

NOTE: The scale varies from 2.5 to 4.1. Six measures of power are assigned points for strength: tenure, appointment power, budget control, veto power, whether governor and legislature belong to the same party, and number of other statewide elected officials.
SOURCE: Adapted from Thad Beyle, www.unc.edu/~beyle/gubnewpwr.html (Sept. 13, 2007).

always. The potential for power and influence must not be confused with action. A governor with strong formal powers enjoys the capacity to serve effectively, but he may choose not to do so or, for various reasons, be unable to utilize the formal powers properly. Alternatively, a governor with weak formal powers can nonetheless be an effective, strong chief executive if she actively and skillfully applies the levers of power available in the constitution and in statutes.

INFORMAL POWERS

No doubt a governor with strong formal powers has an advantage over one without them. But at least equally important for a successful governorship is the exploitation of the informal powers of the office. These powers carry authority and influence that are not directly attached to the governorship through statute or constitution but, rather, are associated with the human being who happens to occupy the governor's mansion. Governors who can master these powers can be highly effective, even in the absence of strong formal powers.

The informal powers help transform the capacity for action into effective action. They react in synergy with the formal powers to create a successful governorship. An incumbent chief executive in the strong governor state of New York will be hopelessly weak unless he also uses his personal assets in performing the multiple roles of the office. Alternatively, a chief executive in a weak governor state such as Oklahoma can be remarkably successful if he fully employs his informal powers to excel in persuading the state to adopt new ideas. The informal powers are not as easy to specify as the formal powers are. However, they generally include such tools of persuasion and leadership as popular support, prestige of the office, previous elected experience, public relations and media skills, negotiating and bargaining skills, pork barrel and patronage; and personal characteristics such as youth, ambition, experience, and energy.

Tools of Persuasion and Leadership

Popular support refers to public identification with and support for the governor and her program. It may be measured in terms of the margin of victory in the primary and general elections or in terms of the results of public opinion polls. Governors can parlay popular support into legislative acceptance of a policy mandate and otherwise channel the pressures of public opinion to their advantage.

Prestige of the office helps the governor open doors all over the world that would be closed to an ordinary citizen. National officials, big-city mayors, corporate executives, foreign officials, and even the president of the United States recognize that the governor sits at the pinnacle of political power in the state, and they treat him accordingly. Governors of California, New York, and Texas—the largest states—almost automatically assume national and even international prominence. Within the state, the governor typically makes use of the prestige of the office by inviting important individuals for an official audience, or perhaps to a special meal or celebration at the mansion.

Previous electoral experience is a valuable asset. Those who have made their way up the state's political ambition ladder by serving in the state legislature or as attorney general or lieutenant governor, have learned how to find their way through political briar patches and avoid tar pits.[40] They can also take advantage of political friends and allies they cultivated along the way.

Other informal powers may be defined in terms of leadership skills. *Public relations and media skills* help the governor command the "big mike": the captive attention of the press, radio, and television. Any governor can call a press conference at a moment's notice and get a substantial turnout of the state's major media representatives, an advantage enjoyed by precious few legislators. Some chief executives appear regularly on television or radio to explain their policy positions and initiatives to the people. Michigan Governor Jennifer Granholm offers a weekly radio address and podcast. Others write a weekly newspaper column or blog for the same purpose. Frequent public appearances, staged events, telephone calls, correspondence, MySpace entries, and "public interest" advertisements delivered through the mass media can also help the governor develop and maintain popular support.

Effective governors, knowing instinctively that the media can be a strong ally in carrying out their programs and responsibilities, cultivate the press like a flower garden. But media relations are a two-way street. The media expect the governor to be honest, forthright, and available. If she instills respect and cooperation, the governor's media relations can be "of incalculable value in his contest for the public eye and ear."[41] After all, most or all of what the public knows about the governor comes from the media.

But popular support may erode when governors' actions alienate the voters. Jesse Ventura, for example, was elected Reform Party governor of Minnesota in 1998. The ex–Navy Seal, pro wrestler, radio personality, and actor captivated the voters with his unconventionality and straight talk. But following a *Playboy* interview in which he dismissed organized religion as a "sham" and made other controversial statements, Ventura's popular support plummeted and his legislative priorities followed suit. Ventura's clout diminished significantly, and he did not seek re-election.[42] More recently, Nevada Governor Jim Gibbons' support dropped to just 28 percent within six months of taking office. Gibbons had made several poorly thought out policy proposals (e.g., to sell water rights under state highways) and endured an FBI investigation into helping a friend secure lucrative military contracts.[43]

Negotiating and bargaining skills are leadership tools that help the governor to convince legislators, administrators, interest groups, and national and local officials to accept his point of view on whatever issue is at hand. These skills are of tremendous assistance in building voting blocs in the legislature, particularly in divided-power settings where hyperpluralism—such as exists in national politics—must be avoided. They also help persuade new businesses to locate in the state and effectively represent a state's interests before the national government. Governor Ed Rendell used his persuasive powers in Pennsylvania to accomplish far-reaching policy changes in education, health care for children, and alternative energy.[44]

Pork barrel and patronage are aspects of the seamier side of state politics. Although they are utilized much less frequently now than they were before the civil service reforms of the first half of the twentieth century, governors are still known to promise jobs, contracts, new roads, special policy consideration, electoral assistance, and other favors to influential citizens, legislators, donors, and others in return for their support. All governors have discretionary funds with which to help a special friend who has constituents in need. And although patronage appointments are severely limited in most jurisdictions, a personal telephone call from the governor can open the door to an employment opportunity in state government.

Characteristics of a Successful Governor

The *personal characteristics* of an effective governor are nearly impossible to measure. As indicated earlier, leadership is generally agreed to be a very important quality of effective governors. Leadership traits are difficult to define, but former Utah Governor Scott Matheson identified the best governors as "men and women who have the right combination of values for quality public service— the courage to stick to their convictions, even when in the minority, integrity by instinct, compassion by nature, leadership by perception, and the character to admit wrong and, when necessary, to accept defeat."[45]

A successful governor attains her objectives by blending these qualities with the formal and informal powers of office in order to achieve her objectives. For example, following the political campaign to win the election, the governor must conduct a "never-ending campaign" to win the loyalty and support of her cabinet, state employees, the legislature, and the people, if she is to be effective.[46] Sixteen-hour days and one hundred hour workweeks are not uncommon.

Successful governors, particularly those in weak governor states, know how to limit their policy agendas. Realizing that not all things are possible, they focus on a few critical issues at a time and marshal their formal and informal resources behind them. Eventually, the determined governor can wear down opponents. But more important, the successful governor exercises leadership by convincing the public that he is the person to pursue their vision and their interests. He prevails in the legislature by applying the pressure of public opinion and by building winning blocs of votes, and he leads the bureaucracy by personal example. Above all else, the successful governor must be persuasive.

In short, the formal powers of the office are important to any governor, but even strong formal powers do not guarantee success. As noted earlier, they must be combined with the informal powers to be effective. Whatever approach the governor chooses as chief executive, his individual skills are probably more important than formal powers.[47] Evidence of this conclusion is provided by governors who have won and held their state's top job and successfully pursued their policy agendas in the face of significant partisan opposition. A notable example is Arnold Schwarzenegger of California, who combines the politics of pragmatism with outstanding interpersonal skills in exercising leadership.

REMOVAL FROM OFFICE

Upon leaving office, the vast majority of governors simply continue their public service in another venue. Four of the past five presidents were ex-governors. The experience of serving as a state's chief executive is widely believed to be excellent training for the top job in the nation. Former California governor Jerry Brown was the elected mayor of Oakland. Colorado's Roy Romer became superintendent of Los Angeles County schools. Eleven former governors are serving in the U.S. Senate.

Because state chief executives are held to higher standards today than ever before and are constantly under the microscope of the media and watchdog groups, illegal actions or conflicts of interest are likely to be found out and prosecuted. All states but one provide for the impeachment of the governor and other elected officials. (In Oregon, they are tried as regular criminal offenders.) Impeachment proceedings are usually initiated in the state house of representatives, and the impeachment trial is held in the senate. A two-thirds vote is necessary for conviction and removal of the governor in most states. Of the more than 2,100 governors who have held office, only 18 have been impeached and 11 actually convicted and removed from office. Others, most recently Connecticut's John Rowland and New Jersey's James McGreevey, have resigned under fire. Rowland left office amid a scandal involving kickbacks and favors, pled guilty to several charges, and received fifteen to twenty-one months in prison.

McGreevey resigned after a homosexual affair with an appointed agency head was revealed. Former Illinois Governor George Ryan was sentenced to six and one-half years in prison for fraud and racketeering.

But these fallen governors are the gubernatorial black sheep, political throwbacks who spawn media feeding frenzies. They deflect proper attention from the vast majority of hardworking, capable, and honest chief executives who typify the American state governorship today.

OTHER EXECUTIVE BRANCH OFFICIALS

The states elect more than 300 officials to key offices in their executive branches, not counting the fifty governors, ranging from attorneys general and treasurers to railroad commissioners. The four most important statewide offices are described here.

Attorney General

The attorney general (AG) is the state's chief legal counsel. The AG renders formal written opinions on legal issues such as the constitutionality of a statute, administrative rule, or regulation when requested to do so by the governor, agency heads, legislators, or other public officials. In most states, the attorney general's opinions have the force of law unless they are successfully challenged in the courtroom.

The attorney general represents the state in cases in which the state government is a legal party and conducts litigation on behalf of the state in federal and state courts. The AG can initiate civil and criminal proceedings in most states. Attorneys general have actively represented their states in legal actions contesting national government statutes, unfunded mandates, and administrative activities in controversial fields such as consumer rights, education reforms, and business regulation. Activist AGs such as New York's Eliot Spitzer (elected governor in 2006) have taken steps to protect consumers against mail fraud, Medicaid fraud, misleading advertisements by pharmaceutical companies, and other consumer rip-offs.

Attorneys general also took on the powerful tobacco industry, winning $206 billion in reimbursements for state funds spent to provide Medicaid-related health care for residents with smoking-related illnesses. Their collective actions have helped to reform corporate conduct and shift business regulation from the national government to the states. AGs often work together under the auspices of the National Association of Attorneys General to assert and protect the authority of the states in the federal system. Predictably, AG activism has produced a corporate backlash and intense interest and participation in AG elections.

Lieutenant Governor

This office was originally created by the states for two major reasons: to provide for orderly succession to a governor who is unable to fill out a term owing to death or other reasons, and to provide for an official to assume the responsibilities of the governor when the incumbent is temporarily incapacitated or out of the state. Seven states do not see the need for the office: Arizona, Maine, New Hampshire, Oregon, Tennessee, West Virginia, and Wyoming. Others attach little importance to it, as indicated by a very low salary or the absence of official responsibilities. The historical reputation of the lieutenant governor was that of a corpse at a funeral—you are needed for the ceremony but no one is expecting much from you.

But from 2003 to 2005, five lieutenant governors rose to occupy the executive office because of deaths and gubernatorial resignations. The lieutenant governorship in the majority of states has become a more visible, demanding, and responsible position. This trend is likely to continue as state governance grows increasingly complex and as additional states adopt the team election of governor and lieutenant governor. Many lieutenant governors hold important powers in the state senate, including serving as presiding officer, making bill assignments to committees, and casting tie-breaking votes. They are official members of the cabinet or of the governor's top advisory body in twenty-three states.[48] And virtually all lieutenant governors accept special assignments from the chief executive, some of which are quite visible and important. For example, Indiana's lieutenant governor acts as the state's commissioner of agriculture, and Utah's acts as the state's homeland security director. In general, lieutenant governors' salaries, budget allocations, and staff have grown markedly during the past two decades.

A lingering problem is that seventeen states continue to elect the governor and lieutenant governor independently. This system can result in conflict and controversy when, for example, the chief executive is out of state and the two office-holders are political rivals or members of opposing political parties. On several recent occasions a lieutenant governor, assuming command, has proceeded to make judicial appointments, veto legislation, convene special sessions of the legislature, and take other actions at odds with the governor's wishes.

To avoid partisan bickering and politicking in the top two executive branch offices, twenty-five states now require team election. In addition to avoiding embarrassing factionalism, team election has the advantages of promoting party accountability in the executive branch, making continuity of policy more likely in the event of gubernatorial death or disability, and ensuring a measure of compatibility and trust between the two state leaders.

Treasurer

The treasurer is the official trustee and manager of state funds and the state's chief financial officer. He collects revenues and makes disbursements of state monies. (The treasurer's signature is on the paycheck of all state employees and on citizens' state tax refunds.) Another important duty is the investment of more than $3.2 trillion in state funds, including state employee pension monies. The failure to make profitable investments can cost the treasurer his job. West Virginia Treasurer A. James Manchin was impeached for losing $279 million in state funds through bad investments. Other treasurers have been criticized for leaving midterm for lucrative private-sector jobs (Connecticut, New Jersey), accepting gifts from financial firms (Massachusetts), or using their post to raise large sums of money from investment companies for their next election (nearly all states in which the treasurer is elected rather than appointed).

Secretary of State

In the past, the duties of this office were rather perfunctory, entailing record-keeping and election responsibilities. But voting system reforms, e-government, and other changes have substantially elevated the position's responsibilities. Secretaries of state typically register corporations, securities, and trademarks, and also commission people to be notaries public. In their election-related responsibilities, they determine the ballot eligibility of political parties and candidates, verify initiative and referendum petitions, supply election ballots to local officials, file the expense papers and other campaign reports of candidates, maintain voter registration rolls, and conduct voter registration programs. The typical secretary of state also maintains state archives, files agency rules and regulations, publishes statutes and copies of the state constitution, and registers lobbyists.

THE CAPABILITY OF U.S. GOVERNORS

The states have reformed their executive branches to enhance the capability of the governor as chief executive and to make the office more efficient, effective, accountable, and responsive. Indeed, the reforms discussed in this chapter not only have extended the formal powers and capacity of the office but also have improved the contemporary governor's performance in his many demanding roles.

In addition, today's governors are better educated, more experienced in state government, and more competent than their predecessors. Their strength and policy influence are at a zenith. They are better able to employ the informal powers of their office in meeting multiple and complex responsibilities. In sum, there is greater vigor and capability in the governorships than ever before.

CHAPTER RECAP

- The American governorship historically was institutionally weak, with very limited formal powers.
- Today's governors are better qualified, educated, and prepared for the office than governors of the past. But winning the office is increasingly expensive.
- The duties of a governor include making policy, marshaling legislative action, administering the executive branch, serving as master of ceremonies, coordinating intergovernmental relations, promoting economic development, and leading their political party.
- Formal powers of the office, which have strengthened over time, are tenure, appointment, veto, budgeting, reorganizing the executive branch, and staffing.
- To be successful, a governor must master the informal powers of the office and integrate them with the formal powers. Among the informal sources of

power are tools of leadership and persuasion, such as public relations skills and negotiations and bargaining skills.

- Governors who violate the law may be removed from office through impeachment.
- Other key executive branch officials are the attorney general, lieutenant governor, treasurer, and secretary of state.

Key Terms

pork barrel *(p. 145)*	package veto *(p. 153)*
formal powers *(p. 149)*	line-item veto *(p. 153)*
informal powers *(p. 149)*	pocket veto *(p. 153)*
plural executive *(p. 151)*	executive amendment *(p. 153)*
patronage *(p. 152)*	executive order *(p. 156)*

Internet Resources

Each governor has his own website, which can be located through the state homepage or at **www.nga.org**. (the National Governors Association webpage). It features, among other things, governors' biographies, and a subject index on a variety of state and local issues, including the latest State of the State address.

Public Administration: Budgeting and Service Delivery

8

FOCUS QUESTIONS

1. What are the key trends that characterize public administration in state and local government?

2. Who are the key actors in state budgetary processes?

3. What are some of the public administration challenges facing state and local governments?

4. As state and local governments continue to evolve, what would you identify as a recent long-term trend?

---

bureaucracy

The administrative branch of government, consisting of all executive offices and their workers.

Bureaucracy is a paradox. On the one hand, bureaucracy and public employees are sometimes portrayed as "the problem" with U.S. government at all levels. From the ponderous department of social services to the dilatory department of motor vehicles, to the county tax assessor's office, bureaucracy is depicted as all-powerful and out of control, inefficient, wasteful, and drowning in red tape. Public employees (bureaucrats) are often seen as insensitive and uncaring, yet stay in their jobs forever. Nearly everyone, from elected officials—presidents, governors, mayors, and legislators at all levels—to talk-show commentators and even product advertisers have stridently bashed the bureaucrats, blaming them for all imaginable sins of omission and commission (and all too often for their *own* personal shortcomings as well). The answer to the problem is no less than bureaucratic liposuction to "get the fat out."

On the other hand, bureaucracy can be beautiful.[1] Bureaucratic organization is indispensable to public administration. Legislative bodies and chief executives enact public policies through vague laws, depending on a variety of state and local agencies to deal with the specifics, such as operationally defining key components of the policies and putting the policies into effect. Some bureaucracies make our lives more difficult, but others help the quality of our existence by enforcing the laws and punishing the criminals, putting out the fires, repairing and maintaining the roads, and helping the poor and disadvantaged among us.

A theme of this chapter is that state agencies and local departments (the public administration) should not be treated as scapegoats for all the social, economic, and political maladies that befall society. The quality and capacity of public administration have improved markedly in the country's states, municipalities, and counties in terms of the characteristics of employees and the efficiency, effectiveness, and professionalism with which they perform their duties. In fact, studies comparing public employees with cohort groups in the private sector find few important differences between them. Government workers are just as motivated, competent, and ethical as private-sector workers. Moreover, public employees tend to be more sensitive to other human beings, and more highly educated, than their counterparts in business and industry[2] (see Table 8.1). State and local employees are responding to citizens' demands by providing a wider range of services in greater quantities to more people than ever before; and publicly provided services are perceived to be just as good as the same services provided by private firms.[3]

Contrary to popular opinion, government work does not consist of pay without labor. Public employees perform some of the most unpleasant and dangerous (but necessary) tasks imaginable, from taking abused or threatened children away from their parents to caring for the mentally ill and guarding prisoners

TABLE 8.1	**Comparing Public- and Private-Sector Employees**

An extensive analysis of published studies on characteristics of public- and private-sector employees debunks certain stereotypes.

CHARACTERISTIC	ADVANTAGE
Motivation	Equal
Work habits	Equal
Competence	Equal
Personal achievement	Private employees
Educational achievement	Public employees
Values of public service and civic duty	Public employees
Ambition	Private employees
Compassion and self-sacrifice	Public employees
Ethics	Public employees
Helping other people	Public employees
Making a difference	Public employees

SOURCE: Adapted from Richard W. Stackman, Patrick E. Connor, and Boris W. Becker, "Sectoral Ethos: An Investigation of the Personal Values Systems of Female and Male Managers In the Public and Private Sectors," *Journal of Public Administration Research and Theory* 16 (October 2006): 577-97; Norman Baldwin, "Public Versus Private Employees: Debunking Stereotypes," *Review of Public Personnel Administration* 11 (Fall 1990–Spring 1991): 1–27; James L. Perry, "Antecedents of Public Service Motivation," *Journal of Public Administration Research and Theory* 7(2) (1997): 181–97; and Gene A. Brewer, Sally Coleman Selden, and Rex L. Facer II, "Individual Conceptions of Public Service Motivation," *Public Administration Review* 60 (May/June 2000): 254–64.

who hurl feces at them. In truth, dedicated public servants who work for the people should be saluted, not castigated, for jobs well done under difficult conditions. But more often than not, good government workers are the scapegoats for vague and poorly designed statutes and policies, failed political and corporate leadership, and other factors beyond the control of civil servants. It must also be recognized that occasional lapses in government administrative ethics pale in comparison to frequent corporate corruption scandals.

PUBLIC EMPLOYEES IN STATE AND LOCAL GOVERNMENT: WHO THEY ARE, WHAT THEY DO

More than 19.3 million employees work for states and localities. Their numbers have grown steadily since accurate counts were first compiled in 1929. Government work tends to be labor intensive. As a result of this fact and of inflation, personnel expenditures for states and localities have risen even faster than the number of workers. Total payroll costs for state and local governments exceed $700 billion.

Of course, the number of employees varies greatly among jurisdictions. Generally speaking, states and localities with large populations and high levels of per capita income provide more services and thus employ larger numbers of workers than do smaller, less affluent jurisdictions. Employment figures are further influenced by the distribution of functions and service responsibilities between states and their local jurisdictions. A state government may have hundreds of agencies, boards, and commissions. A municipality or county may have dozens of departments, boards, and commissions.

Such figures do not adequately account for the real people who work for states, cities, counties, towns, townships, and school districts. These include the police officer on patrol, the welfare worker finding a foster home for an abandoned child, the eleventh-grade English teacher, the state trooper, and even your professor of state and local government (if you are attending a public institution). Their tasks are as diverse as their titles: sanitation engineer, animal control officer, heavy-equipment operator, planner, physician, and so on. The diversity of state and local government work rivals that of the private sector, although there are important distinctions in the nature of the work (see Table 8.2). From the sewer-maintenance worker to the director of human services, all are public servants—often known as bureaucrats. Approximately one of every six working Americans is employed by government at some level. If bureaucrats are the enemy, we have met them and they are us.

BUDGETING IN STATE AND LOCAL GOVERNMENT

The budget is the very lifeblood of government bureaucracy. Without a budgetary appropriation, state and local organizations would cease to exist. The monies are allocated by legislative bodies, but the politics of the budgetary

TABLE 8.2	**Public Management and Private Management: What Are the Distinctions?**

Public- and private-sector management differ in terms of constraints, clients, accountability, and purpose.

	PUBLIC MANAGEMENT	PRIVATE MANAGEMENT
CONSTRAINTS	Politics, public opinion, resources.	Markets, resources.
CLIENTS	Citizens, legislatures, chief executives, interest groups.	Customers who purchase products or services.
ACCOUNTABILITY	To citizens and elected and appointed officials.	To customers, boards of directors, and shareholders.
PURPOSE	To serve the public interest and the common good.	To make profits and grow the organization.

process involves all the familiar political and bureaucratic players: chief executives, interest groups, other government employees, the general public, firms and industries, and, of course, the recipients of legislative appropriations—the state highway department, the municipal police department, the county sanitation office, and so on. In a phrase, budget making is a highly charged political poker game with enormous stakes. To understand public administration, one must have a grasp of budgetary politics.

An often-quoted definition of politics is Harold Lasswell's famous line: "Politics is who gets what, when, where, and how."[4] The budget document provides hard dollars-and-cents data in answer to this question. It is a political manifesto—the most important one you will find in state and local government. The budget is a policy statement of what government intends to do (or not do), detailing the amount of the taxpayers' resources that will be dedicated to each program and activity. The outcomes of the budgetary process represent the results of a zero-sum game—for every winner there is a loser—because public resources are limited. An extra million dollars for corrections can mean that much less for higher education.

The Budget Cycle

The process of governmental budgeting is best understood as a cycle with overlapping stages, five of which can be identified: preparation, formulation, adoption, execution, and audit (see Figure 8.1). Several stages are simultaneously taking place at any given time. For example, while the 2008 budget is being executed and revenues and expenditures are being monitored to guard against an operating deficit, the governor and the legislature are developing the 2009 budget. Meanwhile, the 2007 budget is being audited to ensure that monies were properly spent and otherwise accounted for.

The budget process has built-in checks and balances, because all spending is approved or audited by more than one agency or branch.

Budgets are normally based on a *fiscal* (financial) *year* rather than on the calendar year. Fiscal years for all but four states run from July 1 through June 30

FIGURE 8.1 **The Budget Process**

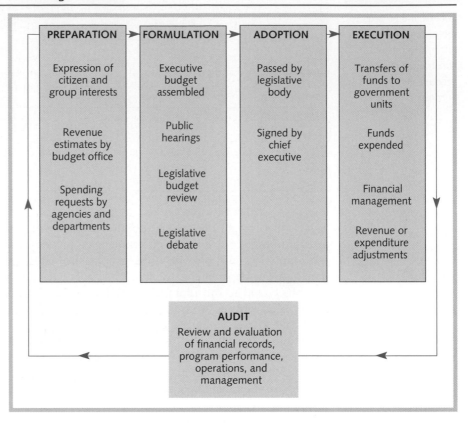

(the exceptions are Alabama, Michigan, New York, and Texas). Twenty-four states, including Montana, Indiana, and Kentucky, have biennial (two-year) budget cycles. Most local governments' fiscal years also extend from July 1 to June 30.

The initial phase of the budget cycle involves demands for slices of the budget pie and estimates of available revenues for the next fiscal year. State and local agency heads join the chorus of interest groups and program beneficiaries seeking additional funding (with no concern for "profits," agencies have little incentive to ask for less funding instead of more). Large state agencies are typically represented by their own lobbyists, or "public information specialists." State and local administrators develop estimates of revenues based on past tax receipts and expected economic conditions, communicating them to their respective state agencies or municipal departments, which then develop their individual spending requests for the fiscal year. Such spending requests may be constrained by legislative and executive "guidance," such as agency or program dollar ceilings and program priorities.

Formulation, or initial development, of the budget document is the responsibility of the chief executive in most states and localities. Exceptions include states in which the balance of power rests with the legislature (such as Arkansas,

Mississippi, and South Carolina) and local governments in which budgeting is dominated by a council or commission. The executive budget of the governor or mayor is presented to the appropriate legislative body for debate, review, and modification. The lengthy review process that follows allows agencies, departments, interest groups, citizens, and other stakeholders to express their points of view. Finally, the legislative body enacts the amended budget.[5]

The state legislature or city council ensures that the final document balances revenues with expenditures. Balanced-budget requirements are contained in the constitutions or statutes of forty-eight states and operate through precedent in Vermont and Indiana. These requirements usually apply to local governments as well. Balanced-budget requirements force state and local governments to weigh projected expenditures against expected revenues, but they may be circumvented to some extent. One popular device is the "off-budget," in which costs and revenues for public enterprises such as government corporations or for special projects are exempt from central review and are not included in budget documents and figures. Another accounting tactic is to borrow money from employee pension funds or next year's revenues to cover the current year's deficit. Perhaps the simplest way to balance next year's budget is to assume extra revenues or savings (realism may take a back seat to political necessity). Before the budget bill becomes law, the chief executive must sign it. Last-minute executive–legislative interactions may be needed to stave off executive vetoes or to override them. Once the chief executive's signature is on the document, the budget goes into effect as law, and the execution phase begins.

During budget execution, monies from the state or local general fund are periodically allocated to agencies and departments to meet payrolls, purchase goods and materials, help average citizens solve problems ranging from a rabid raccoon in the chimney to a car-swallowing sinkhole in the backyard, and generally to try to achieve program goals. If revenues have been overestimated, the chief executive or legislative body must make adjustments to keep the budget in the black. In a crisis, the governor may call the legislature into special session, or impose a variety of money-saving measures, including hiring and travel freezes, layoffs, furloughs, and across-the-board spending reductions. Rainy day funds are tapped as well (see Chapter 12). Local governments implement similar strategies, including spending reductions, tax or fee hikes, short-term borrowing, and delayed or canceled capital expenditures. Eventually, real pain is experienced by many organizations and individuals.

The final portion of the budget cycle involves several types of audits, each with a different objective. Fiscal audits seek to verify that expenditure records are accurate and that financial transactions have been made in accordance with the law. Performance audits examine agency or department activities in relation to goals and objectives, including that government is serving its citizens effectively and efficiently. Operational and management audits review how specific programs are carried out and assess administrators' performance.

The performance measurement and management trend has firm traction in state and local government today, reflecting these governments' genuine determination to improve service provision to citizens.[6]

The Actors in Budgeting

Four main actors participate in the budget process: interest groups, agencies, the chief executive, and the legislative body. Interest groups organize testimony at budget hearings and pressure the other three actors to pursue favored policies and programs. The role of the agency or department is to defend the base—the amount of the last fiscal year's appropriation—and to advocate spending for new or expanded programs. Agency and department heads are professionals who believe in the value of their organization and its programs, but they often find themselves playing Byzantine games to get the appropriations they want, as set forth in Table 8.3.

TABLE 8.3	The Games Spenders Play	
The following are tactics used by state and local officials to maximize their share of the budget during negotiations and hearings with governors, local chief executives, and the legislative body.	**MASSAGE THE CONSTITUENCY**	Locate, cultivate, and utilize clientele groups to further the organization's objectives. Encourage them to offer committee testimony and contact legislative members on your behalf.
	ALWAYS ASK FOR MORE	If your agency or department doesn't claim its share of new revenues, someone else will. The more you seek, the more you will receive.
	SPEND ALL APPROPRIATED FUNDS BEFORE THE FISCAL YEAR EXPIRES	An end-of-year surplus indicates that the elected officials were too generous with you this year; they will cut your appropriation next time.
	CONCEAL NEW PROGRAMS BEHIND EXISTING ONES	Incrementalism means that existing program commitments are likely to receive cursory review, even if an expansion in the margin is substantial. An announced new program will undergo comprehensive examination. Related to this game is camel's nose under the tent, in which low program start-up costs are followed by ballooning expenses down the road.
	HERE'S A KNIFE; CUT OUT MY HEART WHILE YOU'RE AT IT	When told that you must cut your budget, place the most popular programs on the chopping block. Rely on your constituency to organize vigorous opposition. Alternatively, state that all your activities are critically important so the elected officials will have to decide what to cut (and answer for it to voters).
	A ROSE BY ANY OTHER NAME	Conceal unpopular or controversial programs within other program activities. And give them appealing names (for instance, call a sex education class "Teaching Family Values").
	LET'S STUDY IT FIRST (AND MAYBE YOU WON'T BE RE-ELECTED)	When told to cut or eliminate a program, argue that the consequences would be devastating and should be carefully studied before action is taken.

(*cont. on next page*)

TABLE 8.3

SMOKE AND MIRRORS	Support your requests for budget increases with voluminous data and testimony. The data need not be especially persuasive or even factual, just overwhelming. Management writer James H. Boren calls this "bloatating" and "trashifying.
A PIG IN A POKE	Place an unneeded item in your budget request so you can gracefully give it up while protecting more important items.
END RUN	If the chief executive initiates a budget cut, run quickly to friends in the legislature.
EVERY VEIN IS AN ARTERY	Claim that any program cut would so completely undermine effectiveness that the entire program would have to be abandoned.

Political scientist Aaron Wildavsky described the basic quandary of agency and departmental representatives as follows:

> Life would be simple if they could just estimate the costs of their ever-expanding needs and submit the total as their request. But if they ask for amounts much larger than the appropriating bodies believe is reasonable, their credibility will suffer a drastic decline. . . . So the first decision rule for agencies is: do not come in too high. Yet the agencies must also not come in too low, for the assumption is that if the agency advocates do not ask for funds they do not need them.[7]

What agency heads usually do is carefully evaluate the fiscal-political environment. They take into consideration the previous year's events, current and estimated agency expenditures, the composition of the legislature, policy statements by the chief executive, the strengths of clientele groups, and other factors. Then they put forward a figure somewhat larger than they expect to get.

The chief executive has a much different role in the budget process. In addition to tailoring the budget to his program priorities as closely as possible, he acts as an economizer. Individual departmental requests must be reconciled, which means that they must be cut, since the sum total of requests usually greatly exceeds estimated revenues. Of course, an experienced governor or mayor recognizes the games played by administrators; she knows that budget requests are likely to be inflated in anticipation of cuts. In fact, various studies on state and local budgeting indicate that the single most influential participant is the chief executive.[8] Not surprisingly, astute administrators devote time and other resources to cultivating the chief executive's support for their agency's or department's activities.

The role of the legislative body in the initial stage of the budget cycle is essentially to respond to and modify the initiatives of the chief executive. The governor, mayor, or city manager proposes, and the legislature or council reacts. Later in the budget cycle, the legislative body performs another important function through its review of agency and department spending and its response to constituents' complaints.

Pervasive Incrementalism

In a perfect world, budgeting would be a purely rational enterprise. Objectives would be identified, stated clearly, and prioritized; alternative means for accomplishing them would be considered; revenue and expenditure decisions would be coordinated within the context of a balanced budget.

That is how budgeting *should* be done. But state and local officials have to allocate huge sums of money each year in a budgetary environment where objectives are unclear or controversial and often conflict with one another. It is nearly impossible to prioritize the hundreds or thousands of policy items on the agenda. Financial resources, time, and the capacity of the human brain are severely stretched.

To cope with such complexity and minimize political conflict over scarce resources, decision makers "muddle through."[9] They simplify budget decision-making by adopting decision rules. For example, instead of searching for the optimal means for addressing a public policy problem, they search only until they find a feasible solution. As a result, they sacrifice comprehensive analysis and rationality for **incrementalism** in which small adjustments (usually an increase) are made to the nature and funding base of existing programs. Thus the policy commitments and spending levels of ongoing programs are usually accepted as a given—they become the base for next year's funding. Decisions are made on a very small proportion of the total budget: the increments from one fiscal year to the next. If the budget has to be cut, it is done decrementally; small percentage adjustments are subtracted from the base. In this way, political conflict over values and objectives is held to a minimum.

The hallmarks of incremental budgeting are consistency and continuity: The future becomes an extension of the present, which is itself a continuation of the past. Long-range commitments are made, then honored indefinitely. This is not to say that state and local budgeting is a simple affair. On the contrary: It is as tangled and intricate as the webs of a thousand spiders on methamphetamines.

Types of Budgets

A budget document can be laid out in various ways, depending on the purposes one has in mind: control, management, and planning. Historically, *control*, or fiscal accountability, has been the primary purpose of budgeting, incrementalism the dominant process, and the line-item budget the standard document.

Control Through Line-Item Budgets The **line-item budget** facilitates control by specifying the amount of funds each agency or department receives and monitoring how those funds are spent. Each dollar can be accounted for with the line-item budget—which lists every object of expenditure, from police uniforms to toilet paper—on a single line in the budget document. Line-item budgets show where the money goes, but they do not tell us how effectively the money is spent.

Budgeting for Management and Planning Budget formats that stress *management* and *planning* are intended to help budget makers move beyond the

incrementalism

A decision-making approach in the budgetary process in which the previous year's expenditures are used as a base for the current year's budget figures.

line-item budget

A budget that lists detailed expenditure items such as personal computers and paper, with no attention to the goals or objectives of spending.

narrow constraints of line items and incrementalism toward more rational and flexible decision-making techniques that help attain program results. Chief executives and agency officials seek to ensure that organizational units properly carry out priorities set forth in the budget—the management aspect of budgeting. Formal program and policy evaluations are a necessary step in ensuring proper performance and public accountability. The planning part involves orienting the budget process toward the future by anticipating needs and contingencies. A budget format that emphasizes planning is one that specifies objectives and lays out a financial plan for attaining them.

Several techniques permit budgeting for management and planning, but the most important today is performance budgeting. In **performance budgeting,** the major emphasis is on services provided and program results. The idea is to focus attention on how effectively work is being done rather than on what is being acquired. Whereas line-item budgets are input oriented, performance budgets are output and outcome oriented. Governments decide what they want to accomplish and measure these accomplishments versus expenditures. For example, the performance of a fire department can be evaluated by response times to emergency calls and by how quickly a fire is contained once firefighters arrive at the scene. By focusing on program objectives and work performance, performance budgets can assist managers, elected officials, and citizens in improving the quality of government operations.[10]

Capital Budgets The budget formats described above apply to operating budgets whose funds are depleted within a year. Capital outlays are made over a longer period of time and are composed of big ticket purchases such as hospitals, university buildings, libraries, new highways, and new information systems. They represent one-time, nonrecurring expenditures that call for special funding procedures, or a **capital budget.** Because such items cannot be paid for within a single fiscal year, governments borrow the required funds, just as most individuals do when buying a house or an expensive automobile. The debt, with interest, is paid back in accordance with a predetermined schedule.

Capital projects are funded through the sale of general obligation or revenue bonds. *Bonds* are certificates of debt sold by a government to a purchaser, who eventually recovers the initial price of the bond plus interest. *General obligation bonds* are paid off with a jurisdiction's regular revenues (from taxes and other sources). In this instance, the "full faith and credit" of the government is pledged as security. *Revenue bonds* are usually paid off with user fees collected from use of the new facility (for example, a parking garage, auditorium, or toll road). Payments for both types of bonds are scheduled over a period of time that usually ranges from five to twenty years. The costs of operating a new facility, such as a school or sports arena, are met through the regular operating budget and/or user fees.

performance budgeting

Budgeting that is organized to account for the outcomes of government programs.

capital budget

A budget that plans large expenditures for long-term investments, such as buildings and highways.

HUMAN RESOURCE POLICY IN STATE AND LOCAL GOVERNMENT: FROM PATRONAGE TO MERIT

Whether the tasks of state and local government are popular (fighting crime, educating children) or unpopular (imposing and collecting taxes and fees), serious (saving a helpless infant from an abusive parent), or mundane (maintaining the grass on municipal sports fields), they are usually performed by public employees. The 5 million state workers and 13.3 million city, county, and town employees are the critical links between public policy decisions and how those policies are implemented. Agencies and departments must be organized to solve problems and deliver services effectively, efficiently, and reliably. Human resource (personnel) rules and procedures must determine how public employees are recruited, hired, paid, and fired.

In the nation's first decades, public employees came mainly from the educated and wealthy upper class and, in theory, were hired on the basis of fitness for office. During the presidency of Andrew Jackson (1829–1837), who wanted to open up national government jobs to all segments of white, male society, the *patronage* system was adopted to fill many positions. Hiring could depend on party affiliation and other political alliances rather than on job-related qualifications.

Patronage became entrenched in many states and localities where jobs were awarded almost entirely on grounds of partisan politics, personal friendships, family ties, or financial contributions. This system made appointees accountable to the governor, mayor, or whoever appointed them, but it did nothing to ensure honesty and competence. By the beginning of the Civil War, the spoils system permeated U.S. governments at all levels. The quality of public service plummeted.

The Merit System

merit system

The organization of government personnel providing for hiring and promotion on the basis of knowledge, skills, and abilities rather than patronage or other influences.

The concept of the **merit system** is usually associated with the national campaign for passage of the Pendleton Act of 1883. Two key factors led to its realization. First, Anglo-Saxon Protestants were losing political power to urban political machines dominated by "new" Americans of Catholic faith and Irish, Italian, and Polish descent. Second, scandals rocked the administration of President Ulysses S. Grant, and spawned a public backlash that peaked with the assassination of President James Garfield in 1881 by an insane attorney seeking a political appointment. The Pendleton Act set up an independent, bipartisan *civil service* commission to make objective, merit-based selections for federal job openings.

neutral competence

The concept that public employees should perform their duties competently and without regard for political considerations.

The *merit principle* was to determine all personnel-related decisions. Those individuals best qualified would receive a job or a promotion based on their knowledge, skill, and abilities. Far from perfect, the merit system was thoroughly overhauled by the Civil Service Reform Act of 1978. As a result of the Pendleton Act, the negative effects of patronage politics in national selection practices were mostly eliminated. **Neutral competence** became the primary criterion for obtaining a job, as public servants were expected to perform their work competently and in a politically neutral manner.

New York was the first state to enact a merit system, in 1883, the year of the Pendleton Act, and Massachusetts followed in 1884. The first municipal merit system was established in Albany, New York, in 1884; a year later, Cook County, Illinois, became the first county with a merit system. (Ironically, both Albany and Cook County (Chicago) were later consumed once again by machine politics and spoils-ridden urban governance).

Many states and numerous local governments followed with merit-based civil service systems of their own. Congressional passage of the 1939 amendments to the Social Security Act of 1935 gave additional impetus to such systems. This legislation obligated the states to set up merit systems for employees in social service and employment security agencies and departments that were at least partly funded by national grants-in-aid under the Social Security Act. Thus, all states are now required to establish a merit system for a sizable segment (around 20 percent) of their work force; most of them have in fact developed comprehensive systems that encompass almost all state employees. Common elements of these modern personnel systems include recruitment, selection, and promotion according to knowledge, skills, and ability; regular performance appraisals; and employee incentive systems.

Some merit systems work better than others. In a handful of states and localities, they are mere formalities—lifeless skeletons around which a shadowy world of patronage, spoils, favoritism, and incompetence flourishes.[11] Such conditions came to public attention when terrorists boarded and hijacked two commercial aircraft at Boston's Logan Airport on September 11, 2001. For years, gubernatorial patronage appointees with little or no experience in security or law enforcement had run Logan's security operations.[12]

Rigid personnel rules, a lack of training programs, and inadequate salaries continue to plague some jurisdictions. Political control over merit-system employees is limited everywhere because most cannot be fired without great difficulty. Georgia and Florida are exceptions: In these states, new employees are hired on contracts and not granted tenure in the job.

State and Local Advances

On balance, however, state and local personnel systems have been greatly improved, and the process continues. Nonnational governments are experimenting with recruitment and testing innovations, pay-for-performance plans and other incentive systems, participative management innovations, new performance-appraisal methods, web-based training programs, the decentralization of personnel functions, and many other concepts. Virtually every state is reforming its civil service in some way.[13] General public dissatisfaction with government at all levels, combined with increasing needs for government to become more sophisticated and responsive to its clients, means that efforts to "reinvent" human resource management are certain to grow.

These reforms are designed to make the executive branch leaner and more responsive to the chief executive; to improve service efficiency and effectiveness; and, through decentralization of authority, to enhance flexibility for chief executives, agency heads, city managers, and other officials. Reformers remain dedicated to the principle of protecting the civil service from unnecessary and gratuitous interference by politicians with patronage considerations in mind. But they also want to increase the capacity of government executives to manage programs and people in their organizations and to achieve desired results.

Merit-System Controversies

As we shall see, state and local governments have taken the lead in addressing controversial questions that involve merit-system principles and practices, including representative bureaucracy, sexual harassment, and labor unions.

Representative Bureaucracy The concept of representative bureaucracy suggests that the structure of government employment should reflect major sexual, racial, socioeconomic, religious, geographic, and related components in society. The assumptions behind this idea are that (1) bureaucrats have discretion; (2) a work force representative of the values, points of view, and interests of the people it governs will be responsive to their special problems and concerns; and (3) a representative bureaucracy provides strong symbolic evidence of a government "of the people, by the people, and for the people." In some situations representative bureaucracy has "active" implications. Empirical research indicates that although organizational socialization and professionalism are stronger predictors of public policy preferences than racial, sexual, and other personal characteristics,[14] women and minority bureaucrats sometimes use their discretion to improve the treatment of, and outcomes for, minority clients. For instance, female bureaucrats tend to be more active in representing female child support recipients than men are.[15] The symbolic aspects of representative bureaucracy are important. A government that demonstrates the possibility of social and occupational mobility for all sorts of people gains legitimacy in the eyes of its citizens and expands the diversity of views taken into account in bureaucratic decisions.

A controversial question is how to *achieve* a representative work force, particularly at the upper levels of government organizations, without sacrificing the merit principle. *Equal employment opportunity (EEO)*—the policy of prohibiting employment practices that discriminate for reasons of race, sex, color, religion, age, disability, or other factors not related to the job—is mandated by federal law. This policy has been the law for well over a hundred years; yet progress was very slow until the past three decades or so, when **affirmative action** policies were adopted throughout government.

affirmative action

Special efforts to recruit, hire, and promote members of disadvantaged groups to eliminate the effects of past discrimination.

Affirmative action recognizes that equal opportunity has not been sufficient because employment discrimination persists. Governments must take proactive steps to hire and retain those categories of workers legally defined as "protected classes," who have suffered discrimination in the past. These measures may be adopted voluntarily, but they are required under certain conditions specified by the U.S. Equal Employment Opportunity Commission (EEOC), the regulatory body created to enforce EEO, and, in some instances, by the courts. These measures include goals, timetables, and other preferential selection and promotion devices intended to make the work forces of public and private organizations more representative of the racial, sexual, and other characteristics of the available labor pool.

Under affirmative action, the absence of overt discrimination in employment is not sufficient; organizations may implement preferential hiring and promotion schemes to redress existing imbalances. The legitimacy of affirmative action policies imposed on employers by the EEOC was seriously questioned by a series of U.S. Supreme Court decisions during the past two decades[16] and by state legislative actions and referendums.

Obviously, affirmative action is highly controversial. Establishing specific numerical goals and timetables for hiring and promoting minorities does not necessarily correspond with selection or promotion of the best person for the job. In other words, affirmative action appears to conflict with the merit principle. It has also alienated many white males, who feel that they have become victims of reverse discrimination.

Legal clashes among the federal courts, the Congress, and the states and localities continue but have not produced a coherent interpretation of affirmative action's legal standing. Three examples illustrate the complexity of issues surrounding affirmative action policy. The first concerns a 1992 lawsuit against the University of Texas Law School filed by four white applicants (three men and a woman), who alleged that they had not been admitted despite having LSAT scores higher than those of black and Hispanic applicants who were accepted. The first federal judge to hear this case, in *Hopwood* v. *Texas,*[17] ruled against the white applicants. But on appeal, the Fifth Circuit Court judges agreed that the university had violated the students' constitutional rights. According to the court, the use of race as a selection criterion "is no more rational . . . than would be choices based upon the physical size or blood type of applicants." The Fifth Circuit Court's decision applied to universities in Texas, Louisiana, and Mississippi.

Texas attorney general Dan Morales appealed to the U.S. Supreme Court, which refused to hear the case, thereby keeping the circuit court's ruling in effect. Yet, to Texas's astonishment, the U.S. Department of Education warned the state, in an official letter, that Texas could lose all federal financial aid if it ended its affirmative action programs as ordered by the courts! After a furious reaction by Texas's powerful congressional delegation, the Department of Education backed down.

National confusion and uncertainty about affirmative action are further illustrated by the 1996 passage in California of Proposition 209, which amended the state constitution by prohibiting race and gender consideration in contracting decisions and in hiring for state and local jobs. The initiative was approved by nearly 55 percent of the voters. Soon, however, a federal judge blocked enforcement on the grounds that "Prop 209" was discriminatory and therefore unconstitutional. About six months later, the Ninth Circuit Court of Appeals reinstated the standing of Proposition 209, an action that was upheld by the U.S. Supreme Court. In 1998, Washington voters approved an antidiscrimination initiative, and in 2000 Governor Jeb Bush of Florida eliminated racial preferences in his state through an executive order.

The third recent example of confusion and complexity involves a pair of U.S. Supreme Court rulings in 2003 on admissions procedures at the University of Michigan.[18] The Court invalidated a point system used to select undergraduates that awarded additional points for minority status, but it upheld the law school's consideration of race as a nonquantified "plus" in its admissions decisions.

Despite such confusion and ugly political invective, substantial progress toward representative bureaucracy has been made, especially in recruiting and hiring protected-class individuals for entry-level positions. Granted, minorities and women continue to bump against a "glass ceiling" as they try to penetrate the upper levels of state and local agencies, as well as "glass walls" that restrict their access to certain occupations, agencies, or departments.[19] But gradual progress is being seen even with respect to this final barrier to representative bureaucracy. The number of female city managers rose from 100 in 1986 to some 450 today, and the percentage of Latino professionals in state and local government has grown dramatically in recent years. Female and minority employment at all levels of state and local government exceeds that in the private sector.[20]

Indeed, state and local governments today widely recognize the need to recruit, motivate, and manage a work force that reflects an increasingly diverse general population. When employees working together differ in terms of gender, color, religion, customs, and other characteristics, misunderstandings and miscommunications are inevitable. The astute public manager helps employees recognize and accept such differences while maintaining and even raising levels of organizational productivity and effectiveness.[21]

Sexual Harassment Sexual harassment has long been a problem in public and private employment, but it has only recently gained widespread recognition. Sexual harassment can consist of various behaviors: unwanted touching or other physical contact of a sexual nature, implicit or overt sexual propositions, or (in one of its worst forms) extortion of a subordinate by a supervisor who demands sexual favors in return for a promotion or a raise. A "hostile working environment" that discriminates on the basis of gender also constitutes sexual harassment.[22] Examples in this category include repeated—and unwelcome—leering, sexual joking or teasing, and lewd calendars or photographs at the workplace. Isolated incidents of sexual teasing or innuendo do not constitute sexual harassment.[23] Sexual harassment is illegal according to federal and state law, and it is a form of punishable employee misconduct under civil service rules. It is increasingly being prosecuted in the courts.

Sexual harassment is common in the workplace: Surveys of women reveal that at least half of the respondents report being a victim.[24] Approximately 15 percent of men have experienced sexual harassment. Such behavior subverts the merit principle when personnel decisions such as hiring or promotion are influenced by illegal or discriminatory considerations of a sexual nature, or when an employee cannot perform his or her assigned duties because of sexual harassment. Sexual harassment can exact a significant price on organizational productivity, not to mention the costs of monetary settlements with victims. Unfortunately for the recipient of unwanted sexual attention, there are seldom any witnesses. The matter becomes one person's word against another's. And when one of the parties is the supervisor of the second party, a formal complaint may be decided in favor of the boss.

Much of the official activity aimed at stopping sexual harassment has been concentrated in the states, with local governments rapidly following suit. Michigan was the first to adopt a sexual harassment policy, in 1979; since then, nearly every other state has adopted a statewide sexual harassment policy through legislation or executive order. States offer employee-training programs that help workers and supervisors identify acts of sexual harassment, establish procedures for effectively addressing it, and enforce prompt, appropriate disciplinary action against offenders.

The consequences of sexual harassment go well beyond the personal discomfort, stress, or injury suffered by victims. The problem also results in significant financial costs to organizations whose employees lose productive work time. Such misconduct is unacceptable today in a national work force that is almost 50 percent female.

Unions Nearly always controversial in government, *public-employee unions* present a potentially serious threat to the merit principle. They usually insist on seniority as the primary criterion in personnel decisions, often seek to effect changes in merit-system rules and procedures that benefit their membership, and regularly challenge management authority. Moreover, unions aggressively seek higher pay and benefits, threatening to drive up the costs of government and, in some instances, prompting tax increases.

Until the 1960s, unionization was largely a private-sector phenomenon. Federal legislation protected the rights of workers in industry to organize and engage in **collective bargaining** with their employers over wages, benefits, and working conditions. Workers then organized in record numbers. By the late 1950s, however, private-sector union growth began to decline for a number of reasons, including corporate opposition, the shift in the U.S. economy from manufacturing to services, and the globalization of labor markets.

Unionization in state and local government developed and flourished in the 1960s and 1970s, some thirty years after the heyday of private-sector unions, more than tripling during the 1960s alone. Why the sudden growth? In retrospect, several reasons are apparent.

First, the rise of unionism in government was spurred by the realization by state and local employees that they were underpaid and otherwise maltreated in comparison to their private-sector counterparts, who had progressed so well with unionization and collective bargaining. Second, the bureaucratic and impersonal nature of work in large government organizations encouraged unionization to preserve the dignity of the workers. A third reason for the rise of state and local unionism was the employees' lack of confidence in many civil service systems. Not only were pay and benefits inadequate, but grievance processes were controlled by management, employees had little or no say in setting personnel policies, and merit selection, promotion, and pay were often fraught with management favoritism.

Perhaps most important, the growth of unions in government was promoted by a significant change in the legal environment of labor relations. The rights of state and local employees to join unions and bargain collectively with management were guaranteed by several U.S. Supreme Court rulings, state legislation, local ordinances, and various informal arrangements that became operative

collective bargaining

A formal arrangement in which representatives of labor and management negotiate wages, benefits, and working conditions.

City workers rally at the Oklahoma state capitol in 2005 to support legislation that permits them to engage in collective bargaining.
SOURCE: AP/Wide World Photos.

during the 1960s and 1970s. Wisconsin was the first state to permit collective bargaining for state workers, in 1959. Today, forty-two states specifically allow at least one category of state or local government employees to engage in collective bargaining.

The extent of unionization and collective bargaining is greatest in the states of the Midwest and Northeast—the same areas so fertile for the growth of private-sector unions. A handful of traditionalistic states, including Arizona, Mississippi, Utah, Virginia, and North and South Carolina, continues to resist the incursion of state and local unions (see Figure 8.2). Public employees in these jurisdictions have the legal and constitutional right to join a union, but their government employers do not have a corresponding duty to bargain with them over wages, benefits, or conditions of work.

Approximately 34 percent of state and 46 percent of local government workers belong to unions, compared with only 8 percent of workers in private industry. The highest proportions of union workers are found in education, highways, public welfare, police protection, fire protection, and sanitation.[25]

The surge in the fortunes of state and local unions was partially arrested by the taxpayer revolt of the late 1970s and by President Reagan's successful effort to "bust" a federal air traffic controllers' union. Further resistance to unions developed in the 1990s and continues today as governments downsize and priva-

| FIGURE 8.2 | **Collective Bargaining Rights in the States** |

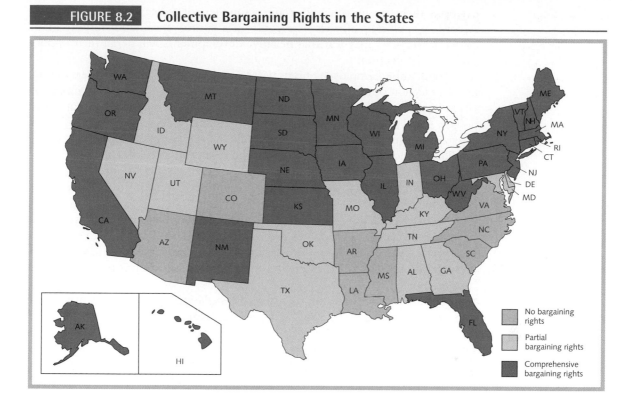

tize, and seek greater efficiencies. Taxpayer resistance has helped stiffen the backbones of public officials, who had been criticized in some jurisdictions for giving the unions too much.

As a result of these factors, unionism in state and local government has leveled off in some jurisdictions and there are tentative signs of reversals in others. However, unions have registered gains in membership in several states in the 2000s and continue their aggressive organizing efforts throughout the United States. Unions will remain an important and highly visible component of many state and local government personnel systems.

What is the impact of collective bargaining in state and local government? Market forces, such as profit levels and the supply and demand for labor, largely determine the outcomes of bargaining between a union and a firm in the private sector. In government, however, political factors are much more important. The technical process of negotiating over wages and other issues in government is very similar to that in business. But the setting makes government labor relations much more complex, mostly because the negotiating process culminates in the political allocation of *public* resources.

Four factors make government labor relations highly political. First, public officials are under greater pressure than private employers to settle labor disputes. Public services are highly visible and often monopolistic in nature; for example, there are no other convenient suppliers of police and fire protection. Accordingly, elected officials who confront a controversial labor dispute in an "essential service" may fear that negative developments will derail their opportunity for re-election.

Second, public-employee unions wield political clout. Their members can influence election outcomes, particularly at the local level. A recalcitrant mayor or city council member who opposes a hefty wage increase may suffer defeat at the polls in the next election if the municipal union members vote as a bloc. Unions actively engage in politics by raising money, writing letters to the editor about candidates, knocking on doors to get out the vote, formally endorsing candidates, or using any of the other electoral techniques employed by interest groups. Many unions have professional lobbyists to represent them at the state capitol or in city hall.

A third politicizing factor in government labor relations is the symbiotic relationship that can develop between unions and elected officials. In exchange for special consideration at the bargaining table and perhaps elsewhere, the unions can offer public officials two valued commodities: labor peace and electoral support.

Finally, a hard-pressed union can use the strike or a related job action (such as a slowdown or a picket line) as a political weapon. In the private sector, a strike is not likely to have widespread public repercussions unless it involves goods or services that the nation relies on for its economic well-being (such as air transportation or communications). In government, however, a strike can directly involve the health and safety of all the citizens of a jurisdiction. For instance, a 2005 strike of 33,700 subway and bus workers left millions of commuters in New York City on street corners and in snarled traffic. A general strike involving police officers, firefighters, and sanitation workers has the potential to turn a city into filthy, life-threatening anarchy. At a minimum, any strike leaves the public inconvenienced. Strikes and other job actions by public employees are illegal in most jurisdictions, although twelve states permit work stoppages by "nonessential" workers under strictly regulated conditions. However, teachers, health care workers, firefighters, and others sometimes walk off the job anyway. The nightmare of a defenseless populace terrorized by acts of violence during a police strike, or by a crazed arsonist during a firefighter strike, has convinced many an elected official to seek prompt settlement of government-labor impasses.

Given these politicizing factors, one might expect unions in government to be extravagantly successful at the bargaining table, but quite the opposite is true Public-employee unions have raised wages and salaries an average of 4 to 8 percent, depending on the service, place, and time period under consideration (for example, teachers earn around 5 percent more, and firefighters around 8 percent more, if represented by a union). These figures are much lower than those representing the union-associated wage impacts that have been identified in the private sector. Greater success has come in the form of better benefits, such as pensions and health care insurance. It should be noted that union-driven wage and benefit hikes in the private sector are absorbed through profits, layoffs, productivity gains, or higher product prices. In government, by contrast, the choices are to raise taxes or fees, cut services, increase productivity, or contract out to a private firm.

Certain personnel impacts have also been associated with collective bargaining in government. Clearly, unions have gained a stronger employee voice in management decision making. All personnel-related issues are potentially negotiable, from employee promotion procedures to retention in the event of a reduction in force. As a result of collective bargaining, many government employers have altered civil service rules, regulations, and procedures. In heavily unionized jurisdictions, two personnel systems coexist uncomfortably—the traditional civil service system and the collective bargaining system.[26] Certainly the rights of public employees have been strengthened by unions.

Generally speaking, governments and collective bargaining have reached an uneasy accommodation. The principle of merit in making human resource management decisions is still largely in place; and it is usually supported strongly by the unions, so long as seniority is fully respected as an employment decision rule. In an increasing number of jurisdictions, unions are cooperating with management to increase productivity in government services through participative decision-making techniques, labor–management partnerships, and worker empowerment programs.

THE POLITICS OF BUREAUCRACY

In an ideal democracy, political officials popularly elected by the people would make all decisions regarding public policy. They would delegate to public administrators in the executive branch the duty of carrying out these decisions through the agencies of state and local government. In the real world of bureaucratic politics, however, the line dividing politics and administration is lightly drawn. Politicians frequently interfere in administrative matters, as when a legislator calls an agency head to task for not hiring a favored constituent. Administrators practice politics at the state capitol and in city hall by participating in and influencing policy formulation decisions.

Joining Administration and Politics

Bureaucrats are intimately involved in making public policy, from the design of legislation to its implementation. Government workers are often the seedbed for policy ideas that grow to become law, in large part because they are more familiar with agency, departmental, and clientele problems and prospective solutions than anyone else in government. It is not unusual, for instance, for law enforcement policy to originate with police administrators or higher-education policy to be the brainchild of university officials.

Once a bill does become law, state and local employees must interpret the language of the legislation to put it into effect. Because most legislation is written in very general terms, civil servants must apply a great deal of **bureaucratic discretion** in planning and delivering services, making rules for service delivery,

bureaucratic discretion

The ability of public employees to make decisions interpreting law and administrative regulations.

adjudicating cases and complaints, and otherwise managing the affairs of government. All states have legal systems for hearing and acting on disputes over agency rules and regulations, such as environmental permits and social service eligibility. These administrative procedures permit individuals, firms, and local governments to challenge agency rules and regulations before an administrative law judge, who issues an order settling the dispute.

In a very real sense, the ultimate success or failure of a public policy depends on the administrators who are responsible for its implementation. Experienced legislators and chief executives understand this, and they bring relevant administrators into the legislative process at a very early stage. The knowledge and expertise of these administrators are invaluable in developing an appropriate policy approach to a specific problem, and their cooperation is essential if a policy enacted into law is to be carried out as the lawmakers intend.

Thus bureaucratic power derives from knowledge, expertise, information, and discretionary authority. It also comes from external sources of support for agency activities—that is, from the chief executive, legislators, and interest groups. Those who receive the benefits of government programs—the clientele, stake-holders, or customers—are also frequently organized into pressure groups. All government programs benefit some interest—agricultural policy for the farm community, tourism policy for the business community, public assistance policy for the poor—and these **clientele groups** often are capable of exerting considerable influence in support of policies that benefit them. Their support is critical for securing the resources necessary to develop and operate a successful government program. They serve as significant political assets to state agencies and municipal and county departments that are seeking new programs or additional funding from legislative and executive bodies, and they can become fearsome political in-fighters when their program interests are threatened.[27] Often, clientele and other concerned interest groups form ad hoc coalitions with relevant government agencies and legislative committees to dominate policymaking and implementation in a particular policy field.

The problem of politics and administration, then, has two dimensions. First, elected officials have the duty of holding administrators responsible for their decisions and accountable to the public interest, as defined by the constitution and by statute. Second, political oversight and intrusion into administrative activities should be minimized so that administrative decisions and actions are grounded in objective rules and procedures—not in the politics of favoritism. For example, legislators have the duty of ensuring that decisions by a state department of environmental protection guard the public from harmful effects of pollution while treating polluting companies fairly. Nevertheless, state representatives should not instruct agency employees to go easy on a favored business constituent. Most government agencies discharge their tasks competently and professionally, and therefore require little direct oversight. Occasionally, however, a rogue agency or department head may strike out in the wrong direction.

An example of the proper balance of politics and administration is the attempt to influence public administrators by legislative officials. This typically occurs when legislators and council members perform casework for members of their constituency. Although the legislator may occasionally seek favorable treat-

clientele group

Groups that benefit from a specific government program, such as contractors and construction firms in state highway department spending programs.

ment that borders on illegality, the bulk of legislative casework comprises responses to citizens' inquiries or complaints, or requests for clarification of administrative regulations. Such legislative casework is useful because it promotes both feedback on the delivery of services and helpful exchanges of information between elected officials and administrators. If inquiries determine bias in the means by which services are being delivered, corrective political actions can be taken.

In sum, state and local politics are intricately joined with administration. Public policy is made and implemented through the interaction of elected officials, interest groups, and public administrators. Nonetheless, the vast majority of administrative decisions are based on the neutral competence and professionalism of public employees.

This is not to say that such decisions are never made on the basis of political favoritism. Sometimes political pressures influence bureaucratic discretion. On the whole, however, state and local services are provided in an unbiased fashion through the application of professional norms and standards.

REINVENTING GOVERNMENT

State and local government employment has burgeoned at a rate much faster than that of population growth. In Texas, for instance, the number of state workers jumped from 223,000 in 1990 to 364,000 in 2007. The total state and local government payroll exceeds about $600 billion per year. Explanations for this huge expansion in the size and costs of government are numerous, including federal mandates, expanding levels of services, partisan politics, and the power of incremental budgeting.

Are the quantity and quality of services better than ever? Not according to most citizens, as we pointed out at the beginning of this chapter. Still, taxpayer ire and criticism of government at all levels seems to have peaked in 2001, when the heroic actions of public employees and military personnel in response to terrorist events helped citizens once again understand the value of public service. Calls for making government more efficient, effective, and responsive have also played a role. Many new strategies are being tried in an effort to solve this quite "vexing puzzle for public administrators since time immemorial"[28] by improving the performance, productivity, and responsiveness of state and local governments.

new public management

An international movement to improve government efficiency and effectiveness through market-based solutions.

The most far-reaching approach is called **new public management,** (NPM) based on a widely read book named *Reinventing Government* by David Osborne and Ted Gaebler.[29] According to NPM proponents, governments today are preoccupied with rules, regulations, and hierarchy; their bureaucracies are bloated, inefficient, and altogether poorly suited for meeting the demands made on them. The solution is for governments to free up managers to tap the powers of entrepreneurialism and market competition to design and provide efficient and effective services to state and local "customers." In short, governments should "steer, not row," by stressing a facilitative or cooperative approach to getting services to citizens rather than delivering all services directly. Among the alternative service-delivery systems are public–private partnerships, volunteerism, voucher plans, and technical assistance. Once transformed, the governments would be enterprising, mission driven, outcome oriented, focused on their customers' needs, and prepared to "do more with less."

Among the formidable obstacles to such profound change in government activities and behavior are labor-intensive tasks such as teaching and policing that do not lend themselves readily to labor-saving technology; rule-bound civil service systems, which tend to discourage management entrepreneurialism and risk taking; the inevitable inertia that plagues public organizations having no bottom line and few market-driven incentives; the difficulties of innovating in organizations created essentially to regulate; the need for politicians to buy into and support the movement, which implies greater autonomy and discretion for administrative agencies, but more risks and more mistakes as well; and the certain opposition by powerful vested interests, such as public-employee unions, that feel threatened by change.

Undeterred by the carping critics and maligning malcontents, many state and local governments have adopted a reinventing attitude in tackling various problems. Principally, they have placed their bets on (1) the privatization of government services, and (2) e-government.

Privatization

Privatization shifts government functions to private or nonprofit organizations through such service arrangements as vouchers, franchises, public–private partnerships, and contracting out. It is a widely heralded reform that garners much support today, especially among conservatives, Republicans, and others who want to see a "businesslike" approach to government. Virtually any government service is a candidate for contracting out (outsourcing), from jails to janitorial work, from teaching to trash collection. (In theory, most government facilities could even be sold to private interests and operated as businesses; airports and bridges are obvious examples.) The purported benefits of privatization include cost savings, higher-quality services, the acquisition of highly specialized skills, and more efficient service delivery. It is a popular strategy for reducing service costs. To date, privatization has been most frequently used to outsource vehicle towing, human resource management tasks, solid waste collection, building maintenance and security, street repair, ambulance services, printing, data processing, and social welfare services.[30]

In choosing the privatization route to reinventing government, Massachusetts has contracted out mental health care, prison health care, various highway maintenance functions, and operations of interstate highway rest stops, among many other functions. Florida has outsourced projects valued at $1.6 billion.[31] Riverside, California, has privatized operations of its public libraries, while Chicago outsources window washing, sewer cleaning, and compost processing. Privately built and operated toll roads and bridges operate in a growing number of states.

Still, privatization isn't as easy as it sounds, and it doesn't guarantee savings.[32] It usually elicits virulent opposition from public-employee unions, who fear the loss of jobs or reductions in pay and benefits. Unless governments carefully negotiate and then monitor the quality and effectiveness of privatized services, performance may decline, and costs may actually rise. Contracts that are vaguely worded or filled with loopholes, and insufficient contract oversight on the part of some jurisdictions, have resulted in cost overruns, shoddy services, and fraud or corruption by the contractors. Successful outsourcing requires not only careful government planning, design, and analysis of what the jurisdiction and its citizens need and want to have done but also a recognition that government accountability cannot be negotiated. The state, county, or city must remember that ultimately *it* will be held accountable for successful, reliable delivery of a service. Successful contract monitoring requires careful inspections, comprehensive performance reports, and assiduous investigations of citizen complaints.[33]

To keep contractors honest, some governments use multiple, competing firms, government agencies, or nonprofit organizations to deliver the same service to different agencies or departments. Arizona state employees, for instance, compete head to head with a national firm in administering public assistance programs. Such collaboration between governments, nonprofit organizations, and private firms saved Indianapolis some $100 million in four years through negotiated arrangements in wastewater treatment, recycling, sewer billing, street sweeping, and many other services.[34]

Is privatization worthwhile? Local officials believe that outsourcing improves service delivery in most cases, and some research suggests that privatization saves cities up to 20 percent for some service categories but little or nothing for others. There are many notable failures of privatization, particularly those involving sweetheart deals and no-bid contracts.[35] It is not a cure-all for the problems besetting states and local governments, but privatization does represent one potentially useful alternative for reinventing government.

E-Government

e-government

The use of information technology to simplify and improve interactions between governments and citizens, firms, and other entities.

E-government involves reinventing, or reengineering, the way a variety of government activities are conducted, and making the face of government more user-friendly. Some improvements are rather mundane and commonsensical. For instance, most states permit online tax filing and renewal of auto licenses and registrations. Chicago, Denver, New York City, and other cities have launched 311 call centers for citizens to report service problems. Other improvements are more futuristic. Arizonans can vote in primary elections on the Web and view live proceedings of the state legislature through "digital democracy." New York City and Washington State have mounted computer-synchronized attacks on crime that electronically track incidents and suspects, spot emerging crime patterns, and coordinate some crime-fighting activities with other state and local jurisdictions. Management of personnel systems has been vastly improved in Wisconsin through online job bulletins, walk-in testing services, and rapid hiring of employees for hard-to-fill positions. Delaware's podcasts allow downloads of breaking state news.

Unmistakably, we are well on the road to electronic government. "Virtual offices" operating through the Internet are establishing convenient, 24-7 connections among citizens, businesses, nonprofit organizations, and their governments. From a home or office personal computer or a conveniently located PC in the neighborhood library or kiosk, citizens can obtain everything from English-language lessons online in Boston to legal aid from "Victor, the cyber-lawyer" in Arizona. Massive filing systems for documents and other hard copy are no longer needed. Instead, paperless offices use imaging technology to scan, store, and access important records of marriages, births, deaths, business licenses, and a host of other documents. Table 8.4 shows state rankings on quality of e-government.

Despite much enthusiastic rhetoric, three hurdles are slowing the diffusion of e-government: the substantial investments required to pay for the computer hardware and trained personnel; the absence of staff expertise; unresolved legal questions of liability, privacy, and security; and the difficulty of integrating soft-

TABLE 8.4   **Overall State E-Govt Ratings, 2006 and 2007**
(2006 ranking in parentheses)

RANK	STATE	RATING OUT OF 100 PTS	RANK	STATE	RATING OUT OF 100 PTS
1.	Delaware	65.6 (44.8)	26.	North Carolina	42.5 (41.9)
2.	Michigan	64.0 (48.5)	27.	Washington	42.4 (45.4)
3.	Maine	62.0 (43.8)	28.	Louisiana	41.9 (40.6)
4.	Kentucky	56.2 (42.9)	29.	Illinois	41.8 (46.9)
5.	Tennessee	54.1 (45.7)	30.	Rhode Island	41.7 (40.6)
6.	Massachusetts	53.8 (42.5)	31.	Colorado	41.7 (36.8)
7.	Maryland	53.5 (39.5)	32.	Iowa	41.1 (42.0)
8.	Texas	51.3 (51.7)	33.	New Hampshire	41.0 (40.1)
9.	New Jersey	50.0 (51.5)	34.	Arizona	40.8 (39.5)
10.	Utah	47.0 (48.1)	35.	Florida	40.8 (41.6)
11.	Montana	46.9 (47.8)	36.	Kansas	40.4 (42.0)
12.	California	46.0 (40.8)	37.	Alaska	40.1 (28.3)
13.	Georgia	45.6 (38.0)	38.	Hawaii	39.5 (35.3)
14.	Oklahoma	44.9 (37.3)	39.	Virginia	39.3 (40.8)
15.	Minnesota	44.4 (44.9)	40.	Idaho	39.1 (40.8)
16.	Indiana	44.4 (46.6)	41.	South Dakota	39.0 (41.1)
17.	Oregon	44.3 (49.1)	42.	Wisconsin	38.4 (36.5)
18.	Nebraska	44.3 (43.6)	43.	Vermont	38.2 (38.6)
19.	Connecticut	44.2 (41.5)	44.	Nevada	38.1 (37.3)
20.	Pennsylvania	43.7 (46.4)	45.	Alabama	37.2 (28.4)
21.	New York	43.5 (47.3)	46.	Arkansas	36.7 (33.8)
22.	Missouri	42.9 (43.0)	47.	Mississippi	33.1 (33.4)
23.	Ohio	42.6 (44.1)	48.	New Mexico	32.9 (34.3)
24.	North Dakota	42.6 (44.9)	49.	West Virginia	31.4 (33.6)
25.	South Carolina	42.5 (44.0)	50.	Wyoming	28.6 (29.0)

SOURCE: Darrell M. West, "State and Federal E-Government in the United States, 2007"accessed September 19, 2007 at www.InsidePolitics.org/egovtdata.html.

ware across multiple agencies and departments. Nevertheless, the potential of e-government to make government more accessible, understandable, and efficient is enormous.[36]

Is New Public Management simply a fad? Definitely not. Responsive states and localities have been reinventing their operations and services ever since they were created, and will continue to do so for as long as they exist. In the short run, some governments will be reinvented, or at least changed in fundamental ways, but others continue to do things the old way. Change is politically risky, and inertia is a powerful force. Ultimately, it is the responsibility of citizens and the elected officials who represent them to bring about change and reforms.

THE QUALITY OF PUBLIC ADMINISTRATION

Despite the quantity of criticism hurled at government agencies, departments, and workers by the popular media, elected officials, and others, the quality of public administration in state and local government has improved markedly. Of course, there is considerable variation among jurisdictions; that capacity is generally of a higher quality in affluent, highly educated, and urban environments.

Results of a study of state government administrative performance are found in Table 8.5. The Government Performance Project, conducted by *Governing*

TABLE 8.5	Rating the States: A Public Administration Report Card				
STATE	**MONEY**	**PEOPLE**	**INFRASTRUCTURE**	**INFORMATION**	**GRADE OVERALL**
Alabama	C	C+	D	C	C–
Alaska	C	C+	C+	C	C+
Arizona	B	B	B–	B–	B
Arkansas	B–	C	C+	C+	C+
California	D	C–	C	C	C–
Colorado	C–	C+	C+	C+	C+
Connecticut	C	B	C+	C–	C+
Delaware	A	B–	B+	B	B+
Florida	C+	B–	B+	B	B–
Georgia	B–	A	C+	B–	B
Hawaii	C	B	C–	D	C
Idaho	B+	B	C+	C+	B–
Illinois	B	C	C+	C+	C+
Indiana	C	C	B–	C	C+
Iowa	B+	B	B	B	B
Kansas	B+	B–	B–	B–	B

(cont. on next page)

TABLE 8.4

STATE	MONEY	PEOPLE	INFRASTRUCTURE	INFORMATION	GRADE OVERALL
Kentucky	B+	B	B+	B	B+
Louisiana	B+	B	C+	A–	B
Maine	B–	B–	B	C+	B–
Maryland	B	B–	A–	C+	B
Massachusetts	C+	C+	C–	C+	C+
Michigan	B	B	B+	B+	B+
Minnesota	A–	B+	B	B+	B+
Mississippi	B–	C+	C+	C+	C+
Missouri	B	B–	B–	A–	B
Montana	C+	C+	B–	C	C+
Nebraska	B+	B–	B+	C+	B
Nevada	C+	C+	B+	B–	B–
New Hampshire	C	C+	C+	C–	C
New Jersey	C+	B	B–	C	B–
New Mexico	B	C+	D+	B	C+
New York	C+	B–	B+	C+	B–
North Carolina	B–	C+	C+	C+	C+
North Dakota	B–	B–	B–	C	B–
Ohio	B+	B–	A–	C+	B
Oklahoma	B–	B–	C–	C	C+
Oregon	D	B–	B	B	C+
Pennsylvania	B+	B–	B+	B	B
Rhode Island	C+	D+	B–	C+	C+
South Carolina	B	B+	A–	C+	B
South Dakota	B+	B–	B	D	B–
Tennessee	B–	C–	B–	C+	C+
Texas	B	B	B–	B	B
Utah	A	B+	A	A–	A–
Vermont	B+	B	B–	B–	B
Virginia	A	A–	A–	A–	A–
Washington	A–	B+	B	A–	B+
West Virginia	B–	C	C	C+	C+
Wisconsin	B–	B	C	B–	B–
Wyoming	B	D+	C	C	C

NOTE: *Definitions:* **Money:** using a long-term perspective to make budget decisions, using a transparent budget process, balancing revenues and expenditures, managing procurement activities, and systematically using financial controls and reporting. **People:** strategic work force planning, effective hiring and retention practices, work force training and development, managing employee performance; **Infrastructure:** capital planning, project monitoring and maintenance, internal coordination; **Information:** strategic policy direction, performance budgeting and management, program evaluation, e-government.
SOURCE: Adapted from "Grading the States," a special of *Governing* (February 2005).

magazine and the Maxwell School of Citizenship and Public Affairs at Syracuse University, examined state performance in managing key administrative areas: money, people, infrastructure, people, and information.

Administrative quality is a critical factor in support of the revitalization and responsiveness of states and localities. State and local governments, particularly through partnerships with private and nonprofit organizations, have the capacity to accomplish more and on a grander scale than ever before; this trend is continuing. The basics of providing services, from disposing of dead animals to delivering healthy human babies, will continue to depend on government employees with high standards of performance and professionalism.

CHAPTER RECAP

- The quality and capacity of public administration have greatly improved in the great majority of the states and local governments.
- State and local government employment has grown rapidly.
- State and local operating budgets must be balanced each year.
- Interest groups, agencies, the chief executive, and the legislative body are the four principal actors in the budgetary process.
- Budgets tend to expand (or contract) incrementally.
- The trend in accounting for revenues and expenditures is performance-based budgeting.
- Most state and local jobs are part of a merit system and are filled based on knowledge, skills, and experience.
- Affirmative action has led to gains in advancement of minorities and women in state and local employment, but it is very controversial.
- States and localities are addressing the problem of sexual harassment in public agencies.
- Unions and collective bargaining present special challenges to many state and local governments.
- Bureaucratic discretion makes public employees important decision makers.
- The NPM movement, aimed at reinventing government through privatization, e-government, and other steps, is a long-term trend.

Key Terms

bureaucracy *(p. 166)*

incrementalism *(p. 174)*

line-item budget *(p. 174)*

performance budgeting *(p. 175)*

capital budget *(p. 175)*

merit system *(p. 176)*

neutral competence *(p. 176)*

affirmative action *(p. 178)*

collective bargaining *(p. 181)*

bureaucratic discretion *(p. 185)*

clientele group *(p. 186)*

new public management *(p. 187)*

e-government *(p. 189)*

Internet Resources

All major municipalities and states have webpages. Many provide links to jobs, NPM initiatives, service-provision information, and other data.

Innovative, award-winning websites include Indianapolis's "Electronic City Hall" at **www.indygov.org;** Service Arizona at **www.servicearizona.ihost.com;** NC@YourService at **www.ncgov.com;** and Delaware's at **www.Delaware.gov.**

An informative public-employee union website is that of the American Federation of State, County and Municipal Employees at **www.afscme.org.**

An Internet-based clearinghouse on GIS is maintained by the Center for Technology in Government at **www.ctg.albany.edu/gisny.html.** Another interesting site on technology and e-government is **www.govtech.net.**

For a step-by-step illustration of a state budget process, see **www.state.ny.us/dob/citizen/process/process.html.**

You can play a budget simulation for New York City at **www.gothamgazette.com/budgetgame.html.**

To view streaming video of public meetings in Indiana, see **www.stream.hoosier.net/cats.**

Information on the Government Performance Project can be found at **www.maxwell.syr.edu/Campbell/gpp.html** and at **www.governing.com.**

The Judiciary

FOCUS QUESTIONS

1. What are the various methods by which state judges are selected?

2. What are the tradeoffs in terms of independence and accountability?

3. Judicial decisionmaking is influenced by what factors?

4. How are states reforming their courts?

*I*n the case of *Barnes* v. *Glen Theatre Inc.* (1991), a prudish U.S. Supreme Court ruled that nude dancing, being dangerous to "order and morality," is not protected as free expression under the First Amendment of the U.S. Constitution. This case, which arose in Indiana, was tried in the federal courts under national constitutional law. But under Ohio's "Eleventh Commandment" of 2007, patrons of strip clubs and the performers themselves are barred from touching "the naughty bits" at the risk of receiving six months in jail and a $1000 fine.[1]

Yet in Boston, a city once known for banning all manner of objects and activities deemed to be immoral, totally naked women grind, bump, and pirouette at tacky cabarets, fully confident that their activities are legal. In Massachusetts, the voluntary display of a naked body has been protected under the *state* constitution as a form of expression since the state supreme court ruled it so in 1984.[2] As the U.S. Supreme Court has become increasingly conservative, from the Chief Justiceship of Earl Warren (1953–1969) to today's Roberts Court, state courts have become more popular with individuals and groups advocating liberal causes such as civil rights, free speech, and freedom of expression. All sorts of conflicts and problems find their way to state and local courts, from the profound (abortion rights) to the profane (nude dancing). And courts at this level are very busy; New York State's cases alone outnumber those filed in all federal courts by a factor of 9 to 1. Many of the state courts are innovative in their decision making and administration; in addition, all are far more accessible to the people and responsive to their concerns than are the federal courts.

State supreme courts sometimes act as policymakers. As the third branch of government, the judiciary is, after all, the final authority on the meaning of the language of laws and constitutions, as well as the ultimate arbiter of disputes between the executive and legislative branches. It also makes public policy through rulings on questions of political, social, and economic significance, and may serve as the last chance for minority interests to defend themselves from the decisions of the majority. As noted in Chapter 3, state courts have become more active policymakers in recent years and have increasingly based important decisions on state constitutions rather than on the national constitution. And as with the other branches of state government, their structures and processes have been greatly reformed and modernized. In our lifetimes, nearly all of us will experience the judicial branch as direct participants. At times, the courts are more accessible to us than are the other branches of government. Disputes that cannot be resolved through ordinary legislative, executive, and political processes frequently wind up before a judge, as litigation.

The work of the fifty state court systems is divided into three major areas: civil, criminal, and administrative. In **civil cases,** one individual or corporation sues another over an alleged wrong. Occasionally, a governmental body is party to a civil action. Typical civil actions are divorces, property disputes, and suits for damages arising from automobile or other accidents. **Criminal cases** involve the breaking of a law by an individual or a corporation. The state is usually the plaintiff; the accused is the defendant. Murder, assault, embezzlement, and disorderly conduct are common examples. **Administrative cases** concern court actions such as probating wills, revoking driver's licenses, or determining custody of a child. Some administrative cases involve administrative law judges and quasi-judicial (less formal) proceedings.

State courts adjudicate (take actions to administer justice) by interpreting state statutes, the state and federal constitutions, and common law. In developing and deciphering the **common law,** courts are concerned with the legal rules and expectations that have developed historically in a state through the citizens' customs, culture, and habits, and that have been given standing through the courts. The most important applications of common law today concern enforcing contracts (contract law), owning and selling property (property law), and establishing liability for death or injuries to people as well as damage to property (tort law).

civil case

A case that concerns a dispute involving individuals or organizations.

criminal case

A case brought by the state against persons accused of violating state law.

administrative case

A case in which a government agency applies rules to settle a legal dispute.

common law

Unwritten law based on tradition, custom, or court decisions.

THE STRUCTURE OF STATE COURT SYSTEMS

State courts have evolved in response to changes in their environment. In colonial days, they developed distinctly, influenced by local customs and beliefs. Owing to a shortage of trained lawyers and an abiding distrust of English law, the first judges were laymen who served on a part-time basis. It did not take long for the courts to become overwhelmed with cases: Case overloads were reported as long ago as 1685.[3] More than three centuries later, case backlogs still plague our state judiciaries.

As the population and the economy grew, so did the amount of litigation. Courts expanded in number and in degree of specialization. However, their development was not carefully planned. Rather, new courts were added to existing structures. The results were predictably complex and confusing, with overlapping, independent jurisdictions and responsibilities. For instance, Chicago offered an astounding array of jurisdictions, estimated at one time to number 556.[4] State court systems were beset as well by a host of other serious problems, including administrative inefficiency, congestion, and excessive delays. In short, the American system of justice left much to be desired.

The organization of the state courts is important because it affects the quality and quantity of judicial decisions and the access of individuals and groups to the legal system. It also influences how legal decisions are made. An efficiently organized system, properly staffed and administered, can do a better job of deciding a larger number of cases than a poorly organized system can. Court structure is of great interest to those who make their living in the halls of justice—namely, lawyers and judges. It can also be an issue of concern to citizens who find themselves in court.

The Two Tiers of Courts

Most states today have a two-tiered court structure: trial courts and appellate courts. There are two types of trial courts: those of limited jurisdiction, and major trial courts. Each tier, or level, has a different *jurisdiction*, or range of authority. **Original jurisdiction** gives courts the power to hear certain types of cases first, in contrast to **appellate jurisdiction**, which gives the courts power to review cases on appeal after they have been tried elsewhere.

Trial courts, which comprise the lower tier, include (1) minor courts of limited jurisdiction and (2) major trial courts of general jurisdiction.

Limited jurisdiction trial courts, also known as special trial courts, handle minor, specialized cases, such as those involving juveniles, traffic offenses, and small claims. Most states have three to five courts of limited jurisdiction, with names that reflect the type of specialized case: traffic court, police court, probate court, municipal court, and so on. Criminal cases here are usually restricted by law to misdemeanor violations of municipal or county ordinances that are punishable by a small fine, a short jail term, or both. Additional courts of limited jurisdiction, sometimes called boutique courts, have been created to deal with special types of cases or circumstances. For example, all states have created drug courts with the dual aims of processing drug-related offenses more efficiently and reducing the recidivism (return to jail or prison) rates of drug offenders on probation or parole. "Water courts" in Colorado and Montana hear disputes over water rights. In Charleston, South Carolina, "Livability Court" convenes regularly to hear complaints against miscreants accused of damaging the quality of life, including parking violators, barking dogs, and homeowners with unkempt lawns.[5]

Present in almost all states are *small-claims courts,* which offer a relatively simple and inexpensive way to settle minor civil disputes without either party

original jurisdiction
The power of a court to hear a case first.

appellate jurisdiction
The power of a court to review cases previously decided by a lower court.

limited jurisdiction trial courts
Courts with original jurisdiction over specialized cases such as juvenile offenses and traffic violations.

having to incur the financial and temporal burdens of lawyers and legal proce-dures. Small-claims courts are usually divisions of county, city, or district trial courts. In the cases they hear, the plaintiff (the person bringing the suit) asks for monetary recompense from the defendant (the individual or firm being sued) for some harm or damage. Claims are limited to varying amounts, usually around $1,000.

The proceedings are informal. Each party presents to a judge the relevant facts and arguments to support her case. The party with the preponderance of evidence on his side wins. Most disputes involve tenant-landlord conflicts, prop-erty damage, or the purchase of goods (for example, shoddy merchandise or the failure of a customer to pay a bill).

major trial court

Court of general jurisdiction that handles major criminal and civil cases.

The second type of trial court is the **major trial court,** which exercises gen-eral authority over civil and criminal cases. Most cases are filed initially under a major trial court's original jurisdiction. However, trial courts also hear cases on appeal from courts of limited jurisdiction. Major trial courts are often organized along county or district lines. Their names—circuit courts, superior courts, dis-trict courts, courts of common pleas—vary widely.

supreme court

The highest state court, beyond which there is no appeal except in cases involving federal law.

intermediate appellate court

A state appellate court that relieves the case burden on the supreme court by hearing certain types of appeals.

The upper tier of the two-tiered state court system consists of appellate courts: **supreme courts** (sometimes called courts of last resort) and, in most states, **intermediate appellate courts.** Oklahoma and Texas have two supreme courts, one for criminal cases and the other for civil disputes. Thirty-eight states have intermediate appellate courts (Alabama, Oklahoma, Oregon, Texas, Penn-sylvania, and Tennessee have two, typically one each for criminal and civil cases). Most intermediate appellate courts are known as courts of appeals. Their work generally involves cases on appeal from lower courts. Thus, these courts exercise appellate jurisdiction. By contrast, state supreme courts have original jurisdic-tion in certain types of cases, such as those dealing with constitutional issues, as well as appellate jurisdiction.

Intermediate appellate courts constitute the most notable change in the structure of the state court system during the past thirty years. They are intended to increase the capability of supreme courts by reducing their caseload burden, speeding up the appellate process, and improving the quality of judicial decision making. The bulk of the evidence points to moderate success in achieving each of these objectives. Case backlogs and delays have been reduced, and supreme court justices are better able to spend an appropriate amount of time on signif-icant cases. Counteracting this positive trend, however, is the growing number of mandatory appeals, such as those for death penalty cases, that make up more than 60 percent of the caseload.

If a state supreme court so chooses, it can have the final word on any state or local case except one involving a national constitutional question, such as First Amendment rights. Some cases can be filed in either federal or state court. For example, a person who assaults and abducts a victim and then transports him across a state line can be charged in state court with assault and in federal court with kidnapping. Some acts violate nearly identical federal and state laws; pos-session or sale of certain illegal drugs is a common example. Other cases fall en-tirely under federal court jurisdiction, such as those involving treason, mail theft, or currency-law violations.

Thus, there exists in the United States a *dual system* of courts that is sometimes referred to as *judicial federalism*. Generally, state courts adjudicate, or decide, matters of state law, whereas federal courts deal with national law. The systems are separate and distinct. In some instances, however, there is jurisdictional overlap and even competition for a case. Following the arrests of Beltway snipers John Muhammad and Lee Malvo in 2003, Virginia, Maryland, and the U.S. Department of Justice all sought to bring the multiple murder case to trial first (six victims were killed in Maryland, three in Virginia, and one in the District of Columbia). Virginia was selected for the initial prosecution.

Although state courts cannot overturn federal law, they can base certain rulings on the federal constitution. Recently, state courts have decided cases governed by both state and federal law in areas such as hate crimes, the right to die, and gay rights. It is very unusual for a case decided by a state supreme court to be heard by the U.S. Supreme Court or any other federal court. An important exception to the custom occurred in the aftermath of the 2000 presidential election, when the U.S. Supreme Court overturned a Florida Supreme Court decision that had ordered a recount of ballots in three counties. The intervention of the nation's highest court effectively awarded the presidency to George W. Bush.

Structural Reforms

The court reform movement that swept across the states in the 1960s and 1970s sought, among other things, to convert the state courts into more rational, efficient, and simplified structures. A driving goal was to increase the capacity and responsiveness of state and local judicial systems. One important legacy of that movement is the *unified court system*.

Oregon State Supreme Court Justice Wallace P. Carson, Jr., speaks to attorneys in a case involving the legality of same-sex marriages. *SOURCE:* AP/Wide World Photos.

Although the two tiers of state courts appear to represent a hierarchy, in fact they do not. Courts in most states operate with a great deal of autonomy. They have their own budgets, hire their own staff, and use their own procedures. Moreover, the decisions of major and specialized trial courts usually stand unchallenged. Only around 5 percent of lower-court cases are appealed, mostly because great expense and years of waiting are certain to be involved.

Unified court systems consolidate the various trial courts with overlapping jurisdictions into a single administrative unit and clearly specify each court's purpose and jurisdiction. The aim of this arrangement, which includes centralized management and rule making, is to make the work of the courts more efficient, saving time and money and avoiding confusion. Instead of a system whereby each judge runs her own fiefdom, such responsibilities as rule making, record-keeping, budgeting, and personnel management are standardized and centralized, usually under the authority of the state supreme court.

Centralization relieves judges from the mundane tasks of day-to-day court management so that they can concentrate on adjudication. Additional efficiencies are gained from *offices of court administration,* which exist in all states. Court administration in an increasing number of states involves actively managing, monitoring, and planning the courts' resources and operations.

Information technology is permitting tremendous improvements in how the courts manage criminal cases. In Los Angeles County, which has the largest local government justice system in the country, a Consolidated Criminal History Reporting System, called "Cheers," consolidates the databases of fifty law enforcement agencies, twenty-one prosecutor's offices, twenty-four municipal courts, and sixty-two other authorities. Judges and other law enforcement authorities have instant access to case histories of defendants, as well as to computerized fingerprint-matching technology.[6] Responsiveness to the public is also growing. An increasing number of state courts are electronically disseminating court documents, judicial rulings, and general information such as instructions for jury duty, maps showing directions to the courthouse, and answers to commonly asked questions about the courts. Some display photographs and biographies of judges, many permit interested citizens to ask questions via e-mail, and others even provide performance evaluations of judges and broadcast cases live over the Internet.[7] (See "Internet Resources" at the end of the chapter.)

Despite consolidation and centralization, court structures and processes continue to vary widely among the states, as shown in Figure 9.1. Generally, the most modern systems are found in the "newer" states, including Alaska and Hawaii, while some of the most antiquated are situated in southern states, among them Arkansas and Georgia.

HOW JUDGES ARE SELECTED

In large part, the quality of a state court system depends on the selection of competent, well-trained judges. According to the American Bar Association (ABA), the leading professional organization for lawyers, judges should be

| FIGURE 9.1 | **Simplicity and Complexity in State Court Systems** |

State court systems can vary from the simple to the very complex, as illustrated by Alaska and Georgia.

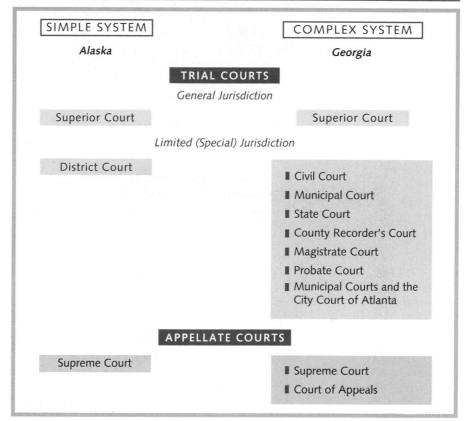

| SIMPLE SYSTEM | COMPLEX SYSTEM |
| *Alaska* | *Georgia* |

TRIAL COURTS

General Jurisdiction

| Superior Court | Superior Court |

Limited (Special) Jurisdiction

| District Court | ▮ Civil Court
▮ Municipal Court
▮ State Court
▮ County Recorder's Court
▮ Magistrate Court
▮ Probate Court
▮ Municipal Courts and the City Court of Atlanta |

APPELLATE COURTS

| Supreme Court | ▮ Supreme Court
▮ Court of Appeals |

SOURCE: State Court Organization, 1998. Washington D.C.: U.S. Bureau of Justice Statistics.

chosen on the basis of solid professional and personal qualifications, regardless of their political views and party identification. Judges should have "superior self-discipline, moral courage, and sound judgment."[8] They should be good listeners, broadly educated, and professionally qualified as lawyers. An appellate or general trial court judge should also have relevant experience in a lower court or as a courtroom attorney.

For a great many years, however, controversy has swirled over the selection of state judges. Should they be elected by popular vote? Should they be appointed by the governor? By the legislature? Many critics insist that judicial selection be free from politics and interest-group influences. Others claim that judges should regularly be held accountable to a majority of the people or to elected officials for their decisions.

The conflict between judicial independence and accountability is manifest in the types of selection systems used in the states: legislative selection, partisan popular election, nonpartisan popular election, the merit plan, and gubernatorial appointment. Most states use a single selection system for all appellate and

FIGURE 9.2   **Appellate and Major Trial Court Selection Plans**

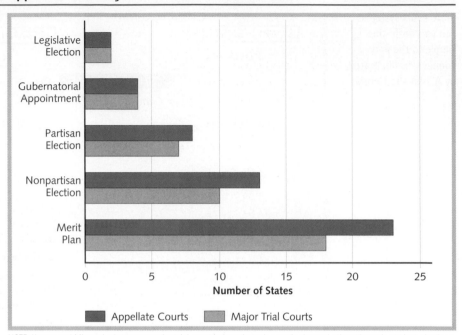

NOTE: Kansas and Missouri select some major trial court judges through a merit plan and others through partisan elections.
SOURCE: Adapted from Council of State Governments, *Book of the States*, vol. 39 (Lexington, KY: Council of State Governments, 2007): 263.

major trial court judges. The others take separate approaches to selecting judges, depending on the tier. Figure 9.2 shows the popularity of these selection techniques for appellate and major trial courts. Some states have rather elaborate systems. Oklahoma, for example, utilizes a merit plan for the supreme court and court of criminal appeals, nonpartisan elections for its other appellate courts and district courts, and city council appointment of municipal judges.

Legislative Selection

In South Carolina and Virginia, the legislature elects judges by majority vote from among announced candidates. Not surprisingly, the vast majority of judges selected under this plan are former legislators (in South Carolina, the proportion has been close to 100 percent).[9] In these two states, a judgeship is viewed as a highly valued reward for public service and a prestigious cap to a legislative career.

Few people other than legislators approve of legislative election. Indeed, the method is open to criticism. The public has no role in either choosing judges or re-electing them, so democratic accountability is minimal. The judges may be independent, but since the major criterion for selection is service as a legislator, they often lack other qualifications. Legislative service has little connection to the demands of a judgeship.

Popular Election

Judges on one or more courts face elections in thirty-nine states. Some are listed on the ballot by party identification; others are not. In theory, elections maximize the value of judicial accountability to the people. Judges must run for office on the same ticket as candidates for other state offices. Like other candidates, they must raise and spend money for their election campaigns and publicly engage political issues.

Partisan Popular Election This plan enjoyed enormous popularity during the Jacksonian era as a way to create a judiciary answerable to the voters. Most of the partisan election states are located in the South. In theory, partisan elections maximize the value of judicial accountability to the people.

Nonpartisan Popular Election This plan won favor during the first half of the twentieth century, when reformers sought to eliminate party identification in the election of judges and certain other officials in state and local government. Political parties are prohibited from openly taking sides in nonpartisan judicial elections. In reality, they sometimes play a covert role in such contests. The vast majority of judges have a political party preference. Most list it in the official biographies that are available to interested voters during campaigns. A disadvantage of nonpartisan popular elections is that they tend to reduce voter participation because incumbent judges are less likely to be challenged and party identification is an important voting cue for many citizens.

The Problems with Popular Elections Voter turnout is very low in many judicial elections, whether partisan or nonpartisan. This fact is a major criticism of both methods of electing judges: The winners may not be truly accountable to the people, which is the principal advantage commonly associated with elections. Low rates of voter interest and participation frequently combine with low-key, unexciting, and issueless campaigns to keep many incumbent judges on the bench as long as they run for re-election. One recent study indicates that less than 10 percent are defeated.[10] Still, this is comparable to state legislative races. And research finds that the electorate can be mobilized by candidates or circumstances in individual states.[11] In the 2000s, judges have been more vulnerable to defeat, particularly in partisan states.

Two more problems have become increasingly troublesome: the politicization of judicial races and the creeping realization that campaign donations influence decisions from the bench. The American Bar Association Code of Judicial Conduct forbids judicial campaigning on legal issues, but this prohibition is increasingly overlooked in close contests and in elections where crime-related concerns, such as the death penalty or an accused murderer freed on a legal technicality, claim voters' attention. As in other electoral contests, negative campaigning is on the rise in judicial elections. Judicial candidates today energetically sling mud at their opponents for allegedly letting drug dealers free, being corrupt or lazy, and acting soft on crime. Several states have moved to restrict aggressive judicial politicking through new ethics rules and other limitations. When challenged in federal courts, however, such restrictions are usually overturned as intrusions on the candidates' First Amendment rights to free speech.[12]

Even more serious is the problem that occurs when judges elected on a partisan ballot are accused of pandering to special interests during election campaigns and of favoring them in court decisions. In Texas, for instance, supreme court justices deciding a $10.5 billion judgment against Texaco in favor of Pennzoil were criticized for accepting huge campaign contributions from both parties. In some recent Ohio supreme court rulings all seven justices have accepted campaign money from lawyers for the plaintiffs or defendants.[13] Nonpartisan elected judges have been open to similar charges, especially because political action committees (PACs) have boosted their contributions to candidates for state court judgeships. Recent research has found systematic empirical evidence that judicial decisions have followed dollars. Similar conclusions have been drawn from research on judicial decision making in Alabama and Ohio.[14]

In addition, popular elections are criticized for the growing amount of money necessary to win a state judgeship. In some cases, the implication is that judges have sacrificed their independence and professionalism for crass electoral politics. Following the trend set in executive and legislative contests, judicial campaign spending surged to $34.4 million in 2006 in states that elect judges.[15] In a heated 2004 race for an Illinois Supreme Court seat, two candidates spent about $4.5 million each. The geographical district in which they ran (it was not a statewide contest) had experienced high-profile personal injury and product liability litigation, including a $10.1 billion product liability award against Phillip Morris Tobacco Company. The largest campaign contributors are usually trial lawyers, corporations, and corporate lawyers, and other groups with an interest in judges' decisions, such as labor unions, business interests desiring to limit the amount of jury awards through tort reform, and various professions, such as insurance or medicine.[16]In some states, attorneys allege that judges "shake them down" for campaign contributions.[17] A supreme court justice was brought down in West Virginia largely through the efforts of a CEO, who, with a pending lawsuit before an unfriendly judge, invested $2.3 million in that judge's opponent.[18]

It looks as though judges running for election are forfeiting their independence in certain legal disputes while offering accountability only to the highest bidders instead of to the general public. If indeed, justice is for rent, neither independence nor accountability is achieved and faith in the legal system is being eroded. According to the president of the Ohio State Bar Association, "The people with money to spend who are affected by court decisions have reached the conclusion that it's a lot cheaper to buy a judge than a governor or an entire legislature, and he can probably do a lot more for you."[19] The sentiment is supported by recent research showing a positive correlation between campaign contributions and judges' decisions.[20]

If it is unethical for a judge to rule on a case in which he or she has accepted money from one or more of the interested parties, then it would be difficult to bring together enough judges to hear cases in some states. Increasingly, the general sentiment is that judges should be both qualified and dignified, and that elections do not further either objective. North Carolina and Wisconsin have launched public financing for judges' campaigns to help contain spiraling costs. Other states are imposing spending restrictions and penalties for false campaign advertising.[21]

Merit Plan

Dissatisfaction with the other methods for selecting judges has led to the popularity of the so-called *merit plan*. Incorporating elements of gubernatorial appointment and elective systems, the merit plan attempts to provide a mechanism for appointing qualified candidates to the bench while permitting the public to evaluate a judge's performance through the ballot box.

First recommended by the ABA in 1937 and strongly supported today by virtually the entire legal community, the merit plan has been adopted by nearly all of the states that have changed their selection systems since 1940. Missouri became the initial adopter in that year. Since then another twenty-three states have adopted the merit plan, and others are considering merit selection.

Three Steps Commonly referred to as the Missouri Plan, the basic merit plan involves three steps:

1. A judicial nominating commission meets and recommends three (or more) names of prospective judges to the governor. Members of this bipartisan commission usually include a sitting judge (often the chief justice), representatives chosen by the state bar association, and laypersons appointed by the governor. The nominating commission solicits names of candidates, investigates them, chooses those it believes to be the best-qualified individuals, and then forwards their names and files to the governor.
2. The governor appoints the preferred candidate to the vacant judgeship.
3. A retention election is held, usually after one or two years, in which the newly appointed judge's name is placed before the voters on a nonpartisan ticket. The voters decide whether or not the judge should be retained in office. If she is rejected by a majority vote, the judicial nominating commission begins its work anew. Subsequent retention elections may be held every eight or twelve years, depending on the merit plan's provision.

Various hybrids of the basic plan are also in use. For example, the California Plan for choosing appellate judges begins when the governor identifies a candidate for a vacancy on the bench and sends that person's name to the Commission on Judicial Appointments. The commission, composed of two judges and the attorney general, hears testimony regarding the nominee and votes to confirm or reject. The new judge is then accepted or rejected in a retention election in the next regularly scheduled gubernatorial contest. Thus, although the governor appoints, the new judge is subject to confirmation by both the Commission on Judicial Appointments and the voters. In New Mexico's multistage merit plan, a judge is nominated by a commission and appointed by the governor. During the next general election the judge must run in a partisan election.

If she wins, she must run unopposed in a nonpartisan retention election on the next general-election ballot.

The object of the merit plan is to permit the governor some appointive discretion while removing politics from the selection of judges. If it works as intended, election or direct gubernatorial appointment is replaced with a careful appraisal of candidates' professional qualifications by an objective commission. The process is intended to ensure both the basic independence of judges and their accountability to the people.

The Politics of Merit Selection The merit plan looks great on paper, but in practice it has not fulfilled its promise. First, it certainly has not dislodged politics from judicial selection. A judgeship is too important a political office in any state ever to be immune from politics. It is a prized job and an important point of judicial access for numerous individuals, firms, and interest groups, especially the powerful state bar association.

Studies of judicial nominating commissions show that politics—partisan and otherwise—is rampant in the review and nomination of candidates.[22] For better or worse, the legal profession often dominates the process. Counting the judge who presides over the nominating commission, lawyers make up a commission majority in most of the states. Bar association lobbying is often the prime reason that merit plans are adopted in the first place. However, the legal profession is not monolithic in its politics, often dividing into two camps: plaintiff's attorneys and defendant's attorneys.

Furthermore, governors' influence can be exceptionally strong. The laypersons he appoints to the nominating commission may hold the judge in awe, but they are there to represent the governor's point of view and sometimes to promote specific candidates or the agenda of the governor's political party. The member who is a judge may also respect the governor's preferences, particularly if he owes his appointment to that chief executive.

A second criticism of the merit plan is that the procedure intended to ensure judicial accountability to the people—the retention election—rarely generates voter interest and seldom results in the departure of an incumbent judge from office. Turnout in retention elections is normally very low and, on average, favors the incumbent by more than 70 percent.[23] Few incumbent judges have been voted out in retention elections—only a handful in sixty years. In most cases, then, merit selection essentially means a lifetime appointment.

However, voter backlashes have occurred against judges whose decisions are distinctly out of step with public opinion. In 1986, California Chief Justice Rose Bird and two associate justices were swept from the state supreme court by large margins in retention elections, as voters reacted negatively to a series of supreme court rulings that significantly expanded the rights of the accused and of convicted felons. Bird had voted to overturn all sixty-one capital punishment cases brought to the court during a period when polls showed 80 percent support for the death penalty in California.[24] Ten years later, Tennessee Supreme Court Justice Penny White was rejected in a retention election for failing to support the death penalty for the perpetrator of a particularly heinous crime.[25]

The final charge leveled against the merit plan is that despite reformers' claims to the contrary, it does not result in the appointment of better-qualified judges or of more women and minorities. When background, education, experience, and decision making are taken into account, judges selected through the merit plan are comparable to those selected through other plans. A large majority are white males. Most leave private practice for the bench in their forties and stay there until retirement. Approximately 20 percent come from a family in which the father or grandfather held political office (often a judgeship).[26] And a substantial majority were born, raised, and educated in the state in which they serve.

Gubernatorial Appointment

All gubernatorial appointment states are former colonies, reflecting the early popularity of the plan. As a method per se, gubernatorial appointment rates fairly high on independence, since the judge is appointed without an election; but it is weak on accountability because the judge is directly beholden to only one person for his or her job.

Although only four states formally recognize it, gubernatorial appointment is in fact the most common method for selecting a majority of appellate and major trial court judges in the United States. Judges in states with popular elections or merit plans often resign or retire from office just before the end of their term.[27] Under most state legal systems, the governor has the power to make interim appointments to vacant seats until the next scheduled election or the commencement of merit-plan selection processes. The governor's temporary appointee then enjoys the tremendous advantage of running as an incumbent for the next full term. Gubernatorial appointment is also used to replace a judge who dies before the expiration of the term.

What criteria does a governor apply in making appointments to the bench? Political considerations usually come first. The governor can use the appointment to reward a faithful legislator, to shore up support in certain regions of the state, to satisfy the demands of party leaders and the state legal establishment, or to appeal to women's or minority groups.[28]

Which Selection Plan Is Best?

The ongoing debate over which selection plan best achieves a healthy balance of (1) judicial independence from interest groups, attorney organizations, and other influences and (2) accountability to the people is unlikely to be settled. Legislative selection and gubernatorial appointment probably maximize the value of judicial independence, but may be the least desirable; judges selected under these systems tend to come from a rather specific political occupation (the legislature), and the general public has little opportunity to hold them accountable. Judicial accountability is maximized when judges and judicial candidates must face voters, but few incumbents are defeated in elections. However, significant policy issues involving the courts can rouse voters to the polls in certain instances, meaning that elected judges who want to stay on the bench must pay attention to public opinion.

None of the judicial selection systems produces "better" judges, although gubernatorial appointment is more likely to benefit women than the other selection systems are.[29] And minorities have not done well under any selection plan. Latinos and African Americans fill fewer than 5 percent of state court seats. Gubernatorial appointment and legislative election apparently increase the selection opportunities for African American judges, but significant gains probably await the development of a larger pool of Latino and black attorneys.

Politics, of course, is what raises all judges into office, regardless of the selection method. According to research by political scientists, what matters is the path a judge takes to the bench. Those chosen through elective systems tend to view the judiciary through a more political—as opposed to juridical—lens than do those who reach the bench through gubernatorial or merit appointment systems. Elected judges also tend to be more activist in their decision making, and they are more likely to dissent from other judges in their opinions than are appointed judges.[30] Voter preferences carry extra weight in the decision making of judges facing competitive elections, particularly with respect to issues of criminal justice, abortion rights, and same-sex marriage. Those in merit-plan states have less to fear from an angry minority in the electorate; they can be guided more by personal ideological preferences and their interpretation of the law.

In other words, judges who attain their jobs through electoral politics tend to behave like elected officials in the executive and legislative branches of state government by emphasizing political—rather than legal—factors in their decision making.[31] The irony is that voters prefer to elect their judges but they fear that campaign contributions influence what judges decide in court.[32]

Removal of Judges

Like anyone else, judges can and do break the law, go mad, suffer senility, or become physically incapable of carrying out their responsibilities. If a judge displays serious deficiencies, he must be removed from the bench. Forty-five states provide for impeachment, wherein charges are filed in the state house of representatives and a trial is conducted in the senate. Other traditional means for removing justices include the legislative address and popular recall. In the legislative address, both houses of the legislature by two-thirds vote must ask the governor to dismiss a judge. Popular recall requires a specified number of registered voters to petition for a special election to recall the judge before the term has expired. Angry Nevada voters attempted to recall six supreme court justices in 2003 for ruling invalid a popular tax limitation initiative. But these traditional mechanisms are cumbersome and uncertain, and hence seldom successful.

Today, states generally use more practical methods to remove judges. Problems related to senility and old age are avoided in at least thirty-seven states by a mandatory retirement age (generally seventy years) or by the forfeiture of pensions for judges serving beyond the retirement age. Such measures have the added benefit of opening up the courtrooms to new, and younger, judges, even in situations where advancing age does not impair performance.

Most states have established special entities to address behavioral problems. *Courts of the judiciary,* whose members are all judges, and *judicial discipline and removal commissions,* composed of judges, lawyers, and laypersons, are authorized to investigate complaints about judges' qualifications, conduct, or fitness. These entities may reject allegations if they are unfounded, privately warn a judge if the charges are not serious, or hold formal hearings. Hearings may result in dismissal of the charges, recommendation for early retirement, or, in some states, outright suspension or removal.

The discipline, suspension, or removal of state court judges is uncommon, but it becomes necessary in all states at one time or another. Judges have been found guilty of drunkenness and drug abuse; sexual misconduct with witnesses and defendants; soliciting and accepting bribes; buying and selling verdicts; and just about every other kind of misconduct imaginable. Sometimes judicial ethics seems to be in seriously short supply. In Rhode Island, a state seldom celebrated as a paragon of political virtue, two consecutive supreme court chief justices vacated the bench when faced with impeachment. One resigned in 1986 following allegations and testimony that he associated with criminals and had adulterous relations with two women in a Mafia-linked motel—among other things. And in 1994, another pleaded guilty to fixing friends and relatives' speeding tickets, using court money to pay for personal expenses, assigning $45,000 in court work to a legal partner, and ordering his secretary to destroy financial records.[33] In 2003, Alabama Chief Justice Roy Moore was removed by the Court of the Judiciary for defying federal court orders to remove a 2½-ton Ten Commandments monument he had installed in the state judicial building.

JUDICIAL DECISIONMAKING

What factors influence the rulings of state court judges? Why are some courts widely recognized as liberal (California and Hawaii) and others as conservative (Arizona and Mississippi)? Why does a prosecutor "judge shop" and prefer to file a case before one judge rather than another? Isn't justice supposed to be blind, like its symbol of the woman holding the scales?

Judges, alas, are mortal beings just like the rest of us. The legal formalities and jargon of the courtroom tend to mask the fact that judges' decisions are no less discretionary and subjective than the decisions of a governor, legislator, or agency head. Before we examine the factors that affect judicial decision making, however, we must distinguish between the legal settings of appellate courts and trial courts.

In and Out of the Trial Court

plea bargaining

Negotiation between a prosecutor and a criminal defendant's counsel that results in the defendant's pleading guilty to a lesser charge or pleading guilty in exchange for a reduced sentence.

Approximately 90 percent of all civil and criminal cases are actually resolved outside of the courtroom. In many civil cases, the defendant never appears in court to defend himself, thereby implicitly admitting guilt, and so loses the case by default. Other civil cases are settled in a pretrial conference between the defendant and the plaintiff (where, for instance, payments on an overdue debt might be rescheduled) or through voluntary dispute resolution procedures.

The process of settling criminal cases out of court at the discretion of the prosecutor and the judge is called **plea bargaining.** Although some defendants plead guilty as originally charged, acknowledging guilt for a lesser charge is more typical in criminal proceedings. With the possible exceptions of the victim and the general citizenry, everyone benefits from plea bargaining, a fact that accounts for its extensive use. The accused gets off with lighter punishment than she would face if the case went to trial and she lost. The defense attorney frees up time to take on additional legal work. The prosecuting attorney increases his conviction rate, which looks good if he has political ambitions. The judge helps cut back the number of cases awaiting trial. Even police officers benefit by not having to spend time testifying (and waiting to testify) and by raising the department's clearance rate (the number of cases solved and disposed of).

Out-of-court settlements through plea bargaining are negotiated in a very informal atmosphere in the judge's chamber, or between attorneys in the halls of the court building, or over drinks in a neighboring pub. This is a disturbingly casual way to dispense justice. The process is secretive and far removed from any notion of due process. The prosecuting (district) attorney enjoys enormous discretion in making deals. Often her propensity to settle depends on the length of her court docket or her professional relationship with the accused's attorney, not on the merits of the case. All too often, an innocent person pleads guilty to a lesser offense for fear of being wrongly convicted of a more serious offense, or because he cannot post bail and doesn't want to spend any unnecessary time behind bars. Equally disturbing—particularly to a victim—is the fact that plea bargaining can soon put a guilty person back on the streets, perhaps to search for another victim.

Nonetheless, plea bargaining is widely practiced. It is almost inevitable when the prosecutor's case hinges on weak evidence, police errors, a questionable witness, or the possibility of catching a bigger fish. Negotiation of a guilty plea for a lesser offense can occur at any stage of the criminal justice process.

If the accused is unable to reach a compromise with the prosecuting attorney, he faces either a **bench trial** by a single judge or a **trial by jury.** Both involve a courtroom hearing with all the legal formalities. In some jurisdictions and for certain types of cases, the defendant has a choice. In other situations, state legal procedures specify which trial format will be utilized. A jury is always mandatory for murder cases.

In a bench trial, the judge alone hears all arguments, determines the facts, and makes rulings on questions of law. Jury trials depend on a panel of citizens who decide the facts of the case; the judge instructs the jury on the applicable law. Although juries and judges would usually come to identical decisions, the uncertainty introduced by twelve laypersons is usually great enough to convince a defendant to choose a bench trial. Only 2 percent of all cases are resolved by jury trial.[34]

Attorneys seek to limit the unpredictable nature of juries by extensively questioning individuals in the jury pool. Each side in the dispute has the right to strike the names of a certain number of potential jurors without giving a specific reason. Others are eliminated for cause, such as personal knowledge of the case or its principals. In high-stakes cases, the jury selection process involves public opinion surveys, individual background investigations of potential jurors, and other costly techniques.

bench trial
A trial by a single judge, without a jury.

trial by jury
A trial in which a jury decides the facts and makes a finding of guilty or not guilty.

Inside the Appellate Court

Appellate courts are substantially different from trial courts. No plaintiffs, defendants, or witnesses are present. The appeal consists of a review of court records and arguments directed by the attorneys, who frequently are not the same lawyers who originally represented the parties. Appellate court rulings are issued by a panel of at least three judges, who decide if legal errors have occurred. Unlike decisions in most trial courts, appellate court decisions are written and published. The majority vote prevails. Judges voting in the minority have the right to make a formal, written dissent that justifies their opinion.

State supreme courts vary dramatically in ideology. The supreme courts in Hawaii, Rhode Island, and Maryland are much more liberal than those in Arizona, Mississippi, and New Hampshire. There is marked variation in the dissent rates of state appellate courts. Some courts maintain a public aura of consensus on even the most controversial matters by almost always publishing unanimous opinions. Justices may disagree, but they do not necessarily dissent. Other courts are racked by public disputes over legal questions. Personal, professional, partisan, political, and other disagreements can escalate into open hostility over casework. As an Illinois chief justice has observed, "dissents are born not of doubt but of firm convictions." Supreme courts in states such as California, New York, Michigan, and Mississippi have a history of contentiousness, whereas others, like those in Rhode Island and Maryland, are paragons of harmony. Dissent rates appear to be positively related to state socioeconomic and political complexity, such as urbanization and partisan competition. More dissent occurs in courts with a large number of justices and in states with intermediate appellate courts. The more time the justices have at their disposal, the more likely they are to find reasons to disagree.

Influence of the Legal System

In addition to the facts of the case itself, judicial decision making is influenced by factors associated with the legal system, including institutional arrangements, accepted legal procedures, caseload pressures, and the ease with which certain interested parties gain access to the legal process.

Institutional Arrangements The level, or tier, of court is a structural characteristic that influences decision making. Trial court judges enforce legal norms and routinely *apply* the law as it has been written and interpreted over the years. The trial court permits direct interpersonal contacts among the judge, the jury, and the parties (usually individuals and small businesses). Divorce cases, personal injury cases, and minor criminal cases predominate in trial courts.

Appellate courts are more apt to interpret the law and create public policy. Cases typically involve governments and large corporations. State constitutional issues, state–local conflicts, and challenges to government regulation of business are the kinds of issues likely to be found in appellate courts. A particular case in a high court sometimes has an enormous impact on public policy, as judges depart from established precedent or offer new interpretations of the law. In 2003, the supreme court of Wisconsin essentially overturned a 1998 constitutional amendment guaranteeing the right to carry a concealed weapon; the Massachusetts supreme court legalized same-sex marriages; and Nevada's highest court nullified a state constitutional provision that two-thirds of the legislature had to approve a tax increase. Florida's supreme court struck down an education voucher system in 2006, and New Jersey's instructed the legislature to recognize gay marriages.

Another important institutional arrangement is the selection procedures for judges. For instance, judicial decisions may be influenced by partisan electoral competition. Especially when a judge facing re-election votes on an issue highly salient to voters, public opinion can affect the judge's ruling.[35] Death penalty cases provide a good example of this point. A study of judicial decision making in Texas, North Carolina, Louisiana, and Kentucky found that judges seeking re-election tend to uphold death sentences. In these traditionally conservative states, a decision in support of the death penalty helps to avoid pre-election criticism from political opponents.[36]

precedent

The legal principle that previous court decisions should be applied to future decisions.

Legal Procedures and Precedent On the basis of **precedent,** the principles and procedures of law applied in one situation are applied in any similar situation. In addition, lower courts are supposed to follow the precedents established by higher courts. An individual decision may seem unimportant, but when it is taken in the context of other, similar cases it helps judicial policy evolve. Through this practice, the doctrine of equal treatment before the law is pursued. When lower-court judges refuse to follow precedent or are ignorant of it, their decisions can be overturned on appeal. Of course, conflicting precedents may relate to a case; in such instances, a judge is permitted to choose among them in justifying his ruling A previous ruling may become obsolete, may be manifestly absurd, or may simply clash with a judge's values or points of view.

Where do judges look to find existing precedent? Within a state, supreme court decisions set the norms. Supreme courts themselves, however, must scan the legal landscape beyond state boundaries. In the past, decisions of the U.S. Supreme Court heavily influenced those of the state supreme courts. Increasingly, however, state supreme courts are practicing doctrinal diversity and looking to one another for precedent. State appellate judges borrow from the experiences of other states. They especially tend to rely on the more professional, prestigious supreme courts, such as those of Massachusetts and New York. State courts also tend to "network" with courts in the same region of the country, where cultural and other environmental factors are similar.[37]

Caseload Pressures Caseload affects the decisions of judges. The number of cases varies in accordance with crime rates, socioeconomic characteristics of the jurisdictions, state laws, the number of judges, and many other variables. It stands to reason that the quality of judicial decision making is inversely related to caseload. Judges burdened by too much litigation are hard-pressed to devote an adequate amount of time and attention to each case before them.

Access to the System The final legal-system characteristic affecting judicial decisions is the access of individuals, organizations, and groups to the court system. Wealthy people and businesses are better able to pay for resources (attorneys, legal research, alternative dispute settlement, etc.) and therefore enter the legal system with a great advantage over poorer litigants. Special-interest groups also enjoy certain advantages in influencing judicial decisions. (Perhaps this helps account for why African Americans and Latino defendants tend to receive harsher sentences than white defendants.)[38] They often have specialized knowledge in areas of litigation, such as environmental or business regulation. Lobbying by interest groups is much less prominent in the judicial branch than in the legislative and executive branches, but groups can affect outcomes by providing financial aid to litigants in important cases, by filing amicus curiae (friend of the court) briefs supporting one side or the other in a dispute, or, in popular election systems, making monetary contributions to a judge's re-election campaign.

The states have implemented several reforms to increase access to the judicial system for those who are disadvantaged. For example, court interpreter training is now available in states with large Latino populations. Physical and communication barriers are being removed so that persons with disabilities can fully participate in all aspects of the legal system. Racial, ethnic, and gender biases against attorneys, plaintiffs, defendants, witnesses, and other court participants are being addressed (although women tend to receive less severe sentences than men who commit similar crimes).[39] Night courts remain open past closing hours for people who have difficulty getting off their day jobs to appear in court. And daycare is being provided for children of plaintiffs, defendants, witnesses, and jurors. Gradually, the state courts are responding to changes in the nature of society.

Personal Values, Attitudes, and Characteristics of Judges

Simply put, judges do not think and act alike. Each is a product of his or her individual background and experiences, which in turn influence decisions made in the courtroom. Studies of state court justices have found that decisions are related to the judges' party identification, political ideology, prior careers, religion, color, age, and sex. In other words, personal characteristics predispose a judge to decide cases in certain ways.

For example, Democratic judges tend to favor the claimant in civil rights cases, the injured party in liability (tort) cases, the government in tax disputes, the employee in worker's compensation cases, the government in business regulation cases, the defendant in criminal contests, the union in disagreements with management, and the tenant in landlord–tenant cases. Republicans tend to support the opposite side on all these issues. Female judges, who presently occupy one of every four state supreme court seats, are more supportive of women on sex discrimination and other feminist issues, more likely to favor the accused in death penalty and obscenity cases, and, in general, are more liberal than their male colleagues.[40] And, finally, the judge's race appears to have little effect on the sentences handed down to black and white defendants, although according to one study, African American judges tend to be tougher on defendants than Latino judges are.[41] Obviously, these distinctions do not hold in all situations, but the point is that "justice" is an opaque concept.

JUDICIAL FEDERALISM

During the 1950s and 1960s, the U.S. Supreme Court was far and away the leading judicial actor in the land. Under the Chief Justiceship of Earl Warren (1953–1969) and his liberal majority, the Court handed down a long series of rulings that overturned racial segregation, mandated legislative reapportionment, extended voting rights, and expanded the rights of accused criminals. Significant reversals of state court decisions were commonplace.

Beginning with Chief Justice Warren Burger (1969–1986) and a growing faction of conservative justices, however, the Supreme Court changed directions in the 1970s and 1980s.[42] Since 1988, a conservative majority has been in control. The Court has been less intrusive in state and local affairs and has, through its own caution, flashed a green light to state courts inclined to activism (see Chapter 2). The result is **judicial federalism,** in which state courts look first to state constitutional and statutory law in rendering legal judgments on important state and local issues once addressed mostly by the federal courts.

> **judicial federalism**
> A trend in which state constitutional and statutory law are consulted and applied before federal law.

Judicial Activism in the States

Judicial activism is a term with value-laden and ideological dimensions. When associated with politically liberal Court decisions, it is decried by conservatives. However, some conservative judges are also tagged as activists. Whether liberal or conservative, all tend to show strong ideological tendencies.

An objective definition of judicial activism, then, points to court-generated change in public policy that is perceived as illegitimate by opponents who favor the status quo.[43] Judicial activism is in the eye of the beholder. All too often an "activist" judge is one who does not decide a case the way one *thinks* she should.

Regardless of one's feelings on the matter, state supreme courts have clearly become *more* activist by expanding into new policy areas. They are more likely to be involved in the policymaking process by making decisions that affect policy in the executive branch, and they even appear to preempt the lawmaking responsibility of the legislature when they invalidate a statute based on constitutional grounds. Examples of new judicial federalism include the following:

> **judicial activism**
> Judges' making of public policy through decisions that overturn existing law or effectively make new laws.

- California, Connecticut, and Massachusetts courts have expanded women's right to abortion on demand and the right to state financial aid for abortions. (Virginia, on the other hand, requires parental consent before an abortion for a woman under legal age.)
- Although the U.S. Supreme Court has upheld state sodomy prohibitions, courts in New York, Pennsylvania, and other states have struck down sodomy laws as violations of the right to privacy, as spelled out in state constitutions.

And, as noted above, the Massachusetts Supreme Court has recognized the state constitutional right for same-sex couples to wed.

- Oregon's supreme court rejected a U.S. Supreme Court decision that provided guidelines for declaring certain printed and visual materials to be obscene. The Oregon court noted that its state constitution had been authored "by rugged and robust individuals dedicated to founding a free society unfettered by the governmental imposition of some people's views of morality on the free expression of others." The court went on to declare, "In this state, any person can write, print, read, say, show or sell anything to a consenting adult even though that expression may be generally or universally considered 'obscene.'"[44]

How can the state courts override the decisions of the highest court in the land? The answer is that they are grounding their rulings in their own constitutions instead of in the national Constitution. In several decisions, the U.S. Supreme Court has upheld the right of the states to expand on the minimum rights and liberties guaranteed under the national document. Of course, when there is an irreconcilable conflict between state and federal law, the latter prevails.

Current Trends in State Courts

The new wave of state court activism is not carrying all the ships of state with it. Many state supreme courts remain caught in the doldrums, consistently endorsing—rather than repudiating—U.S. Supreme Court decisions. Some of them are so quiet, as one wag suggested, "that you can hear their arteries harden." But even traditionally inactive courts, such as those in Wisconsin and North Carolina, have been stirred into independent actions recently, and the trend is continuing. The U.S. Supreme Court is likely to have a conservative majority for many years to come, permitting the state courts to explore the legal landscape further. Meanwhile, state court activism seems to be contagious, as courts utilize their own information and case networks instead of those of the Supreme Court.

Of course, with rare exceptions, judges cannot seize issues as governors and legislators can; they must wait for litigants to bring them to the courthouse. And although judges can issue rulings, they must depend on the executive and legislative branches to comply with and enforce those rulings. Nonetheless, many state supreme courts are becoming more active in the policymaking process.[45] The reluctance of the federal courts to address important and controversial issues comprehensively has resulted in more cases for state supreme courts to decide.

State court activism does have some negative points. First, some courts may overstep their authority and try to go too far in policymaking, intruding into the proper domain of executive and legislative actors. The Nevada Supreme Court's nullification of a two-thirds majority on tax hikes is a rather extreme example. One problem is that judges have little expertise in the substance of public policy or in the policymaking process. They have no specialized staff to perform in-depth policy research on particular policy issues, and they cannot realistically depend on lawyers to do policy research for them. After all, lawyers are trained and practiced in legal reasoning, not social science or political science. Second, state courts are increasingly issuing policy decisions that have significant budgetary implications. Court rulings on school finance, prison overcrowding, and treatment of the mentally ill have severely affected state budgets. Such court actions rarely take into account their related financial effects. A third problem is that in the context of state constitutional rights, geography is limiting. A state-by-state approach may not be appropriate for such policies as civil rights, clean air, or safe food, which should be equal for all citizens.

ADMINISTRATIVE AND ORGANIZATIONAL IMPROVEMENTS

We have already discussed several important judicial reforms: intermediate appellate courts; court unification and consolidation; merit selection plans for judges; more practical means for disciplining and removing judges; administrative and organizational improvements, including those of a financial nature. This last category deserves further consideration.

Financial Improvements

The exorbitant costs of some trials can bankrupt local jurisdictions if state financial assistance is not forthcoming. For example, one child molestation case in Los Angeles County lasted two and a half years and carried a tab of $15 million. (Neither of the two defendants was convicted.) The price tag for a murder trial and subsequent appeals can also be counted in the millions. If an accused murderer elects to retain a public defender, this single case can threaten the financial viability of an entire local court system.[46] Given such contingencies, more than half of the states have assumed full financial responsibility for the operation of state and local courts.

Another financial reform, centralized budgeting, has been adopted by more than half of the states. Also referred to as *unified court budgeting,* this reform entails a consolidated budget for all state and local courts that details all personnel, supplies, equipment, and other expenditures. It is intended to enhance financial management and help maintain judicial independence from the executive and legislative branches. A unified court system, centralized management and financing, and unified budgeting are all similar in that they share the objective of bringing a state's entire court system under a single authoritative administrative structure.

Dealing with Growing Caseloads

Recently, court reformers have recognized the need to deal more effectively with case backlogs. State courts confront more than 100 million new cases each year. Some judges hand down more than 300 opinions annually. Delays of two years or more have not been uncommon for appellate court hearings, and the unprecedented pressure is growing.

Excessive caseloads are caused by numerous factors, including the greater propensity of losing parties to appeal lower-court decisions, the tremendous growth in litigation, huge increases in drug-related and drunk-driving cases, and poor caseload management procedures. Exacerbating the problem is the sheer number of lawyers in the United States, which accounts for nearly two-thirds of all the lawyers in the world (nearly one million at last count).

The paramount concern is that long delays thwart the progress of justice. The quality of evidence deteriorates as witnesses disappear or forget what they saw, and victims suffer from delays that prevent them from collecting damages for injuries incurred during a crime or an accident. Innocent defendants can be harmed by the experience of being held in prison for long periods while awaiting trial.

Reducing excessive caseloads is not a simple matter. Common sense dictates establishing intermediate appellate courts and adding new judgeships. But much like a new highway draws more traffic, intermediate appellate courts, by their very existence, tend to attract more appeals. And although additional judges can speed up the trial process in lower courts, they may also add to appellate backlogs. Expanding the number of judges in an appellate court is also problematic; hearings may actually take longer because of more input or factional divisions among judges.

The stubborn persistence of case backlogs has led to some interesting and promising new approaches.

1. *Alternative dispute resolution.* Almost all states today use mediation, arbitration, or other techniques to help settle litigation prior to or in between formal courtroom proceedings. Mediation involves a neutral third party who tries to help the disputants reach a voluntary settlement. Arbitration consists of a binding ruling by a neutral party in favor of one disputant or the other. In a growing number of states, civil litigants in search of timely settlement hire private judges to arbitrate their disputes.

2. *Fines against lawyers and litigants.* New laws or court rules provide for judges to levy monetary fines against lawyers and litigants guilty of delaying tactics, frivolous litigation, or standards violations that require cases to be heard within a specified time period.

3. *Case management systems.* Judges can take charge of their dockets and impose an aggressive case management system. Although individual systems vary widely, a typical approach is multitracking, or differentiated case management. It distinguishes between simple and complex cases, as well as between frivolous and potentially significant cases, and treats them differently. Complex and significant cases are waved on down the traditional appellate track. Simple and frivolous cases take a shorter track, usually under the direction of staff attorneys. In Vermont, this case management system is called the "rocket docket." Experiments with multitracking have been successful in reducing case delays in Arizona, Maine, New Hampshire, and other states. As noted above, another case management innovation designed to speed up the wheels of justice is *boutique courts,* in which environmental law disputes,

drug cases, or others with special characteristics are heard by judges in specialized courts.

4. *New technology.* Technological innovations are also improving the quality and quantity of court operations. Electronic databases (for example, LEXIS and WESTLAW) store case information and legal research and transmit information from law offices to courts. Electronic filing of court documents helps track child support payments, court administrative systems, and traffic tickets. Videotaping of witnesses' testimony is commonplace. Arraignment procedures, during which suspects are formally charged, are videotaped to save time or to prevent potential problems from a disruptive defendant. Video courtrooms, in which trials are filmed, create a more accurate trial record and cost much less than a written transcript by a court stenographer. Lawyers in high-tech courtrooms speed up proceedings by using Power Point, video clips, and Internet sources, all displayed for jurors on individual flat screen monitors. Audio-visual technology permits hearings, motions, pleas, sentencing, and other proceedings to be conducted long distance between jail and courthouse, thereby both saving money and enhancing security.

5. *Performance standards.* The National Center for State Courts has developed performance standards for state trial courts to aid self-assessment and improvement.[47] A growing number of states are not only adopting quantitative indicators of the speed with which cases are processed but also trying to measure broader concerns such as access to justice; fairness and integrity; public trust and confidence; and the quality of judges' decision making.

Compensating the Judges

At first glance, judicial salaries seem high enough. In 2007, state supreme court judges earned an average of $137,998.[48] (The variation is great: California justices make $210,000; their counterparts in Montana are paid only $101,000.) Trial court judges were paid 10 to 20 percent less. However, these amounts are substantially below what an experienced, respected attorney can expect to make. A successful lawyer who gives up private practice for the bench must be willing to take a considerable cut in income. Unlike legislators, state judges are permitted very little outside income. Therefore, it is reasonable to ask whether the best legal minds will be attracted to judgeships, given that judicial compensation is relatively low. This dilemma exists at all levels and in all branches of public service, from the municipal finance officer to the highway patrol officer, because most state and local government compensation lags behind pay for comparable jobs in the private sector. If we expect our judges, law enforcement officers, and other public employees to be honest, productive, and highly qualified, they must be compensated adequately. Recent salary increases for state judges seem to reflect this principle.

Judicial Performance Evaluation

Who judges the judges? In popular election and merit system states, the voters hold judges accountable. But voters have no voice in gubernatorial and legislative selection states. And even when judicial elections are held, how much do the voters really know about the candidates?

Judicial performance evaluation (JPE) offers an objective process to assess the performance of judges. Voters are educated, and judges can use results of evaluation for self-improvement. First adopted by Alaska in 1975, JPE programs are now mandated in eighteen other states and under active consideration in several others. JPE involves confidential surveys of attorneys, court professionals, witnesses, jurors, and other court participants. Respondents are questioned about how the judge interprets the law, manages his workload, and interacts with people in the courtroom, among other factors.[49]

Indications are that JPE can contribute to judicial self-improvement and provide valuable, job-related information on judges' performance to the voters. Used appropriately, JPE helps preserve the hallmark characteristics of independence and accountability of the judiciary.[50]

State Courts in the 2000s

Like the other two branches of government, the state judiciary has been reformed significantly. Court systems have been modernized and simplified, intermediate appellate courts have been added, processes have been streamlined, and case delays have been reduced. Disciplinary and removal commissions now make it easier to deal with problem judges, and JPE furnishes useful data on the performance of judges. But courts are still striving for greater independence from political pressures and favoritism and more accountability for their actions. Justice may at times appear to be an ephemeral ideal, and an expensive one at that; but it is more likely to be approximated in state judicial decisions today than ever before. But the courts, like the rest of society, are no longer immune to the technological age. New innovations and approaches will follow the recommendations of commissions in states now studying the needs of state judicial systems in the twenty-first century.

Court modernization and reform have been accompanied by increased judicial activism. The newly assertive state courts have far surpassed the federal courts in public policy activism. They sometimes blatantly disagree with federal precedents and insist on decisions grounded in state constitutional law rather than in the national constitution. In short, the state courts are actively responding to public concern with the administration of justice and, by inference, to the perennial issues of crime and criminal justice.

CRIME AND CRIMINAL JUSTICE

The judiciary is the critical institutional link to the policy problem of crime. Governors exercise criminal justice policy leadership, legislatures determine what constitutes violations of the law and establish sentencing rules, and law enforcement personnel enforce the law—but it is the courts that decide questions of guilt or innocence and impose punishments.

Sometimes the criminal justice system misfires, with dreadful consequences as the result. People may be convicted for crimes they did not commit. For instance, concern is growing that innocent people are being put to death by state justice systems. DNA testing makes identification of a killer a statistical certainty when such evidence is available, and more states are demanding that DNA evidence be submitted before extinguishing a person's life. A growing number of inmates are being exonerated and released from prison after being proven innocent by DNA testing. Wrongful convictions can result from lack of solid evidence of a crime, dishonest police claims of a confession, incompetent legal representation, and many other factors. But the critical element in avoiding such problems is the court.

There is much controversy today regarding what should be done with properly convicted criminals. The debates over correctional policy range from the desirability of capital punishment to what, if anything, to do about "victimless" crimes such as prostitution and drug use. To an important degree, the role of the courts in applying the law and in sentencing is significantly restricted by sentencing mandates. Judges once exercised great discretion in deciding the number of years for which an offender should be sentenced to prison. But the current approach is *determinate sentencing,* in which offenders are given mandatory terms that they must serve without possibility of parole. Over half the states have enacted "three strikes and you're out" laws, which mandate tough sentences—perhaps even life without parole—for habitual felons who are convicted of a third serious crime. The goal is to reduce sentencing disparity among judges, but this approach comes at the expense of flexibility. Isn't it more appropriate to make the punishment fit the crime? Longer sentences, combined with a greater propensity toward locking up people convicted of nonviolent crimes, have also led to tremendous growth in the nation's prison population, even while the United States has been experiencing a significant reduction in crime levels.

The United States imprisons a higher proportion of its citizens than any other nation. More than 2.2 million Americans are behind bars. The number of prisoners is growing about 3 percent annually. Approximately one-half of all prisoners are considered nonviolent offenders, convicted of such crimes as consuming or dealing drugs, passing bad checks, and burglary. There is a striking inconsistency in the lockup rate of African Americans, who are seven times more likely to be incarcerated than whites. One in ten African Americans is locked up today.

Prison overcrowding has produced a serious—and expensive—policy dilemma for the states, which have been busily experimenting with methods to ease the problem. Three basic strategies are being employed: back-door strategies, front-door strategies, and capacity enhancement. *Back-door strategies* are designed to extract inmates from correctional institutions before they serve their full sentences. Early release, probation, and parole remain options in many states. A useful measure is electronic house detention, whereby a released inmate wears a transmitter (usually on the ankle) that emits a steady signal to a receiver in his or her home. Failure to detect a signal causes the receiver to dial a central computer that brings the matter to the attention of law enforcement officials. This technique is much less expensive than incarceration, and it enables offenders not only to work to pay their own share of the program's costs but also to repay their victims financially. (The central computer is programmed to "know" when the inmates are permitted to be away from home.)

Front-door strategies are intended to keep offenders out of prison in the first place by directing them into alternative programs. Creative sentencing grants judges the flexibility to design punishments that fit the crime, yet permit the offenders to remain in society. A popular alternative sentence is community service, which ranges from cleaning up parks or streets to working in a hospital. Some sentences are creative indeed. A judge in Wake County, North Carolina, has been known to seize valuable items of clothing and personal stereos from larceny offenders. A municipal judge in Colorado requires young offenders to listen to musical artists they don't like, such as Wayne Newton or Barney the Dinosaur. And in California, judges have the option of offering child molesters surgical or chemical castration. Other front-door approaches include intensive probation supervision, which combines house arrest with intrusive surveillance for nonviolent criminals, and boot camps, in which young, first-time offenders are given the option of either doing jail time or spending several months in "shock incarceration." The latter involves rigorous Marine boot camp–style training intended to promote self-discipline.

Capacity enhancement usually entails construction and operation of new prison facilities—a seriously expensive undertaking that has hamstrung many a state budget. Some states have chosen the privatization route to capacity enhancement. Prisons run by firms such as Correctional Corporation of America are now found in thirty-nine states. Savings appear to be marginal, and troubling legal questions have arisen concerning violations of inmate rights, the training and aptitude of guards, the quality of food and lodging, and related issues.

Crime and corrections present major challenges to state and local governments. How they meet these challenges will go a long way toward determining their future role in American federalism. More innovation and experimentation are certain to occur.

CHAPTER RECAP

- State courts are organized into two tiers: appellate courts and trial courts.
- The five methods for selecting judges are legislative election, partisan election, nonpartisan election, the merit plan, and gubernatorial appointment. Each selection plan has certain advantages and disadvantages—there is no "one best way."
- Many factors influence judicial decision making, including institutional arrangements; legal procedures; case precedent; caseload pressures; access to the legal system; and personal values, attitudes, and characteristics of judges.
- Judicial federalism is related to increased capability and judicial activism in many state courts.
- Efforts to reform state courts are in full swing, including financial improvements, better caseload management, and improved compensation for judges.
- Crime rates are down but incarceration rates are rising. Alternatives to imprisonment are being tested in the states.

Key Terms

civil case *(p. 196)*

criminal case *(p. 196)*

administrative case *(p. 196)*

common law *(p. 196)*

original jurisdiction *(p. 197)*

appellate jurisdiction *(p. 197)*

limited jurisdiction trial courts *(p. 197)*

major trial court *(p. 198)*

supreme court *(p. 198)*

intermediate appellate court *(p. 198)*

plea bargaining *(p. 209)*

bench trial *(p. 210)*

trial by jury *(p. 210)*

precedent *(p. 212)*

judicial federalism *(p. 214)*

judicial activism *(p. 214)*

Internet Resources

The National Center for State Courts maintains a list of courts and their web addresses at **www.ncsc.dni.us/.** This is a rich source of information on the courts, including state court decisions.

Interesting sites include the following: California at **www.courtinfo.ca.gov/,** Florida at **www.flcourts.org,** and Alaska at **www.alaska.net/~akctlib/ homepage.htm.**

The American Bar Association's website provides an analysis of current controversial cases and other legal information. It is located at **www.abanet.org.**

The Law Forum Legal Resources site, located at **www.lawforum.net,** has links to all on-line state and local courts. For a detailed examination of all states' judicial systems, see **www.ajs.org/select11.html.**

To watch live performances of Indiana's court proceedings, see **www.in.gov/ judiciary/webcast/.**

Information on Florida's Ninth Judicial Circuit Court's webcast may be viewed at **www.governmentvideo.com/articles/publish/article_182.shtml.** This site also has interesting information on shooting video depositions, perimeter security, and other law enforcement concerns.

State–Local Relations

10

FOCUS QUESTIONS

1. How would you characterize state–local government relationships, from the state perspective and from the local perspective?

2. What are the three types of common state–local organizations?

3. Regionalism may be a solution to what major issue in state–local relations?

New crime-fighting technology has led to the creation of DNA databases in many major cities around the country. And although these databases may be useful in convicting the guilty and acquitting the innocent, their existence has raised questions about privacy and security. State databases are linked to the Combined DNA Index System run by the FBI and are subject to their regulation and procedures, but local databases are not. However, that may be changing. In 2007, New York became the first state to consider legislation to restrict the operation of local databases.[1] Can state governments impose limitations on their localities? The answer is an emphatic "yes." A state can supersede the local governments within its boundaries.

The relationship between states and their communities is often strained. On the one hand, state government gives local governments life. States create the rules for their localities. On the other hand, state governments historically have not treated their local governments very well. It appears, however, that states have realized that mistreating their governmental offspring is counterproductive, and many have launched a sometimes-uncoordinated process of assistance and empowerment of local government.

Capturing this evolution is the statement of the National Conference of State Legislatures (NCSL) Task Force on State–Local Relations: "Legislators should place a higher priority on state–local issues than has been done in the past. The time has come to change their attitude toward local governments—to stop considering them as just another special interest group and to start treating them as partners in our federal system."[2] Stronger, more competent local governments are an asset to state government.

THE DISTRIBUTION OF AUTHORITY

Dillon's rule

A rule that limits the powers of local government to those expressly granted by the state or those powers closely linked to the expressed powers.

In essence, local governments are creatures of their states. In the terminology of Chapter 2, the relationship is that of a unitary system: the state holds all legal power. Federal and state courts have consistently upheld the dependency of localities on the state since Iowa judge John F. Dillon first laid down **Dillon's rule** in 1868. Dillon's rule established that local governments may exercise only those powers explicitly granted to them by the state, those clearly implied by these explicit powers, and those absolutely essential to the declared objectives and purposes of the local government. Any doubt regarding the legality of a specific local government power is resolved in favor of the state.[3] This perspective runs counter to the more Jeffersonian conception that local governments are imbued with inherent rights.[4]

In the words of the U.S. Advisory Commission on Intergovernmental Relations (ACIR), "State legislatures are the trustees of the basic rules of local governance in America. The laws and constitutions of each state are the basic legal instruments of local governance."[5] The ACIR statement denotes the essence of the distribution of authority between a state and its localities. In short, it is up to the state to determine the amount and type of authority a local government may possess. As specified by Dillon's rule, localities depend on the state to grant them enough power to operate effectively.

The Amount and Type of Authority

The amount and type of authority that states give their local governments vary widely. Some states grant their localities wide-ranging powers to restructure themselves, impose new taxes, and take on additional functions. Others, much more conservative with their power, force local governments to turn to the legislature for approval to act. Empowerment also depends on the type of local government. General-purpose governments such as counties, cities, and towns typically have wider latitude than special-purpose entities like school districts. (The concept of general-purpose governments is discussed in Chapter 11.) Even among general-purpose governments, there are different degrees of authority; counties tend to be more circumscribed than cities in their ability to modify their form of government and expand their service offerings. In general, states' regulatory reach is great. For example, states may regulate local governments':

- finances (by establishing debt limits and requiring balanced budgets),
- personnel (by setting qualifications for certain positions and prescribing employee pension plans),
- structure (by establishing forms of government and outlawing particular electoral systems),
- processes (by requiring public hearings and open meetings and mandating financial disclosure),
- functions (by ordering the provision of public safety functions and proscribing the pursuit of enterprise activities),

- service standards (by adopting solid waste guidelines and setting acceptable water-quality levels).

The preceding list makes the point: The state capitol casts a long shadow.

Building codes offer an illustration of the variability in state–local authority. Researcher Peter May examined all fifty states to determine the amount of discretion allowed local governments to adopt and enforce building codes.[6] He found several different patterns. Twelve states (Kentucky and Michigan among them) played an aggressive role, imposing mandatory building codes on their local governments and overseeing local compliance. Thirteen states (including Indiana and Wyoming) had mandatory local codes but stopped short of state review or oversight. The rest of the states gave their local governments more leeway. In eight states (Iowa and Nebraska among them), local governments themselves decided whether to enforce the state building code. And in seventeen states (including Delaware and Oklahoma), there were no comprehensive building codes; thus local governments were free to design and enact their own **ordinances.** The building code example underscores an important point: States vary in their treatment of local government.

Devolution, the shift in power from the national government to the states, has also occurred between states and their local governments. In the state–local case, it is called **second-order devolution.** The more recently a state has adopted its constitution, the more likely the document is to contain provisions that strengthen local governments.[7] Many state constitutions set forth a provision for **home rule,** which although it falls short of actual local self-government, is an important step in the direction of greater local decisionmaking.[8] (In a few states, home rule provisions are statutory, not constitutional.) And local jurisdictions tend to be extremely protective of whatever power they have wrested from state government. For example, the beleaguered Baltimore school system resisted a state plan to take over the schools in 2004 because, in the words of one local official, "the solution to the problems in Baltimore city starts with Baltimore city."[9]

ordinance
Enacted by the governing body, it is the local government equivalent of a law.

second-order devolution
A shift in power from state government to local government.

home rule
The legal ability of a local government to run its own affairs, subject to state oversight.

A State–Local Tug of War

Local governments want their states to provide them with adequate funding and ample discretion. Local officials are supremely confident of their abilities to govern, given sufficient state support. These same local officials express concern that neither their policymaking power nor their financial authority has kept pace with the increased administrative responsibilities placed on them by state government. The recognition and correction of such conditions are the states' responsibility. Clearly, states are not at all hesitant to exercise power vis-à-vis their local jurisdictions. Consider these contemporary examples:

- Concerned that Florida cities might follow the example of Santa Fe, New Mexico, and require firms to provide higher minimum pay than the federal minimum wage, Sunshine State legislators passed a bill in 2003 to prevent local governments from doing so.[10]
- When state revenues fell below expectations in 2002, North Carolina's governor made up the difference by taking $200 million in tax money that had been earmarked for localities.[11]

- After a local jurisdiction's aggressive use of its power to take property, Colorado lawmakers in 2004 introduced bills designed to restrict localities' power to take land.[12]

A persistent theme runs through the preceding list: State government can impose its will on local governments. Still, states and localities are not invariably at each other's throats; plenty of examples of state–local partnerships exist, such as Florida's and Palm Beach County's joint effort to attract biotechnology industries. The county has purchased the land and is building a research facility ($200 million); the state is paying the facility's operating costs for seven years ($300 million).[13] Still, the relationship between a state and its local governments often involves conflict as each level tries to exert its will.

The diagram presented in Figure 10.1 reflects the two fundamental ways states can influence the authority of local governments. One way is through the vertical state–local government relationship—states can choose to retain power (centralize) or disperse power (decentralize). The other way is horizontal—the power relationships of local governments to each other. Combining the two dimensions, vertical and horizontal, produces the four square-shaped boxes on the right half of the diagram.[14] Box A reflects a state that centralizes vertically and horizontally; Box C is a state that decentralizes on both dimensions. In a metropolitan area in "A" states, there are few local governments, and they lack power. In states characterized by the pattern described in box "C," many local governments exist and they enjoy substantial power. The states depicted by boxes B and D have one centralizing feature and one decentralizing feature. Each state decided a long time ago the square in which it belongs.

FIGURE 10.1   Typology of Governance Structure of Metropolitan Regions

SOURCE: David K. Hamilton, David Y. Miller, and Jerry Paytas, "Exploring Horizontal and Vertical Dimensions of the Governing of Metropolitan Regions," Urban Affairs Review 40 (November 2004): 152. Copyright 2004 by Sage Publications Inc. Journals. Reproduced with permission from Sage Publications Inc. Journals in the format Textbook via Copyright Clearance Center.

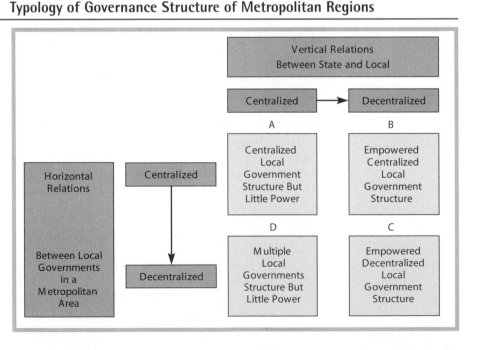

The ability of states and localities to work together effectively has gotten a real test with the issue of homeland security. Concerned that state and local governments were ill-prepared to respond to a disaster in a comprehensive and cooperative way, the federal government funded two antiterrorism exercises in 2005. One simulation, a bomb and chemical weapon attack, took place in Connecticut; the other, a bioterror incident, was set in New Jersey.[15] The exercises exposed weaknesses in response capability, especially in communications among responders. The results of the mock disasters sent state and local officials throughout the nation back to the drawing boards to try to determine how to improve their response systems. One outcome has been the creation of "all-hazards" emergency operations plans that identify and assign responsibilities to state and local agencies—and to nonprofit organizations—in the event of a disaster. These plans are designed to improve coordination and communication not only vertically (between the state government and localities) but also horizontally (among local jurisdictions).

State Mandates

Although local governments generally want increased autonomy, state governments have shared their policymaking sphere with reluctance. Rather than let these "subgovernments" devise their own solutions to problems, states frequently prefer to impose a solution. For instance, when solid waste management became a concern in Florida, the state legislature's reaction was to require counties to establish recycling programs. Not only were counties required to initiate programs, they were ordered to achieve a recycling rate of 30 percent.[16] This kind of requirement or order is an example of a *mandate*. Unfunded mandates are a persistent source of friction between state and local levels of government.

From the perspective of state government, mandates are necessary to ensure that vital activities are performed and desirable goals are achieved. State mandates promote uniformity of policy from one jurisdiction to another (for instance, regarding the length of the public school year or the operating hours of precinct polling places). In addition, they promote coordination, especially among adjacent jurisdictions that provide services jointly (as with a regional hospital or a metropolitan transportation system).

Table 10.1 provides some perspective on how those at the local level see the mandates issue. Based on a survey of local officials in Minnesota, the data in the table indicate that resistance to mandates is not uniform; that is, it depends on the policy area.[17] Mandates for infrastructure, public safety, and environmental protection, especially if funded at least partially by the state, are acceptable to local officials. But in areas such as recreation, economic development, and general government administration, a large subset of those surveyed believe that mandates are not appropriate. Recognizing that funding is one of the key considerations, many states have adopted **mandate-reimbursement requirements.** These measures require states either to reimburse local governments for the costs of state mandates or to give local governments adequate revenue-raising capacity to pay for them.

From their vantage point, local officials offer several suggestions for fixing the mandate problem. Three solutions supported by more than 80 percent of the respondents to the Minnesota survey are:

mandate-reimbursement requirements

Measures that take the financial sting out of state mandates.

TABLE 10.1	Minnesota Local Officials' Views on State Mandates			
	MANDATES ARE APPROPRIATE . . .			MANDATES ARE NOT APPROPRIATE REGARDLESS OF STATE FUNDING
	. . . EVEN WITH NO STATE FUNDING	. . . IF THEY ARE PARTIALLY STATE FUNDED	. . . IF THEY ARE FULLY STATE FUNDED	
POLICY AREA				
Economic development	6	30	24	40
Environment	6	40	48	6
General government administration	6	32	26	40
Health services	2	25	44	2
Infrastructure	2	56	31	11
Public safety	2	47	37	10
Recreation	2	33	21	41
Welfare and human services	1	20	25	2

NOTE: The numbers indicate the percentage of Minnesota local officials responding to the survey who agree with each statement.
SOURCE: "Minnesota Local Officials' Views on State Mandates," from Lawrence J. Grossback, "The Problem of State-Imposed Mandates: Lessons from Minnesota's Local Governments," *State and Local Government Review* 34 (Fall 2002): 183–97. Reprinted with permission of Carl Vinson Institute of Government, University of Georgia (www.vinsoninstitute.org).

- The state should provide a clear statement of the rationale behind the mandate; in other words, the state should justify its action.
- Localities should be given greater flexibility in implementing the provisions of the mandate.
- Financial aid to local governments should be increased so that they can deal with mandates effectively.[18]

As might be expected, these solutions are substantially less popular with state officials. But certainly, more communication between state policymakers and local officials, especially at the outset, would reduce some of the friction generated by mandates. Allowing local governments more leeway in implementation, either through extension of time or variation in rules, would lessen the punch that mandates pack. Even more central to any type of mandate reform is adequate state funding of mandates. This action would go a long way toward improving state–local relationships.

An Uneasy Relationship

A conflicted relationship exists between states and local governments when it comes to money. Cities, counties, and other local governments will always live within the constitutional constraints of their states. Localities enjoy their own sources of revenue—property taxes, user fees, and business license fees—but depend on the states for much of their income. They suffer the frustration of having to cope with rising expenditure demands from their residents while their authority to raise new monies is highly circumscribed by state law. No wonder they turn to the national government to bail them out when times are tough.

But by far the single largest source of local revenues is the state. About 40 percent of all state expenditures goes to local governments. Like federal grants-in-aid, however, state grants come with lots of strings attached. Most state dollars are earmarked for public education and social welfare; other state assistance is targeted for roads, hospitals, public safety, and public health. The result is that local governments have little spending discretion. During bad economic times, states have a tendency to push a portion of their own budget shortfalls down to their already struggling local governments.

Naturally, great diversity characterizes the levels of encumbered (earmarked) and unencumbered state assistance to local jurisdictions, much of which is related to the distribution of functions between a state and its localities. Highly centralized states such as Hawaii, South Carolina, and West Virginia fund and administer at the state level many programs that are funded and administered locally in decentralized states such as Maryland, New York, and Wisconsin. In states where taxation and expenditure limitations have hampered the ability of local jurisdictions to raise and spend revenues, the trend has been toward fiscal centralization. Greater centralization has also resulted from state efforts to reduce service disparities between wealthy and poor jurisdictions, and to lessen the dependence of local governments on the property tax.

What Local Governments Want from the States

What local governments want from their states and what they actually get may be worlds apart. Today, states and their local jurisdictions conduct nearly constant dialogue over financial matters. More and more often today, the states are willing to recognize and want to respond to local financial problems—subject, of course, to their own fiscal circumstances, citizen demands for tax relief, and their judgment as to what is best for all state residents.

Simply put, what localities want most is *more money.* But they also want more control over how it is spent and the independent power to raise it. Taxpayer resistance, reductions in federal grants-in-aid, and pressing infrastructure needs have left local jurisdictions in a financial bind. State governments must provide help, and in general they have done so. State aid for all local governments has grown steadily, substantially outstripping inflation over the past three and one-half decades.

Most increases in state aid are devoted to education, corrections, health care, and social services. But many states also distribute a portion of their tax revenues based on local fiscal need, thus tending to equalize or level economic disparities between local jurisdictions.

The specific means for sharing revenues takes many forms. Most of the states make special payments in lieu of taxes to local governments where state buildings or other facilities are located. Such payments are of particular concern to capital cities, in which large plots of prime downtown property are occupied by state office buildings.

In addition to more money, local governments want the *legal capacity to raise additional revenues themselves,* especially through local option sales and income taxes. A share of gasoline, tobacco, and other tax benefits is greatly appreciated, as is the authority to impose impact fees on developers of residential property. The key is local option, whereby jurisdictions decide for themselves which, if any, taxes they will exact. More than two-thirds of the states have authorized an optional sales or income tax for various local governments, and some permit localities to adopt optional earmarked taxes. For example, Florida empowers its counties to place an accommodations tax on local hotel and motel rooms. Revenues from the tax are dedicated to tourism development projects. Local option taxes are attractive because they provide local jurisdictions with the flexibility to take action as they see fit in response to local needs. What protects citizens against taxaholic local legislative bodies in the aftermath of the taxpayer revolt is the state requirement that local tax hikes must be approved by the voters in a referendum.

As noted in the State Mandates section of this chapter, *localities also want limitations on and reimbursements for state mandates.* Local governments believe that they should not have to obey *and* pay, and that states should reimburse them for expenses incurred in carrying out mandates. Most states have responded to this request by attaching fiscal notes to any proposed legislation or administrative regulation or rule that involves local governments; these notes estimate the local costs and fiscal impact of implementing the legislation.

STATE–LOCAL ORGANIZATIONS

Legal, administrative, and financial ties link state and local governments. Additional interaction occurs when state governments establish organizations such as local government study commissions and advisory panels of local officials. Among the most prevalent structures are task forces, advisory commissions on intergovernmental relations, and departments of community affairs.

annexation

The addition of unincorporated adjacent territory to a municipality.

Task forces tend to be focused organizations set up by the governor or the state legislature in response to a perceived local-level problem. If a state wants to investigate the ramifications of changing its **annexation** statutes, the legislature might create a task force on annexation and boundary changes (or something similar), composed of state and local officials, community leaders, and experts on the subject of annexation. First, the task force would collect information on how other states handle the annexation question; next; it would conduct a series of public hearings to get input from individuals and groups interested in the issue; and, finally, it would compile a report that included recommendations suitable for legislative action. Its work completed, the task force would then disband, although individual members might turn up as advocates when the task force's recommendations receive legislative attention. Task forces are quick organizational responses to local problems that have become too prominent for state government to ignore. A task force is a low-cost, concentrated reaction that undertakes specific tasks and, in some instances, actually influences legislative deliberations.

In an ongoing, comprehensive effort at state–local cooperation, twenty-three states have created state-level *advisory commissions on intergovernmental relations,* modeled after the commission, now defunct, created by the U.S. Congress in 1959. State-level ACIRs are designed to promote more harmonious, workable relations between the state and its governmental subdivisions. They are intended to offer a neutral forum for discussion of long-range state–local issues—a venue where local officials can be listened to and engaged in focused dialogue; conduct research on local developments and new state policies; promote experimentation in intergovernmental processes, both state–local and interlocal; and develop suggested solutions to state–local problems.[19] To prevent their recommendations from gathering dust on a shelf, many state-level ACIRs have added marketing and public relations to their list of activities. Generally, state-level ACIRs return real benefits to local government. Whether in their narrowest form (as arenas for discussion of local issues) or in their broadest (as policy developers and initiators), ACIRs are useful to state and local governments. But their greatest impact occurs when they are given the authority and resources to do something more than simply discuss issues. Indiana's ACIR, for instance, has four primary duties:

- to promote better understanding of the process of government and the outcomes of policy decisions;
- to improve communication between all levels of government and its citizens;
- to foster long-term planning between all levels of government; and
- to promote research on the impacts of mandates and policy changes.[20]

Another way in which states can generate closer formal ties with their local governments is through specialized administrative agencies. All fifty states have created *departments of community affairs* (*DCAs*) that are involved in local activities. They have different labels (Kentucky calls its DCA the Department for Local Government; Washington's is the Department of Community, Trade and Economic Development), but their function is similar: to offer a range of programs and services to local governments. DCAs are involved in housing, urban revitalization, antipoverty programs, and economic development; they also offer local governments such services as planning, management, and financial assistance. DCAs vary on several dimensions: their niche in state government, the sizes of their budget and staff, and whether they include an advisory board of local officials. Compared to state-level ACIRs, DCAs function much more as service deliverers and much less as policy initiators. Therefore, these two types of organizations tend to complement rather than compete with one another. Both function as advocates for local government, however, at the state level.

METROPOLITICS: A NEW CHALLENGE FOR STATE GOVERNMENT

State governments often find their dealings with local governments to be confounded by the side effects of urban change. Regardless of which state we examine, its urban areas show the effects of three waves of suburbanization. An early wave occurred during the 1920s, when automobiles facilitated the development of outlying residential areas. Although the dispersion slowed during the Great Depression and World War II, its resurgence in the 1950s triggered a second wave, during which retail stores followed the population exodus, the so-called malling of America. Now a third wave of suburbanization is upon us, one fueled by what has been called America's "exit ramp economy." Office, commercial, and retail facilities are increasingly located along suburban freeways.[21] This phenomenon is occurring nearly everywhere, from New York City to San Diego, from Milwaukee to Miami. This third wave has caught the attention of state governments.

As a result of the transformation of American **metropolitan areas,** central cities have lost some of their prominence as the social, economic, and political focal points. People have moved to surrounding **suburbs** and beyond; businesses and firms have sprung up in the hinterlands; communities have formed their own service and taxing districts. The outward flow of people and activities has fundamentally altered metropolitan areas, creating a multiplicity of local governments. The de-emphasis of the central city suggests the need for changes in outmoded state government policy toward metropolitan jurisdictions. A serious concern is that rapid, unplanned growth is producing sprawl. A logical question is: What is state government doing while all of this is occurring? The answer: more than it used to, as the next section of the chapter explains.

Urban Sprawl versus Smart Growth

Population growth is, of course, something that states and localities desire. But the consequences of rapid and unplanned population growth test the capability of governments to provide services efficiently and effectively. As growth spills beyond city limits into unincorporated areas, as **edge cities** spring up along interstate highways, the result is often traffic congestion and overcrowded schools. Far from the central city, subdivisions and strip malls sprout up on land that was recently forests and farms. It costs a lot of money for government to provide infrastructure—streets, water and sewer lines, schools—to these new developments. Meanwhile, many inner cities, where the infrastructure is already in place, are plagued by empty storefronts, vacant lots, and abandoned factories. Many states and localities have struggled to balance the benefits of new growth against the attendant costs.

Sprawling Growth One of the hottest issues of the early twenty-first century is **urban sprawl,** a term that carries negative connotations. It refers to development beyond the central city that is characterized by low densities, rapid land consumption, and dependence on the automobile. It is often called leapfrog development because it jumps over established settlements. Exit-ramp communities and edge cities are a manifestation of sprawl. Urban sprawl is resource intensive and costly, and it is also the subject of much political debate.

Las Vegas, Nevada, may offer the best contemporary example of a fast-growing central city. According to the city's statistics, "two hundred new residents arrive in Las Vegas every day; a house is built every fifteen minutes."[22] According to an official in the county's public works department, "Traffic is probably 100 times worse than it was 10 years ago."[23] Maintaining an adequate water supply is a persistent problem in this desert city. As human settlement pushes ever outward to lower-cost

metropolitan area
A central city of at least 50,000 people, the adjacent suburbs, and the surrounding county (or counties); often called an urban area.

suburbs
Populated areas, often residential in character, on the outskirts of a central city. Some suburbs have their own governments, some do not.

edge cities
New boom towns featuring retail shops and malls, restaurants, office buildings, and housing developments, far from the central city.

urban sprawl
Development characterized by low population density, rapid land consumption, and dependence on the automobile.

land, local government is pressed to provide schools, parks, and roads. Growth has outstripped the infrastructure needed to support it. The mayor of Las Vegas proposed a $2,000 per house **impact fee** to mitigate the effects of growth, but the city lacked the authority to levy the fee. The Nevada legislature had to approve the proposal before it could take effect. Meanwhile, the nearby suburban communities of North Las Vegas and Henderson are growing even faster than the city of Las Vegas itself. Other places do not have the furious pace of development that the Las Vegas area has, but they face serious challenges related to growth nonetheless. Table 10.2 lists the concerns of five cities in different parts of the United States.

Rapid growth can spark serious conflict in a community. Consider the case of Fillmore, a city of 13,000 in southern California. After losing many of its orange groves to new housing and commercial developments, concerned residents were able to place an initiative on the ballot that would require voter approval for development beyond the current city limits. The initiative was called Save Openspace and Agricultural Resources or SOAR. City officials countered with their own, less restrictive, initiative: Vision 2020. Pundits characterized the ensuing battle as citrus groves versus Starbucks and sport-utility vehicles.[24] The campaigns for and against the measures were intense and, in the end, *both* initiatives were defeated by voters. In the aftermath, Fillmore's city council decided to establish **greenbelts** on two sides of the town to preserve some of the city's open space and agricultural base.

The relentless creep of urban sprawl has prompted reactions in many states and communities. In 2006, 128 open space protection measures appeared on ballots throughout the country; 99 of them passed.

impact fee

A fee, levied by a government on developers, that is intended to shift some of the societal costs of growth to the developer.

greenbelts

Open spaces in which development is limited.

TABLE 10.2	**Growth–Related Challenges Facing Five Metropolitan Areas**

METROPOLITAN AREA	GROWTH-RELATED CHALLENGES
Albuquerque, NM	Providing enough water to support growth. Conducting land-use planning in an area surrounded on three sides by federal and tribal land.
Atlanta, GA	Addressing an average daily commute that is among the highest in the nation. Improving air quality in an area where ozone pollution exceeds the Clean Air Act standard.
Burlington, VT	Maintaining the area's rural character. Maintaining traditional downtown centers and villages.
Columbus, OH	Preserving farmland. Providing the water-sewer infrastructure needed to support growth.
Fresno, CA	Preserving prime agricultural land in the metropolitan area—which includes the highest-producing agricultural county in the nation. Maintaining an adequate water supply.

SOURCE: U.S. General Accounting Office, *Local Growth Issues—Federal Opportunities and Challenges* (Washington, D.C.: U.S. GAO, September 2000), p. 88.

These measures committed more than $5.7 billion for land conservation, much of it in the form of tax increases.[25] For instance, in Cobb County, Georgia, and Ravelli County, Montana, land conservation bonds in the amount of $40 million and $10 million, respectively, met with public approval. But the largest single land conservation measure was in California where voters approved $2.25 billion for acquisition and protection of open lands. And it may be in California that the sprawl issue receives it severest test, at least in terms of scale. By 2025, experts predict that another 18 million new housing units will be constructed in the Golden State.[26] Although some of the new housing will replace existing structures, most of it will be built on what is now open space.

Smart Growth The majority of land-use decisions occur at the local level. Many states have begun to provide localities with more tools to manage growth. Hawaii was a pioneer in this effort with its State Land Use Law, adopted in 1961; Vermont and Oregon got on board in 1970 and 1973, respectively, with growth management acts designed to control the pace of development and protect environmentally sensitive areas. The **smart growth** movement is an effort by governments to reduce the amount of sprawl and minimize its impact.

Maryland was one of the first states to take action to limit sprawl. Calling sprawl "a disease eating away at the heart of America," Governor Parris Glendening signed the Smart Growth Areas Act into law in 1997.[27] In effect, the state rewards local governments that target new growth to areas that already have infrastructure, and it denies state funding for infrastructure projects that encourage sprawl. Several other states moved quickly to follow Maryland's lead. The following year, Arizona adopted a Growing Smarter Act; by 2003, another twenty states had taken antisprawl actions of one sort or another.[28] A particularly ambitious plan was New Jersey's Blueprint for Intelligent Growth (BIG). Had BIG been adopted as originally drafted, huge portions of the Garden State would have been off-limits to additional development, much to the dismay of many local officials and builders.[29] Although the far-reaching antisprawl proposal was eventually pared down, it was clear that in New Jersey, as in many other places, state governments are reestablishing themselves as major influences in local governments' land-use decisions.

A word of caution is necessary. Not everyone thinks that sprawl is so bad. In fact, to some, sprawl is simply the consequence of the unfettered workings of a market economy.[30] Given a choice, they contend, Americans prefer a spread-out, car-centered lifestyle. Obviously, there is some truth to that argument. Smart growth inevitably means higher density, that is, smaller lot sizes and taller buildings to accommodate more people. High-rise condominium complexes and soaring office towers appeal to some folks, but to most suburbanites, increased density is not something they want.[31]

smart growth

Government efforts to limit urban sprawl by managing growth.

Regional Governance

A **regional government** is a structure put in place because of the interdependence of proximate communities. As noted in the preceding section, a typical metropolitan area is fragmented, that is, it is comprised of many local governments. Under a regional government, local jurisdictions give up some of their

regional government

An areawide structure for local governance, designed to replace multiple jurisdictions.

power and authority to a larger government in exchange for areawide solutions to local problems. State legislatures are important players in this process because, aside from the state constitution, they create the rules of the regional game. Their actions either facilitate or hinder local government reorganization into regional units.

city–county consolidation

The merger of city and county governments into a single jurisdiction.

City–County Consolidation In the United States, the closest thing to regional government is **city–county consolidation,** whereby area jurisdictions are absorbed into a single countywide government. Structure and function are unified. In a pure consolidation, one police department, one fire department, one water and sewer system serve the entire area. The functions of local government—public safety, public works, health and human services, community and economic development, and recreation and arts programs—are provided by a single jurisdiction. Thirty-two city–county consolidated governments operate in the United States. Some of these consolidated governments reflect political decisions of the nineteenth century, such as the city–county governments of Philadelphia, San Francisco, and New Orleans. Among the most prominent mergers of the past forty years are those of Indianapolis–Marion County, Indiana; Jacksonville–Duval County, Florida; Nashville–Davidson County, Tennessee; and more recently, Louisville–Jefferson County, Kentucky.

Regional government seems so rational, yet it has proven to be quite difficult to achieve. Voters typically defeat proposals to consolidate city and county government. At various times, voters have rejected the mergers of Des Moines and Polk County, Iowa; Spokane and Spokane County, Washington; Wilmington and New Hanover County, North Carolina; and Knoxville and Knox County, Tennessee, to name but a few. Opponents of jurisdictional consolidation often include city and county governing boards, city and county employees, and taxpayer organizations. Support for merging governments typically comes from the local Chamber of Commerce, real estate developers, local newspapers, and civic organizations.[32]

To reformers, this lack of success is perplexing. The logic is straightforward: If small local governments in a metropolitan area merge to form a larger local government, two positive outcomes will occur. First, stubborn public policy problems can be tackled from an areawide perspective. For example, the pollution generated by city A but affecting city B can be handled as a regional problem rather than as a conflict between the two cities. Second, combining forces produces *economies of scale* in service delivery. Instead of a situation in which each jurisdiction constructs and operates jails, for example, one large regional facility can be maintained, providing jail service at a lower cost to each participating jurisdiction. These anticipated outcomes are persuasive arguments in favor of consolidation. In 2004, the county executive of Erie County, New York, proposed doing away with both the city of Buffalo and Erie County to create a new Greater Buffalo regional government.[33] This bold proposal came on the heels of the cash-strapped city's agreement to let the county take over its parks and its water system. Consolidation talk could be heard elsewhere, in Pittsburgh, Pennsylvania; Milwaukee, Wisconsin; Memphis, Tennessee; Fresno, California; Cedar Rapids, Iowa; and Tucson, Arizona.

Regional government does not always perform as expected, however. Research has shown that city–county consolidation does not necessarily reduce the costs of government, and may even increase them.[34] Another criticism of regional government is that it can be inaccessible and destructive of the hard-won political gains of minorities. Compared with a city or town government, regional government is farther away, both literally and figuratively. Residents of small towns fear the loss of identity as their community gets swept into bigger government. The effect on minority political strength is no less troublesome. Because the proportionate number of minorities may be lessened when jurisdictions are combined, their voting strength can be diluted. For instance, African Americans comprised 34 percent of pre-merger Louisville, Kentucky, but only 19.5 percent of consolidated Louisville–Jefferson Metro Government.[35]

A competing perspective on regional government comes from **public choice theory.** According to this theory, the existence of many jurisdictions in a metropolitan area gives people options, that is, they can choose to live in the central city, in nearby suburbs, or in the county. Each of these jurisdictions offers a particular mix of tax rates, policies, and public services. In deciding where to reside or open a business, individuals seek places that are in line with their own tax, policy, and service preferences.[36] To public choice theorists, consolidating cities and counties or creating regional governments robs people of important choices and creates inefficiencies. The consolidation of the city of Louisville and Jefferson County borrowed a page from public choice theory when, in a political compromise, it left 80 smaller jurisdictions in the county out of the merger. Figure 10.2 shows the boundaries of preconsolidated Louisville and Jefferson County, as well as the other jurisdictions.

public choice theory

The theory that individuals shop around to find a local government whose taxes and services are in line with their own preferences.

FIGURE 10.2   **Louisville, Jefferson County, and Small Cities**

Although the districts have similar population sizes, their shapes and territorial sizes vary. SOURCE: H.V. Savitch and Ronald K. Vogel, "Suburbs Without a City: Power and City-County Consolidation," *Urban Affairs Review*, 39 (July 2004): 769. Copyright 2004 by Sage Publications Inc. Journals. Reproduced with permission of Sage Publications Inc. Journals in the format Textbook via Copyright Clearance Center.

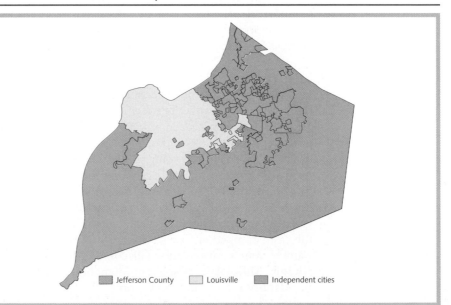

Jefferson County   Louisville   Independent cities

A City and Its Suburbs The former mayor of Albuquerque, David Rusk, after thinking long and hard about the relationship between a central city and its suburbs, jumped into the regionalism debate with this statement: "The real city is the total metropolitan area—city and suburb."[37] He uses the concept of elasticity (and inelasticity) to signify the ability of a city to expand its city boundaries (or not). In a sense, a city's elasticity is its destiny. Elastic cities have been able to capture suburban growth; by adjusting their boundaries through annexation, they can keep pace with urban sprawl. Conversely, many inelastic cities trapped in existing boundaries have suffered population loss and tax-base erosion, resulting in higher levels of racial and class segregation.

The solution offered is a familiar one: metropolitan (or regional) government. But to be effective, the metropolitan government must include the central city and at least 60 percent of the area's population. How to do this? It depends on the characteristics of the metropolitan area. In single-county metropolitan areas, empowerment of the urban county would effectively create metropolitan government, as would city–county consolidation. And in multi-county metropolitan areas, a single regional government could be created out of existing cities and counties. Obviously, the restructuring of local governments in these ways would engender substantial opposition; as Rusk acknowledges, however, there are few alternatives in areas with low elasticity.

The argument for a metropolitan-wide government is simple: Because economies are essentially regional in nature, governance can (and should) be, too. As discussed earlier, however, regional governance has never been a popular alternative in this country. Overcoming traditional antiregionalism sentiment will not be easy, but regional approaches may be necessary for effective competition in an increasingly global economy. And there is some evidence that thinking regionally is gaining favor. Maybe the mayor of Missoula, Montana (population 57,000), said it best when he commented: "It is not possible for Missoula to understand itself, or its future, except in a regional context. The city draws its strength from the region."[38]

It's Up to the States Both Portland, Oregon, and the Twin Cities area of Minnesota, have embraced regionalism. In Oregon, Portland joined with its suburbs and outlying jurisdictions to develop a regionwide vision for the future. The 2040 Plan, as it is called, aims at accommodating orderly growth while maintaining a desirable quality of life in the region. The planning process involved extensive public participation, including citizen surveys and public forums. In addition, the plan's backers launched media campaigns and loaned videos to acquaint residents with the proposal. The 2040 Plan is enforced by an elected, regionwide council that works to secure the compliance of local governments.[39]

In the Minneapolis–St. Paul area of Minnesota, jurisdictions contribute 40 percent of their new commercial and industrial tax base to a regional pool. The money in this pool is redistributed to communities throughout the region on the basis of financial need, thereby reducing fiscal disparities across jurisdictions. Thus, for instance, a new industry locating in one city becomes a benefit to neighboring cities as well. With regional tax-base sharing as a start, Minnesota went even further in 1994 when the state legislature placed all regional

A new housing development brings urban sprawl to a bucolic setting of farms, meadows, and hills.
SOURCE: © Construction photography/Corbis

sewer, transit, and land-use planning in the hands of a regional organization—the Metropolitan Council of the Twin Cities.[40] This significantly empowered council makes crucial decisions about growth and development in the Twin Cities area from a regional perspective.

In the final analysis, it is up to state government to provide a sufficiently supportive environment in which regionalism can take root. It was Oregon and Minnesota that created the legal environment for Portland and the Twin Cities, respectively. As political scientists Margaret Weir, Harold Wolman, and Todd Swanstrom declared in their research on city–suburban coalitions, "states are critical players; they set the terms and conditions under which regionalism occurs."[41] They have to because the natural tendency for officials in cities and their suburbs is to see each other as rivals rather than allies or partners.

councils of governments

Formal organizations of general-purpose governments in an area, intended to improve regional coordination.

Regional Coordination Councils of Governments (COGs), or regional planning commissions, are examples of regional coordination. They do not involve a formal merger or combination of governments; instead, COGs are loose collections of local governments designed to increase communication and coordination in an area. State governments, in fact, were not active in the creation of COGs; national government programs spurred their development. For example, the federal government requires states to use planning organizations such as COGs to coordinate transportation programs in urban areas.[42]

Although areawide planning is the most common activity of councils of government, they also perform other tasks. Member governments can turn to these councils for technical assistance (such as help in writing federal grant applications), professional services (planning, budgeting, engineering, legal advice), and information (economic data for the region).

The impact of these councils has been less significant than their creators hoped, but they have had two positive effects. First, councils have elevated the concept of areawide policy planning from a pipe dream to a reality. They have been heavily involved in criminal justice, water quality, housing, and especially transportation planning. Second, councils have substantially improved the operational capacity of rural local governments by providing expertise to small local jurisdictions that cannot afford to hire specialized staff.

Some localities have taken a more informal route to regional coordination through service-sharing. In service-sharing, jurisdictions agree to consolidate specific services, cooperate in their provision, or exchange them. For instance, recreational facilities may be provided jointly by several jurisdictions, one government may rent jail space from another, or county residents may use the city library in return for city residents' use of the county's solid waste landfill. Service-sharing arrangements are popular because they hold the promise of greater efficiency in service delivery, *and* they do not threaten the power and autonomy of existing jurisdictions the way consolidation does. These agreements provide for a modicum of regional governance . . . without a regional government.

STATES AND THEIR RURAL COMMUNITIES

When the local Dairy Queen closes its doors, a small town in rural America knows that it is in trouble. The Dairy Queen, like the coffee shop on Main Street, serves as a gathering place for community residents. Its demise symbolizes the tough times that a lot of rural communities face. In fact, some analysts argue that the major distinctions in regional economics are no longer between Sunbelt and Frostbelt, or East Coast and West Coast, but between metropolitan America and the countryside.[43] America's economy is flourishing, but several old rural towns in the Great Plains states have became veritable ghost towns. Isolated rural areas located miles from an interstate highway, without a coastline or a major city nearby, and lacking an economic engine are particularly at risk.

The decline of rural America has provoked a question: What can state governments do to encourage the right kind of growth in rural areas? Short of pumping enormous amounts of money into the local economy, they can encourage the expansion of local intergovernmental cooperation, whereby small rural governments join together to increase their administrative capacity to deliver services and achieve economies of scale. Two state actions facilitate such cooperation. One is the reforming of state tax codes so that jurisdictions can share locally generated tax revenues, similar to the Twin Cities example discussed earlier. Rather than competing with one another for a new manufacturing plant or a shopping mall, local governments can cooperate to bring the new facility to the area; regardless of where this facility is located, all jurisdictions can receive a portion of the tax revenue. A second useful state action is the promotion of statewide land-use planning. As one observer has noted, "Currently too many rural local governments engage in wasteful intercommunity competition, mutually antagonistic zoning, and contradictory development plans."[44]

Some small towns in Kansas have resurrected a strategy from bygone days in an effort to reverse population loss: offering free land to families who will build a home on the parcel. For example, Marquette, a town of 500 people in central Kansas, had given away 80 free lots and had seen its population reach 620 within two years.[45] Some of these proverbial one stoplight towns offer additional inducements to new residents: free water and sewer hookups, no-cost building permits, and memberships at nearby golf courses. In the words of a regional economist, "Rural places have to find a new way to compete, and that comes from being entrepreneurial."[46] Another action that may bear fruit is the effort to foster business by installing high-speed Internet connections to isolated rural areas. Indiana created its I-Light program to bring broadband to its farming communities; Alabama and Alaska give tax credits to broadband firms committed to investing in rural areas.[47]

The federal government has also stepped in. In 1990, a new federal initiative offered states a means of redesigning their rural development efforts. Concerned that existing rural programs were fragmented and only partially successful, the national government selected eight states for a pilot study. In those states, newly established Rural Development Councils brought together—for the first time—federal, state, and local officials involved in rural development. And rather than mandating the structure of the councils and their agendas, the federal government assumed a hands-off posture and simply provided the necessary start-up funds. In the ensuing years, each council designed its own initiative aimed at specific conditions and problems confronting the state. Mississippi, for example, worked on a tourism and recreation project, South Dakota developed an online resource database, and Washington undertook the issues of affordable housing and job retraining.[48] During the decade many successful projects were completed. The promise of these state-based interorganizational networks is substantial; thinking optimistically, the federal government extended the initiative to another thirty-seven states.

THE INTERACTION OF STATES AND LOCALITIES

Constitutionally, state governments are supreme in their dealings with local governments. New York City, Los Angeles, and Chicago are large, world-class cities, but even they have to follow the dictates of their respective state governments. Even so, power does not flow in only one direction. The political realities are such that these cities and their smaller counterparts influence what happens in their state capitols. Suffice it to say, the state–local relationship is subject to constant adjustment. A Governor's Task Force to Renew Montana Government, for instance, adopted several provisions aimed at diminishing the influence of the state in what are considered purely local issues. But in a different vein, when Philadelphia's mayor proposed closing some fire stations to cut costs, state legislators intervened, passing a bill to prevent the city from doing so.[49] (The governor of Pennsylvania, a former mayor of Philadelphia, vetoed the bill, saying it infringed on the city's home rule power.)

Some issues or problems require a statewide, uniform response, while others are the particular concern of a single local jurisdiction. Consider the problem of drought, a condition that has affected most of the western states since 2000. Some areas of Colorado, such as Denver, have been especially hard hit. A local agency, Denver Water, is responsible for water management in the city; a state agency, the Colorado Water Conservation Board, has statewide authority. To address the drought problem, both agencies had to work together. The comments of a hydrologist capture the situation, "There needs to be a state coordinating mechanism, but it needs to be sensitive to the local context."[50] Thus, even with the constitutional superiority of the state, the state–local relationship is much more nuanced.

When he was elected governor of New York, George Pataki said that, "as a former mayor, I know firsthand the importance of freeing our cities, towns, and counties from the heavy hand of state government."[51] But as Governor Pataki quickly learned, a governor has to engage in big-picture, statewide thinking, and it is awfully tempting to impose the state's will on those same localities. To make sure their voice is heard, many local governments do what those in California do: hire lobbyists to represent their interests in the state legislature. Localities in the Golden State spent nearly $40 million lobbying lawmakers in 2006.[52] Even so, cities and counties found themselves on the losing side of several key measures, including one that diverted funds for local transportation projects to the state. The state–local relationship can be rocky indeed.

CHAPTER RECAP

- States vary in the amount and type of authority they give their local governments. The general trend has been toward increased state assistance and empowerment of localities, but some states continue to keep their local governments on a short leash.
- The issue of mandates is a particularly contentious state–local matter.
- Local governments want more money from the state, more power to generate revenues, and more control over how the revenues are spent.
- Three types of state–local organizations are common: task forces, advisory commissions on intergovernmental relations, and departments of community affairs.

- Urban sprawl has become a major issue in state–local relations. States have begun to adopt "smart growth" laws that are designed to help localities manage growth.
- Regionalism continues to be advocated as a solution to many local problems. More jurisdictions are creating regional organizations to link their local governments.
- With many rural communities in decline, states are seeking ways of revitalizing them.
- Even as the interaction of states and localities becomes more positive, the tug of war between the two levels continues.

Key Terms

Dillon's rule *(p. 224)*
ordinance *(p. 225)*
second-order devolution *(p. 225)*
home rule *(p. 225)*
mandate-reimbursement
  requirements *(p. 227)*
annexation *(p. 230)*
metropolitan area *(p. 232)*
suburbs *(p. 232)*
edge cities *(p. 232)*

urban sprawl *(p. 232)*
impact fee *(p. 233)*
greenbelts *(p. 233)*
smart growth *(p. 234)*
regional government *(p. 234)*
city–county consolidation *(p. 235)*
public choice theory *(p. 236)*
councils of governments *(p. 238)*

Internet Resources

The National Association of Regional Councils maintains a website at **www .narc.org/.** It shows the differences and similarities of regional councils across the country.

The Association of Bay Area Governments' award-winning site can be found at **www.abag.ca.gov.**

The website for the regional planning agency that deals with 184 cities and 6 counties in Southern California is **www.scag.ca.gov.**

For information on the activities of a state-level ACIR, see the Tennessee ACIR at **www.state.tn.us.tacir/.**

The Urban Institute's site for research on economic and social policy can be found at **www.urban.org.** It is a useful source of information on states and localities.

The Sierra Club presents its case against urban sprawl at **www.sierraclub.org/ sprawl.**

Iowa's rural development council maintains a website at **www.iowarural.org.** Other states with rural development councils have websites also.

Local Government: Structure and Leadership

11

CHAPTER OUTLINE

Five Types of Local Governments

Leadership in Local Government

Communities and Governance

FOCUS QUESTIONS

1. What are the five types of local governments, and what is the primary role of each?

2. Which of these is the most prevalent?

3. Of the various offices in local governments, which one is the most central?

4. What are some of the key changes in city governance?

*A*n article appearing in a 2006 issue of the magazine *Governing* posed a particularly provocative question: "Can Dallas Govern Itself?" The story went on to detail the "political chaos and bureaucratic mismanagement" that has plagued America's ninth-largest city for years. A local columnist criticized the city's governmental structure as "the weak-weak-weak system—weak mayor, weak manager, weak city council."[1] So, it would seem that it was time for a change. However, when given the opportunity to replace the structure with a strong mayor form of government, Dallasites voted "no." It seems that residents did not want a new structure—they just wanted the one they had to work better. In a word, they wanted *leadership*.

What do citizens want from local governments? The answer is, to be governed well. They want governmental structures that work and leaders who are effective. They want jurisdictions with adequate capacity to resolve the tough public problems of our times. But as this chapter demonstrates, the goal of being "governed well" is hard to achieve. Even with improved capacity, local governments confront a series of difficult challenges.

FIVE TYPES OF LOCAL GOVERNMENTS

Local government is the level of government that fights crime, extinguishes fires, paves streets, collects trash, maintains parks, provides water, and educates children. Some local governments provide all of these services; others, only some. A useful way of thinking about them is to distinguish between general-purpose

**general-purpose
local government**

A local government that
performs a wide range
of functions.

**single-purpose
local government**

A local government, such
as a school district,
that performs a
specific function.

and single-purpose local governments. **General-purpose local governments** are those that perform a wide range of governmental functions. These include three types of local governments: counties, municipalities, and towns and townships. **Single-purpose local governments,** as the label implies, have a specific purpose and perform one function. School districts and special districts are single-purpose governments. (Native American reservations are not a type of local government, even though tribal governments perform many local government functions.) In the United States, the number of local governments exceeds 87,800. Figure 11.1 shows the number of local governments at two points in time: 1952 and 2002. The greatest change occurred among single-purpose local governments: a dramatic decrease in the number of school districts and a large increase in the number of special districts.

American local governments were not planned according to some grand design. Rather, they grew in response to a combination of citizen demand, interest-group pressure, and state government acquiescence. As a consequence, no rational system of local governments exists. What does exist is a collection of au-

---

FIGURE 11.1   **Numbers of Local Governments, by Type of Government: 1952 Versus 2002**

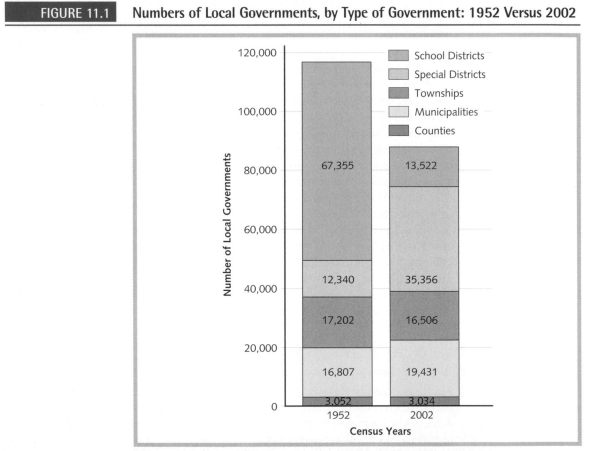

SOURCE: U.S. Bureau of the Census, "Government Units in 2002," 2002 *Census of Governments,* p. 8.

tonomous, frequently overlapping jurisdictional units. The number of local governments varies from state to state. Consider the case of Pennsylvania and its 5,031 local jurisdictions: 66 counties, 1,018 cities, 1,546 townships, 1,885 special districts, and 516 school districts.[2] Nevada, on the other hand, has a grand total of 210 local governments.

Being so close to the people offers special challenges to local governments. Citizens are well aware when trash has not been collected or when libraries do not carry current bestsellers. Moreover, they can contact local officials and attend public hearings—and they do. A recent survey asked a national sample of Americans about their interaction with government. More than 40 percent said that they had contacted an elected local official or attended a community meeting.[3] The interactive nature of local government makes the questions of capacity and responsiveness all the more critical.

Counties

State governments have carved up their territory into 3,034 discrete, general-purpose subunits called counties (except in Louisiana, where counties are called parishes, and in Alaska, where they are called boroughs). Counties exist everywhere, with only a few exceptions. The exceptions include Connecticut and Rhode Island, where there are no functional county governments; Washington, D.C., which is a special case in itself; municipalities in Virginia that are independent jurisdictions and are not part of the counties that surround them; and cities like Baltimore and St. Louis, which are not part of a county because of past political decisions. Also, there are jurisdictions—Philadelphia and San Francisco, for example—that are considered cities but are actually consolidated city–county government structures.

Counties vary dramatically in terms of size. At one extreme is Los Angeles County, California, which, with its more than 9 million residents, is larger than many states. Loving County, Texas, at the other extreme, has fewer than 100 people spread over its 673-square-mile territory.

Why We Have County Government Counties were created by states to function as their administrative appendages. In other words, counties were expected to manage activities of statewide concern at the local level. Their basic set of functions traditionally included property tax assessment and collection, law enforcement, elections, record-keeping (land transactions, births, and deaths), and road maintenance.[4]

The twin pressures of modernization and population growth have placed additional demands on county governments. As a result, their service offerings expanded and now include health care and hospitals, pollution control, mass transit, industrial development, social services, and consumer protection.[5] The more new services that a county provides, the more it is delivering city-type services to its residents and businesses.[6] As a result, counties are increasingly regarded less as simple functionaries of state government than as important policymaking units of local government. Thirty-eight states have adopted home rule provisions for at least some of their counties.[7] This has made it easier for counties to change their organizational structure and reform their practices.

How County Governments Are Organized The traditional structure of county government is based on an elected governing body, usually called a board of commissioners or supervisors, that is the central policymaking apparatus in the county. The board enacts county ordinances, approves the county budget, and appoints other officials (such as the directors of the county public works department and the county parks department). One of the board members acts as presiding officer. Historically, this form of government has been the most popular; more than half of U.S. counties still use it, although its predominance is decreasing. A typical county commission has three or five members and meets in regular session twice a month.

The board is not omnipotent, however, several other county officials are elected, thereby forming a plural executive structure. In most places, these officials include the sheriff, the county prosecutor (or district attorney), the county clerk (or clerk of the court), the county treasurer (or auditor), the county tax assessor, and the coroner. These officials can become powerful political figures in their own right through their control of bureaucratic units. Figure 11.2 sketches the typical organizational pattern.

There are two primary criticisms of this type of organization. First, it has no elected central executive official, like the mayor of a city or the governor of a

FIGURE 11.2	Traditional Organization of County Government

The most common form of county government lacks a central executive.

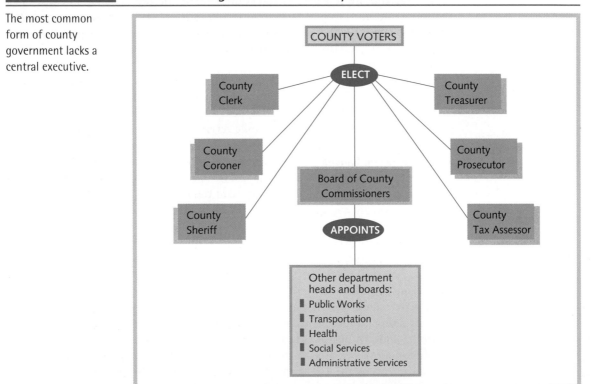

state. County government is run by a board. Second, it does not have a single professional administrator to manage county government, the way a city manager does in a municipality. Elected officials are responsible for administering major county functions.

These criticisms have led to calls for reform of the structure of county government. Two alternative county structures have emerged. In one, called the *county council–elected executive plan,* the voters elect an executive officer in addition to the governing board. The result is a clearer separation between legislative and executive powers—in effect, a two-branch system of government. The board still has the power to set policy, adopt the budget, and audit the financial performance of the county. The executive's role is to prepare the budget, administer county operations (in other words, implement the policies of the board), and appoint department heads. Nearly 400 counties have adopted this arrangement. In the other alternative structure, the *council-administrator plan,* the county board hires a professional administrator to run the government. The advantage of this form of government is that it brings to the county a highly skilled manager with a professional commitment to efficient, effective government. Approximately 1,000 counties have variations of the council-administrator structure.

Determining the most effective structural arrangements for county government is an ongoing issue. Defections from the long-standing commission form of county government and experimentation with alternatives continue, especially in the most populous counties. In 2007, Los Angeles County, which employs 100,000 people and has a budget of $20 billion, empowered its county administrator by giving him the power to hire and fire most department heads.[8] Does structure matter? If results from new research in Florida counties can be extended to other states, the answer is yes. Among fast-growing counties in the Sunshine State, the adoption of a reformed structure led to an expansion of the counties' services to its residents.[9]

The Performance of County Government Counties are now more prominent than they were in the old days when they were considered the shadowy backwaters of local governments. As urban populations spill beyond the suburbs into the unincorporated territory of counties, the pressure on local governments grows.[10] A county and the cities located within it may find themselves at odds on myriad issues. The county–state relationship is rocky, primarily because of spiraling costs of state-imposed mandates for programs such as indigent services and long-term health care. In addition, counties are expected to tackle tough dilemmas of affordable housing and land-use planning at the same time that they are expanding their services to include such matters as disaster preparedness and consumer protection.

Clearly the pressures on county government are many. One novel idea for relieving the burdens on counties was suggested in California, where the legislature considered a proposal to divide the state into seven regions that would be governed by thirteen-member elected boards.[11] These regional "supergovernments" would assume many of the development and infrastructure functions currently assigned to county governments. Although the bill did not pass, the performance of county government remains an issue in many parts of the nation. In Massachusetts, where cities and towns provide most local services, the state legislature has abolished several counties, contending that they were superfluous in the Bay State.[12] Clearly, county governments must continue to modernize and focus on the big picture or run the risk of being bypassed. With that in mind, voters in Allegheny County, Pennsylvania (the Pittsburgh area), approved a restructuring plan in 2005 that merged several elected county positions and made some elective offices appointed.[13]

Municipalities

Municipalities are cities; the words are interchangeable because each refers to a specific, populated territory, typically operating under a charter from the state government. Cities differ from counties in terms of how they were created and what they do. Historically, they have been the primary units of local government in most societies—the grand enclaves of human civilization.

Creating Cities A city is a legal recognition of settlement patterns in an area. In the most common procedure, residents of an area in a county petition the state for a charter of **incorporation.** The area slated for incorporation must meet certain criteria, such as population or density minimums. In most cases, a referendum is required. The referendum enables citizens to vote on whether they wish to become an incorporated municipality. If the incorporation measure is successful, then a **charter** is granted by the state, and the newly created city has the legal authority to elect officials, levy taxes, and provide services to its residents. Not all cities have charters, however. Most California cities, for example, operate under general state law rather than a charter. New cities are created every year. For instance, during a single six-year period, 145 places incorporated around the country (and 33 cities disincorporated, or ceased to exist as official locales). Although most new cities tend to be small, some begin with sizable populations. For example, more than 86,000 people were living in Sandy Springs, Georgia, when the city incorporated in 2005.

Like counties, cities are general-purpose units of local government. But unlike counties, they typically have greater decision-making authority and discretion. Almost all states have enacted home rule provisions for cities, although in some states, only those cities that have attained a certain population size can exercise this option. (One of the few states without home rule for cities, New Hampshire, sought to provide it through a constitutional amendment in 2000. The measure was defeated by voters.) In addition, cities generally offer a wider array of services to their citizenry than most counties do. Police and fire services, public works, parks, and recreation are standard features, supplemented in some cities by publicly maintained cemeteries, city-owned and -operated housing, city-run docks, city-sponsored festivals, and city-constructed convention centers. City government picks up garbage and trash, sweeps streets, inspects restaurants, maintains traffic signals, and plants trees.

City Governmental Structure Nearly all city governments operate with one of three structures: a mayor–council form, a council–manager form, or a city

incorporation

The creation of a municipality through the granting of a charter from the state.

charter

A document that sets out a city's structure, authority, and functions.

commission form. In each structure, an elected governing body, typically called a city council, has policymaking authority. What differentiates the three structures is the manner in which the executive branch is organized.

1. *Mayor–council form.* In the mayor–council form of government, executive functions such as the appointment of department heads are performed by elected officials. This form of government can be subdivided into two types, depending on the formal powers held by the mayor. In a **strong-mayor-council structure,** the mayor is the source of executive leadership. As noted later in the chapter, strong mayors run city hall the way governors run the statehouse. They are responsible for daily administrative activities, the hiring and firing of top-level city officials, and budget preparation. They have a

strong-mayor-council structure

The mayor is empowered to perform the executive functions of government and has a veto over city council actions.

| FIGURE 11.3 | **Mayor–Council Form of Government** |

The primary difference between these two structures concerns the power and authority possessed by the mayor. Strong mayors are more ideally situated to exert influence and control.

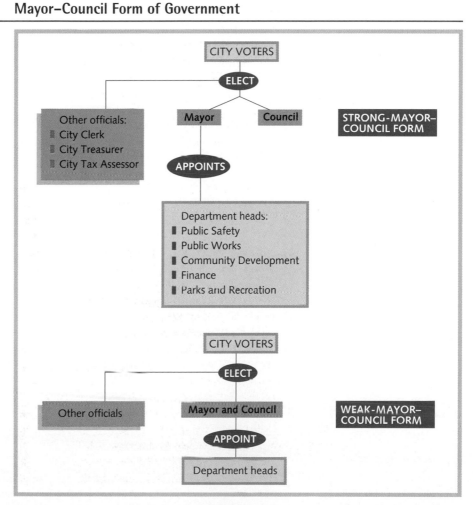

potential veto over council actions. The **weak-mayor-council structure** limits the mayor's role to that of executive figurehead. The council (of which the mayor may be a member) is the source of executive (and legislative) power. The council appoints city officials and develops the budget, and the mayor has no veto power. He performs ceremonial tasks such as speaking for the city, chairing council meetings, and attending ribbon-cutting festivities. A structurally weak mayor can emerge as a powerful political figure in the city, but only if he possesses informal sources of power. Figure 11.3 highlights the structural differences between the strong- and weak-mayor–council forms of city government.

Mayor–council systems are popular both in large cities (populations greater than 250,000) and in small cities (populations less than 10,000). In large cities, the clash of conflicting interests requires the leadership of an empowered politician, a strong mayor. Some large cities, in which the administrative burdens of the mayor's job are especially heavy, have established the position of general manager or chief administrative officer to assist the mayor. In small communities, the mayor–council structure is a low-cost, part-time operation.

2. *Council–manager form.* The council–manager form of government emphasizes the separation of politics (the policymaking activities of the governing body) from administration (the execution of the policies enacted by the governing body). Theoretically, the city council makes policy, and administrators execute policy. Under this structure, the council hires a professional administrator to manage city government. Figure 11.4 sketches this structure.

The administrator (usually called a city manager) appoints and removes department heads, oversees service delivery, develops personnel policies, and prepares budget proposals for the council. These responsibilities alone make the

---

FIGURE 11.4 | **Council–Manager Form of Government**

The council–manager form places administrative responsibility in the hands of a skilled professional. The intent is to make the operation of city government less political.

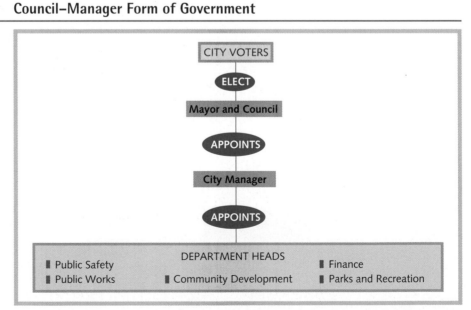

CITY VOTERS

ELECT

Mayor and Council

APPOINTS

City Manager

APPOINTS

DEPARTMENT HEADS

▪ Public Safety
▪ Public Works
▪ Community Development
▪ Finance
▪ Parks and Recreation

FIGURE 11.5	**City Commission Form of Government**

Executive leadership is fragmented under a commission form of government. Individually, each commissioner heads a department; together they run city hall.

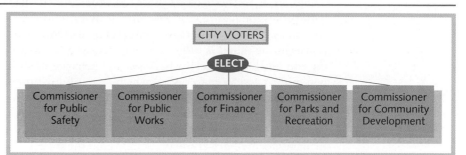

manager an important figure in city government. But, add to them the power to make policy recommendations to the city council, and the position becomes even more powerful. When offering policy recommendations to the council, the manager is walking a thin line between politics and administration.[14] Managers who, with the acquiescence of their council, carve out an activist role for themselves may be able to dominate policymaking in city government.[15]

More than half of U.S. cities use the council–manager form of city government. Among cities of 25,000 to 75,000, the council-manager structure predominates; it is also popular in homogeneous suburban communities and in the newer cities of the Sunbelt region. Examples of large cities with a council-manager structure include Dallas, Phoenix, and San Diego.

3. *City commission form.* Under the city commission form of government, illustrated in Figure 11.5, legislative and executive functions are merged. Commissioners make policy as members of the city's governing body; they also head the major departments of city government. They are both policymakers and policy executors. One of the commissioners is designated as mayor simply to preside over commission meetings.

The appeal of the commission structure was its ostensible reduction of politics in city government. But almost as fast as the commission form of government appeared on the scene, disillusionment set in. One problem stemmed from the predictable tendency of commissioners to act as advocates for their own departments. Each commissioner wanted a larger share of the city's budget allocated to her department. Another problem had to do with politicians acting as administrators: Elected officials do not always turn out to be good managers. The result was that public enthusiasm for the commission form declined. By 1990, when Tulsa, Oklahoma, replaced its commission system with a mayor–council form, only a few cities were operating with a commission structure. Notable among them was Portland, Oregon, with its modified commission form of government.

Which Form of City Government Is Best? Experts disagree about which city government structure is best. Most would probably agree that structures lacking a strong executive officer are generally less preferable than others. By that standard, the weak-mayor–council and the commission forms are less favorable.

The strong-mayor–council form of government is extolled for fixing account-ability firmly in the mayor's office, and the council–manager system is credited with professionalizing city government by bringing in skilled administrators to run things. Yet strong-mayor structures are criticized for overconcentrating power in the mayor's office; council–manager forms are taken to task for placing too much power in the hands of an unelected city manager. Thus, it is up to community residents to decide which form of government they want. In 2004, Richmond, Virginia, switched from a weak-mayor structure to a strong-mayor form while El Paso, Texas, abandoned its strong-mayor structure and joined the ranks of council–manager cities. In 2006, San Diego ditched its council-manager form of government, empowered the mayor, and added a chief operating officer who reports to the mayor. For some cities, a hybrid form that combines features of several structures may be the answer.[16] For instance, both Oakland, California, and Cincinnati, Ohio, amended their council–manager form of government by adding a strong-mayor position *and* retaining the position of city manager. Some mayor-council systems have added a chief administrative officer with powers similar to a city manager to their structures. These hybrid or adapted forms defy easy classification. Debate over the best form of government continues; the best advice for cities may be to use whichever form of government works while remaining receptive to structural improvements.

Towns and Townships

Towns and townships are general-purpose units of local government, distinct from county and city governments. Only twenty states, primarily in the North-east and Midwest, have official towns or townships. In some states these small jurisdictions have relatively broad powers; in others they have a more circum-scribed role.

How Do We Know a Town When We See One? In New England, towns of-fer the kinds of services commonly associated with cities and counties in other states. Many New England towns continue their tradition of direct democracy through a **town meeting** form of government. At a yearly town assembly, residents make decisions on policy matters confronting the community. They elect town officials, pass local ordinances, levy taxes, and adopt a budget. In other words, the people who attend the town meeting function as a legislative body. Although the mechanism of the town meeting exemplifies democracy in action, it often falls short of the ideal. One concern is the relatively low rate of citizen participation in meetings. Often, fewer than 10 percent of a town's voters actually attend the meeting. Larger towns in Connecticut and Massachusetts rely on representatives elected by residents to vote at the meetings.

Towns in New England, along with those in New Jersey, Pennsylvania, and to some degree Michigan, New York, and Wisconsin, enjoy fairly broad powers. In large measure, they act like other general-purpose units of government. In the remainder of the township states (Illinois, Indiana, Kansas, Minnesota, Missouri, Nebraska, North Dakota, Ohio, and South Dakota), the nature of town-ship government is more rural. Rural townships tend to stretch across thirty-six

town meeting

An annual event at which a town's residents enact ordinances, elect officials, levy taxes, and adopt a budget.

square miles of land (conforming to the surveys done by the national government before the areas were settled), and their service offerings are often limited to roads and law enforcement. A part-time elected board of supervisors or trustees commonly rules the roost in townships. In addition, some of the jobs in government may be staffed by volunteers rather than salaried workers. However, the closer these rural townships are to large urban areas, the more likely they are to offer an expanded set of services to residents.

The Future of Towns and Townships The demise of the township type of government has long been expected. As rural areas become more populated, they will eventually meet the population minimums necessary to become municipalities. In 2000, for instance, residents of a Minnesota township decided to incorporate as a municipality to ward off annexation by a neighboring city.[17] Some towns face a different problem. Many are experiencing a substantial population exodus and, in the process, losing their reason for existence. These towns may die a natural death, with other types of government (perhaps counties or special districts) providing services to the remaining residents. The question is whether towns and townships are needed in twenty-first-century America.

Towns and townships have not sat idly by as commentators speculated on their dim future. They formed an interest group, the National Association of Towns and Townships (NATaT), to lobby on their behalf in Washington, D.C. NATaT spawned a spinoff organization, the National Center for Small Communities, to provide training and technical assistance to towns. Many small towns have embarked upon ambitious economic development strategies: industrial recruitment, tourism promotion, and amenity enhancement.[18]

Special Districts

Special districts are supposed to do what other local governments cannot or will not do. They are created to meet service needs in a particular area. Special districts can be formed in three different ways:

- states can create them through special enabling legislation,
- general-purpose local governments may adopt a resolution establishing a special district,
- citizens may initiate districts by petition, which is often followed by a referendum on the question.

public authority
A type of special district funded by nontax revenue and governed by an appointed board.

Some districts have the power to levy taxes; others rely on user fees, grants, and private revenue bonds for funding. Taxing districts typically have elected governing boards; nontaxing districts—called **public authorities**—ordinarily operate with appointed boards.[19] The United States has approximately 35,000 special districts and that number is increasing. (See Figure 11.1.)

Not all special districts are organized alike. Ninety-two percent of them provide a single function, but the functions vary. Natural resource management, fire protection, housing and community development, and water and sewer service are the most common. The budget and staff size of special districts range from minuscule to mammoth. Some of the more prominent include the Port Authority of New York and New Jersey, the Chicago Transit Authority, and the Los Angeles County Sanitation District.

Why Special Districts Are Needed Special districts overlay existing general-purpose local governments and address deficiencies in them.[20] Three general categories of deficiencies are worth examining: technical conditions, financial constraints, and political explanations.

First are the *technical conditions* of a general-purpose local government. In some states, cities cannot extend their service districts beyond their boundaries. Moreover, the problem to be addressed may not fit neatly within a single jurisdiction. A river that runs through several counties may periodically overflow its banks in heavy spring rains—a problem affecting small portions of many jurisdictions. A flood control district covering only the affected areas of these jurisdictions may be a logical solution. Problems of scale must also be considered. A general-purpose local government simply may not be able to provide electric service to its residents as efficiently as a special utility district that covers a multitude of counties. Finally, states may prohibit jurisdictional co-venturing that would allow jurisdictions to offer services jointly. For instance, operation of a two-county library requires that a special two-county library district be established.

A second set of deficiencies has to do with *financial constraints*. Local general-purpose governments commonly operate under debt and tax limitations. Demands for additional services that exceed a jurisdiction's revenue-raising ceiling or lead to the assumption of excessive debt cannot be accommodated. By using special districts, existing jurisdictions can circumvent the debt and tax ceilings. Special districts are better suited than general-purpose governments for service-charge or user-fee financing, whereby the cost of the service can be directly apportioned to the consumer (as with water or sewer charges).

Technical and financial deficiencies of general-purpose local governments help to explain the creation of special districts, but *political explanations* shed even more light. Restrictive annexation laws and county governments with limited authority are political facts of life that encourage the use of special districts. For residents of an urban fringe area, a public service district (which may provide more than one service) may be the only option. Some special districts owe their existence to a federal mandate. For example, national government policy has spurred the establishment of soil conservation and flood control districts throughout the country.

Once created, a special district may become a political power in its own right. In places where general-purpose governmental units are fully equipped legally, financially, and technically to provide a service, they may encounter resistance from special-district interests fighting to preserve the district.

Concerns About Special Districts The arguments in favor of special districts revolve around their potential for efficient service provision and the likelihood that they will be responsive to constituents whose demands are not otherwise being met.[21] But for the most part, scholarly observers look at special districts with a jaundiced eye. The most frequently heard complaint is that special districts lack accountability. The public is often unaware of their existence, so they function free of much scrutiny. A study of 100 airport and seaport districts found that those with an elected governing board were no more likely to be responsive to public preferences than were those with appointed boards.[22] And, as research by Nancy Burns reminds us, the establishment of special districts is a costly political act.[23] Well-placed groups such as businesses, developers, and homeowners' associations are among the beneficiaries of special-district creation. One thing is certain: The proliferation of special districts complicates the development of comprehensive solutions to public problems. It is not uncommon for cities and counties to be locked in governmental combat with the special districts in their area. All of these governmental units tend to be turf-protecting, service-providing rivals. Special districts may actually drive up the costs of service delivery. Research on 300 metropolitan areas, which compared services provided by special districts with those provided by general-purpose governments, found districts had a higher per-capita cost.[24]

Cognizant of these concerns, state governments are looking more closely at special districts and the role they play in service delivery. Several states have taken actions that give their general-purpose local governments more input into the state's decision to create special districts.

School Districts

School districts are a type of single-purpose local government. They are a distinct kind of special district and, as such, are considered one of the five types of local government. The trend in school districts follows the theory that fewer is better. Despite serving as a source of community identity, small districts were so expensive to maintain that consolidations have occurred throughout the nation. (See Figure 11.1.)

School Politics The school board is the formal source of power and authority in the district. It is typically composed of five to seven members, usually elected in nonpartisan, at-large elections. Their job is to make policy for the school district. One of the most important policy decisions involves the district budget—how the money will be spent.

School districts are governed by these boards and managed by trained, full-time educational administrators. Like city governments, school districts have invested heavily in the reform model of governance, and the average district has become more professional in operation in the past forty years. An appointed chief administrator (a superintendent) heads the school district staff, the size of which varies according to the size of the district.

Revamping public education has been a hot topic for the past decade. Concern over mismanagement of funds and low student achievement has led some states to shift control of schools away from the school district itself and place it in the hands of city government. Cleveland and Detroit are two of the most prominent examples; and in 2006, the new mayor of Washington, D.C., Adrian Fenty, took control of the District's public school system. At the same time, other school districts have sought to decentralize, shifting power to the individual school level. This school-based management approach has meant greater involvement of the private sector in some schools; in others it has enhanced the role of parents.

Parental influence in school district policy is most clearly emerging in the matter of **school choice.** School districts around the country have begun to adopt measures that allow parents to decide whether their child will attend the neighborhood school or one elsewhere in the district, perhaps a charter school. In effect, schools are competing for students. Schools are anxious to attract students because district and state funds are allocated on a per-pupil basis. To increase their appeal, some schools specialize in a particular academic area, such as arts or sciences; others emphasize certain teaching styles. Advocates of parental choice claim that this approach offers poor families some of the options that wealthy families have always had with private schools. They argue that competition among schools will generate creativity and responsiveness among teachers and principals.

School District Issues Among the myriad challenges faced by school districts is one persistent conundrum: how to secure sufficient funding for public education. Although the relationship is a bit more complex than "you get what you pay for," there is widespread agreement that children in well-funded school districts are better off educationally than those in poorly funded ones.

Serious disparities in school funding, caused by great differences in the available property taxes that provide most of the revenue, have led to the increasing financial involvement of state government in local school districts. State governments use an **equalization formula** to distribute funds to school districts in an effort to reduce financial disparities. Under this formula, poorer school districts receive a proportionately larger share of state funds than wealthier districts do. Although these programs have increased the amount of funding for education, they have not eliminated the interdistrict variation. Wealthier districts simply use the state guarantee as a foundation on which to heap their own resources. Poorer school districts continue to operate with less revenue. This situation prompted many state supreme courts around the country to declare their public-school finance systems unconstitutional. Legislatures have struggled to design new, more equitable financial arrangements. Michigan lowered property taxes for schools and substituted sales taxes and other revenues. Other states have established lotteries and earmarked the proceeds for education. The issue of money for schools is one that stays at the top of legislative agendas, year in and year out.

school choice

Market-based approach to education improvement that permits parents to choose which school their child will attend. Examples include charter schools and voucher programs.

equalization formula

A means of distributing funds (primarily to school districts) to reduce financial disparities among districts.

LEADERSHIP IN LOCAL GOVERNMENT

In 2005, Antonio Villaraigosa defeated incumbent James Hahn to become mayor of America's second largest city, Los Angeles. The last time that the City of Angels had a Latino mayor was 1872 when the vast metropolis was little more than a frontier outpost of 6,000 people. Villaraigosa's election was hailed as "a crowning symbol of Latinos' growing clout in California," while he himself was heralded as a politician to watch. Why was Villaraigosa able to defeat the sitting mayor?

Chalk it up to an electorate in the mood for change: polls showed public sentiment favoring a new direction for the city. Plus, it didn't hurt that the challenger was an adept campaigner with a knack for raising money. But winning the office was just the first step; next came an even tougher challenge—governing Los Angeles. Inundated with advice from friends and foes alike, the new mayor would do well to heed to the guidance offered by the *Los Angeles Times:* "Run an honest, open City Hall."[25]

Leadership goes hand in hand with governance. Regardless of the jurisdiction, leadership can make the difference between an effectively functioning government and one that lurches from one crisis to another. The terms that conjure up images of leadership in local government circles these days include *initiative, persistence, entrepreneurship, innovation,* and *vision*. These words share a common element: They denote activity and engagement. Leaders are people who "make a difference."[26]

Real questions about who is running the show in local government do arise. At the risk of being accused of naiveté, we might suggest that "the people" run government, local and otherwise. Unfortunately, there is much evidence to persuade us otherwise. But we should not become too cynical, either. Citizen preferences do have an impact on public policy decisions. Can we assume, therefore, that those who occupy important positions in government, such as the mayor and the city council, are in fact in charge? Are they the leaders of the community?

In sorting through the issue of who's running the show, we find that several different theories have been advanced. In general, they revolve around the concentration of power and the influence of different groups. For instance, **elite theory** argues that a small group of leaders called an elite possesses power and rules society;[27] **pluralist theory,** conversely, posits that power is dispersed among competing groups, whose clash produces societal rule.[28] Another approach, **regime analysis,** contends that certain individuals and groups possess systemic power and enjoy a strategic advantage in influencing government decisions.[29] It is important to remember that not all communities are organized alike; furthermore, even within a single community, power arrangements shift as time passes and conditions change. A case in point is Athens, Georgia, where the rock group R.E.M. has become a power broker on many issues in the community.[30]

> **elite theory**
>
> A theory of government asserting that a small group possesses power and rules society.

> **pluralist theory**
>
> A theory of government asserting that multiple open, competing groups possess power and rule society.

> **regime analysis**
>
> An approach asserting that certain individuals and groups possess systemic power and enjoy a strategic advantage in influencing government decisions.

Mayors and Managers

Mayors tend to be the most prominent figures in city government primarily because their position automatically makes them the center of attention. Successful mayors blend vision with communication skills and, even more important, an ability to get results.

Differences Between Strong and Weak Mayors As discussed earlier in the chapter, strong mayors are different from weak mayors. It is important to note that these labels refer to the *position,* not to the person who occupies it. Similarly, a structure creates opportunities for leadership, not the certainty of it. True leaders are those who can take what is structurally a weak-mayor position and transform it into a strong mayorship in practice.

A strong-mayor structure establishes the mayor as the sole chief executive who exercises substantive policy responsibilities. Directly elected by the voters rather than selected by the council, a strong-mayor serves a four-year (not a two-year) term of office and has no limitations on re-election. She also has a central role in budget formulation, extensive appointment and removal powers, and veto power over council-enacted ordinances. The more of these powers a mayor has, the stronger her position is and the easier it is for her to become a leader.

A weak-mayor structure does not provide these elements. Its design is such that the mayor shares policy responsibilities with the council and perhaps a manager, and serves a limited amount of time in office. (In an especially weak-mayor system, the job is passed around among the council members, each of whom takes a turn at being mayor.) A weak-mayor structure usually implies strong council involvement in budgetary and personnel matters.

Some observers argue that large, diverse communities grappling with complex problems are better served by a structure that fixes leadership and accountability in the mayor's office.[31] Others fear that a too-powerful mayor could run amok, building political machines based on the exchange of benefits. Structural differences can indeed have consequences, but the individuals who work within structures are the essential factor. As David Morgan and Sheilah Watson note, "Even in council–manager communities—where mayors have the fewest formal powers—by negotiating, networking, and facilitating the efforts of others, mayors clearly rise above the nominal figurehead role."[32] In the words of one politician: "It's your leader, not your form of government."[33]

African American Mayors, Women Mayors In the past, few African Americans or women were elected to the top job in America's largest cities. Like so many aspects of local politics, this too has changed. These days, it is not uncommon to find African Americans and women leading major U.S. cities.

Today's black mayors have been called a new generation by some observers because they consider themselves problem solvers, not crusaders; political pragmatists, not ideologues.[34] For example, in his successful 2006 campaign for mayor of Newark, New Jersey, Cory Booker's message was about hard work . . . and hope. On his campaign website he proclaimed, "Working together we're going to make Newark's neighborhoods safe and our schools safe. . . . Bringing real change to Newark won't be easy."[35]

Table 11.1 lists big-city African American mayors and the African American population percentage in the cities they lead. The increased success of blacks in mayoral elections has led some scholars to speak of deracialization, or the de-emphasis of race as a campaign issue for black candidates seeking white voter support.[36] Instead of making racial appeals, candidates offer a race-neutral platform that stresses their personal qualifications and political experience.[37] In cities where the white electorate outnumbers the black electorate, such as Columbus and Buffalo, neither Michael Coleman nor Byron Brown could have been elected without the support of white voters. Deracialization works both ways. Baltimore, a majority African American city, had a black mayor from 1987 to 1999, a white mayor from 1999 to 2007, and a black mayor since then.

TABLE 11.1	African American Mayors in Big Cities, 2008

CITY*	AFRICAN AMERICAN PERCENTAGE OF POPULATION	MAYOR
Philadelphia, PA	43.2	Michael Nutter
Detroit, MI	81.6	Kwame Kilpatrick
Columbus, OH	24.5	Michael Coleman
Memphis, TN	61.4	Willie Herenton
Washington, D.C.	60.0	Adrian Fenty
Baltimore, MD	64.0	Sheila Dixon
New Orleans, LA	67.3	C. Ray Nagin
Cleveland, OH	51.0	Frank Jackson
Atlanta, GA	61.4	Shirley Franklin
Oakland, CA	41.7	Ron Dellums
Cincinnati, OH	42.9	Mark Mallory
Buffalo, NY	37.2	Byron Brown
Newark, NJ	53.5	Cory Booker
Birmingham, AL	73.5	Bernard Kincaid
Baton Rouge, LA	50.0	Melvin Holden

*Cities with populations of 200,000 or more, listed in descending order according to size.
SOURCE: National Conference of Black Mayors, Atlanta, Ga., www.ncbm.org/members_of_ncbm.html (October 10, 2007). Reprinted by permission of the National Conference of Black Mayors.

More women, too, are running for and winning local elective offices. The data from cities with populations of 30,000 or more are instructive. In 1973, fewer than 2 percent of the cities in that population range had female mayors; a quarter century later, the proportion of cities with women mayors had increased to 21 percent, a level around which it has fluctuated. The list of female mayors at the helm of cities with populations of 200,000 or more appears in Table 11.2. The ranks of female mayors of major cities nearly increased by one in 2004 when Donna Frye, a member of San Diego's city council, ran against the incumbent mayor. Frye, competing as a write-in candidate, lost in a hotly disputed election. At issue were 5,547 ballots in which voters had written in Frye's name but neglected to fill in the small oval next to the write-in line. Election officials did not count these ballots because state law requires that the ovals be filled in for a write-in vote to count. Frye's supporters contended that, regardless of the ovals, voter intent was clear: a vote for Frye. Had those ballots been counted, Frye would have won by 3,439 votes.[38]

Studies of female mayoral candidates have dispelled several electoral myths.[39] For example, women do not appear to experience greater difficulty in raising money or gaining newspaper endorsements than men do. Women mayors, however, do tend to be political novices. Few female mayors in Florida, for instance,

| TABLE 11.2 | **Women Mayors in Big Cities, 2007** |

CITY*	MAYOR
Baltimore, MD	Sheila Dixon
Sacramento, CA	Heather Fargo
Virginia Beach, VA	Meyera Oberndorf
Atlanta, GA	Shirley Franklin
Tulsa, OK	Kathryn Taylor
Tampa, FL	Pam Iorio
Plano, TX	Pat Evans
Glendale, AZ	Elaine Scruggs
Chula Vista, CA	Cheryl Cox
Scottsdale, AZ	Mary Manross

*Cities with populations of 200,000 or more, listed in descending order according to size.
SOURCE: Center for American Women and Politics, "Women Mayors in U.S. Cities 2007," www.cawp.rutgers.edu/Facts/Officeholders/mayors-cur.html (October 11, 2007).

had held elective office before their mayoral election; if they had, it was usually a city council seat. Other research indicates that mayors, regardless of gender, see their political environments similarly, which makes sense: Successful local politicians know their communities.

City Managers City managers (as well as county administrators and appointed school superintendents) exemplify the movement toward reformed local government. Local government reform was a **Progressive Era** movement that sought to depose the corrupt and inefficient partisan political machines that controlled many American cities. To the reformers, local government had become too political; what was needed, they believed, was a government designed along the lines of a business corporation. To achieve their goals, reformers advocated such fundamental structural changes in local government as the abolition of partisan local elections, the use of at-large electoral systems, and the installation of a professionally trained city manager. Altering the structure of local government has had profound consequences for local government leadership. City managers—the professional, neutral experts whose job it is to run the day-to-day affairs of the city—have become key leaders.

In the original conception, managers were to implement but not formulate policy. Administration and politics were to be kept separate. The managers' responsibility would be to administer the policies enacted by the elected officials—the city councils—by whom they were hired (and fired). But it is impossible to keep administration and politics completely separate. City managers are influenced not only by their training and by the councils that employ them but also by their own political ideologies.[40] When it comes to making choices, they balance professional norms, the politics of the issue, and their own predispositions.

Progressive Era

A period in the early twentieth century that focused on reforming or cleaning up government.

Hence city managers typically end up being far more influential on the local government scene than their neutral persona might suggest.

According to the International City/County Management Association, the city managers' professional association, the role of the manager is to help the governing body function more effectively. "Managers—and their staffs—need to build political capacity so they can assist the elected body in framing community issues."[41] Ways in which the manager can assume a larger role in policymaking include proposing community goals and service levels; structuring the budget preparation, review, and adoption process so that it is linked to goals and service levels; and orienting new council members to organizational processes and norms. The approach has had the intended effect. James Svara, who surveyed officials of large cities, concluded that managers have become "more assertive in attempting to focus the council on long-range concerns and in shaping the tone of the policymaking process."[42] Another indisputable role for the manager is as an information source for the busy, part-time city council.

City Councils

Local legislatures include city councils, county commissions, town boards of aldermen or selectmen, special-district boards, and school boards. They are representative, deliberative, policymaking bodies. In this section we focus on city councils, because that is where most of the research has taken place; but many of the points made are applicable to the other local legislative bodies, especially county commissions and school boards. And although the ensuing discussion focuses on patterns across councils, it is important to remember that there may be significant variations from one city to another. For example, in some communities, council members receive high salaries, are assisted by clerical and research staff, and have no limits on the number of terms they can serve. In Chicago, for instance, city council members (called **aldermen**) earn more than $98,000 per year, have office staffs and can serve an unlimited number of four-year terms. (To put it in perspective, the mayor of Chicago has an annual salary of $216,000.) In other places, council service is considered a volunteer activity, with members receiving little compensation.

aldermen

A label used in some communities for members of a local legislative body, such as a city council.

City Council Members: Old and New A former member of the city council of Concord, California, defines "the good old days" on local governing boards with this comment: "When I first came on the city council, it was like a good-old-boys' club."[43] The standard view was that the city council was a part-time, low-paying haven for public-spirited white men who did not consider themselves politicians. Most councils used at-large electoral mechanisms, so individual council members had no specific territorially-based constituency. Council members considered themselves volunteers. Research on city councils in the San Francisco Bay–area cities in the 1960s found that these volunteer members were fairly unresponsive to public pressures and tended to vote their own preferences.[44]

Today, the circumstances have changed. City councils are less white, less male, and less passive than they were in the past. City councilors are more engaged and active. Some of this change is due to modifications in the electoral mechanism

at-large elections

Citywide (or countywide) contests to determine the members of a city council (or county commission).

district (ward) elections

Elections in which the voters in one district or ward of a jurisdiction (city, county, school district) vote for a candidate to represent that district.

such as the abandonment of at-large or citywide elections and the switch to district (or ward) elections. In **at-large elections,** a city voter can vote for as many candidates as there are seats to be filled. In **district (ward) elections,** a city voter can vote only in the council race in her district. From the perspective of candidates, the at-large system means that a citywide campaign must be mounted; with districts, the candidate's campaign is limited to a specific area of the city. Figure 11.6 displays the district map for the Phoenix city council, which elects eight councilors from districts with the mayor (who is also a member of the council) running at-large. Other cities have chosen to retain some at-large council seats while dividing the city into electoral districts. Houston, a strong-mayor city, is an example: Of the fourteen members of the Houston city council, five are elected at large, and nine are elected from districts. (Table 11.3 shows the wide variation both in council size and in number of members elected at large and from districts.) Changes in election mechanisms signaled a change in council composition. There are more African Americans, Latinos, and women

---

FIGURE 11.6 | **City Council Districts in Phoenix, 2008**

Each city council district in Phoenix contains approximately 190,000 people.
SOURCE: City of Phoenix, http://phoenix.gov/citygov/map .html (November 15, 2007).

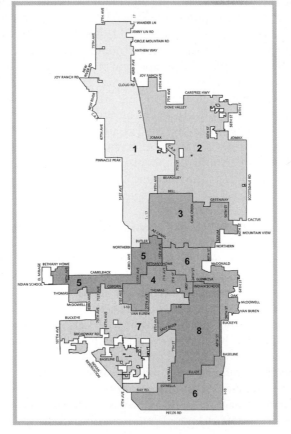

| TABLE 11.3 | City Councils of the Twenty Largest U.S. Cities |

CITY	2000 ESTIMATED POPULATION	COUNCIL SIZE	NUMBER ELECTED AT-LARGE	NUMBER ELECTED FROM DISTRICTS
New York, NY	8,214,426	51	0	51
Los Angeles, CA	3,849,378	15	0	15
Chicago, IL	2,833,321	50	0	50
Houston, TX	2,144,491	14	5	9
Phoenix, AZ	1,512,986	9	1	8
Philadelphia, PA	1,448,394	17	7	10
San Antonio, TX	1,296,682	11	1	10
San Diego, CA	1,256,951	8	0	8
Dallas, TX	1,232,940	14	0	14
San Jose, CA	929,936	10	0	10
Detroit, MI	871,121	9	9	0
Jacksonville, FL	794,555	19	5	14
Indianapolis, IN	785,597	29	4	25
San Francisco, CA	744,041	11	0	11
Columbus, OH	733,203	7	0	7
Austin, TX	709,893	7	7	0
Memphis, TN	670,902	13	0	13
Ft. Worth, TX	653,320	9	1	8
Baltimore, MD	631,366	19	1	18
Charlotte, NC	630,478	12	5	7

SOURCE: "Annual Estimates of the Population for Incorporated Places Over 100,000," U.S. Census Bureau (July 2006); individual city websites.

on city councils than ever before, and councils are taking their governance roles quite seriously.

Much research has been done on the impact of structural considerations—for example, the at-large election format, the size of the council, and the use of nonpartisan elections—on minority council representation.[45] Other factors such as the size of the minority group, its geographical concentration, and its political cohesiveness affect electoral success. In general, a higher proportion of African American council members can be found in central cities that use a mayor–council structure and in southern cities with large black populations. Councils with higher-than-average Hispanic representation tend to be found in the West, particularly the Southwest, in larger central cities using council–manager structures. Thus far, Asian representation has been clustered primarily in the Pacific Coast area in larger council–manager central cities. And Native American representation is highest in very small communities using commission structures in the southwestern and Pacific Coast regions of the country. The increase in non-whites on councils has policy consequences. Data from 351 city council members indicate that nonwhites pursue a more liberal policy agenda than whites.[46]

Given the finite number of council seats in any community and the fact that more groups are now clamoring for representation, two outcomes are possible: Minority groups may try to build coalitions, or they may opt for a more independent, competitive approach. Although temporary electoral coalitions have emerged in a few cities, it appears that interminority group competition is on the rise. Research in ninety-six cities demonstrates, for example, that an increase in the Latino population has a negative effect on black representation on city councils.[47] Another interesting question is the extent to which the concept of deracialization can be extended to Latinos and Asian Americans in their bids for local offices. Research on the Little Saigon area of Orange County, California, showed evidence of racial bloc voting in every election for city council or school board between 1998 and 2002 in which a Vietnamese American competed against a white candidate.[48]

Local governing boards in cities and counties are becoming more diverse in another way: The number of openly gay and lesbian elected officials is increasing. The Gay and Lesbian Victory Fund is a PAC that provides technical and financial support for openly gay and lesbian candidates, many of whom are seeking local offices. Christine Quinn, who in 2006 became speaker of New York City's council, is one of the most prominent; Sam Adams, a city commissioner in Portland, Oregon, is another. A study focusing on cities and counties that had antidiscrimination ordinances in place revealed several findings about the election of gays and lesbians. Based on that sample of jurisdictions, gay and lesbian electoral success was more likely in larger cities; in jurisdictions with higher numbers of nonfamily households (such as university communities); and in places with partisan, district election of council members.[49] The limited nature of the sample makes it difficult to generalize to all localities, but the research yields interesting findings about council diversity.

Councils in Action: Increasing Conflict In earlier times, when members of the council came from the same socioeconomic stratum and when they shared a common political philosophy, governing was a lot easier. Members of the council could come together before the meeting and discuss the items on the agenda. That way, they could arrive at an informal resolution of any particularly troubling items and thereby transform the actual council meeting into a rubber-stamp exercise. No wonder that the majority of council votes were often unanimous; members were merely ratifying what they had already settled on.

Council members elected by districts report more factionalism and less unanimity than do their counterparts elected at large. The growing tendency of cities to move away from complete reliance on at-large electoral mechanisms suggests that council discord will be on the rise in the future. Fifty-five percent of the city council members responding to a national survey reported that such conflict was a serious source of frustration to them.[50] Ten years earlier, only 33 percent had voiced a similar concern. High levels of council conflict have other consequences. Research on city managers has shown a link between council conflict and managerial burnout.[51] Burned-out city managers perform poorly and often leave the city or the profession itself. Conflict-management skills can assist novice managers in their dealings with the council.

Battles with the Mayor Relationships between a city council and the mayor can be conflictual, to say the least. In fact, they can be downright hostile. A former mayor of Philadelphia did not pull any punches when he referred to the city council as "the worst legislative body in the free world."[52] In Salt Lake City, the new mayor, Rocky Anderson, took several actions at odds with the city council when he assumed office in 2000. He vetoed several of the council's pet projects, and he took action unilaterally through executive orders when the council was indecisive on an issue. In the mayor's words, "You don't ask the council . . . you just do it."[53] Needless to say, the city council in Salt Lake City took offense at the mayor's attitude and actions.

Council-mayor conflict is not necessarily unproductive. Conflict is expected in a political system that operates on the foundation of separation of powers. Clashes between the legislative branch and the executive branch can produce better government. But when the disagreements between the council and the mayor escalate to the point of gridlock, effective governance is stymied.

Nonprofit Organizations in the Community

nonprofit organizations

Private sector groups that carry out charitable, educational, religious, literary, or scientific functions.

Nonprofit organizations have become increasingly important in communities. Many of these organizations have become fully integrated into the world of local government and politics. Four types of governmentally active nonprofit organizations can be identified:

- Civic nonprofits
- Policy advocates
- Policy implementers
- Governing nonprofits[54]

The first type, civic nonprofit organizations, plays a watchdog role, monitoring government and educating the public. A local citizen's league acts in this way, attending city council meetings and publicizing council decisions. Policy advocates, the second type, move beyond the provision of information to become active supporters of particular policies or programs. For instance, if an education advocacy group endorses year-round schools, it would lobby the school board vigorously in support of such a policy change. The third type of nonprofit organization, policy implementers, actually delivers services, often through a contract with a local government. For example, homeless shelters in many communities are operated by nonprofit groups supported by city funds, federal grants, and charitable contributions. Governing nonprofits, the fourth type, are different because they may work through or with local government but they also act independently. These nonprofits are the most powerful of the four types because they offer an alternative venue for decision making.

Nonprofit organizations of all types have become omnipresent in localities throughout the nation. In Detroit, for example, groups such as New Detroit and Detroit Renaissance have become important players in the city's politics.[55]

New Detroit has more of a social agenda, focusing on race relations and education reform. Detroit Renaissance, a smaller organization made up of the corporate elite from the Detroit area, has concentrated its energies on economic renewal. For thirty years, these organizations have advocated ambitious reforms and new policies, and while not always successful, they have influenced local decisions.

COMMUNITIES AND GOVERNANCE

Let us return to the governance issue that was raised early in this chapter and has been alluded to throughout it: How do we know when a community is well governed? This chapter is full of examples of communities that have restructured their governments in hopes of improving governance. Voters oust incumbents and elect new council members in a similar effort. Once in office, many big-city mayors adopt a pragmatic approach, an orientation that is independent of race or ethnicity. It is a back-to-basics approach to governing, one that emphasizes service delivery, balanced budgets, and working with the private sector to cure the city's ills. Jurisdictions with workable structures and effective leaders have an advantage, to be sure.

Although there is no set of universally accepted criteria for evaluating the quality of governance, several organizations have come up with proxy measures. For example, the National Municipal League annually bestows its "All-America City" designation on jurisdictions (both cities and counties) that successfully tackle community problems in a collaborative way. Among the All-America Cities in 2007 were Santa Rosa, California; Polk County, Florida; and Dubuque, Iowa.[56] Another effort is that of the Government Performance Project (GPP), which gauges the management practices and performance of major cities. In their latest evaluation, GPP researchers gave top grades to Austin, Indianapolis, Milwaukee, Phoenix, and San Diego.[57]

The governance question goes back to Plato and Aristotle, and we are unlikely to resolve it here. Local governments and their leaders are confronting their problems and challenges by trying new ideas, exploring alternatives, and reaching out for solutions. No doubt about it: this can be a tough task. Consider the case of Philadelphia. In 2007, voters elected a new mayor to take control of a city plagued by high rates of violent crime, pervasive poverty, and persistent unemployment; in addition, its school system had been taken over by state government. Not only that, a budget crisis loomed, and the contracts with public employee unions were due to be renegotiated. Despite the circumstances, the new mayor was optimistic, stating, "What I'm hoping to lead is literally the renaissance of Philadelphia."[58] His upbeat tone is shared by mayors elsewhere. New York City Mayor Michael Bloomberg, when asked whether he would run for higher office, responded this way: "I think I have a better job than the governor and the president."[59]

CHAPTER RECAP

- There are five types of local governments: counties, municipalities, towns and townships, special districts, and school districts. There are more than 87,800 local governments in the United States.
- Counties were created by states to serve as their local administrative arms, while cities operate with a charter of incorporation, and typically have more power than counties.
- Special districts are both the most prevalent and the least understood of the five types of local government.
- School districts have many concerns, but one persistent issue is the availability of sufficient funding for public education.
- The public wants well-governed communities. Local governments redesign their structures in hopes of improving governance. A primary issue in redesigning structures is the role of the executive.
- Mayors tend to be the central figures in city politics and government, even if they operate in formally weak-mayor structures.
- City managers, as top-level appointed officials, have become policy leaders.
- City councils have changed from the good-old-boy clubs of the past. They are more active, they are more diverse, and there is more conflict on the council.
- Nonprofit organizations have become increasingly important in communities.

Key Terms

general-purpose local government *(p. 244)*

single-purpose local government *(p. 244)*

incorporation *(p. 248)*

charter *(p. 248)*

strong-mayor-council structure, *(p. 249)*

weak-mayor-council structure *(p. 249)*

town meeting *(p. 252)*

public authority *(p. 253)*

school choice *(p. 256)*

equalization formula *(p. 256)*

elite theory *(p. 257)*

pluralist theory *(p. 257)*

regime analysis *(p. 257)*

Progressive Era *(p. 260)*

aldermen *(p. 261)*

at-large elections *(p. 262)*

district (ward) elections *(p. 262)*

nonprofit organizations *(p. 265)*

Internet Resources

Most of the five types of government are represented by national associations, which have useful websites: **www.naco.org** (National Association of Counties); **www.nlc.org** (National League of Cities); **www.natat.org** (National Association of Towns and Townships); **www.nsba.org** (for school districts, the relevant website is that of the National School Boards Association).

To explore a specific school district, such as the City of Philadelphia's school district, see **www.phila.k12.pa.us.**

Special districts, by virtue of their specialized nature, tend to have function-specific national organizations. For example, to learn about the National Association of Conservation Districts, see **www.nacdnet.org.** A fifteen-county district, the Colorado River Water Conservation District, whose website can be found at **www.crwcd.org,** is an example of an individual special district. One of the most famous special districts is the Port Authority of New York and New Jersey; its website is **www.panynj.gov.**

Over time, cities and counties have found that maintaining websites is a good way to connect with the public. See, for example, the website for Miami–Dade County at **www.miamidade.gov.** The website for the city of Los Angeles can be found at **www.ci.la.ca.us;** the web site for the county is at **lacounty.info.** To learn more about the largest county in Michigan, go to **www.waynecounty .com.** You can find information about the Big Apple at **www.nyc.gov;** while **www.houstontx.gov** and **www.cityofboston.gov** are the websites for the cities of Houston and Boston, respectively.

The U.S. Conference of Mayors, the association of mayors of cities with populations of 30,000 or more, has a web presence: **www.usmayors.org.**

Specialized constituency groups often have their own organizations and web sites, as does the National Conference of Black Mayors at **www.ncbm.org.**

The web site for the Center for American Women and Politics at Rutgers University, **www.cawp.rutgers.edu,** contains a wealth of data on women and politics.

Information about the city and county management profession can be found at the International City/County Management Association's website: **www .icma.org.**

An important outlet for the latest scholarly research on local politics is the journal *Urban Affairs Review* (**http://uar.sagepub.com/**).

Taxing and Spending

CHAPTER OUTLINE

FOCUS QUESTIONS

1. What are the two basic principles of state and local financial systems?

2. Among the variety of state and local taxes, what are the three major ones and what are some of the primary criteria for evaluating them?

3. What are some of the consequences of taxpayer resistance?

4. How would you characterize state and local financial relationships?

*E*ight months of tough negotiations came to a head the night of September 30, 2007, when Governor Jennifer Granholm made good on her threat to shut down Michigan state government if the legislature did not produce a budget to her liking. Suffering from the infirmities of the U.S. auto industry and a housing slowdown, Michigan's lawmakers had been unable to come to agreement on how to repair a $1.75 billion budget deficit. In play were income and sales tax hikes, extension of the sales tax to more services, and spending cuts. Finally, in the early morning hours of October 1, the legislature heeded Granholm's call to "put loyalty to Michigan over loyalty to party" and enacted a budget.[1] The state income tax rate was raised, the sales tax was applied to tanning beds, landscaping, carpet cleaning, and more than twenty other services, to pull in estimated new revenues of $1.3 billion. Three prisons and two state police labs were closed, state workers were laid off, and spending was cut to make up the remainder of the deficit.

Such fiscal drama is not unusual in state capitals. Indeed, it is increasingly the norm whenever revenues do not equal expenditures over the fiscal year. Sometimes budget problems are relatively isolated in a handful of states. At other times, serious problems sweep across the states, forcing all of them to make difficult choices.

This chapter deals with state and local finance: the politics and policies of taxing and spending. It is a topic of continuing, visceral interest in state and local

269

jurisdictions, and an activity characterized by much change and experimentation. From taxpayer revolts to spending mandates, the fiscal landscape has changed profoundly. More change is certain as state and local governments strive to meet taxpayer service demands economically and creatively.

THE PRINCIPLES OF FINANCE

A major purpose of government is to provide essential services to citizens. But this costs money: Equipment must be purchased and employees must be paid. Governments raise needed funds through taxes, fees, and borrowing. In a democracy, the voters decide what range and quality of services they desire and register those opinions through elected representatives. Sometimes, when elected officials don't listen, voters revolt and take matters directly into their own hands.

Two basic principles describe state and local financial systems: *interdependence* and *diversity*. State and local fiscal systems are closely interlinked and heavily influenced by national financial activities. Intergovernmental sharing of revenues is a pronounced feature of our interdependent federal fiscal system. Yet our state financial structures and processes are also highly diverse. Though affected by national activities, their own economic health, and competitive pressures from one another, the states enjoy substantial autonomy in designing individual revenue systems in response to citizens' policy preferences.

Interdependence

own-source revenue

Monies derived by a government from its own taxable resources.

intergovernmental transfers

The movement of money or other resources from one level of government to another.

State governments raise huge amounts of money. In 2005, the states and localities garnered about $2.5 trillion. Most of this money is **own-source revenue,** gathered from taxes, charges, and fees applied to people, services, and products within the jurisdiction of each level of government. Nonnational governments also benefit from **intergovernmental transfers.** The national government contributes about 30 percent of all state and local expenditures; however, 64 percent of this federal money is passed through to *individual* recipients such as those receiving Medicaid. For their part, states pass on more than $400 billion to their cities, counties, and special-purpose governments.[2] Some of the states are economic powerhouses. California's $1.7 trillion total economy is the fifth largest in the world, just ahead of France.

Local governments rely heavily on the states, and to a lesser degree on the national government, for financial authority and assistance. *Only the states* can authorize localities to levy taxes and fees, incur debt, and spend money. State constitutions and laws place many conditions on local government taxing and spending. As federal aid declined in importance, states increased their monetary support of local governments through state grants-in-aid and revenue sharing; they also assumed financial responsibility for activities previously paid for by localities—in particular, school and social welfare costs. The emergence of the states as senior financial partners in state–local finance has been challenged in some states (especially those without state income taxes) by the need for large local tax increases to fund school improvements or local services.

State–local finances are linked very closely to activities of the national government. For instance, when the federal government changes the tax code, it can wreak havoc on those thirty-five states that base their own income tax on that of the federal government. Congress's phase-out of the estate tax was projected to cost the states upwards of $5 billion in 2007 alone.[3]

countercyclical aid

A transfer of federal dollars to states and localities to counteract a downturn in the economic cycle.

When national monetary and fiscal policies push the nation into recession, state and local governments suffer most. This fact is sometimes recognized by Congress, which may send substantial amounts of **countercyclical aid** to the states and localities to help them recover from the ravages of recession. Special aid is targeted to states suffering from natural disasters, including hurricanes, floods, and fires.

Diversity

The second basic principle of state and local finance systems is diversity of revenue sources. Each level of government depends on one type of revenue device more than others. For the national government it is the income tax; for the states, the sales tax; and for local governments, the property tax. But diversity triumphs among the states. Differences in tax capacity (wealth), tax effort, and tax choices are obvious even to the casual observer. Most states tax personal income and merchandise sales, but a handful of them do not. A majority of states operate lotteries and pari-mutuel betting facilities.

Some states, such as Maine and New York, tax with a heavy hand. Others, including New Hampshire and Alaska, are relative tax havens. Most fall somewhere in the middle. If the basic objective of taxing is to pluck the maximum number of feathers from the goose with the minimum amount of hissing, the wealthy states hold a great advantage, since they can reap high tax revenues with much less effort than poor states, which must tax at high rates just to pull in enough money to pay for the basics. Per-capita state and local tax revenues vary from $5,752 in New York to $2,569 in Alabama. The U.S. average is $3,698.[4] There is a close relationship between state wealth (as measured by personal income) and tax burden. Table 12.1 shows how the states compare in state and local tax burdens (taxes, controlling for personal income). Tax levels can reflect such factors as citizen attitudes, population characteristics and trends, business climate, and the quality as well as quantity of government services. And taxing is only one means of plucking the public goose. State and local governments increasingly rely on fees and charges for services rendered. Examples include entrance fees for parks and recreation facilities; sewer and garbage fees; and motor vehicle fees.

tax capacity

The taxable resources of a government jurisdiction.

tax effort

The extent to which a jurisdiction exploits its taxable resources.

There is an important difference between **tax capacity,** the potential ability to raise revenues from taxes, and **tax effort,** the degree to which a state exploits its fiscal potential. High tax capacity is associated with high levels of urbanization, per-capita income, economic development, and natural resources. But simply because a state has high revenue-raising capacity does not necessarily mean that it will maximize its tax-collecting possibilities. Indeed, many states with high revenue potential, such as Alaska and Wyoming, actually tax at relatively low rates, indicating low tax effort.[5] Tax effort depends largely on the scope and level of services desired by the people.

| TABLE 12.1 | State and Local Tax Burdens, 2007, in Descending Order |

STATE	STATE/LOCAL TAXES AS A % OF INCOME	STATE/ LOCAL RANK	STATE	STATE/LOCAL TAXES AS A % OF INCOME	STATE/ LOCAL RANK
Vermont	14.1	1	Utah	10.7	27
Maine	14.0	2	Massachusetts	10.6	28
New York	13.8	3	Mississippi	10.5	29
Rhode Island	12.7	4	Colorado	10.4	30
Ohio	12.4	5	Arizona	10.3	31
Hawaii	12.4	6	Georgia	10.3	32
Wisconsin	12.3	7	Virginia	10.2.	33
Connecticut	12.3	8	Missouri	10.1	34
Nebraska	11.9	9	Idaho	10.1	35
New Jersey	11.6	10	Nevada	10.1	36
Minnesota	11.5	11	Oregon	10.0	37
California	11.5	12	Florida	10.0	38
Arkansas	11.3	13	North Dakota	9.9	39
Michigan	11.2	14	New Mexico	9.8	40
Kansas	11.2	15	Montana	9.7	41
Washington	11.1	16	Wyoming	9.5	42
Louisiana	11.0	17	Texas	9.3	43
Iowa	11.0	18	South Dakota	9.0	44
North Carolina	11.0	19	Oklahoma	9.0	45
Kentucky	10.9	20	Alabama	8.8	46
West Virginia	10.9	21	Delaware	8.8	47
Illinois	10.8	22	Tennessee	8.5	48
Maryland	10.8	23	New Hampshire	8.0	49
Pennsylvania	10.8	24	Alaska	6.6	50
Indiana	10.7	25	U.S. average	11.0	
South Carolina	10.7	26			

SOURCE: "State and Local Taxes as a Percentage of Personal Income, 2008, in Descending Order" data from Tax Foundation (www.taxfoundation.org). Reprinted by permission of the Tax Foundation.

REVENUES

Although the state and local finance systems have their own strengths, weaknesses, and peculiarities, certain trends can be found in all of them. The property tax is always unpopular. It is no longer a significant source of state revenue;

| FIGURE 12.1 | **Distribution of Total State and Local Tax Revenue by Source** |

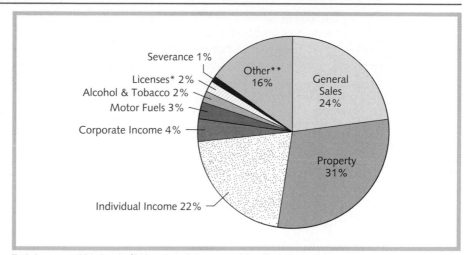

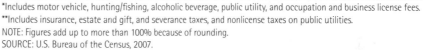

*Includes motor vehicle, hunting/fishing, alcoholic beverage, public utility, and occupation and business license fees.
**Includes insurance, estate and gift, and severance taxes, and nonlicense taxes on public utilities.
NOTE: Figures add up to more than 100% because of rounding.
SOURCE: U.S. Bureau of the Census, 2007.

its contribution to total own-source local revenues, though, is still strong. User fees and other miscellaneous charges are gradually increasing. States continue to depend heavily on the sales tax, but alternatives are being used more widely. Revenues from the federal government make up almost 22 percent of the total. In fact, revenue diversification is an important trend in all state and local tax systems (see Figure 12.1).

Criteria for Evaluating Taxes

Numerous criteria can be used to evaluate taxes. What one person or interest group likes about a tax may be what another detests. Nevertheless, most political scientists and economists agree that among the most important criteria are equity, yield, elasticity, ease of administration, political accountability, and acceptability.

Equity If citizens or firms are expected to pay a tax, they should view it as fair. In the context of taxation, equity usually refers to the distribution of the tax burden in accordance with ability to pay: High income means greater ability to pay and, therefore, a larger tax burden. Equity has other dimensions as well, such as the relative tax burden on individuals versus firms and the impact of various types of taxes on income, age, and social class.

regressive tax

A tax in which the rate falls as the base or taxable income rises.

Taxes may be regressive, progressive, or proportional. A **regressive tax** places a greater burden on low-income citizens than on high-income citizens. Thus the ability-to-pay principle is violated, with the result that upper-income groups contribute a smaller portion of their incomes than lower-income groups do. Most state and local levies, including property and sales taxes, are regressive. For example, both low-income and high-income people would pay, say, a 7 percent sales tax. The latter will likely make more purchases and contribute more total dollars in sales tax, but at a lower percentage of their total income than the low-income individuals.

A **progressive tax** increases as a percentage of a person's income as that income rises. The more you make, the greater proportion of your income is extracted by the progressive tax. Thus, those who are better able to pay carry a heavier tax burden than the poor. Among the states, California's personal income tax is most progressive, varying from 2.0 to 10.3 percent of taxable income. The more you earn, the higher your *income tax bracket*.

A **proportional tax,** sometimes called a **flat tax,** burdens everyone equally, at least in theory. For instance, a tax on income of, say, 10 percent that is applied across the board is a proportional tax. Whether you earn $100,000 or $10,000, you pay a flat 10 percent of the total in taxes. Of course, it can be argued that a low-income person is more burdened by a proportional tax than a high-income person (as in the case of the sales tax).

In place of ability to pay, some people advocate the **benefit principle.** Under this principle, those who reap more benefits from government services should shoulder more of the tax burden than people who do not avail themselves of service opportunities to the same degree. As a hypothetical example, it might be argued that parents whose children attend public schools should pay higher taxes for education than should senior citizens, childless couples, or single people without children. The benefit principle is the theoretical underpinning for user fees, which charge a taxpayer directly for services received. The unfortunate downside is that it disadvantages those who have the least ability to pay.

Yield Taxes can also be evaluated on the basis of efficiency, or how much money they contribute to government coffers compared to the effort expended to collect them. The administrative and other costs of applying a tax must be taken into consideration when determining yield. Taxes that return substantial sums of money at minimal costs to the government are preferred to taxes that require large outlays for moderate revenues. Income and sales taxes have high yields because they raise large sums of money at low expense. Property taxes have lower yields because they are more expensive to assess and collect. Yield depends on base and rate. The broader the tax base, the higher the yield. For example, a sales tax applied to all purchases yields much more than a sales tax on cigarette purchases, and a $2 per pack tax produces more revenue than a 25 cents per pack tax.

Elasticity This criterion is related to yield. Tax yields should be automatically responsive to changes in economic conditions, and revenue devices should expand or contract their yields as government expenditure needs change. Specifically, as per capita income grows within the state and its localities, revenues should keep pace without increases in the tax rate. Tax reductions should accompany economic recession and declines in per capita income, so that citizens' tax burdens are not increased during hard times. The progressive income tax is considered to be elastic because revenues increase as individuals earn more money and

progressive tax

A tax in which the rate rises as the base or taxable income rises.

proportional (flat) tax

A tax in which people pay an identical rate regardless of income or economic transaction.

benefit principle

The principle that taxes should be levied on those who benefit directly from a government service.

move into higher tax brackets and decline as income falls. User fees, for example, generally do not move in tandem with economic conditions and are therefore considered to be inelastic.

Ease of Administration Taxes should be simple to understand and compute. They should also be easy to apply in a nonarbitrary fashion and difficult to evade. Income taxes are fairly easy to collect because most are deducted from employee paychecks and remitted to the state by employers. Local property taxes are difficult to administer because of the time and expense involved in regularly appraising property values and the inherent subjectivity of placing a dollar value on buildings and land. The sales tax is easy to administer at the time and place of sale, and nearly impossible to evade. (Exceptions to this rule involve out-of-state catalog and Internet sales and consumers who cross state borders to avoid high sales taxes on merchandise, cigarettes, gasoline, and alcohol.)

Political Accountability Tax increases should not be hidden. Instead, state and local legislative bodies should have to approve them deliberately—and publicly. Citizens should know how much they owe and when it must be paid. For example, some state income taxes are silently hiked as wages rise in response to cost-of-living increases. After inflation is accounted for, taxpayers make the same income as they did before, but they are driven into a higher income bracket for tax purposes. This phenomenon, known as bracket creep, can be eliminated by **indexing** income tax brackets to changes in the cost of living.

indexing
A system in which tax brackets are automatically adjusted to account for inflation.

Acceptability The type and mix of taxes imposed should be congruent with citizen preferences. No tax commands wild enthusiasm, but some are less disagreeable than others. Tax acceptability varies from place to place depending on numerous factors, including equity implications and the perceived pain of paying. Large, one-time payments, such as the annual property tax, inflict greater pain than small, frequently paid sales taxes. And a tax on someone else is always preferable. As Senator Russell Long of Louisiana put it many years ago, "Don't tax me, don't tax thee; tax that man behind the tree."

Major State and Local Taxes

The principal types of taxes are those on property, sales, and income. Various other miscellaneous taxes also provide much-needed revenue for state and local governments.

Property Tax Taxes on personal and corporate property account for 31 percent of tax revenues. States hardly utilize the property tax at all today—about 4 percent of their total revenues—but local governments continue to depend on this fiscal workhorse for three-quarters of all their own-source revenues. Other revenue sources have augmented the property tax so that overall, its proportionate contribution has diminished. As always, there is considerable state-by-state variation. New Hampshire, which has no sales or income taxes, depends on property taxes for more than half of its total state and local tax revenues.

The best feature of the property tax is that it is certain; owners of property must pay it or the government may seize and sell their land, buildings, or other taxable possessions. But it has lost acceptability in recent years because it tends to be regressive, lacks political accountability, is hard to administer, and sometimes must be paid in a large lump sum. At first thought, it seems that property taxes cannot be truly regressive, because only those people who own property pay taxes on it directly; however, renters pay property taxes indirectly through their monthly rent checks to the landlord. When property tax assessments climb, so do rental charges. Property taxes can also violate the ability-to-pay principle when housing values spiral upward, as they recently did in Utah, Colorado, Oregon, and Arizona. Retirees and other homeowners on fixed incomes discover with alarm that their annual property tax bills are rising sharply as housing prices escalate.

Just this sort of situation helped precipitate California's Proposition 13, which was credited with kicking off a taxpayer revolt across the United States. In the Los Angeles and San Francisco Bay areas during the 1970s, property taxes doubled and then tripled in only a few years. Some senior citizens were forced to sell their homes to pay their property tax. Proposition 13 reduced property tax bills by approximately $7 billion in the first year; and it imposed strict limitations on the ability of local governments to raise property and other taxes in the future. California dropped from being the eighth-highest property tax state to the twenty-eighth. This illustrates the problem of political accountability: When property values rise to lofty heights, taxpayers' bills keep pace, even though elected officials do not explicitly vote to hike property taxes.

Property taxes are difficult to administer and are somewhat arbitrary. The process of levying an annual fee on "real property" (land and buildings) begins with a government assessor's making a formal appraisal of the market value of the land and the buildings on it. Then property values are "equalized" so that similarly valued real estate is taxed at the same level. Next, an assessment ratio is applied to the property. For instance, houses might be assessed for tax purposes at 80 percent of market value. A rate is placed on the assessed value to calculate the annual tax amount. (Assessed at $100,000, taxed at a ratio of .80 and a rate of $3 per $100 [30 mils], a house would produce a tax due of $2,400.) Determining market value may seem fairly straightforward, but ultimately the appraised value depends on the findings of the assessor, who may or may not be properly trained for the job or be fully aware of conditions in the local housing market. Property can thus be underappraised or overappraised. For the sake of equity, property should be appraised regularly (for example, every five years). Otherwise, property that does not change ownership becomes increasingly undervalued.

Property tax systems are further criticized for exempting certain types of real estate and buildings. Government buildings such as hospitals and state offices are not taxed, even though they utilize police and fire protection, trash collection, and other local government services. Churches, synagogues, mosques, and related property used for religious purposes are also partly or wholly exempted in the vast majority of jurisdictions, as is property owned by charitable and nonprofit organizations.

circuit breaker

A limit on taxes applied to certain categories of people, such as the poor or the elderly.

In an effort to make property taxation more equitable and more in keeping with ability to pay, most states have enacted some form of **circuit breaker.** For instance, the property of low-income individuals is excluded from taxation in some states; others assign lower assessment ratios to the homes of senior citizens or set a top limit on the tax according to the owner's income (for example, 4 percent of net income). Many states have "truth in taxation" laws that roll back property taxes as appraised values rise rapidly. Most also offer homestead exemptions, in which owner-occupied homes are taxed at lower rates or assessed at lower values than rental homes or business property. Massachusetts municipalities permit seniors to earn credits against their tax bills through public service activities.

Despite such attempts to make property tax fairer, differences in property values among cities, counties, and school districts have important implications for the quality and distribution of services. Jurisdictions with many wealthy families, capital-intensive industries, or rapid construction growth can provide high levels of services with low tax rates, whereas areas with weak property tax bases must tax at high rates merely to yield enough revenues to maintain minimal services. Residential property tax rates vary widely in individual cities. For example, the rate is $2.99 per $100 of assessed value in Houston but only $0.38 in Honolulu. Altering the unequal distribution of property values is essentially beyond the control of local governments. As a result, "wealthy suburbs remain wealthy, poor communities remain poor, and services remain unequal."[6] Inequity in school funding has been the target of a growing number of lawsuits. In Michigan, the legislature significantly reduced property taxes for public education and asked voters to substitute either sales tax increases or higher income taxes. Voters opted overwhelmingly for a 2¢ sales tax increase accompanied by a 50¢-per-pack cigarette tax hike. Dramatic property tax relief measures have also been adopted recently in Florida, Maine, and Washington.

Sales Tax States currently collect more of their revenues from the general sales and gross receipts tax than from any other source. It accounts for about one-third of total own-source state taxes. (Again, see Figure 12.1.) Only five states do not levy a general sales tax: Alaska, Delaware, Montana, New Hampshire, and Oregon. State sales tax rates vary from 7.25 percent in California and 7 percent in Rhode Island, Tennessee, New Jersey and Mississippi, to 2.9 percent in Colorado. Some states, particularly those that do not have personal income taxes, are exceptionally dependent on the sales tax: Florida, Washington, and Tennessee derive approximately 60 percent of their own-source revenues from the sales tax.

The sales tax has remained in favor for two major reasons. First, citizen surveys have consistently shown that when a tax must be raised, voters prefer the sales tax. Although the reasons are not entirely clear, this tax is perceived to be fairer than other forms of taxation. Second, there is an abiding belief that high state income taxes depress economic development.[7] Moreover, the property tax is widely detested.

Thirty-three states authorize at least some of their municipalities and counties to levy local sales taxes. When state and local sales taxes are combined, the total tax bite can be painful. In Arkansas cities, the purchase of a $1 item requires up to 11.5¢ in sales tax. The rate on the dollar is 10.5¢ in Oklahoma City. Sales taxes are almost always optional for the local jurisdiction, requiring majority approval by the city or county legislative body. Typically, states impose ceilings on how many pennies the localities can attach to the state sales tax; states also specify which sizes and types of local governments are permitted to exercise this option.

When applied to all merchandise, the sales tax is clearly regressive. Poor folks must spend a larger portion of their incomes than rich people on basics such as food and clothing. Therefore, the sales tax places a much heavier burden on low-income people. Most of the forty-five states with a sales tax alleviate its regressivity by excluding certain necessities. Thirty-five states do not tax food purchased from the grocery store, only five tax prescription drugs, most exempt consumer electric and gas utilities, and six exclude clothing.[8] New Jersey excludes paper products. When the sales tax was extended to paper products in 1990, enraged Jerseyites mailed wads of toilet paper—some of it used—to legislators, who quickly rescinded the tax.

States can improve the yield of the sales tax by broadening the base to include services. In this way, more of the burden is passed on to upper-income individuals, who are heavier users of services. More than half of the states tax services such as household, automobile, and appliance repairs, barber and beauty shop treatments, printing, rentals, dry cleaning, and interior decorating. Hawaii, New Mexico, and South Dakota tax virtually all professional and personal services. New Jersey taxes hair transplants and tummy tucks, while Arkansas taps into tattoos and nose rings. Maryland residents must pay a "flush tax" of $30.00 on their sewer and septic bills to help clean up Chesapeake Bay. However, two states moved too far and too fast with taxes on services. Florida and Massachusetts both broadened the base of their sales tax to services, only to have it repealed shortly afterward through aggressive lobbying efforts by the business community.

These setbacks are likely to be temporary. Services are the largest and fastest-growing segment of the U.S. economy. Eighty-five percent of new jobs are in services. As political journalist Neil Peirce asked, "How can one rationalize taxing autos, videocassettes, and toothpaste, but not piped-in music, cable TV, parking lot services, or $100 beauty salon treatments?"[9] Pet grooming services, legal and financial services, and many others from landscaping to legal work are likely to lose their tax-favored status in years to come, as states extend sales taxes to services incrementally, fighting industry and lobbyists one at a time.

A big battle has been joined over state and local governments' right to tax an enormously promising revenue stream—electronic commerce on the Internet. Twenty-one states were levying taxes or fees on Internet access, data downloads, or goods purchased on the Internet. Then pressures from Internet interests, including servers (for example, America Online), media companies, and retail businesses, led Congress to pass the Internet Tax Freedom Act, which imposes a moratorium on taxation of online sales. State and local officials strongly oppose such limitation, estimating that it costs them as much as $20 billion in annual revenues as more and more goods are purchased on the Internet. Already states estimate that they forfeit $5 billion a year in uncollected taxes from inter-state catalog sales. Only catalog sales to citizens living in a state in which the mail-order firm has a physical presence are now taxed. A rapidly growing number of states require citizens to declare and pay such sales taxes in their annual state income tax returns, usually to no avail because of difficulty of enforcement.

Internet taxation is both complicated and controversial, and it has become a compelling issue for the states. A 1992 U.S. Supreme Court ruling blocked taxation of catalog sales on the grounds that it violated the Commerce Clause—a ruling that has obvious applicability to taxing Internet commerce today.[10] Congress has been tied in knots over the issue, as have the governors. No less than the fiscal integrity of state revenue systems is at stake. If states lose billions of dollars to a tax-free Internet, how will the gaping budget holes be filled? What about Main Street retailers whose prices are made less competitive by the amount of the sales tax? Yet it would be a heavy burden indeed for vendors to comply with the tax laws of 7,600 taxing jurisdictions in the United States.

A compromise is the streamlined sales tax (SST), wherein states collapse all their local sales tax rates into one (or just a few) statewide rates, resulting in a manageable number of Internet tax jurisdictions.[11] This approach has the added value of laying the foundation for taxing mail-order catalog sales.

Seemingly a simple proposition, simplification of multistate sales tax systems has presented such Zen-like puzzlers as: Are marshmallows food or candy? Are "fruit beverages" food or soft drink? Still, as of 2007, twenty-two states had passed the SST model legislation.[12] Elasticity is not a strong point of the sales tax—although its productivity falls when consumer purchases slow and rises as consumers boost their spending. Broadening the base helps. A few states have attempted to make the sales tax more responsive to short-term economic conditions by increasing it on a temporary basis, to make up lower-than-anticipated revenues, then reducing it when needed monies are collected. A problem with these tactics, however, is that consumers tend to postpone major purchases until the tax rate falls.

The sales tax is relatively simple for governments to administer. Sellers of merchandise and services are required to collect it and remit it to the state on a regular basis. Political accountability is also an advantage because legislative bodies must enact laws or ordinances to increase the sales tax rate. And, as we have observed, the sales tax is the least unpopular of the major taxes.

Income Tax Most states tax personal and corporate income. Wisconsin was the first, in 1911, two years before the national government enacted its own personal income tax. Forty-one states have broad-based taxes on personal income; two (Tennessee and New Hampshire) limit theirs to capital gains, interest, and dividends. Only Alaska, South Dakota, Florida, Texas, Nevada, Washington, and Wyoming leave all personal income untaxed. The latter three also refuse to tax corporate income. Personal income taxes garner 22 percent of all state and local own-source taxes (see Figure 12.1), and the corporate tax brings in 4 percent. Fifteen states permit designated cities, counties, or school districts to levy taxes on personal income.

State and local income taxes are equitable when they are progressive. This contingency normally entails a sliding scale, so that high-income filers pay a greater percentage of their income in taxes than low-income filers do. Most of the states do not levy a personal income tax on people whose earnings fall below a certain floor—say, $5,000. Overall, personal income taxes in the states are moderately progressive and are gradually becoming more so. Six states, however, tax income at a flat rate varying from 3.0 percent in Pennsylvania to 5.3 percent in Massachusetts.

Personal and corporate income taxes are superior to other taxes on the criteria of yield and elasticity. By tapping virtually all sources of income, they draw in large sums of money and respond fairly well to short-term economic conditions. Through payroll withholding, income taxes are fairly simple to collect. Also, many states periodically adjust income tax rates in response to annual revenue needs.

As mentioned earlier, political accountability can be problematic with respect to income taxes during periods of rising prices. Unless income tax rates are indexed to inflation, cost-of-living increases push salaries and corporate earnings into higher tax brackets. At least seventeen states have adopted indexing.

Miscellaneous Taxes A wide variety of miscellaneous taxes are assessed by state and local governments. "Sin taxes" raise a small but rapidly growing percentage of all state revenues. All states tax cigarettes, and many have boosted these taxes recently. New Jersey discourages smokers with a $2.58-per-pack tax and Rhode Island posts a tax of $2.46. Some cities levy additional taxes on smokes, bringing the price of some premium brands to $8 a pack. South Carolina, a tobacco state, charges only 7¢ per pack. This startling disparity in prices has led to a flourishing trade in cigarette smuggling from low- to high-tax states.

Recently the states experienced the equivalent of winning the lottery. A court settlement with tobacco companies is sending an estimated total of $246 billion into state coffers over a period of years. However, the payments are based on cigarette sales in each state, and this quantity has been declining. Ideally, states would spend their shares on smoking prevention and health care services. But few strings are attached, and many states are spending their windfall on economic development initiatives and balancing the budget.

Alcoholic beverages are also taxed in all fifty states, with rates varying according to classification: beer, wine, or spirits. Beer guzzlers should steer clear of Alaska, where the tax per gallon of beer is $1.07. Frequent imbibers are invited to visit Wyoming, where the tax is only 2¢ per gallon. (The eighteen states that hold monopolies on wholesale distribution of alcoholic beverages or that have their own state-run liquor stores are not accounted for in these figures.) Ironically, as drinking and smoking have declined during the past few years, so have their tax-based revenues. Clearly, raising alcohol and tobacco taxes helps to curtail these "sins." It has been suggested that marijuana and other "recreational" drugs be legalized so that they, too, can be taxed.

Though not a "sin," gasoline falls under taxation's shadow as well. The highest state tax on driving is New York's (39¢ per gallon). The lowest is in Oklahoma (7.5¢). All states also tax vehicles and vehicle licenses.

Most states tax death in one form or another. Estate taxes must be paid on the money and property of a deceased person before the remainder is disbursed to the survivors. Sixteen states tax those who inherit substantial assets (typically valued at more than $675,000). Rates are generally staggered according to the value of the estate and the relationship to the deceased. As noted above, however, a reduction—and proposed abolition—of the federal estate tax foretell a slow death knell for some such state taxes as well.

Other miscellaneous sources of revenue include hunting and fishing licenses, business licenses, auto license fees, parking tickets, and traffic violation fines. One interesting instrument is the jock tax. Some twenty states and several cities require professional athletes to pay a prorated income tax for games played in their jurisdiction. For highly paid baseball, basketball, and football players, the jock tax burns. New York Yankees star Alex "A-Rod" Rodriguez recently forked over a season's jock tax of $149,582 to California.

User Fees

Setting specific prices on goods and services provided by state and local governments is one time-proven method that clearly pursues the *benefit principle:* Only those who use the goods and services should pay. Examples include college tuition, water and sewer charges, and garbage collection assessments. Toll roads and bridges are coming back in fashion as well. Today, user fees are being applied broadly as state and especially local officials attempt to tie services to their true costs. Such fees are increasingly being levied on "nonessential" local government services, such as parks and recreation, libraries, airports, and public transit. The average American pays more than $1,456 a year in user fees.[13]

User fees offer several advantages. If priced accurately, they are perfectly appropriate under the benefit principle, and they enjoy a relatively high level of political acceptability. But those people who do not have enough money to purchase the goods and services may have to do without—a circumstance that violates the ability-to-pay principle. A good case in point is higher education, which is shifting increasingly from state funding to tuition funding. (Fortunately, rebates, scholarships, fee waivers, and reduced-fee schedules mitigate ability-to-pay difficulties among low-income residents.)

User fees are structured to yield whatever is needed to finance a particular service. An added benefit is that service users who do not live in the taxing jurisdiction must also pay the price, say, for a day in the state park. Elasticity may be achieved if the amount of the charge is varied so that it always covers service costs. In many instances user fees can be levied without the specific permission of the state.

Because service users must be identified and charged, some user fees can be difficult to administer. Political accountability is low because the charges can be increased without legislative action. However, a special advantage of user fees is that they can be employed to ration certain goods or services. For instance, entrance charges can be increased to reduce attendance at an overcrowded public facility, or varied according to the day of the week in order to encourage more efficient utilization. If the municipal zoo has few visitors on Mondays, it can cut the entrance fee on that day of the week by one-half.

| TABLE 12.2 | Rating State and Local Taxes According to Six Criteria |

TAX	EQUITY	YIELD	ELASTICITY	EASE OF ADMINISTRATION	POLITICAL ACCOUNTABILITY	ACCEPTABILITY
Property	C	B	C	D	D	D
Sales	D	B	B	B	A	B
Personal and corporate income	B	A	B	B	C	C
User fees	C	B	A	C	C	B

NOTE: A = excellent, B = good, C = fair, D = poor.

An increasingly popular and specialized form of user charge is the local impact fee, or exaction, requiring private land developers to contribute roads, sewers, and other infrastructure as a price for local regulatory approval for development projects, such as subdivisions or factories. The cost of infrastructure is shifted to private firms and, ultimately, to those who purchase or use their buildings or facilities. A related concept applied through a special sales tax on travel-related services is the travel tax. Here, taxes on lodging, rental cars, and other services paid largely by out-of-towners are imposed at rates averaging 12 percent. Table 12.2 rates major taxes and fees based on the six criteria discussed at the beginning of this section.

Severance Tax

States blessed with petroleum, coal, natural gas, and minerals have for many years taxed these natural resources as they are taken from the land and sold. A fortunate few are able to "export" a substantial portion of their tax bite to people living in other states. However, in-staters must pay the same tax rate as out-of-staters.

A large majority of states (thirty-nine) place a severance tax on some form of natural resources, but just ten states collect 90 percent of all severance tax revenues. Taxes on oil and natural gas account for around 50 percent of total state revenues in Alaska. Wyoming brings in about 45 percent of its revenues from severance taxes on coal, oil, and gas. (Perhaps this explains why these states are able to forgo personal income taxes.) Several states are rather creative in applying the severance tax. Washington levies the tax on oysters, salmon, and other food fish;[14] and Louisiana, on freshwater mussels.

Severance taxes are popular in states rich in natural resources, because they help keep income, property, and sales taxes relatively low. Severance tax revenues also help to pay for environmental damage resulting from resource extraction operations, such as strip mining. The major disadvantage is that a state economy too dependent on severance taxes can be damaged badly if the price of its natural resources declines, as Alaska experiences from time to time with depressed crude oil prices. Even so, natural resources have been individually enriching for

Alaskans. For more than twenty years every man, woman, and child resident of Alaska has received a rebate from the state's Permanent Fund. Checks totaled $1,575 per person in 2007. Established primarily with severance taxes on petroleum, the $40 billion Permanent Fund's reserves are diversified through investments in office buildings, industrial complexes, stocks, and bonds.[15]

Gambling: Lotteries and Casinos

The lottery is an old American tradition; initially established in the 1600s, it was popular from the colonial days until the late 1800s. Lotteries flourished throughout the country as a means of raising money for such good causes as new schools, highways, canals, and bridges. But scandals and mismanagement led every state and the national government to ban "looteries." From 1895 to 1963, no legal lotteries were operated. Then New Hampshire established a new one, followed in 1967 by New York. Since then forty-one states have created lotteries.

Several factors account for the rebirth of "bettor government." First, lotteries can bring in large sums of money—more than 7 percent of all state tax revenues in Rhode Island and South Dakota in one recent year, for example. Second, they are popular and entertaining. And they are voluntary—you do not have to participate. In addition, lotteries help relieve pressure on major taxes. In some states, net lottery earnings take the place of a 1¢ increase in the sales tax. Finally, state ownership of a game of chance offers a legal and fair alternative to illegal gambling operations such as neighborhood numbers games or betting (parlay) cards.

But lotteries also have disadvantages. They are costly to administer and have low yields. Prize awards must be great enough to encourage future ticket sales; the higher the payout, the more people play. New games must be created to retain enthusiasm. Ticket vendors must be paid commissions. And tight (as well as expensive) security precautions are required to guarantee the game's integrity. As a result, lotteries generate only a small percentage of most states' total revenues, usually less than 3 percent of own-source income.[16] The average yield for players is low as well: About 50 percent of the total revenues is returned to players in prize money. This is far below the returns of other games of chance, such as slot machines, roulette, or craps. Although many states earmark lottery proceeds for popular programs, especially education, the result is often a shell game. For instance, Florida's lottery officially benefits schools and colleges, but in reality lottery money simply *replaces* general-fund revenues, rather than actually enhancing education funding.[17]

Lotteries can also be attacked on the grounds of equity and elasticity. Although the purchase of a ticket is voluntary and thus seemingly fair, studies indicate that low-income individuals are more likely to play. Participation is also higher among African Americans, Latinos, males, older people, and those with low levels of education.[18] The lottery, then, is a regressive way to raise revenues.[19] Furthermore, lotteries tend to encourage compulsive gambling. In recognition of this problem, some states earmark a portion of lottery proceeds for treatment programs. Lotteries are considered inelastic because earnings are cyclical and generally unstable. Sales depend on such factors as the legalized gambling activities in neighboring states, the size of jackpots, and the effectiveness of marketing efforts.

As interstate lottery competition depresses profits, states have adopted other forms of legalized gambling, such as pari-mutuel betting on horse and dog races, racinos with slots at the track, as well as gambling on riverboats, Indian reservations, and at Old West historical sites like mining towns. In a persistent quest for more revenues, many states have legalized casino gambling. Once restricted to Atlantic City and Las Vegas, casino gambling actually now occurs in twenty-three states, including operations on about 400 Native American reservations. Gambling establishments virtually blanket Minnesota and Mississippi. Touted as producers of jobs, tourist dollars, and state revenues, casinos share many of the same disadvantages as lotteries, including diminishing returns as new casinos open across the country.

Illegal Internet gaming sites are thwarting state-sponsored gambling activities. Hundreds of them offer Texas Hold-em and other betting opportunities. And limited state revenue is derived from most tribal casinos. "Cruises to Nowhere" in which the dice are rolled and the cards are dealt once the ship enters international waters tap into the gaming fever in some coastal states. Interactive systems permit couch potatoes to place bets over the Internet. Kansas's "e-scratch" Internet lottery game came online in 2004.

THE POLITICAL ECONOMY OF TAXATION

Spending

Taxes lead to spending. The principle of diversity in state and local finance is evident given what nonnational governments choose to do with their revenues. First, these governments spend a great deal of money. State and local spending has been ascending much faster than the gross national product and the level of inflation. The functional distribution of spending varies from state to state. As indicated in Figure 12.2, education consumes the largest proportion of total state spending, followed by social services, which includes health care.

Within each of these functional categories lies a wide range of financial commitments. For instance, higher-education expenditures in a recent year ran from 16.6 percent of total state and local spending in Utah to only 5.4 percent in New York. South Dakota dedicated 14.9 percent of its spending to highways, whereas New York set aside just 4.4 percent for the same purpose.[20] Such differences represent historical trends, local economic circumstances, and citizens' willingness to incur debt to pay for services. Demographic factors also play a role. For instance, states with high populations of children invest more money in schools than do states with large proportions of senior citizens. State population growth also drives up expenditures for such services as law enforcement, water and sewer systems, and street maintenance. The largest expenditure gains in recent years have been registered in corrections and Medicaid as populations of prisoners and the medically indigent have ballooned.

| FIGURE 12.2 | **Total State and Local Government Spending by Service Delivered** |

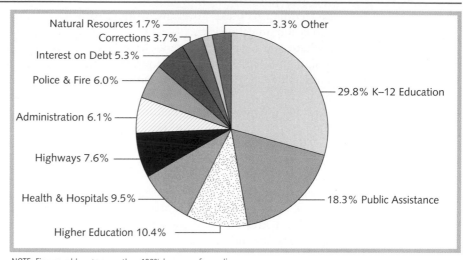

NOTE: Figures add up to more than 100% because of rounding.
SOURCE: U.S. Bureau of the Census, 2005.

One of the most difficult decisions for an elected official is to go on record in favor of raising taxes. The political heat can scorch even the coolest incumbent. But when revenues do not equal service costs and citizens do not want to cut services, raising taxes may be the only answer. However, most people do not want higher taxes. This is the familiar **tax-service paradox:** People demand new, improved, or at least the same level of government services, but do not want to pay for them through higher taxes. For instance, the people of Washington State, in their collective wisdom, voted in a 1999 constitutional referendum to slice taxes. But the very next year they passed another initiative to reduce class size and hike teachers' pay—without providing any new money. Voters in a dozen other states have taken similar action. As a former legislator put it, "I wouldn't say voters are stupid. But the same voter who wants unlimited services also does not want to pay for it. There is a disconnect."[21] Is it any wonder that user charges have become a popular option?

The tax-service paradox reflects a growing alienation between government and its citizens. The widespread belief that government at all levels has become too big and wasteful undoubtedly has some basis in fact. The size and responsibilities of state and local governments have grown dramatically, and waste and inefficiency have sometimes accompanied this growth. But the unwillingness of citizens to accept the inevitable reductions in services that follow tax cuts borders on mass schizophrenia.

Helping promote the tax-service paradox are the news media, which "commonly paint government with the broad brush of incompetence."[22] Prime-time television news capsules on "how government wastes your money" and typical reporting on actions of states and localities focus on the negative while ignoring

tax-service paradox

A situation in which people demand more government services but do not want to pay for them through higher taxes.

the positive. Government-bashing is a popular talk show sport. Meanwhile, state and local government functions have become much more complex and technical, tending to make government more difficult to understand, interact with, and communicate with.

State and local governments have begun responding with outreach efforts designed to educate citizens about what their governments are doing for them and where their tax dollars are going. There are indications that the message has been received in a growing number of states. Taxation and Expenditure Limits (TELS) have been recently defeated by voters in Maine, Nebraska, and Oregon and rolled back in Colorado. New York City's website provides personalized tax receipts, showing what each citizen's tax dollars paid for. Local governments everywhere are striving to write their annual budgets in reader-friendly formats.

political economy

Political choices that have economic outcomes.

Thus, the **political economy**—the set of political choices that frames economic policy—has become enormously perplexing for state and local officials. Several features of the political economy merit additional discussion: the tax revolt, fiscal stress, limited discretion in raising new revenues, and unfunded retiree pensions and health care benefits.

Tax Revolt

Taxpayer resentment of property taxes, and the general perception of government as too big, too costly, and too wasteful, first took on a tangible form in 1978 with the passage of Proposition 13 in California. Today, twenty-seven states have enacted statutory or constitutional limitations on taxing and spending by slashing personal or corporate income taxes, indexing their income taxes to the cost of living, and cutting the sales tax. In most instances, voters took tax matters into their own hands through the initiative process. In other cases, state legislators jumped in front of the parade and cut taxes and spending themselves. The taxpayer revolt continues at a slower pace today. Its legacy, however, remains enormously important. Watchdog organizations such as Americans for Tax Reform, led by famous taxophobe Grover Norquist, insist that candidates for public office sign "no-tax" pledges. Public officials must work hard to justify tax increases; otherwise, they risk a citizen uprising and perhaps political death.

Indeed, the stirrings of new tax revolts are constantly in evidence. Responding to citizen pressure, the Florida legislature rolled back local property taxes in 2007. Oregon voters fanned the flames of tax revolt in 2003 by soundly defeating a proposal to raise personal and corporate income taxes, choosing instead to accept prisoner releases, layoffs of state troopers, and a shortened school year, among other serious budget-balancing consequences. In desperation, the state legislature passed a plan to impose a three-year income tax surcharge. At least Beaver State voters acted civilly. In Tennessee, angry tax protestors stormed the capitol building, screaming obscene insults and hurling rocks at legislators.

taxation and expenditure limitations (TELs)

Restrictions on state and/or local government taxing and spending.

Most state and local jurisdictions managed the fallout of the tax revolt reasonably well. Many of them held large budget surpluses that they utilized to ameliorate the immediate effects of **taxation and expenditure limitations (TELs).** These are restrictions on government taxing and spending, such as limiting the growth in spending to no more than the latest year's growth in per

Florida Governor
Charlie Crist rallies
supporters of property
tax reform in Talla-
hassee.
SOURCE: © AP/Wide World
Photos

capita income. For example, California had a $3 billion surplus with which it temporarily replaced property tax revenues forgone by local governments. Only a handful of states followed California's stringent TELs, which cut property taxes by 60 percent. Forty-one states have some sort of property tax restriction in effect, and many place limitations on other forms of taxation as well. Raising taxes now requires a constitutional amendment, voter approval, or an extraordinary legislative majority in quite a few states. States and localities usually resist reducing service levels, opting instead to shift tax burdens or to find new sources of revenues, such as user charges.[23]

Political and economic consequences of the tax revolt have been much studied. In many cases, TELs have made state and local finance an extraordinarily difficult undertaking: Voters insist on passing spending mandates for education, law enforcement, or other popular programs while at the same time tying the hands of legislatures with restrictions on new revenue raising. So far, TELs have not significantly reduced the size and cost of government as advertised. Political and electoral influences are apparently more important in determining expenditures and size of government. However, TELs have led local governments to depend more on the states and to greater recognition by public officials of the continuing need to consult with the taxpaying public on tax issues.[24]

Fiscal Stress

fiscal stress

Financial pressure on a government from such factors as revenue shortfalls and taxing and spending limitations.

During national and regional economic downturns, many state and local jurisdictions experience severe **fiscal stress:** They struggle to pay for programs and provide services that citizens want and need without taxing the citizens at unacceptably high levels. Many factors contribute to fiscal stress. Typically, adverse social and economic conditions, mostly beyond state and local government control, establish an environment conducive to financial problems. Older industrial cities are particularly vulnerable. Many jobs and manufacturing industries have been lost because of the gradual but compelling shift to a service- and information-based economy and to company relocations to Sunbelt and foreign sites. In cities such as Detroit, Philadelphia, and New York, the exodus of jobs and firms has eroded the value of taxable resources (mostly property); yet citizens left behind have growing service demands. In New Orleans and other Gulf Coast communities, the local tax base was essentially destroyed by Hurricane Katrina in 2005. But ironically, sales tax revenues boomed afterwards as residents rebuilt.

Concentration of the poor and minorities in deteriorating housing, the shortage of jobs, high levels of crime, the illegal drug trade, homelessness, large expanses of blighted property, and related factors have produced crisis-level situations. Declining infrastructure also plagues older cities: water and sewer lines, treatment plants, streets, bridges, sidewalks, and other components of the urban physical landscape are in dire need of restoration or replacement. The estimated amount needed to replace Atlanta's crumbling and leaking drinking water and wastewater systems alone is an astounding $3.9 billion over the next seven years. Pennsylvania needs $11 billion to replace failing bridges throughout the state. Most of these problems, it should be noted, will require national government attention if they are to be addressed effectively. Special factors contributing to state fiscal stress include weak real-estate markets, increasing energy and equipment prices, unfunded federal mandates, and court- and congressionally mandated spending increases in corrections, education, and other areas. Political sources of fiscal stress typically compound the economic problems of older cities. Mismanagement of resources and inefficient procedures and activities are common complaints. For instance, mismanagement and fraud in the San Diego municipal pension system sent the city to the brink of bankruptcy in 2005 and led to the resignation of Mayor Dick Murphy.[25] Pressures from city workers and their unions have also driven up service provision costs in some localities. Thus, service demands and the costs of providing services grow while taxes and intergovernmental revenues decline. This is a well-tested recipe for fiscal stress that evokes fears of bond defaults and even bankruptcy.

New York City offers a thirty-year saga of fiscal stress. People, jobs, and industry fled the city for the suburbs and the Sunbelt in the early 1970s, thereby reducing fiscal capacity. Yet public employees' pay and pensions grew to some of the highest levels in the United States, and welfare payments to the poor and a growing number of unemployed were generous. The City University of New York (CUNY), which was tuition-free at this time, had an enrollment of 265,000 students.

As revenues increasingly lagged behind expenditures, the city government played fiscal roulette with the budget and borrowed huge sums through municipal notes and bonds. Eventually it was poised on the brink of bankruptcy. Defaults on the city's bonds, notes, and other debt instruments seemed imminent. City officials cried out to the national government and New York State for help, but some people had little sympathy for a city that had lived beyond its means for so long.

Aided by national guarantees of new long-term loans, New York State and other large holders of New York City debt finally agreed to a bailout. Had this immense urban financial edifice collapsed, the fiscal shocks would have threatened New York State's economic stability and even resulted in serious fiscal repercussions for other states and localities throughout the United States.

Unfortunately, the Big Apple once again risked being reduced to a seedy core in 1992. It faced a budget deficit of $3.5 billion, a mass exodus of jobs, and the enormous cost of thousands of AIDS and crack babies. Seventy percent of the city's more than 2,000 bridges desperately needed expensive repairs, and water and sewer lines were rupturing regularly. Mayor David Dinkins responded with several actions, including massive layoffs of city employees, closure of libraries and clinics, and shutdown of 25 percent of the city's streetlights.

New York City's fiscal problems cannot be solved overnight. Its 250,000 employees and $50 billion operating budget serve 7 million people spread throughout five boroughs. The city itself is the area's biggest landlord. It owns television and radio stations, a huge higher-education system, and four hospitals. When Mayor Rudolph Giuliani took office in 1994, the operating deficit was pegged at $2.3 billion, even as most of the country was enjoying economic growth. Giuliani, too, cut city employment and targeted various services for budget reductions. New York City continues today to struggle with its vast fiscal problems, with no relief in sight. As the ashes of the Twin Towers cooled in 2001, the new mayor, Michael Bloomberg, wrestling with a deficit of approximately $4 billion in his $43 billion budget, entertained the idea of a state takeover of city finances.[26] His "doomsday budget" included tens of thousands of layoffs, significant service cuts, and large property tax increases. Distressingly, the debts the City is still paying off from the 1970s had to be refinanced. The good news is that New York City's budget deficit had been turned into a surplus in 2007.

Most jurisdictions have not experienced the traumas faced by New York City. Taxpayer revolt and fiscal stress notwithstanding, budgets have been balanced, payrolls met, and most services maintained. When necessary, state officials have swallowed hard, held their noses, and raised taxes. A nine-year economic growth spurt caused the state–local picture to improve rapidly. Yet state officials knew another recession is inevitable, and one returned with a vengeance in 2001, producing what turned out to be their most serious budget crisis since the Great Depression. Gradually, however, states managed to close their budget gaps by 2006 and quickly rediscovered how much more fun it is to spend money than to cut back.

Recessions notwithstanding, some states and localities face chronic fiscal shortfalls because of structural problems deeply embedded in their revenue systems. Structural imbalances result from tax systems developed for radically different state economies of fifty years past.[27]

Limited Discretion

TELs have placed ceilings on rates and amounts of taxation and spending, thus limiting the discretion of the nonnational governments. Other constraining factors, too, keep state and local governments from falling prey to the temptation of taxing and spending orgies. One important factor is interstate competition for jobs and economic development. High-tax states run a serious risk of having jobs, firms, and investments "stolen" by low-tax states.

Earmarking taxes for popular programs also limits state and local taxing and spending discretion. Earmarking is well established: Gasoline taxes have been set aside for road and highway programs ever since automobiles first left ruts in muddy cow pastures. What differs today are the levels of specificity and creativity in earmarking. Approximately 25 percent of state tax revenues are earmarked. Surpluses may accumulate in some dedicated funds, such as highways, whereas other important needs such as education or law enforcement are not sufficiently met. The hands of government officials are tied, however, because they cannot move the funds around. Cigarette buyers in Washington cough up millions of dollars each year to help clean up Puget Sound. Several states earmark penny increases in the sales tax for public education.

Financial discretion is partly determined by one's position on the fiscal food chain. The national government can essentially tax and spend as it wishes, subject only to its highly underdeveloped capacity for self-discipline. States must meet federal spending mandates for Medicaid, corrections, and other functions while somehow balancing their budgets each year. Local governments, in addition to suffering reductions in state aid during tough times in this game of "shift and shaft federalism," must comply with an increasing number of state spending mandates even as their legal authority to raise revenues remains highly circumscribed in most states. In some ways, then, local governments are not masters of their own fiscal fate.[28]

Pensions and OPEB

When the Governmental Accounting Standards Board (GASB) issued standards requiring state and local governments to publicly report the funding status of employee pensions and health care benefits, most respondents were caught with their financial pants down. As noted above, for years most states and many local governments have been underfunding the future liabilities of employee retirement benefits. The Indiana Teachers Retirement Plan owes $9 billion to present and future retirees; Illinois owes nearly $10 billion to state employees and California is a shocking $27 billion in debt.[29]

Even more serious are the unfunded future liabilities of health care for retirees and their families. California is in the red for $70 billion, New Jersey for $60 billion, and New York for $54 billion. The larger the state employment numbers, the higher the future debt in most cases. But on a per capita basis, other states are hard hit. Alaska is underfunded at more than $7,000 per person and Hawaii for nearly $4,400 per resident.

There are several reasons for these huge future retirement and health care obligations. The baby boom bulge in the government work force has now reached retirement age. Unwise state borrowing from pension funds during difficult economic times is a major cause in some jurisdictions. And, of course, legislators have a tendency to spend today and worry about the future later (or let the next generation of legislators worry about it).

Addressing the problem will require innovative thinking as well as aggressive pre-funding of the future liabilities. The good thing about the GASB standards is that states and localities are being pressed to account for these future problems now. The bad thing is that in some cases tax increases and reductions in promised benefits for government employees will have to be implemented.

MANAGING MONEY

Every state except Vermont is constitutionally or statutorily mandated to balance its budget each fiscal year. In turn, the states require their local governments to balance *their* budgets. However, these requirements apply only to *operating budgets,* which are used for daily financial receipts and disbursements. Capital budgets, used for big purchases that must be paid for over time (for example, a new bridge or school building), typically run substantial deficits. Operating budgets may also run in the red during the fiscal year, so long as expenditures equal revenues at the end of the year. Consequently, the reliability of revenue estimates is a vital consideration.

Estimating Revenues

Until fairly recently, state and local governments estimated their annual revenues simply by extrapolating from past trends. This incremental approach is simple, inexpensive, and works well during periods of steady economic growth; but it fails miserably during years of boom or bust.[30] The finance officers of states and most larger cities and counties are much more sophisticated today. Using computer software, they employ econometric modeling to derive mathematical estimates of future revenues. Economic forecasting firms and/or academics assist or provide independent projections.

Econometric modeling places key variables in equations to predict the fiscal-year yield of each major tax. A wide variety of variables are used, including employment levels, food prices, housing costs, oil and gas prices, consumer savings levels, interest rates, intergovernmental aid projections, and state and local debt obligations. Because state and local economies are increasingly linked to national and international factors, estimates often include measures for the value of the dollar, international trade and investment, and national fiscal policy.

Two critical factors determine the accuracy of revenue estimates: the quality of the data and the validity of the economic assumptions. Indeed, econometric modeling of state and local economies can be a voyage into the unknown. Data problems include difficulty in measuring key variables; periodic revisions of historical economic data, which require new calculations; and modifications in tax laws or fee schedules. But the major sources of error are the economic assumptions built into the models. Examples are legion. The national economy may not perform as expected; energy prices may plummet or soar; natural or human disasters may disrupt state or local economic growth. Recessions are particularly damaging to fiscal stability because state and local taxes are highly sensitive to economic downturns.

Rainy Day Funds

Because a balanced budget is mandatory but estimation errors are inevitable, nearly all states and many localities establish contingency or reserve funds.

Popularly known as rainy day funds, these savings accounts help insulate budgets from fiscal distortions caused by inaccurate data or faulty economic assumptions; they are also available for emergencies. In years of economic health, the funds accumulate principal and interest. When the economy falters, governments can tap their savings accounts to balance the budget and avoid imposing tax and fee increases.[31]

During the sunny days of the 1990s, the states filled up their contingency funds to 7.7 percent of total spending. Amidst the recessionary storms of the early 2000s, they were forced to dip into them.[32] The task of balancing the budget is especially daunting in local governments, given their lack of economic diversity, dependency on state taxes and financial aid, and sensitivity to economic dislocations. The departure of a single large employer can disrupt a local economy for years. So the potential advantages of such funds are numerous in the fragile fiscal context of cities and counties.

Other Financial Management Practices

State and local governments, of necessity, are becoming more knowledgeable about how to manage cash and investments. Cash reserves that once sat idly in non-interest-bearing accounts or a desk drawer are now invested in money market accounts, U.S. Treasury bills, certificates of deposit, and other financial instruments so that governments can maximize interest earnings. Most states have local government investment pools that manage billions of dollars in short-term assets. The process of spending and collecting monies is also manipulated to advantage. For example, large checks are deposited on the day they are received; conversely, payable checks are drawn on the latest date possible. In general, state and local financial management today resembles that of a large corporation instead of the mom-and-pop approach of years ago. After all, the nonnational governments spend and invest more than $1.2 trillion annually.

The most important state or local investment is usually the public-employee pension fund. These retirement accounts comprise about $3.0 trillion in assets. In the past, they were conservatively managed and politically untouchable. Today, however, they tend to be invested in more aggressive instruments such as corporate stock. They also represent a tempting honey pot for financially suffering states whose governors have dipped their hands in the funds and pulled out billions to balance the budget. And as described above, most retirement plans have very large unfunded liabilities.

State and local investments must not be managed too aggressively, as the case of Orange County, California, demonstrates. One of the nation's largest and wealthiest local jurisdictions, Orange County became the largest in history to file for federal bankruptcy in 1994. The county's financial nightmare commenced when its investment pool manager, Robert L. Citron, placed millions of dollars in financial instruments called derivatives. These instruments "derive" their value from underlying assets such as stocks, bonds, or mortgages. The derivatives' value changes when the price of the underlying assets changes. Orange County lost $1.5 billion when its derivatives, which were tied to interest rates, declined precipitously in value. In effect, Citron was borrowing money from stocks, bonds, and other assets to bet on the direction of interest rates. He lost, and so did Orange County's taxpayers.[33]

Long-Term Borrowing Like corporations, state and local governments issue long-term debt obligations, typically for five to twenty-five years. Bonds are the most common form of long-term borrowing. Because of federal and state tax breaks for investors, the nonnational governments are able to finance bonded indebtedness at significantly lower rates than corporations. There are three conventional types of bonds: general obligation bonds, revenue bonds, and industrial development bonds.

The principal and interest payments on **general obligation bonds** are secured by the "full faith, credit, and taxing power" of the state or local jurisdiction issuing them. General obligation bonds are used to finance public projects such as highways, schools, and hospitals. Lenders are guaranteed repayment so long as the bond-issuing government is solvent; defaults are nearly nonexistent, but downgrades of cities' credit worthiness occur from time to time.

Revenue bonds are backed up by expected income from a specific project or service; examples include a toll bridge, a municipal sewer system, or mortgage loans. Revenue bonds are payable only from the revenues derived from the specified source, not from general tax revenues. Because they typically represent a riskier investment than general obligation bonds, they command a higher rate of interest.

The **industrial development bond (IDB)** is a type of revenue bond. The payment of principal and interest on IDBs depends solely on the ability of the industry using the facilities financed by the bond to meet its financial obligation. If the user fails to make payments, creditors can seize and sell any real or personal property associated with the facility. Private interests, such as shopping malls or firms, are the primary beneficiaries of IDBs. Conventionally, these private-purpose bonds are issued by local governments to attract economic activity and investments; in fact, they are frequently used to furnish loans at highly favorable interest rates to small- or medium-size firms.

Limits on Borrowing Almost all states place constitutional or statutory restrictions on their own and local government borrowing. Some set maximum levels of indebtedness; others require popular referenda to create debt or to exceed specified debt limits. They tightly restrict local government debt, especially general obligation bonds. (State-imposed constraints normally do not apply to revenue bonds.)

The bond market places its own informal limitations on debt by assessing the quality of bonds, notes, and other debt instruments. Investors in government bonds rely on Moody's Investors Service, Standard and Poor's Corporation, Fitch Ratings, and other investment services for ratings of a jurisdiction's capacity to repay its obligations. Criteria taken into consideration in bond ratings include existing debt levels, unfunded future liabilities, rainy day funds, market value of real estate, population growth, per capita income, employment levels, and other measures of financial health and solvency. Highly rated bond issues receive

---

general obligation bond

A debt instrument supported by the full financial resources of the issuing jurisdiction.

revenue bond

A bond that is paid off from income derived from the facility built with the bond proceeds.

industrial development bond (IDB)

A bond issued to fund the construction of a facility to be used by a private firm.

ratings of *Aaa, Aa,* and *A.* Variations of *B* indicate medium to high risk. A rating of *C* is reserved for bonds in immediate danger of default. The average interest rate on risky low-rated bonds usually exceeds that of top-rated ones by one and a half to two percentage points; this translates into a considerable difference in interest payments. Bond ratings tend to rise during periods of economic growth but can drop rapidly during recessions, driving up borrowing costs.

States can consolidate the bond sales of smaller municipalities and counties through a **bond bank.** These banks help provide increased management capacity to less-experienced local governments and, through economies of scale, save them significant sums of money.

bond bank

A state-administered fund that aggregates local government debt instruments and sells them as a package at a reduced interest rate.

STATE AND LOCAL SPENDING

What do state and local governments choose to do with their revenues? First of all, they spend a great deal of money. To provide a closer look at how governments spend their (and your) money, we examine three policy areas: economic development, education, and health and welfare.

Economic Development

In 2003, sport utility vehicles began rolling off the assembly line at a new Nissan plant—not in Japan, but in Mississippi. Luring the automaker to the Magnolia State was an incentive package that included $295 million in job training, infrastructure improvements, and tax breaks. Why was the state willing to pay the big bucks? There are four related reasons. First was Nissan's four thousand jobs, which would generate a $160 million annual payroll. Second, the state hoped that Nissan would have a ripple effect and attract other industries to the area. Third, the state believed that winning Nissan's business added some much-needed luster to Mississippi's tarnished image. And, last but not least: If Mississippi had not come through with an attractive incentive package, its neighbor to the east, Alabama, would have.[34] The motto for state economic development may well be "You've got to pay to play."

Economic development strategies vary greatly. Some states still engage in a form of smokestack chasing by dangling tax breaks, subsidies, and other financial inducements before firms, hoping to recruit them from other locations. Travel and tourism are also big business. States publicize their natural resources, cultural amenities, cuisine, and casinos—whatever it takes to attract tourism dollars. Advertising campaigns are developed around catchy slogans, such as "Restart Your Engines" in Indiana and "Possibilities . . . Endless" in Nebraska.

Dance, theater, and opera are used as development strategies in some metropolitan areas. These performing arts not only attract tourism dollars; they also appeal to high-technology firms and their ranks of well-paid, culturally sensitive knowledge workers, and they attract a "creative class" of educated, talented, young professionals.[35] Arts-led downtown economic revivals are occurring today in cities as diverse as Providence, Rhode Island; Beaumont, Texas; and Newark, New Jersey.

The professional sports realm is another economic development tool, although its economic advantages for beneficiaries other than the owners are greatly disputed. Professional sports and big-league cities go hand-in-hand. Hosting a professional sports team is a sign that a city has arrived. Still, acquiring a professional baseball, basketball, hockey, or football team is not inexpensive and the strategy is being called into doubt.[36] Cities and states compete against one another frantically, offering to build hugely expensive playing facilities and to invest millions of dollars in new highways and other infrastructure.

Increasingly, state and local governments are casting their acquisitive eyes beyond national borders, looking abroad for international trade and development opportunities. Foreign markets are often important for manufacturers of state products, and foreign investors can provide new jobs and tax revenues. States actively market themselves and their local governments, often sending the governor and other high-ranking officials on trade promotion missions overseas. For in-state firms, the state may arrange financing and technical support to help them initiate new international opportunities.

Economic development remains a high priority for all of the states, but critics are asking troubling questions: Do subsidies, tax breaks, and other giveaways really pay off? Does government spend too much in pursuit of more economic growth? Does more economic growth come at the cost of environmental problems and lower quality of life? And has interstate competition for firms become dysfunctional and damaging, as firms play one state off another in a greedy game designed to extort the taxpayer?

Education Policy

Education consumes more of state and local budgets than any other function. Some $500 *billion* is spent on elementary and secondary education by states and localities each year. That comes to around $7,830 per pupil. Citizens have high—but largely unrealized—expectations for the public schools. The schools, it is said, are failing to make the grade.

Critics claim that public education has four major problems. First, standards have declined. Students are being taught how to feel good about themselves instead of how to read, write, calculate, and think. Second, too little is expected of students, many of whom are functionally illiterate upon graduating and poorly prepared for either work or higher education. (Students are also alleged to be poorly motivated and lazy, and more concerned with Facebook or MySpace, the latest TV show, computer game, or sports contest than with their schoolwork.) Third, the quality of teachers has declined. University programs for training teachers are weak and misdirected, and the teachers themselves are underprepared for their classroom duties. Finally, critics blame the education bureaucracy: There are too many administrators and too few teachers. The result is red tape, excessive paperwork, and inefficiency.

Who answers these charges? The president and Congress regularly debate the problems of K–12 education. Many federal actions are more symbol than substance. An exception is the No Child Left Behind (NCLB) law of 2002, which significantly raised federal mandates and testing requirements (and related costs) on local schools. (NCLB has been roundly criticized by state officials and educators for its over-emphasis on testing and unrealistic goals). The national government also contributes money for public education—about 8.3 percent of all K–12 spending.

But the primary policy and financial responsibilities for education continue to reside with the state and local governments, which actually have been actively engaged in education innovation and reform for nearly three decades. Pay is being hiked to attract and keep more capable classroom teachers. Standards are being raised through strengthened curricula and stricter promotion and graduation requirements. Student-teacher ratios are being reduced. Outcomes-based education strives to hold students, teachers, and administrators accountable for student performance. And various techniques for "school choice" are being assessed, including magnet schools, charter schools, voucher plans, and virtual schools.

Progress *is* taking place, but public education remains perhaps the most perplexing—and important—policy challenge for state and local governments. The quality of public schools is clearly related to economic development, social and behavioral conditions, and the overall quality of life in the United States. But progress does not come cheaply or easily. Smaller classrooms mean more teachers and classroom space. And attracting and retaining qualified teachers requires competitive pay and benefits.

Social Welfare and Health Care Policy

Poverty in the United States has many faces, as does the programmatic response to alleviating it. Numerous public assistance and health care programs have been established to help ease the problems and pains of the poor, elderly, and disadvantaged.

Social welfare and health care policies include national programs such as Medicare (medical care for the aged) and Food Stamps, as well as state-developed programs like General Assistance. State and local governments also administer and share funding on several programs, such as Medicaid (medical care for the poor), various employment and housing programs, and the "social insurance" programs included under Social Security and Unemployment Compensation.

Despite a major overhaul of public assistance policy by the federal government, which replaced the unpopular Aid to Families with Dependent Children program, with the Temporary Assistance for Needy Families (TANF) program, any search for innovative policymaking in social welfare and health care leads directly to the states. Two major policy initiatives have dominated the states' agenda during the past several years: saving the children and turning welfare checks into paychecks.

The plight of the nation's children is both sad and perplexing. Divorce rates are high (almost one-half of all children experience a family divorce), and the number of irresponsible fathers who refuse to support their offspring is disheartening (the child support rate is only about 50 percent). Single mothers who work often find it difficult to secure affordable, high-quality daycare for their kids. Finally, many children are born not only into poverty but also into illness. Lack of prenatal care, parental drug abuse, inadequate diets, and related factors cause many mothers to give birth to premature, sickly, and underweight infants.

Several programs seek to help such unfortunate children. Head Start, a federally funded program that many states augment with their own efforts, provides preschool education, medical and dental care, and social services for more than one million three- to five-year-olds. The federal Family Support Act of 1988 requires the states to withhold court-ordered child support payments from the wages of absentee parents. And through DNA techniques, states are often able to establish paternity for children born out of wedlock.

Daycare for children of working and single parents is garnering much attention as states and localities subsidize daycare programs through tax breaks and experiment with various child-care arrangements. Several states guarantee child-care assistance to poor families.

Welfare checks are being turned into paychecks under the 1996 federal Welfare Reform Act's Temporary Assistance for Needy Families (TANF) program, which relies heavily on state innovation and creativity. Instead of simply handing over welfare checks to recipients, states are requiring them to prepare for and find gainful employment. The goal, of course, is to help welfare recipients leave the welfare rolls altogether. Wisconsin, for example, offers transportation assistance, generous child-care benefits, health care subsidies, and drug counseling for unemployed welfare recipients. Those who cannot find jobs must perform community service or pursue further job training or education. Like all other states, Wisconsin has recorded a substantial drop in its welfare rolls since implementing TANF.

Given Congress's inability to address the matter of health care effectively, health care reform has become largely a state-driven policy. Although the quality of health care technology in the United States is unsurpassed, the "system" is inordinately expensive and, for many, dysfunctional. Some 46 million Americans remain uninsured and, therefore, largely dependent on government for medical services. The costs for these services have soared to more than $2 trillion annually—16 percent of the national economy and the highest of any country in the world. Medicaid alone, funded by the states at a rate exceeding $300 billion annually, consumes more than 20 percent of the typical state budget. These expenses reflect the care of 56 million recipients. In the national policy vacuum, states have aimed at expanding health care coverage to the uninsured, containing escalating costs, and maintaining the quality of health care. All states are involved in reforming health care, but their approaches vary markedly. For example, many states subsidize health care programs for poor children. Maine and Massachusetts operate extensive health care programs with universal coverage for those unable to afford health care insurance. Oregon has established a health care rationing system that ranks illnesses and conditions according to their priority for state Medicaid expenditures. Under this system, child immunization, birth control, and maternal health care receive high priority; terminal AIDS and the common cold come last. Several states control the costs of prescription drugs, and some states facilitate importing them at lower prices from Canada.

Unless and until Congress and the president agree on a national health care approach, the states will take the lead and reform will continue at a lively pace. The principal concerns continue to be rising costs (particularly for Medicaid) and gaps in insurance coverage, problems that the national government could help resolve through courageous action.

CURRENT ISSUES IN STATE AND LOCAL FINANCE

State and local governments are experiencing significant long-term problems in political economy. Tax systems designed for a primitive industrial age are badly out of step with today's service- and information-based global economy. Beset with its own chronic, self-inflicted financial travails and a record high budget deficit from wars and other spending, the budget-impaired federal government is no longer a reliable fiscal partner. The keys to surviving the inevitable financial problems in states and localities are intergovernmental cooperation, burden sharing, capacity building, and citizen comprehension of the basic tax-service relationship.

The spiraling costs of Medicaid, corrections, and public education are burdens that cannot be shouldered by a single level of government. Mandates without money are certainly no help. When mandates and program responsibilities are pushed to a different rung of the federal ladder, funds should follow. Local governments in particular need more revenue-raising authority and broader tax bases to pay for the services they deliver. Most states have been receptive to these principles; the federal government requires further education.

The need for increasing state and local capability and responsiveness by reinventing and reinvigorating government has perhaps never been greater. The financial structures and processes of state and local governments must be made more appropriate to the social and economic environment in which they operate, which includes a service-based economy, global markets, aging baby boomers, and the changing gender, racial, and ethnic composition of the labor force. Special challenges to state and local governments are not being met sufficiently by present revenue systems.

Education is also needed for taxpayers, who do not always grasp the relationship between taxes paid and services rendered. Resistance to new or existing taxes is to be expected, but campaigns can educate citizens that the result of reducing or eliminating taxes will be fewer or lower quality services.

CHAPTER RECAP

- The two basic principles of state and local financial systems are interdependence of the three levels of government and diversity of revenue sources.
- Among the criteria for evaluating taxes are equity, yield, elasticity, ease of administration, political accountability, and acceptability.
- The major state and local taxes are those that are assessed on property, sales, and income. A variety of other taxes and fees are also imposed.
- Legalized gambling and gaming also raise money.

- Taxpayer resistance has produced tax and expenditure limitations in many states; increased sensitivity of state and local officials to taxpayer preferences; and, in some cases, fiscal stress for governments.
- State and local governments estimate annual revenues and set aside money in rainy day funds for emergencies and contingencies.
- State and local financial relationships are characterized by sharing and cooperation, but also by conflict over mandates and limited local discretion.

Key Terms

own-source revenue *(p. 270)*
intergovernmental transfers *(p. 270)*
countercyclical aid *(p. 271)*
tax capacity *(p. 271)*
tax effort *(p. 271)*
regressive tax *(p. 273)*
progressive tax *(p. 274)*
proportional (flat) tax *(p. 274)*
benefit principle *(p. 274)*
indexing *(p. 275)*
circuit breaker *(p. 277)*

tax-service paradox *(p. 285)*
political economy *(p. 286)*
taxation and expenditure limitations (TELs) *(p. 286)*
fiscal stress *(p. 287)*
general obligation bond *(p. 293)*
revenue bond *(p. 293)*
industrial development bond (IDB) *(p. 293)*
bond bank *(p. 294)*

Internet Resources

The National Conference of State Legislatures' Principles of a High Quality Tax System are available at **www.NCSL.org.**

One of the best individual sites on state tax and budget information, including an up-to-date look at "where the money goes," is that of the Texas State Comptroller at **www.window.state.tx.us.**

For current reports in developments, trends, and policy changes in state government finances, see the website of the Center for the Study of the States at SUNY–Albany: **www.stateandlocalgateway.rockinst.org.**

Comparative state and local revenue, tax, and expenditure data may be found at the U.S. Census Bureau's website, **www.census.gov,** and at the Tax Foundation's web address, **www.taxfoundation.org.**

See **www.taxsites.com** for general tax information and official state tax sites.

The Joint Center for Poverty Research focuses on the causes of poverty and the effectiveness of policies aimed at reducing it. Their website is **www.jcpr.org.**

For information on federal and state health care, see the Centers for Medicaid and Medicare Services at **www.cms.hhs.gov/.**

REFERENCES

CHAPTER 1 NEW DIRECTIONS FOR STATE AND LOCAL GOVERNMENT PP. 1–19

1. Governor Eliot Spitzer, "New York State of the State Address 2008," www.stateline.org (January 10, 2008)

2. Bruce Wallin, "State and Local Governments Are American, Too," *The Political Science Teacher* 1 (Fall 1988): 1–3.

3. Mike Sullivan, as quoted in "Wyoming's Governor Signs Law to Restructure State Government," *Denver Post* (March 5, 1989), 8B.

4. "The Innovations Award Winners," *Governing* 21 (October 2007): 1–24.

5. Beth Walter Honadle, "Defining and Doing Capacity Building: Perspective and Experiences," in Beth Walter Honadle and Arnold M. Howitt, eds., *Perspectives on Management Capacity Building* (Albany: State University of New York Press, 1986), 9–23.

6. Katherine Barrett and Richard Greene, "Grading the States, 2005," *Governing* 18 (February 2005): 24–95.

7. Julie Bund and Gene M. Lutz, "Connecting State Government Reform with Public Priorities: The Iowa Test," *State and Local Government Review* 31 (Spring 1999): 73–90.

8. David M. Hedge, *Governance and the Changing American States* (Boulder, Colo.: Westview, 1998).

9. National Education Association, "No Child Left Behind/ESEA: It's Time for a Change!" www.nea.org/esea/titleIcomments.html (August 30, 2007).

10. Terry Sanford, *The Storm Over the States* (New York: McGraw-Hill, 1967), 21.

11. Quoted in ibid.

12. John Herbers, "The New Federalism: Unplanned, Innovative and Here to Stay," *Governing* 1 (October 1987), 28.

13. Sheryl Gay Stolbert, "As Congress Stalls, States Pursue Cloning Debate," *New York Times,* www.nytimes.com (May 26, 2002).

14. Ann O'M. Bowman and Richard C. Kearney, *The Resurgence of the States* (Englewood Cliffs, N.J.: Prentice-Hall, 1986).

15. Sanford, *Storm Over the States.*

16. Ann O'M. Bowman and Richard C. Kearney, "Dimensions of State Government Capability," *Western Political Quarterly* 41 (June 1988): 341–62.

17. Donald P. Haider-Markel, "Policy Diffusion as a Geographical Expansion of the Scope of Political Conflict: Same Sex Marriage Bans in the 1990s," *State Politics and Policy Quarterly* 1 (Winter 2001): 5–26.

18. Craig Savoye, "States Spare Residents from Telemarketers," *Christian Science Monitor* (December 22, 2000), 8.

19. Chris Hamby, " 'Fire-Safe' Cigarette Laws Spread Quickly," www.stateline.org (August 7, 2007).

20. "U.S. Mayors Climate Protection Agreement," www.seattle.gov/mayor/climate/ (September 25, 2007).

21. David Winder, James T. LaPlant, and Larry E. Carter, "State Lawsuits Against Big Tobacco," paper presented at the annual meeting of the Southwestern Political Science Association, San Antonio, April 1999.

22. Derek Cane, "States Sue Music Labels for Price Fixing," http://dailynews.yahoo.com (August 8, 2000).

23. Ann O'M. Bowman, "Trends and Issues in Interstate Cooperation," in *The Book of the States 2004* (Lexington, Ky.: Council of State Governments, 2004), 34–40.

24. Governor George Voinovich, as quoted in "Reassessing Mandates," *State Policy Reports* 11 (October 1993): 16.

25. Brad Knickerbocker, "States Take the Lead on Global Warming," *Christian Science Monitor* (October 10, 2003), 1, 12.

26. Todd Sloane, "Governors Face Mounting Deficits," *City & State* 8 (November 4, 1991): 1, 20.

27. Don Boyd, quoted in "Overview," *2004 State of the States* (Washington, D.C.: Pew Center on the States, 2004), 5.

28. John Holahan et al., *State Responses to the 2004 Budget Crisis: A Look at Ten States* (Washington, D.C.: The Urban Institute, 2004).

29. Ralph Vartabedian, "The Race to Steal Bases Heats Up," *Los Angeles Times,* latimes.com (November 29, 2004).

30. Michael Johnston, "Right and Wrong in American Politics: Popular Conceptions of Corruption," in Arnold Heidenheimer and Michael Johnston, eds., *Political Corruption: Concepts and Contexts* (New Brunswick, N.J.: Transaction, 2002), 173–91; see also, Richard T. Boylan and Cheryl X. Long, "Measuring Public Corruption in the American States," *State Politics and Policy Quarterly* 3 (Winter 2003): 420–38.

31. Kenneth R. Gosselin and Christopher Keating, "Corruption Costs Jobs, Study Says," *Hartford Courant,* www.ctnow.com/news.local (February 25, 2004).

32. Jeff Whelan and Mark Mueller, "Statewide Sting Catches 11 Officials," *Newark Star-Ledger,* www.nj.com/news/ledger (September 7, 2007).

33. "Table 2. Percent of Population by Race and Hispanic or Latino Origin, 2000," U.S. Census Bureau, www.census.gov/population/cen2000/phc-t6/tab02.pdf.

34. U.S. Census Bureau, "Foreign-Born Population Tops 34 Million," www.census.gov/Press-Release (February 22, 2005).

35. Sylvia Moreno, "Flow of Illegal Immigrants to U.S. Unabated," *Washington Post,* www.washingtonpost.com (March 22, 2005).

36. Rodney E. Hero and Caroline J. Tolbert, "A Racial/ Ethnic Diversity Interpretation of Politics and Policy in the States of the U.S.," *American Journal of Political Science* 40 (August 1996): 851–71.

37. U.S. Census Bureau, "Cumulative Estimates of Population Change for the United States, April 1, 2000 to April 1, 2006," www.census.gov (December 21, 2006).

38. U.S. Census Bureau, "Cumulative Estimates of Population Change for Incorporated Places Over 100,000, Ranked by Percent Change: April 1, 2000 to July 1, 2006," www.census.gov/popest/ SUB-EST_2006.html (September 21, 2007).

39. Michael Barone, "The 2012 Seating Plan," *National Journal,* July 21, 2007, 34–38.

40. Daniel J. Elazar, *American Federalism: A View from the States,* 3d ed. (New York: Harper & Row, 1984).

41. Jody L. Fitzpatrick and Rodney E. Hero, "Political Culture and Political Characteristics of the American States: A Consideration of Some Old and New Questions," *Western Political Quarterly* 41 (March 1988): 145–53.

42. Keith Boeckelman, "Political Culture and State Development Policy," *Publius: The Journal of Federalism* 21 (Spring 1991): 49–62; Russell L. Hanson, "Political Culture Variations in State Economic Development Policy," *Publius: The Journal of Federalism* 21 (Spring 1991): 63–81.

43. James P. Lester, "A New Federalism: Environmental Policy in the States," in Norman Vig and Michael Kraft, eds., *Environmental Policy in the 1990s* (Washington, D.C.: Congressional Quarterly Press, 1994), 51–68; Steven A. Peterson and James N. Schubert, "Predicting State Aids Policy Spending," paper presented at the annual meeting of the American Political Science Association, New York City, September 1994.

44. Joel Lieske, "Regional Subcultures of the United States," *Journal of Politics* 55 (November 1993): 888–913.

45. Frederick M. Wirt, "'Soft' Concepts and 'Hard' Data: A Research Review of Elazar's Political Culture," *Publius: The Journal of Federalism* 21 (Spring 1991): 1–13.

46. Emily Van Dunk, "Public Opinion, Gender and Handgun Safety Policy Across the States," paper presented at the annual meeting of the Midwest Political Science Association, Chicago, April 2000.

47. Mark Preston, "The 'Most' Representative State: Wisconsin," CNN, www.cnn.com/2006/POLITICS/ 07/27/mg.thu/index.html (July 27, 2006).

48. Elaine B. Sharp, "Introduction," in Elaine B. Sharp, ed., *Culture Wars and Local Politics* (Lawrence: University Press of Kansas, 1999), 1–20.

49. Jonathan Walters, "Uncivil Disunion," *Governing* 17 (March 2004): 14.

50. John Shannon, "The Return to Fend-for-Yourself Federalism: The Reagan Mark," *Intergovernmental Perspective* 13 (Spring 1987): 34–37; David R. Morgan and Kenneth Kickham, "Modernization among the U.S. States: Change and Continuity from 1960 to 1990," *Publius: The Journal of Federalism* 27 (Summer 1997): 23–39.

51. Alan Ehrenhalt, "The Increasing Irrelevance of Congress," *Governing* 11 (January 1998): 6–7.

52. Kate Brown, as quoted in Rob Gurwitt, "Cookie-Jar Clampdown," *Governing* 20 (April 2007): 36.

CHAPTER 2 FEDERALISM AND THE STATES PP. 20–45

1. Carmine P.F. Scavo, Richard C. Kearney, and Richard J. Kilroy, Jr., "Challenges to Federalism: Homeland Security and Disaster Response," *Publius: The Journal of Federalism* (forthcoming 2008).

2. David B. Walker, *Toward a Functioning Federalism* (Cambridge, Mass.: Winthrop, 1981), 25.

3. James Madison, *The Federalist,* No. 45, 1788.

4. Quoted in Richard Hofstadter, *The American Political Tradition* (New York: Vintage Books, 1948), 9.

5. Quoted in Richard H. Leach, *American Federalism,* No. 45 (New York: W.W. Norton, 1970), 1.

6. Charles S. McCoy, "Federalism: The Lost Tradition?" *Publius* 31 (Spring): 1–14.

7. Forrest McDonald, *States' Rights and The Union: Imperium in Imperio, 1776–1876* (Lawrence: University Press of Kansas, 2000).

8. Quoted in ibid., 1788.

9. Walter Berns, "The Meaning of the Tenth Amendment," in Robert A. Goldwin, ed., *A Nation of States* (Chicago: Rand McNally, 1961), 130.

10. Walker, *Functioning Federalism,* 47–48; Forrest McDonald, *States' Rights and the Union: Imperium in Imperio* (Lawrence The University of Kansas Press, 2000).

11. Hofstadter, *American Political Tradition,* 72.

12. *McCulloch v. Maryland,* 4 Wheaton 316 (1819).

13. *Gibbons v. Ogden,* 9 Wheaton 316 (1819).

14. *National League of Cities v. Usery,* 426 U.S. 833 (1976).

15. *Garcia v. San Antonio Metropolitan Transit Authority,* 105 S. Ct. 1007, 1011 (1985).

16. Ibid. (O'Connor, dissenting).

17. John C. Pittenger, "Garcia and the Political Safeguards of Federalism: Is There a Better Solution to the Conundrum of the Tenth Amendment?" *Publius: The Journal of Federalism* 22 (Winter 1992).

18. *United States v. Lopez,* 115 S. Ct. 1424 (1995). See Kenneth T. Palmer and Edward B. Laverty, "The Impact of *U.S. v. Lopez* on Intergovernmental

Relations," *Publius: The Journal of Federalism* 26 (Summer 1996): 109–26.

19. *Alden* v. *Maine*, 527 S. Ct. 706 (1999).

20. *Kansas* v. *Hendricks*, 117 S. Ct. 2072 (1997).

21. *Printz* v. *United States*, No. 95–1478 (1997).

22. *Coalition for Economic Equity* v. *Wilson*, No. 96–50605 (1997).

23. *Lee* v. *Harcleroad*, No. 96–1824 (1997).

24. *Hill* v. *Colorado*, No. 98–1856 (2000).

25. *Seminole Tribe of Florida* v. *Florida*, 116 S. Ct. 1114 (1996).

26. *College Savings Bank* v. *Florida Prepaid Postsecondary Education Expense Board et al.*, 98 S. Ct. 149 (1999).

27. Nevada Department of Human Resources *v.* Hibbs, S. Ct. 631 (2000).

28. *Federal Maritime Commission* v. *South Carolina Ports Authority*, no. 01–46 (2002).

29. *Tennessee* v. *Lane* 124 S. Ct. 1978 (2004).

30. *Crosby* v. *National Foreign Trade Council*, 2000 US. LEXIS 4134.

29. *Sternberg* v. *Carhart*, 2000 U.S. LEXIS 4484.

31. *Lorillard Tobacco* v. *Reilly*, No. 00–596 (2000).

32. *Bush* v. *Gore et al.*, 00 S. Ct. 949 (2000).

33. Wright, *Understanding Intergovernmental Relations*, 40–42; McDonald, op. cit. (2002).

34. Timothy J. Conlon "Federalism and Competing Values in the Reagan Administration," *Publius: The Journal of Federalism* 16 (Winter 1986): 29–47.

35. Ann O'M. Bowman and Michael A. Pagano, "The State of American Federalism 1989–1990," *Publius: The Journal of Federalism* 20 (Summer 1990): 1–25.

36. John Kincaid and Richard L. Cole, "Public Opinion on Federalism in Canada, Mexico, and USA in 2003," *Publius: The Journal of Federalism* 33:3 (Summer 2003)

37. Jonathan Walters, "'Save Us from the States.'" *Governing* (June 2001): 20–21.

38. Quoted in U.S. Advisory Commission on Intergovernmental Relations, *State Constitutions in the Federal System* (Washington, D.C.: ACIR, 1989), 37.

39. Bill McGarigle, "The Battle Over Ellis Island," www.govtech.net (January 2000): 44–45; Neil MacFarquhar, "Ruling Like Solomon's Favoring New Jersey Splits Ellis Island in Two," *New York Times* (April 2, 1997), A21.

40. "Mandate Monitor," National Conference of State Legislatures 5 (August 2007), 1, accessed at www.ncsl.org/print/standcomm/scbudg/mandate monitorAugust2007.pdf.

41. Donald F. Kettl, "10th Amendment Turf War," *Governing* (October 1998), 13.

42. Marcia L. Godwin, "Innovations Across American States," paper presented at the 2001 annual meeting of the American Political Science Association, August 30–September 2, 2002, San Francisco.

43. See David B. Walker, "The Advent of Ambiguous Federalism and the Emergence of New Federalism

III," *Public Administration Review* 56 (May/June 1996): 271–80.

44. Scavo, Kearney, and Kilroy, Jr., op. cit.; John Kincaid and Richard L. Cole, "Issues of Federalism in Response to Terrorism," *Public Administration Review* 62 (September 2002): 181–92.

45. Samuel H. Beer, "The Future of the States in the Federal System," in Peter Woll, ed., American Government: Readings and Cases (Boston: Little, Brown, 1981), 92.

CHAPTER 3 STATE CONSTITUTIONS PP. 46–66

1. G. Alan Tarr, *Understanding State Constitutions* (Princeton, N.J.: Princeton University Press, 1999).

2. U.S. Advisory Commission on Intergovernmental Relations (ACIR), *State Constitutions in the Federal System*, A-113 (Washington, D.C.: ACIR, 1989), 2.

3. Donald S. Lutz, "The United States Constitution as an Incomplete Text," *Annals of the American Academy of Political and Social Science* 496 (March 1989): 23–32.

4. G. Alan Tarr and Mary Cornelia Porter, "Introduction: State Constitutionalism and State Constitutional Law," *Publius: The Journal of Federalism* 17 (Winter 1987): 5.

5. Donald S. Lutz, "Toward a Theory of Constitutional Amendment," *American Political Science Review* 88 (June 1994): 356; G. Alan Tarr, ed., *Constitutional Politics in the States* (Westport, Conn.: Greenwood Press, 1996), xv.

6. Donald S. Lutz, "The Iroquois Confederation Constitution: An Analysis," *Publius: The Journal of Federalism* 28 (Spring 1998): 99–127.

7. Daniel J. Elazar, "The Principles and Traditions Underlying State Constitutions," *Publius: The Journal of Federalism* 12 (Winter 1982): 11.

8. Quoted in Perry Gilbert Miller, "Thomas Hooker and the Democracy of Early Connecticut," *New England Quarterly* 4 (1931): 695.

9. Bruce Fraser, *The Land of Steady Habits: A Brief History of Connecticut* (Hartford: Connecticut Historical Commission, 1986), 10.

10. John Estill Reeves, *Kentucky Government* (Lexington: University of Kentucky, 1966), 7. As quoted in Penny M. Miller, *Kentucky Government and Politics* (Lincoln: University of Nebraska Press, 1994), 82.

11. Albert L. Sturm, "The Development of American State Constitutions," *Publius: The Journal of Federalism* 12 (Winter 1982): 61.

12. Ibid., 62–63.

13. Paul G. Reardon, "The Massachusetts Constitution Makes a Milestone," *Publius: The Journal of Federalism* 12 (Winter 1982): 45–55.

14. David McCullough, *John Adams* (New York: Touchstone Books, 2001).

15. Quoted in Thomas Parrish, "Kentucky's Fourth Constitution Is a Product of Its 1980 Times," in Thad L. Beyle, ed., *State Government: CQ's Guide to Current Issues and Activities* 1991–92 (Washington, D.C.: Congressional Quarterly Press, 1991), 46.

16. U.S. Advisory Commission on Intergovernmental Relations (ACIR), *The Question of State Government Capability* (Washington, D.C.: ACIR, 1985), 36.

17. David Fellman, "What Should a State Constitution Contain?" in W. Brooke Graves, ed., *Major Problems in State Constitutional Revision* (Chicago: Public Administration Service, 1960), 146.

18. Sturm, "American State Constitutions," 64.

19. David C. Nice, "Interest Groups and State Constitutions: Another Look," *State and Local Government Review* 20 (Winter 1988): 22.

20. Donald S. Lutz, "Patterns in the Amending of American State Constitutions," in G. Alan Tarr, ed., *Constitutional Politics in the States* (Westport, Conn.: Greenwood Press, 1996), 24–27.

21. U.S. Advisory Commission on Intergovernmental Relations (ACIR), *A Report to the President for Transmittal to the Congress* (Washington, D.C.: U.S. Government Printing Office, 1955).

22. National Municipal League, *Model State Constitution,* 6th ed., rev. (New York: National Municipal League, 1968).

23. John J. Carroll and Arthur English, "Traditions of State Constitution Making," *State and Local Government Review* 23 (Fall 1991): 103–109.

24. *Gitlow* v. *New York* 26 U.S. 652 (1925).

25. Ibid., 38.

26. Ibid., 38–42.

27. Council of State Governments, *The Book of the States,* 39 (Lexington, Ky.: Council of State Governments, 2007), 317–318.

28. Janice C. May, "State Constitutions and Constitutional Revision: 1988–89 and the 1980s," *The Book of the States, 1990–91* (Washington, D.C.: Council of State Governments, 1991), 25.

29. Quoted in U.S. Advisory Commission on Intergovernmental Relations, *State Constitutions in the Federal System* (Washington, D.C.: ACIR, 1989), 37.

30. Sturm, "American State Constitutions," 104.

31. W. Brooke Graves, "State Constitutional Law: A Twenty-Five Year Summary," *William and Mary Law Review* 8 (Fall 1966): 12.

32. ACIR, *State Government Capability,* 60.

33. Richard H. Leach, "A Quiet Revolution: 1933–1976," in *The Book of the States, 1975–76* (Lexington, Ky.: Council of State Governments, 1976), 25.

CHAPTER 4 CITIZEN PARTICIPATION AND ELECTIONS PP. 67–88

1. Randal C. Archibold, "Arizona Ballot Could Become Lottery Ticket," *New York Times,* www.nytimes.com (July 17, 2006).

2. Robert D. Putnam, *Bowling Alone: the Collapse and Revival of American Community* (New York: Simon and Schuster, 2000).

3. John D. Griffin and Brian Newman, "Are Voters Better Represented?" *Journal of* Politics 67 (November 2005): 1206–27.

4. William E. Lyons and David Lowery, *The Politics of Dissatisfaction* (Armonk, N.Y.: M. E. Sharpe, 1992).

5. Henry E. Brady, Sidney Verba, and Kay Lehman Schlozman, "Beyond SES: A Resource Model of Political Participation," *American Political Science Review* 89 (June 1995): 271–94; see also Jennifer Jerit, Jason Barabas, and Toby Bolsen, "Citizens, Knowledge, and the Information Environment," *American Journal of Political Science* 50 (April 2006): 266–82.

6. Richard Murray and Arnold Vedlitz, "Race, Socioeconomic Status, and Voting Participation in Large Southern Cities," *Journal of Politics* 39 (November 1977): 1064–72; Fredrick C. Harris, Valeria Sinclair-Chapman, and Brian D. McKenzie, "Macrodynamics of Black Political Participation in the Post-Civil Rights Era," *Journal of Politics* 67 (November 2005): 1143–63.

7. Virginia Sapiro, *The Political Integration of Women* (Urbana: University of Illinois Press, 1983).

8. Any Linomon and Mark R. Joslyn, "Trickle Up Political Socialization: The Impact of Kids Voting USA on Voter Turnout in Kansas," *State Politics and Policy Quarterly* 2 (Spring 2002): 24–36.

9. J. Eric Oliver, "City Size and Civic Involvement in Metropolitan America," *American Political Science Review* 94 (June 2000): 361–73.

10. Kim Quaile Hill and Jan E. Leighley, "Party Ideology, Organization, and Competitiveness as Mobilizing Forces in Gubernatorial Elections," *American Journal of Political Science* 37 (November 1993): 1158–78.

11. "Voter Registration and Turnout, 2000," www.fec.gov/ pages/turnout (January 17, 2005).

12. Committee for the Study of the American Electorate, "Total Turnout as a Percentage of CSAE Nov. Eligibles," www.fairvote.org/reports/CSAE2004electionreport.pdf.

13. "Voter Registration Information," *The Book of the States 2006* (Lexington, Ky.: Council of State Governments, 2006), 280.

14. "Election Reform: What's Changed, What Hasn't and Why, 2000–2006," www.electiononline.org (October 26, 2006).

15. Priscilla Southwell and Justin Burchett, "The Effect of Vote-by-Mail Elections on Voter Turnout," *American Politics Quarterly* 29 (February 2000): 72–80.

16. John M. Broder, "Growing Absentee Voting Is Reshaping Campaigns," *New York Times* (October 22, 2006).

17. "Methods of Nominating Candidates for State Offices," *The Book of the States,* 2006 (Lexington, Ky.: Council of State Governments, 2006), 272–73.

18. John F. Bibby and Thomas M. Holbrook, "Parties and Elections," in Virginia Gray and Russell L. Hanson, eds., *Politics in the American States: A Comparative Analysis,* 8th ed. (Washington, D.C.: Congressional Quarterly Press, 2004).

19. Alexandra Marks, "New York Wrestles with Its 'Party Machine' in Historic Vote," *Christian Science Monitor* (October 31, 2003), 2.

20. Charles S. Bullock III, Ronald Keith Gaddie, and Anders Ferrington, "System Structure, Campaign Stimuli and Voter Falloff in Runoff Primaries," *Journal of Politics* 64 (November 2002): 1210–24.

21. "Instant Runoff Voting," www.instant runoff.com (September 17, 2007).

22. Peter L. Francia and Paul S. Herrnson, "The Synergistic Effect of Campaign Effort and Election Reform on Voter Turnout in State Legislative Elections," *State Politics and Policy Quarterly* 4 (Spring 2004): 74–93.

23. Randall W. Partin, "Economic Conditions and Gubernatorial Elections," *American Politics Quarterly* 23 (January 1995): 81–95.

24. Pamela M. Prah, "Historic Election Year in Governors' Races," www.stateline.org (October 28, 2006).

25. Pamela M. Prah, "2007 Election: Lessons Learned," www.stateline.org (November 8, 2007).

26. Kimberly L. Nelson, *Elected Municipal Councils: Special Data Issue* (Washington, D.C.: International City/County Management Association, 2002).

27. Brian F. Schaffner, Gerald Wright, and Matthew Streb, "Teams Without Uniforms: The Nonpartisan Ballot in State and Local Elections," *Political Research Quarterly* 54 (March 2001): 7–30.

28. Zoltan Hajnal and Jessica Trounstine, "When Turnout Matters: The Consequences of Uneven Turnout in City Elections," *Journal of Politics* 67 (May 2005): 515–36.

29. Arnold Fleischmann and Lana Stein, "Campaign Contributions in Local Elections," *Political Research Quarterly* 51 (September 1998): 673–89.

30. Luis Ricardo Fraga, "Domination Through Democratic Means: Nonpartisan Slating Groups in City Electoral Politics," *Urban Affairs Quarterly* 23 (June 1988): 528–55; Christopher A. Cooper and Anthony J. Nownes, "Citizen Groups in Big City Politics," *State and Local Government Review* 35 (Spring 2003): 102–11.

31. David B. Magleby, "Taking the Initiative: Direct Legislation and Direct Democracy in the 1980s," *PS: Political Science and Politics* 21 (Summer 1988): 600.

32. www.iandrinstitute.org/Montana.htm; www.iandrinstitute.org/Nebraska.htm (May 14, 2005).

33. Elisabeth R. Gerber, et al,. *Stealing the Initiative* (Upper Saddle River, N.J.: Prentice-Hall, 2001).

34. "Fall Ballot Measures 2006," www.iandrinstitute.org (October 21, 2006).

35. Alana S. Jeydel and Brent S. Steel, "Public Attitudes toward the Initiative Process in Oregon," *State and Local Government Review* 34 (Fall 2002): 173–82.

36. Valentina A. Bali, "Implementing Popular Initiatives: What Matters for Compliance?" *Journal of Politics* 66 (November 2003): 1141.

37. Thad Kousser, "The California Governor's Recall," *Spectrum: The Journal of State Government* 77 (Winter 2004): 32–36.

38. Jim Cleary, as quoted in "Fighting City Hall—and Winning," *The State* (May 26, 1987), 7A.

39. Thomas E. Cronin, "Public Opinion and Direct Democracy," *PS: Political Science and Politics* 21 (Summer 1988): 612–19.

40. Charles Mahtesian, "The Endless Struggle over Open Meetings," *Governing* 11 (December 1997): 48–51.

41. Neal Peirce, "Oregon's Rx for Mistrusted Government," *National Journal* 24 (February 29, 1992): 529.

42. Jonathan Walters, "Polling the Populace," *Governing* 20 (April 2007): 66–68.

43. Christopher Swope, "E-Gov's New Gear," *Governing* 17 (March 2004): 40–42.

44. Shane Harris, "Bridging the Divide," *Governing* 13 (September 2000): 36.

45. Mary A. Culp, "Volunteering as Helping," *National Civic Review* 77 (May/June 1988): 224–30.

46. Markus Prior, "News vs. Entertainment: How Increasing Media Choice Widens Gaps in Political Knowledge and Turnout," *American Journal of Political Science* 49 (July 2005): 577–92.

47. Evan J. Ringquist, Kim Quaile Hill, Jan E. Leighley, and Angela Hinton-Andersson, "Lower-Class Mobilization and Policy Linkage in the U.S. States: A Correction," *American Journal of Political Science* 41 (January 1997): 339–44.

48. Rob Gurwitt, "A Government That Runs on Citizen Power," *Governing* 6 (December 1992): 48.

49. Tom W. Rice and Alexander F. Sumberg, "Civic Culture and Government Performance in the American States," *Publius: The Journal of Federalism* 27 (Winter 1997): 99–114.

50. Ibid., 113.

CHAPTER 5 POLITICAL PARTIES, INTEREST GROUPS, AND CAMPAIGNS PP. 89–112

1. Alan Ehrenhalt, "Rivals on the Right," *Governing* 19 (July 2006): 11-12.

2. A. James Reichley, "The Future of the American Two-Party System at the Beginning of a New Century," in John C. Green and Rick Farmer, eds., *The State of the Parties,* (Lanham, Md.: Rowman & Littlefield, 2003), 19-37.

3. Sarah M. Morehouse and Malcolm E. Jewell, "State Parties: Independent Partners in the Money Relationship," in Green and Farmer, *The State of the Parties*, 151–68.

4. Marjorie Randon Hershey, *Party Politics in America*, 11th ed. (New York: Pearson Longman, 2005).

5. The Pew Research Center for the People and the Press, "Political Landscape More Favorable to Democrats," people-press.org/reports/pdf/312.pdf (last visited, September 22, 2007).

6. David Von Drehle, "Culture Clash: Geography, Technology, and Strategy Have Nurtured a Political Split," *Washington Post National Weekly Edition* (May 24–30, 2004), 6–7.

7. James G. Gimpel and Jason E. Schuknecht, "Reconsidering Political Regionalism in the American States," *State Politics and Policy Quarterly* 2 (Winter 2002): 325–52.

8. Malcolm E. Jewell and Sarah M. Morehouse, *Political Parties and Elections in American States,* 4th ed. (Washington, D.C.: Congressional Quarterly Press, 2001).

9. John H. Aldrich, "Southern Parties in State and Nation," *Journal of Politics* 62 (August 2000): 643-70.

10. Ibid.

11. Robert E. Hogan, "Candidate Perceptions of Political Party Campaign Activity in State Legislative Elections," *State Politics and Policy Quarterly* 2 (Spring 2002): 66-85.

12. James Dao, "Churches in Ohio Flex Political Muscle," *New York Times* (March 27, 2005), 12.

13. Scott Lasley, "Explaining Third Party Support in American States," paper presented at the annual meeting of the American Political Science Association, Washington, D.C., 1997, 180–95.

14. Richard L. Berke, "U.S. Voters Focus on Selves, Poll Says," *New York Times* (September 21, 1994), A12.

15. Eric Kelderman, "GOP Rules Amid Bickering in Ga. Statehouse,"www.stateline.org (July 17, 2007); Daniel C. Vocke, "Democrats' Dysfunction Hobbles Illinois," www.stateline.org (September 17, 2007).

16. Stephen C. Craig, "The Decay of Mass Partisanship," *Polity* 20 (Summer 1988): 705-13.

17. Michael Slackman, "Voters Choosing None of the Above, and Parties Scramble," *New York Times,* www.nytimes.com (April 13, 2004).

18. Ibid.

19. Clive S. Thomas and Ronald J. Hrebnar, "Interest Groups in the States," in Virginia Gray and Russell L. Hanson, eds. *Politics in the American States: A Comparative Approach* (Washington, D.C.: Congressional Quarterly Press, 2004), 100–28.

20. Clive S. Thomas and Ronald J. Hrebnar, "2002 State Interest Group Power Update: Results and Tables," manuscript (June 12, 2003), 12.

21. Thomas and Hrebnar, "Interest Groups in the States."

22. Sarah M. Morehouse, "Interest Groups, Parties, and Politics in the American States," paper presented at the annual meeting of the American Political Science Association, Washington, D.C., 1997.

23. Clive S. Thomas and Ronald J. Hrebenar, "Toward a Comprehensive Understanding of the Political Party-Interest Group Relationship in the American States," paper presented at the annual meeting of the Western Political Association, Seattle, 1999.

24. Christopher A. Cooper and Anthony J. Nownes, "Perceptions of Power: Interest Groups in Local Politics," *State and Local Government Review* 37 (Fall 2005): 201–16.

25. Christopher A. Cooper and Anthony J. Nownes, "Citizen Groups in Big City Politics," *State and Local Government Review* 35 (Spring 2003): 102–11.

26. Virginia Gray and David Lowery, "A Niche Theory of Interest Representation," *Journal of Politics* 58 (February 1996): 91-111; Michael T. Heaney, "Issue Networks, Information, and Interest Group Alliances: The Case of Wisconsin Welfare Politics, 1993–99," *State Politics and Policy Quarterly* 34 (Fall 2004): 237–270.

27. Donald P. Haider-Markel, "Interest Group Survival: Shared Interests versus Competition for Resources," *Journal of Politics* 59 (August 1997): 903–12.

28. Clive S. Thomas and Ronald J. Hrebenar, "Interest Groups in the States," in Virginia Gray, Herbert Jacob, and Robert B. Albritton, eds., *Politics in the American States,* 5th ed. (Glenview, Ill: Scott, Foresman/Little, Brown, 1990), 143.

29. Center for Public Integrity, "Ratio of Lobbyists to Legislators (2005)," www.publicintegrity.org (November 1, 2007).

30. Jim Snyder and Jeffrey Young, "Like Congress, State Legislatures Wrestle with Lobbying Reforms," The Hill, www.hillnews.com (May 17, 2006).

31. Virginia Gray and David Lowery, "Trends in Lobbying in the States," in *The Book of the States 2003* (Lexington, Ky.: Council of State Governments, 203), 257–62.

32. Alan Rosenthal, *The Third House* (Washington, D.C.: Congressional Quarterly Press, 1993).

33. Rob Gurwitt, "Cookie-Jar Clampdown," *Governing* 20 (April 2007): 32–39.

34. Ron Faucheux, "The Grassroots Explosion," *Campaigns & Elections* (December/January 1995): 20.

35. Anthony J. Nownes and Patricia Freeman, "Interest Group Activity in the States," paper presented at the annual meeting of the American Political Science Association, San Francisco, 1996.

36. William P. Browne and Delbert J. Ringquist, "Michigan Interests: The Politics of Diversification," paper presented at the annual meeting of the Midwest Political Science Association, Chicago, 1987, 24.

37. Fred Monardi and Stanton A. Glantz, "Tobacco Industry Campaign Contributions and Legislative Behavior at the State Level," paper presented at the annual meeting of the American Political Science Association, San Francisco, 1996, 8.

38. Louay M. Constant, "When Money Matters: Campaign Contributions, Roll Call Votes, and School Choice in Florida," *State Politics and Policy Quarterly* 6 (Summer 2006): 195–219.

39. Daniel M. Shea and Michael John Burton, *Campaign Craft: The Strategies, Tactics, and Art of Political Campaign Management* (Westport, Conn.: Praeger, 2000), 75–98.

40. Jerry Hagstrom and Robert Guskind, "Selling the Candidate," *National Journal* 18 (November 1, 1986): 2619-26.

41. L. Marvin Overby and Jay Barth, "Radio Advertising in American Political Campaigns," *American Politics Research* 34 (July 2006): 451–78.

42. Owen G. Abbe and Paul S. Hernnson, "Campaign Professionalism in State Legislative Elections," *State Politics and Policy Quarterly* 3 (Fall 2003): 223–45.

43. Cleveland Ferguson III, "The Politics of Ethics and Elections," *Florida State University Law Review* 25 (Fall 1997): 463-503.

44. "Statewide Candidate Spending Once Again Climbs to a Record High," www.amss.gov/ocpf/swerept06.pdf (December 5, 2005).

45. "GOP congressman Bobby Jindal Wins Louisiana Governor's Race," www.foxnews.com (October 21, 2007).

46. Donald A. Gross and Robert K. Goidel, "The Impact of State Campaign Finance Laws," *State Politics and Policy Quarterly* 1 (Summer 2001): 80-195.

47. Zach Patton, "Chasing the Shadow," *Governing* 19 (June 2006): 43–45.

48. Eric Kelderman, "Report Ranks Campaign Disclosure Laws," stateline.org (October 17, 2007).

49. Eric Kelderman, "Small Donors Equal Big Bucks for State Party Coffers," stateline.org (July 3, 2004).

50. Ronald D. Michaelson, "Trends in State Campaign Financing," in *The Book of the States 2003* (Lexington, Ky.: Council of State Governments, 2003), 270–80.

51. "Funding of State Elections: Tax Provisions and Public Financing," in *The Book of the States 2000–01* (Lexington, Ky: Council of State Governments, 2000), 229–32.

52. Kedron Bardwell, "Campaign Finance Laws and the Competition for Spending in Gubernatorial Elections," *Social Science Quarterly* 84 (December 2003): 811–25.

CHAPTER 6 STATE LEGISLATURES PP. 113–137

1. Jim Tharpe, "GOP Rules Georgia," *State Legislatures* 31 (July/August 2005): 40–44.

2. Mark C. Ellickson and Donald E. Whistler, "Explaining State Legislators' Casework and Public Resource Allocations," *Political Research Quarterly* 54 (September 2001): 553–69.

3. Ellen Perlman, "The 'Gold-Plated' Legislature," *Governing* 11 (February 1998): 36–40.

4. National Conference of State Legislatures, "Legislator Demographics," www.ncsl.org (September 26, 2007).

5. Lilliard E. Richardson Jr., Brian E. Russell, and Christopher A. Cooper, "Legislative Representation in Single-Member versus Multiple-Member District System: The Arizona State Legislature," *Political Research Quarterly* 57 (June 2004): 337–44.

6. *Reynolds v. Sims,* 84 S.Ct. 1362 (1964).

7. Michael P. McDonald, "A Comparative Analysis of Redistricting Institutions in the U.S., 2001–02," *State Politics and Policy Quarterly* 4 (Winter 2004): 371–95.

8. William March, "Black Voters Win, Lose with Districting," *Tampa Tribune* (April 6, 1998), B-1, B5.

9. Ronald E. Weber, "Emerging Trends in State Legislative Redistricting," *Spectrum* 75 (Winter 2002): 13–15.

10. "Legislative Compensation: Regular Sessions," in *The Book of the States 2006* (Lexington, Ky: Council of State Government, 2006), 84–86.

11. Perlman, "The Gold-Plated Legislature."

12. Peverill Squire, "Member Career Opportunities and the Internal Organization of Legislatures," *Journal of Politics* 50 (August 1988): 726–44.

13. Thomas H. Little, "A Systematic Analysis of Members' Environments and Their Expectations of Elected Leaders," *Political Research Quarterly* 47 (September 1994): 733–47.

14. Keith E. Hamm, Ronald D. Hedlund, and Stephanie S. Post, "Committee Specialization in State Legislatures During the Twentieth Century," paper presented at the annual meeting of the American Political Science Association, Washington, D.C., 1997.

15. Ralph G. Wright, *Inside the Statehouse: Lessons from the Speaker* (Washington, D.C.: Congressional Quarterly Press, 2005).

16. Alan Rosenthal, *Heavy Lifting: The Job of the American Legislature* (Washington, D.C.: Congressional Quarterly Press, 2004).

17. L. Marvin Overby, Thomas A. Kazee, and David W. Prince, "Committee Outliers in State Legislatures," *Legislative Studies Quarterly* 29 (February 2004): 81–107; David W. Prince and L. Marvin Overby, "Legislative Organization Theory and Committee Preference Outliers in State Senates," *State Politics and Policy Quarterly* 5 (Spring 2005): 68–87.

18. Donald R. Songer et al., "The Influence of Issues on Choice of Voting Cues Utilized by State Legislators," *Western Political Quarterly* 39 (March 1986): 118–25.

19. Eric M. Uslaner and Ronald E. Weber, "U.S. State Legislators' Opinions and Perceptions of Constituency Attitudes," *Legislative Studies Quarterly* 4 (November 1979): 563–85.

20. "Bill and Resolution Introductions and Enactments, 2005 Regular Sessions," *The Book of the States 2006* (Lexington, Ky.: Council of State Governments, 2006), 111–12.

21. Alan Rosenthal, "The Legislature as Sausage Factory," *State Legislatures* 27 (September 2001): 12–15.

22. Tom Loftus, *The Art of Legislative Politics* (Washington, D.C.: Congressional Quarterly Press, 1994), 76.

23. Ibid., 77.

24. David C. Saffell, "School Funding in Ohio: Courts, Politicians, and Newspapers," *Comparative State Politics* 18 (October 1997): 9–25.

25. Citizens' Conference on State Legislatures, *The Sometimes Governments: A Critical Study of the 50 American Legislatures,* 2d ed. (Kansas City, Mo.: CCSL, 1973), 41–42.

26. Alan Rosenthal, "The New Legislature: Better or Worse and for Whom?" *State Legislatures* 12 (July 1986): 5.

27. Charles Mahtesian, "The Sick Legislature Syndrome," *Governing* 10 (February 1997): 16–20.

28. Charles W. Wiggins, as quoted in "Is the Citizen Legislator Becoming Extinct," *State Legislatures* 12 (July 1986): 22–25.

29. Representative Vic Krouse, as quoted in ibid., 24.

30. Rosenthal, *Heavy Lifting*; James D. King, "Changes in Professionalism in U.S. State Legislatures," *Legislative Studies Quarterly* 25 (May 2000): 327–43.

31. Peverill Squire, "Measuring State Legislative Professionalism: The Squire Index Revisited," *State Politics and Policy Quarterly* 7 (Summer 2007): 211–27.

32. Richard Nathan, as cited in Kathe Callahan and Marc Holzer, "Rethinking Governmental Change," *Public Productivity Management & Review* 17 (Spring 1994): 202.

33. Brad Bumsted, "Rendell Jumps on Reform Bandwagon," *Pittsburgh Tribune-Review,* www.pittsburghlive.com (last visited March 22, 2007).

34. Stuart Rothenberg, "How Term Limits Became a National Phenomenon," *State Legislatures* 18 (January 1992): 35–39.

35. National Conference of State Legislatures, *"The Effect of Term Limits in the 2006 Elections,"* www.ncsl.org/programs/legman/about/effects0tl-2006.htm (last visited April 6, 2006).

36. Joel A. Thompson and Gary F. Moncrief, "The Implications of Term Limits for Women and Minorities: Some Evidence from the States," *Social Science Quarterly* 74 (June 1993): 300–309.

37. Karen Hansen, "The Third Revolution," *State Legislatures* 23 (September 1997): 20–26; Thad Kousser, "The Limited Impact of Term Limits: Contingent Effects on the Complexity and Breadth of Laws," *State Politics and Policy Quarterly* 6 (Winter 2006): 410–29.

38. Gary Moncrief and Joel A. Thompson, "On the Outside Looking In: Lobbyists Perspectives on the Effects of State Legislative Term Limits," *State Politics and Policy Quarterly* (Winter 2001): 394–411; Joel Thompson and Gary Moncrief, "Lobbying under Limits: Interest Group Perspectives on the Effects of Term Limits in State Legislatures," in Farmer, Rausch, and Green, eds, *The Test of Time: Coping with Legislative Term Limits* (Lanham, Md.: Lexington Books, 2003), 211–24.

39. Robert A. Bernstein and Anita Chadha, "The Effects of Term Limits on Representation: Why So Few Women?" in Rick Farmer, John David Rausch Jr., and John C. Green, eds., *The Test of Time* 147–58; Stanley M. Caress et al., "Effect of Term Limits on the Election of Minority State Legislators," *State and Local Government Review* 35 (Fall 2003): 183–95.

40. John M. Carey, Richard G. Niemi, Lynda W. Powell, and Gary F. Moncrief, "The Effects of Term Limits on State Legislatures: A New Survey of the 50 States," *Legislative Studies Quarterly* 31: (February 2006): 105–34.

41. Daniel A. Smith, "Overturning Term Limits: The Legislature's Own Private Idaho?" *PS: Political Science and Politics* (April 2003): 215–20.

42. Lucinda Simon, "Legislatures and Governors: The Wrestling Match," *State Government* 59 (Spring 1986): 1.

43. Governor Haley Barbour, State of the State Address (January 26, 2004).

44. "New Assembly Leaders Vow New Decorum," *San Jose Mercury News,* www.mercurynews.com (December 30, 2003).

45. Madeleine Kunin, as quoted in Sharon Randall, "From Big Shot to Boss," *State Legislatures* 14 (June 1988): 348.

46. Dianna Gordon, "Virginia's JLARC: A Standard of Excellence," *State Legislatures* 20 (May 1994): 13–16.

47. Brian J. Gerber, Cherie Maestas, and Nelson C. Dometrius, "State Legislative Influence over Agency Rulemaking," *State Politics and Policy Quarterly* 5 (Spring 2005): 24–46.

48. Jerry Brekke, "Supreme Court of Missouri Rules Legislative Veto Unconstitutional," *Comparative State Politics* 19 (February 1997): 32–34.

49. As quoted in Dave McNeely, "Is the Sun Setting on the Texas Sunset Law?" *State Legislatures* 20 (May 1994): 17–20.

50. Ibid.

51. William M. Pearson and Van A. Wigginton, "Effectiveness of Administrative Controls: Some Perceptions of State Legislators," *Public*

Administration Review 46 (July/ August 1986): 328–31.

52. Rosenthal, "The New Legislature," 5.

53. Alan Rosenthal, *The Decline of Representative Democracy,* (Washington, D.C.: Congressional Quarterly Press, 1998), 85.

54. Alan Ehrenhalt, "An Embattled Institution," *Governing* 5 (January 1992): 28–33.

CHAPTER 7 GOVERNORS PP. 138–165

1. Gar Alperovitz, "California Split," *New York Times* (February 10, 2007) accessed on line at www.nytimes.com; Timothy Egan, "Where's Arnold?" *New York Times* (June 7, 2007) accessed on-line at www.nyt.com.

2. For a more detailed discussion of the processes and results of the state government reform movement, see Ann O'M. Bowman and Richard C. Kearney, *The Resurgence of the States* (Englewood Cliffs, N.J.: Prentice-Hall, 1986).

3. Larry Sabato, *Goodbye to Goodtime Charlie: The American Governorship Transformed* (Lexington, Mass.: Lexington Books, 1978), 13.

4. As quoted in George F. Will, "Ashcroft in 2000? He's Playing the Part," *Hartford Courant* (September 9, 1997), A24.

5. Eric Kelderman, "Mr. Smith Goes to Washington and Back," www.stateline.org (November 14, 2005).

6. Thad L. Beyle, "Gubernatorial Elections, Campaign Costs and Powers," in *The Book of the States,* vol. 39 (Lexington, Ky.: Council of State Governments, 2007), 154–162.

7. *Book of the States, 2007,* 159.

8. Ibid.

9. Beyle, "Governors: Elections, Campaign costs, Profiles, Forced Exits, and Powers," in *The Book of the States* vol. 36 (Lexington, KY: Council of State Governments, 2007), 95.

10. Malcolm E. Jewell and David M. Olson, *Political Parties and Elections in the American States,* 3d ed. (Chicago: Dorsey Press, 1988).

11. Peverill Squire, "Challenger Profile and Gubernatorial Elections," *Western Politics Quarterly* 45 (1992): 125–42.

12. Thad Beyle, "The Governors," *The Book of the States 2003* (Lexington, Ky. The Council of State Governments), 179; Robert C. Lowry, James E. Alt, and Karen E. Feree, "Fiscal Policy Outcomes and Accountability in American States," *American Political Science Review* 92 (December 1998): 759–72.; Jason A. MacDonald and Lee Sigelman, "Public Assessments of Gubernatorial Performance: A Comparative State Analysis," *American Politics Quarterly* 27 (April 1999): 201–15.

13. Sharon Sherman, "Powersplit: When Legislatures and Governors Are of Opposing Parties," *State Legislatures* 10 (May/June 1984): 9–12.

14. Sander M. Polster, "Maine's King Makes Independence a Virtue," www.stateline.org (November 30, 1999).

15. As quoted in Alan Ehrenhart, "The Debilitating Search for a Flabby Consensus," *Governing* 9 (October 1996): 8.

16. Josh Goodman, "Against the Grain," *Governing* (October 2006): 32–38.

17. Jennifer Steinhauer, "As States Innovate, Schwarzenegger Blurs Lines," *New York Times* (January 12, 2007), accessed on-line at www.nytimes.com.

18. As quoted in Thad L. Beyle and Lynn R. Muchmore, *Reflections on Being Governor* (Washington, D.C.: National Governors Association, 1978), 45.

19. *Book of the States,* vol. 39, 166.

20. Thad L. Beyle and Lynn R. Muchmore, "The Governor and the Public," in Beyle and Muchmore, eds., *Being Governor,* 24.

21. Cathilea Robinett, "Few Governors Grasp Digital Revolution," *Government Technology* (May 1999): 6.

22. Alan Ehrenhalt, "Ostrich Readings," *Governing* (February 2004).

23. Jonathan Walters, "Full Speed Ahead: Remaking a State through Ideology and Determination," *Governing* (November 2001), 44–51.

24. Jeffrey E. Cohen and James D. King, "Relative Unemployment and Gubernatorial Popularity," *Journal of Politics* 66 (November, 2004): 1267–82.

25. Thad L. Beyle and Lynn R. Muchmore, "The Governor as Party Leader," in Beyle and Muchmore, eds., *Being Governor,* 44–51.

26. John Wagner, "Hunt," *News and Observer* (April 1, 2000), 1 A, 18A.

27. As quoted in Samuel R. Soloman, "Governors: 1960–1970," *National Civic Review* (March 1971): 126–46.

28. As quoted in Coleman B. Ransome, Jr., *The American Governorship* (Westport, Conn.: Greenwood Press, 1982), 121.

29. *Rutan et al.* v. *Republican Party of Illinois,* 1110 S.Ct. 2229, 1990.

30. Beyle, "The Governors . . . ," 216.

31. Rosenthal, *Governors and Legislatures,* 11–12; Charles Barrilleaux and Michael Berkman, "Do Governors Matter? Budgeting Rules and the Politics of State Policymaking," *Political Research Quarterly* 56 (December 2003): 409–417.

32. Daniel C. Vock, "Govs Enjoy Quirky Veto Power," *stateline.org* (April 24, 2007), 1–3, accessed at www.stateline.org.

33. James Conant, "Executive Branch Reorganization: Can It Be an Antidote for Fiscal Stress in the States?" *State and Local Government Review* 24 (Winter 1992): 3–11.

34. Dan Durning, "Governors and Administrative Reform in the 1990s," *State and Local Government Review* 27 (Winter 1995): 36–54.

35. Conant, 3–11.

36. As quoted in Flentje, "Governor as Manager," 70. For a description of failure in reorganization in Florida, see also Less Garner, "Managing Change Through Organization Structure," *State Government* 60 (July/August 1987): 191–95.

37. Ibid.; Michael B. Berkman and Christopher Reenock, "Incremental Consolidation and Comprehensive reorganization of American State Executive Branches," *American Journal of Political Science* 48 (October 2004): 796–812

38. Norma M. Riccucci and Judith R. Saidel, "The Demographics of Gubernatorial Appointees: Toward an Explanation of Variation," *Policy Studies Journal* 29, no. 1 (2000): 11–22.

39. *The Book of the States, 2003:* Table 4.3.

40. Beyle, "The Governors . . . ," 206.

41. Ransome, *The American Governorship,* 156.

42. Matt Bai, "The Taming of Jesse," *Newsweek* (October 15, 1999): 38; Jesse Ventura, *I Ain't Got Time to Bleed: Reworking the Body Politic from the Bottom Up* (New York: Villard, 1999).

43. Pamela M. Prah, "Some Rookie Governors Fumble," stateline.org (March 23, 2007) accessed at www.stateline.org.; Jennifer Steinhauer, "A Rocky Start for Nevada's Governor," *New York Times* on-line (May 30, 2007), accessed at www.nytimes.com.

44. Louis Jacobson, "Keystone State's Gov Looms Large," stateline.org (September 13, 2007), accessed at www.stateline.org.

45. Scott M. Matheson, with James Edwin Kee, *Out of Balance* (Salt Lake City: Peregrine Smith Books, 1986), 186.

46. See Paul West, "They're Everywhere! For Today's Governors, Life Is a Never-Ending Campaign," *Governing* 3 (March 1990): 51–55.

47. Beyle, "Enhancing Executive Leadership," 33.

48. *Book of the States,* 2007, 199–200.

CHAPTER 8 PUBLIC ADMINISTRATION: BUDGETING AND SERVICE DELIVERY
PP: 166–194

1. H. George Frederickson, "Can Bureaucracy Be Beautiful?" *Public Administration Review* 60 (January/February 2000): 47–53.

2. J. Norman Baldwin, "Public versus Private Employees: Debunking Stereotypes," *Review of Public Personnel Administration* 11 (Fall 1990–Spring 1991): 1–27.

3. See, for example, Theodore H. Poister and Gary T. Henry, "Citizen Ratings of Public and Private Service Quality: A Comparative Perspective," *Public Administration Review* 54 (March/April 1994): 155–59.

4. Harold D. Laswell, *Politics: Who Gets What, When, Where, How?* (Cleveland: World, 1958).

5. See Kurt M. Thurmaier and Katherine G. Willoughby, *Policy and Politics in State Budgeting* (Armonk, N.Y.: M. E. Sharpe, 2000); Dall W. Forsythe, *Memos to the Governor,* 2d ed. (Washington, D.C.: Georgetown University Press, 2004).

6. Ellen Perlman, " 'Stat' Fever," *Governing* (January 2007): 48–49.

7. Aaron Wildavsky, "Toward a Radical Incrementalism," in Alfred De Grazia, ed., *Congress: The First Branch of Government* (Washington, D.C.: American Enterprise Institute, 1966).

8. Glenn Abney and Thomas P. Lauth, *The Politics of State and City Administration* (Albany: State University of New York Press, 1986), 110–11, 115, 142–43; Janet M. Kelly and William C. Rivenbark, *Performance Budgeting for State and Local Government* (Armonk, N.Y.: M. E. Sharpe, 2003).

9. Charles E. Lindblom, "The Science of Muddling Through," *Public Administrative Review* 19 (Spring 1959): 79–88.

10. Kelly and Rivenbark, 2003.

11. Jay Shafrtiz, "The Cancer Eroding Public Personnel Professionalism," *Public Personnel Management* 3 (November/December 1974): 486–92; David K. Hamilton, "The Staffing Function in Illinois State Government After Rutan," *Public Administration Review* 53 (July/August 1993): 381–86.

12. H. George Frederickson, "The Airport That Reforms Forgot," *PA Times* (January 2000): 11.

13. Steven W. Hays and Richard C. Kearney, "Anticipated Changes in Human Resource Management: Surveying the Field," *Public Administration Review* 61 (September/October, 2001): 585–97; J. Edward Kellough and Sally Coleman Selden, "The Reinvention of Public Personnel Administration: An Analysis of the Diffusion of Public Personnel Management Reforms in the States," *Public Administration Review* 61 (November/December 2003): 165–76.

14. See, for example, Kenneth J. Meier, "Representative Bureaucracy: An Empirical Analysis," *American Political Science Review* 69 (June 1975): 526–42; and Samuel Krislow and David H. Rosenbloom, *Representative Bureaucracy and the American Political System* (New York: Praeger, 1981), 31–73, 75–107. But see also Kenneth J. Meier, "Latinos and Representative Bureaucracy: Testing the Thompson and Henderson Hypotheses," *Journal of Public Administration Research and Theory* 3 (October 1993): 393–414.

15. Vicky M. Wilkins, "Exploring the Causal Story: Gender, Active Representation, and Bureaucratic

Priorities," *Journal of Public Administration Research and Theory* 17 (2006): 77–94.

16. J. Edward Kellough, "Equal Employment Opportunity and Affirmative Action in the Public Sector," in Steven W. Hays and Richard C. Kearney, eds., *Public Personnel Administration: Problems and Prospects,* 4th ed. (Upper Saddle River, N.J.: Prentice Hall, 2003), 209–24.

17. *Hopwood* v. *Texas* (1996). 78 F.3d 932 (5th Cir. 1990), *cert. denied,* 1996 WL 227009.

18. *Gratz* v. *Bollinger,* No. 97–75321 (E.D. Mich.) (June 22, 2003); *Grutter* v. *Bollinger,* No. 02–241 F.3d 732 (June 23, 2003).

19. Mary E. Guy, "The Difference that Gender Makes," in Hays and Kearney (2003), 256–70; Norma Riccucci and Judith R. Seidel, "The Representativeness of State-Level Bureaucratic Leaders: A Missing Piece of the Representative Bureaucracy Puzzle," *Public Administration Review* 57 (September/October 1997): 423–30; Norma M. Riccucci, *Managing Diversity in Public Sector Workforces* (Boulder, Colo.: Westview Press, 2002).

20. See, for example, Antonio Cisneros, "Hispanics in the Public Service in the Late Twentieth Century," *Public Administration Review* 53 (January/February 1993): 1–7; Riccucci, *Managing Diversity,* 2002.

21. Sonia Ospina and James F. O'Sullivan, "Working Together: Meeting the Challenge of Workplace Diversity," in Hays and Kearney, 2003, 238–55; Riccucci, 2002.

22. *Meritor Savings Bank* v. *Vinson,* 477 U.S. 57 (1986); *Teresa Harris* v. *Forklift Systems, Inc.,* 510 U.S. 17 (1993).

23. *Clark County School District* v. *Breeden,* 532 US. 268 (2001).

24. Sally Coleman Selden, "Sexual Harassment in the Workplace," in Hays and Kearney, 2003, 225–37.

25. www.bls.gov/news.release/unions2.t03.htn (accessed September 18, 2007).

26. Richard C. Kearney, *Labor Relations in the Public Sector,* 3d ed. (New York: Marcel Dekker, 2001), 23–43; Joel M. Douglas, "State Civil Service Systems and Collective Bargaining: Systems in Conflict," *Public Administration Review* 52 (January/February 1992): 162–71.

27. Jeffrey S. Banks and Barry R. Weingast, "The Political Control of Bureaucracies Under Asymmetric Information," *American Journal of Political Science* 36 (May 1992): 509 24.

28. Gerald T. Gabris and Douglas M. Ihrke, "Unanticipated Failures of Well-Intentioned Reforms: Some Lessons Learned from Federal and Local Sectors," *International Journal of Organization Theory and Behavior* 6 (February 2003): 195–225.

29. David Osborne and Ted Gaebler, *Reinventing Government* (New York: Penguin Books, 1993).

30. Keon S. Chi, Kelley A. Arnold, and Heather M. Perkins, "Privatization in State Government: Trends and Issues," *Spectrum: The Journal of State Government* (Fall 2003): 1; Robert Jay Dilger, Randolph R. Moffett, and Linda Struyk, "Privatization of Municipal Services in America's Largest Cities," *Public Administration Review* 57 (January/February 1997): 21–26.

31. Alan Greenblatt, "Sweetheart Deals . . . ," *Governing* (December 2004): 20–25; Eliott D. Sclar, *You Don't Always Get What You Pay For: The Economics of Privatization* (Ithaca, N.Y.: Cornell University Press, 2000).

32. J. D. Greene, "Does Privatization Make a Difference? The Impact of Private Contracting on Municipal Efficiency," *International Journal of Public Administration* 17 (July 1994): 1299–325; George A. Boyne, "Bureaucratic Theory Meets Reality: Public Choice and Service Contracting in U.S. Local Government," *Public Administration Review* 58 (November/December 1998): 474–84.

33. John Rehfuss, "Contracting Out and Accountability in State and Local Governments-The Importance of Contract Monitoring," *State and Local Government Review* 22 (Winter 1990): 44–48; Jonas Prager, "Contracting Out Government Services: Lessons from the Private Sector," *Public Administration Review* 54 (March/April 1994): 176–84.

34. Sclar, *You Don't Always Get . . .*

35. See Sclar, 2000; Katherine Barrett and Richard Greene, "A Balancing Act," *Governing* (March 2005): 59.

36. Donald Norris and Jae Moon, "Advancing E-government at the Grassroots: Tortoise or Hare?" Public Administration Review 65 (1), 64–75.

CHAPTER 9 THE JUDICIARY PP. 195–222

1. W. John Moore, "In Whose Court?" *National Journal* (October 15, 1991): 2396.

2. Aaron Marshall, "Ohio House Makes 'Don't Touch' the Rule in Strip Clubs," www.Cleveland.com (accessed September 22, 2007).

3. Henry Robert Glick and Kenneth N. Vines, *State Court Systems* (Englewood Cliffs, N.J.: Prentice Hall, 1973), 19.

4. Ibid., 21.

5. Kevin Sack, "Where the Bench Orders Some Southern Comfort," *New York Times,* www.nytimes.com (January 29, 2002).

6. Doug Lemov, "Bringing Order to the Courts," *Governing* 10 (February 1997): 58–59.

7. Tom Carlson, "Courts Ride the Information Superhighway," *Judicature* 80 (September/October 1996): 98–100.

8. American Bar Association, *Standards Relating to Court Organization* (New York: ABA, 1974), 43–44.

9. See Charles H. Sheldon and Linda S. Maule, *Choosing Judges: The Recruitment of State and Federal Judges* (Pullman, Wash.: Washington State University Press, 1997).

10. Melinda Gann Hall, "State Supreme Courts in American Democracy: Probing the Myths of Judicial Reform," *American Political Science Review* 95 (June 2001): 315–30.

11. Melinda Gann Hall, "Mobilizing Voters in State Supreme Court Elections: Competition and Other Contextual Forces as Democratic Incentives," a paper presented at the Sixth annual State Politics and Policy Conference, Lubbock, TX (May 19–20, 2006).

12. *Republican Party of Minnesota* v. *White*, U.S. Sup. Ct. No. 01–521 (June 27, 2002).

13. Adam Liptak and Janet Roberts, "Campaign Cash Mirrors a High Court's Rulings," *New York Times* (October 1, 2006), 1, 10.

14. Stephen Ware, "Money, Politics, and Judicial Decisions: A Case Study of Arbitration Law in Alabama," *Journal of Law and Politics* 15 (Fall 1999): 645–86; Madhavi McCall, "The Politics of Judicial Elections: The Influence of Campaign Contributions on the Voting Patterns of Texas Supreme Court Judges," *Politics and Policy* 31 (June 2003): 314–33.

15. "The Best Judges Business Can Buy," *The New York Times* editorial (June 18, 2007): accessed at www.nyt.com June 18, 2006.

16. William Glaberson, "Court Rulings Curb Efforts to Rein in Judicial Races," *New York Times* (October 7, 2000), A1, A4.

17. Alexander Wohl, "Justice for Rent," *The American Prospect* (May 22, 2000): 34–37.

18. Kathleen Hunter, "Money Mattering More in Judicial Elections," www.stateline.org (May 12, 2004): 1–3.

19. Sheila Kaplan, "Justice for Sale," in Thad Beyle, *State Government: CQ's Guide to Current Issues and Activities, 1986–87* (Washington, D.C.: Congressional Quarterly Press, 1987), 151–57.

20. Damon M. Cann, "Justice for Sale? Campaign Contributions and Judicial Decisionmaking," *State Politics and Policys Quarterly* 7 (Fall 2007): 281–97; Chris W. Bonneau, "Campaign Fundraising in State Supreme Court Elections," *Social Science Quarterly* 88 (March 2007).

21. William Glaberson, "States Take Steps to Rein in Excesses of Judicial Politicking," *New York Times* (June 15, 2001), 1–4.

22. See, for example, Richard A. Watson and Ronald C. Downing, *The Politics of the Bench and Bar* (New York: John Wiley and Sons, 1969), 43–48, 136–38.

23. Melinda Gann Hall, "State Supreme Courts in American Democracy: Probing the Myths of Judicial Reform," *American Political Science Review* 95 (June 2001): 315–30.

24. John Culver, "California Supreme Court Election: 'Rose Bird and the Supremes,'" *Comparative State Politics Newsletter* (February 1987), 13.

25. Steven D. Williams, "The 1996 Retention Election of Justice White," *Comparative State Politics* 17 (October 1996): 28–30.

26. John Paul Ryan et al., *American Trial Judges* (New York: Free Press, 1980), 125–30.

27. Philip L. Dubois, *From Ballot to Bench: Judicial Elections and the Quest for Accountability* (Austin: University of Texas Press, 1980), ch. 4.

28. Hall, 319.

29. Kathleen A. Bratton and Rorie L. Spill, "Existing Diversity and Judicial Selection: The Role of the Appointment Method in Establishing Gender Diversity in State Supreme Courts," *Social Science Quarterly* 83 (June 2002): 508–18; Kathleen A. Bratton and Rorie L. Spill, "Existing Diversity and Judicial Selection: The Role of the Appointment Method in Establishing Gender Diversity in State Supreme Courts," *Social Science Quarterly* 83 (June 2002): 504–18.

30. Melinda Gann Hall, "Electoral Politics and Strategic Voting in State Supreme Courts," *Journal of Politics* 54 (1992): 427–46; Melinda Gann Hall, "Toward an Integrated Model of Judicial Voting Behavior," *American Politics Quarterly* 20 (1992): 147–68.

31. James P. Wenzel, Shaun Bowler, and David J. Lanoue, "Legislating from the State Bench: A Comparative Analysis of Judicial Activism," *American Politics Quarterly* 25 (July 1997): 363–79.

32. Chris W. Bonneau, "The Effects of Campaign Spending in State Supreme Court Elections," *Political Research Quarterly* 60 (September 2007): 489–99.

33. "New Questions About Rhode Island Chief Justice," *New York Times* (October 3, 1993), sec. 1, 22; "Ex-Top Judge Ends Rhode Island Appeal with a Guilty Plea," *New York Times* (April 30, 1994), sec. 1, 12; "Justice in Impeachment Inquiry Quits in Rhode Island," *New York Times* (May 29, 1986), A14.

34. Glick and Vines, *State Court Systems*, 78; Kenyon D. Bunch and Gregory Casey, "Political Controversy on Missouri's Supreme Court: The Case of Merit versus Politics," *State and Local Government Review* 22 (Winter 1990): 5–16.

35. Walter V. Schaefer, "Precedent and Policy: Judicial Opinions and Decision Making," in David M. O'Brien, ed., *Judges on Judging: Views from the Bench* (Washington, D.C.: CQ Press, 2004), 108.

36. Hall, "Electoral Politics and Strategic Voting."

37. Melinda Gann Hall, "Justices as Representatives: Elections and Judicial Politics in the American States," *American Politics Quarterly* 23 (October 1995).

38. Gregory A. Caldeira, "The Transmission of Legal Precedent: A Study of State Supreme Courts," *American Political Science Review* 79 (March 1985): 178–93.

39. Gregory A. Caldeira, "Legal Precedent: Structures of Communication Between State Supreme Courts," *Social Network* 10 (1988): 29–55.

40. Stephen Demuth and Darrell Steffensmeier, "Ethnicity Effects on Sentence Outcomes in Large Urban Courts: Comparisons Among White, Black, and Hispanic Defendants," *Social Science Quarterly* 85 (December 2004): 994–1011.

41. S. Fernando Rodriguez, Theodore R. Curry, and Gand Lee, "Gender Differences in Criminal sentencing: Do Effects Vary Across Violent, Property, and Drug Offenses?, *Social Science Quarterly* 87 (June 2006): 318–39.

42. Melinda Gann Hall and Paul Brace, "Justices' Responses to Case Facts: An Interactive Model," *American Politics Quarterly* 24 (April 1996); Donald R. Songer and Kelley A. Crews-Meyer, "Does Judge Gender Matter? Decision Making in State Supreme Courts," *Social Science Quarterly* 81 (September 2000): 750–62.

43. Darrell Steffensmeier and Charles A. Britt, "Judges' Race and Judicial Decision Making: Do Black Judges Sentence Differently?" *Social Science Quarterly* 82 (December 2001): 749–64.

44. Richard C. Kearney and Reginald Sheehan, "Supreme Court Decision Making: The Impact of Court Composition on State and Local Government Litigation," *Journal of Politics* 54 (November 1992): 1008–25.

45. Canon, "Defining the Dimensions," 238–39.

46. As quoted in Stanley M. Mosk, "The Emerging Agenda in State Constitutional Law," *Intergovernmental Perspective* 13 (Spring 1987): 21.

47. Laura Langer and Paul Brace, "The Preemptive Power of State Supreme Courts: Adoption of Abortion and Death Penalty Legislation," *Policy Studies Journal* 33 (2005): 317–39.

48. Brenda Goodman, "Georgia Murder Case's Cost Saps Public Defense System, *The New York Times* (March 22, 2007) accessed at www.nyt.com March 22, 2007.

49. George F. Cole, "Performance Measures for the Trial Courts, Prosecution, and Public Defense," in U.S. Department of Justice, *Performance Measures for the Criminal Justice System* (October 1993), 87–108.

50. Council of State Governments, *The Book of the States*, vol. 39 (Lexington, Ky.: Council of State Governments, 2007), 260.

CHAPTER 10 STATE–LOCAL RELATIONS
PP. 223–242

1. Will Wilson, "DNA Databases Raise Alarms," *Governing* 20 (June 2007): 80.

2. Steven D. Gold, "NCSL State-Local Task Force: The First Year," *Intergovernmental Perspective* 13 (Winter 1987): 11.

3. *Merriam* v. *Moody's Executors*, 25 Iowa 163, 170 (1868). Dillon's rule was first written in the case of *City of Clinton* v. *Cedar Rapids and Missouri Railroad Co.* (1868).

4. Jeffrey I. Chapman, "Local Government Autonomy and Fiscal Stress: The Case of California Counties," *State and Local Government Review* 35 (Winter 2003): 15–25.

5. U.S. Advisory Commission on Intergovernmental Relations, *The Organization of Local Public Economies* (Washington, D.C.: ACIR, December 1987), 54.

6. Peter J. May, "Policy Design and Discretion: State Oversight of Local Building Regulation," paper presented at the annual meeting of the American Political Science Association, San Francisco, 1996.

7. David R. Berman and Lawrence L. Martin, "State-Local Relations: An Examination of Local Discretion," *Public Administration Review* 48 (March/April 1988): 637–41.

8. Dale Krane, Platon N. Rigos, and Melvin B. Hill, Jr., *Home Rule in America: A Fifty State Handbook* (Washington, D.C.: Congressional Quarterly Press, 2001).

9. As quoted in Laura Vozzella and David Nitkin, "City Rejects State Plan, Offers Own School Loan," *Baltimore Sun* (March 9, 2004), 1.

10. "New State Law Bans City Minimum Wage," *Tampa Tribune*, www.tampatrib.com/floridametronews (June 5, 2003).

11. Alan Ehrenhalt, "Devolution's Double Standard," *Governing* 16 (April 2003): 6.

12. Alicia Caldwell, "High Court Pulls Reins on Eminent Domain," *Denver Post*, www.denverpost.com/cda/article (March 2, 2004).

13. Christopher Swope, "States Go for the Biotech Gold," *Governing* 17 (March 2004): 46.

14. David K. Hamilton, David Y. Miller, and Jerry Paytas, "Exploring Horizontal and Vertical Dimensions of the Governing of Metropolitan Regions," *Urban Affairs Review* 40 (November 2004): 147–182.

15. David Kocieniewski and Eric Lipton, "Two States Get High Marks for Five-Day Antiterrorism Exercise," *New York Times*, www.nytimes.com (April 9, 2005).

16. Renu Khator, "Coping with Coercion: Florida Counties and the State's Recycling Law," *State and Local Government Review* 26 (Fall 1994): 181–91.

17. Lawrence J. Grossback, "The Problem of State-Imposed Mandates: Lessons from Minnesota's Local Governments," *State and Local Government Review* 34 (Fall 2002): 183–97.

18. Ibid., 191.

19. Andree E. Reeves, "State ACIRs: Elements of Success," *Intergovernmental Perspective* 17 (Summer 1991): 13.

20. "Indiana Advisory Commission on Intergovernmental Relations," http://iacir.spea.iupui.edu/ (November 12, 2007).

21. Bruce Katz, "Smart Growth: The Future of the American Metropolis?" (Washington, D.C.: Brookings Institution, 2002), 2.

22. William Fulton and Paul Shigley, "Operation Desert Sprawl," *Governing* 12 (August 1999): 16.

23. Ibid., 17.

24. Joseph Giordono, "California Sprawl Spawns Competing Ballot Initiatives," www.stateline.org (May 16, 2004).

25. "Voters Approve Record Amount for Land Conservation," www.tpl.org (October 1, 2007).

26. Daniel B. Wood, "Californians Raise Roof Over New Housing," *Christian Science Monitor* (June 17, 2003), 1, 4.

27. Jayson T. Blair, "Maryland Draws Line Against Sprawl," *Boston Globe* (December 7, 1997), A26.

28. Christopher Swope, "McGreevey's Magic Map," *Governing* 16 (May 2003): 45–48.

29. Iver Peterson, "War on Sprawl in New Jersey Hits a Wall," *New York Times* (October 21, 2003), A15.

30. Christopher R. Conte, "The Boys of Sprawl," *Governing* 13 (May 2000): 28–33; Peter Gordon and Harry W. Richardson, "The Sprawl Debate: Let Markets Plan," *Publius: The Journal of Federalism* 31 (Summer 2001): 131–49.

31. Alan Ehrenhalt, "Breaking the Density Deadlock," *Governing* 20 (March 2007): 11-12.

32. Jered B.Carr and Richard C. Feiock, "Who Becomes Involved in City-County Consolidation?" *State and Local Government Review* 34 (Spring 2002): 78–94.

33. Robert J. McCarthy, "New Unified Government to Be Proposed," *Buffalo News* (February 11, 2004), 1.

34. H.V. Savitch and Ronald K. Vogel, "Suburbs Without a City: Power and City-County Consolidation," *Urban Affairs Review* 39 (July 2004): 758–90.

35. Alan Greenblatt, "Anatomy of a Merger," *Governing* 16 (December 2002): 20–25.

36. Ronald J. Oakerson, *Governing Local Political Economies: Creating the Civic Metropolis* (Oakland, Calif.: Institute for Contemporary Studies, 1999).

37. David Rusk, *Cities Without Suburbs* (Washington, D.C.: Woodrow Wilson Center Press, 1993), 5.

38. Daniel Kemmis, as quoted in Neal R. Peirce, "Missoula's 'Citistate' Claim Marks a New Way to Define Regions," *The News & Observer* (July 1, 1993), 14A.

39. Randolph P. Smith, "Region Idea Works, Oregon City Says," *Richmond Times-Dispatch* (October 30, 1994), Al, A18.

40. Myron Orfield, *American Metropolitics: The New Suburban Reality* (Washington, D.C.: Brookings, 2002).

41. Margaret Weir, Harold Wolman, and Todd Swanstrom, "The Calculus of Coalitions: Cities, Suburbs, and the Metropolitan Agenda," *Urban Affairs Review* 40 (July 2005): 730–60. See also Annette Steinacker, "Metropolitan Governance: Voter Support and State Legislative Prospects," *Publius: The Journal of Federalism* (Spring 2004): 69–93.

42. James F. Wolf and Margaret Fenwick, "How Metropolitan Planning Organizations Incorporate Land Use Issues in Regional Transportation Planning," *State and Local Government Review* 35 (Spring 2003): 123–31.

43. DeWitt John, as cited in William K. Stevens, "Struggle for Recovery Altering Rural America," *New York Times* (February 5, 1988), 8.

44. Jim Seroka, "Community Growth and Administrative Capacity," *National Civic Review* 77 (Jan/Feb. 1988) 45.

45. John Ritter, "Towns Offer Free Land to Newcomers," *USA Today* (February 9, 2005), 1A, 2A.

46. Jason Henderson, quoted in ibid., 2A.

47. Patrik Jonsson, "North Carolina's Gambit to Bring Internet Age to Rural Areas," *Christian Science Monitor* (July 1, 2004): 2–3.

48. Beryl A. Radin et al., *New Governance for Rural America* (Lawrence: University Press of Kansas, 1996).

49. Arthur Holst, "Review of Local Government and the States: Autonomy, Politics, and Policy," *Publius: The Journal of Federalism* 35 (Fall 2005): 644–45.

50. Christopher Conte, "Dry Spell," *Governing* 16 (March 2003): 20–24.

51. George Pataki, "Governor Pataki Offers $1 Billion Plan to Help Local Governments," Press Release, January 10, 1997.

52. Patrick McGreevy, "Cities, Counties Pay Price for Capital Clout," *Los Angeles Times,* www.latimes.com/news/local (September 12, 2007).

CHAPTER 11 LOCAL GOVERNMENT: STRUCTURE AND LEADERSHIP PP. 243–268

1. Jim Schutze, quoted in Rob Gurwitt, "Can Dallas Govern Itself?" *Governing* 19 (August 2006): 42.

2. *2002 Census of Governments,* vol. 1, *Government Organization* (Washington, D.C.: U.S. Census Bureau, 2005).

3. Council for Excellence in Government 2000, www.excelgov.org (July 9, 2003).

4. Victor S. DeSantis and Tari Renner, "Governing the County: Authority, Structure, and Elections," in David R. Berman, ed., *County Governments in an Era of Change* (Westport, Conn.: Greenwood, 1993), 15–28.

5. J. Edwin Benton and Donald C. Menzel, "County Services: The Emergence of Full-Service Government," in Berman, ed., *County Governments in an Era of Change,* 53–69.

6. Christopher Hoene, Mark Baldassare, and Michael Shires, "The Development of Counties as Municipal Governments," *Urban Affairs Review* 37 (March 2002): 575–91.

7. Dale Krane, Platon N. Rigos, and Melvin B. Hill, Jr., *Home Rule in America: A Fifty State Handbook* (Washington, D.C.: Congressional Quarterly Press, 2001).

8. Alan Greenblatt, "New Clout in a Big County," *Governing* 20 (May 2007): 22–23.

9. J. Edwin Benton, "The Impact of Structural Reform on County Government Service Provision," *Social Science Quarterly* 84 (December 2003): 858–74.

10. Ellen Perlman, "The Fiscal Fast Lane," *Governing* 18 (March 2005): 42–44.

11. "Counties Out of Date," *State Legislatures* 17 (March 1991): 17.

12. Jonathan Walters, "The Disappearing County," www.governing.com (July 5, 2000).

13. Jerome I. Sherman, "6 Elected Row Officers Become 3 Appointed," *Pittsburgh Post-Gazette*, www.post-gazette.com (May 18, 2005).

14. James H. Svara, *Official Leadership in the City* (New York: Oxford University Press, 1990).

15. David R. Morgan, Robert E. England, and John P. Pelissero, *Managing Urban America*, 6th ed. (Washington D.C.: Congressional Quarterly Press, 2007).

16. H. George Frederickson, Gary A. Johnson, and Curtis Wood, *The Adapted City: Institutional Dynamics and Structural Change* (Armonk, N.Y.: M.E. Sharpe, 2004).

17. Melissa Conradi, "But Definitely Not St. Ventura," *Governing* 14 (January 2001): 16.

18. Gary A. Mattson, "Municipal Services and Economic Policy Priorities Among Florida's Smaller Cities," *National Civic Review* 79 (September/October 1990): 436–45.

19. Kathryn A. Foster, *The Political Economy of Special Purpose Government* (Washington, D.C.: Georgetown University Press, 1997).

20. John C. Bollens, *Special District Governments in the United States* (Berkeley: University of California Press, 1957).

21. Barbara Coyle McCabe, "Special District Formation Among the States," *State and Local Government Review* 32 (Spring 2000): 121–31.

22. Michael A. Molloy, "Local Special Districts and Public Accountability," paper presented at the annual meeting of the Midwest Political Science Association, Chicago, 2000.

23. Nancy Burns, *The Formation of American Local Governments* (New York: Oxford University Press, 1994).

24. Foster, *The Political Economy of Special Purpose Government.*

25. Michael Finnegan and Mark Z. Barabak, "Villaraigosa Sweeps Past Hahn in Historic Victory," *Los Angeles Times*, www.latimes.com (May 18, 2005); "A Bigger, Bolder Mayor," *Los Angeles Times,* www.latimes.com (May 18, 2005).

26. Jameson W. Doig and Erwin C. Hargrove, eds., *Leadership and Innovation* (Baltimore: Johns Hopkins University Press, 1987).

27. Floyd Hunter, *Community Power Structure* (Chapel Hill: University of North Carolina Press, 1953); and *Community Power Succession* (Chapel Hill: University of North Carolina Press, 1980).

28. Robert Dahl, *Who Governs?* (New Haven, Conn.: Yale University Press, 1961).

29. Clarence N. Stone, *Regime Politics: Governing Atlanta, 1948–1988* (Lawrence: University Press of Kansas, 1989).

30. Tom Lassetter, "Rock Group Takes on Ga. Town's Political Network," *The State* (July 25, 1999), A15.

31. Rob Gurwitt, "The Lure of the Strong Mayor," *Governing* 6 (July 1993): 36-41; Terrell Blodgett, "Beware the Lure of the 'Strong' Mayor," *Public Management* 76 (January 1994): 6–11.

32. David R. Morgan and Sheilah S. Watson, "The Effects of Mayoral Power on Urban Fiscal Policy," paper presented at the annual meeting of the American Political Science Association, New York City, September 1994.

33. Thomas P. Ryan, Jr., as quoted in Jane Mobley, "Politician or Professional? The Debate Over Who Should Run Our Cities Continues," *Governing* 1 (February 1988): 42–48.

34. W. John Moore, "From Dreamers to Doers," *National Journal* (February 13, 1988): 372–77.

35. Cory Booker, "Fighting for Newark's Future," (audio) www.corybooker.com/main/cfm (July 5, 2006).

36. Huey L. Perry, "Deracialization as an Analytical Construct in American Urban Politics," *Urban Affairs Quarterly* 27 (December 1991): 181–91; Nicholas O. Alonzie, "The Promise of Urban Democracy: Big-City Black Mayoral Service in the Early 1990s," *Urban Affairs Review* 35 (January 2000): 422–34.

37. Mary E. Summers and Philip A. Klinkner, "The Daniels Election in New Haven and the Failure of the Deracialization Hypothesis," *Urban Affairs Quarterly* 27 (December 1991): 202–15.

38. Philip J. LaVelle, "S.D. Political Hounds Catch First Scent of Recall Bid," *San Diego Union-Tribune,* www.signonsandiego.com (January 4, 2005).

39. Several of these studies are summarized in Susan A. MacManus and Charles S. Bullock III, "Women and Racial/Ethnic Minorities in Mayoral and Council Positions," in International City/County Management Association, *The Municipal Year Book 1993* (Washington, D.C.: International City/County Management Association, 1993), 70–84.

40. Clifford J. Wirth and Michael L. Vasu, "Ideology and Decision Making for American City Managers," *Urban Affairs Quarterly* 22 (March 1987): 454–74.

41. Martin Vanacour, "Promoting the Community's Future," in Charldean Newell, ed., *The Effective Local Government Manager*, 3rd ed. (Washington, D.C.: International City/County Management Association, 2004), 84–85.

42. James H. Svara, "Conflict and Cooperation in Elected-Administrative Relations in Large Council-Manager Cities," *State and Local Government Review* 31 (Fall 1999): 173–89.

43. Larry Azevedo, as quoted in Alan Ehrenhalt, "How a Liberal Government Came to Power in a Conservative Suburb," *Governing* 1 (March 1988): 51–56.

44. Kenneth Prewitt, *The Recruitment of Political Leaders: A Study of Citizen-Politicians* (Indianapolis: Bobbs-Merrill, 1970).

45. MacManus and Bullock, "Women and Racial/Ethnic Minorities in Mayoral and Council Positions," 70–84; Joshua G. Behr, *Race, Ethnicity and the Politics of Redistricting* (Albany, N.Y.: SUNY Press, 2004).

46. Bari Anhalt, "Minority Representation and the Substantive Representation of Interests," paper presented at the annual meeting of the American Political Science Association, San Francisco, 1996.

47. Paula D. McClain and Steven C. Tauber, "Racial Minority Group Relations in a Multiracial Society," in Michael Jones-Correa, ed., *Governing American Cities: Immigrants and Inter-Ethnic Coalitions, Competition, and Conflict* (New York: Russell Sage Foundation, 2001).

48. Christian Collett, "Bloc Voting, Polarization, and the Panethnic Hypothesis: The Case of Little Saigon," *Political Research Quarterly* 67 (August 2005): 907–933.

49. James W. Button, Kenneth D. Wald, and Barbara A. Rienzo, "The Election of Openly Gay Public Officials in American Communities," *Urban Affairs Review* 35 (November 1999): 188–209.

50. James Svara, "Council Profile: More Diversity, Demands, Frustration," *Nation's Cities Weekly* 14 (November 18, 1991): 4.

51. James B. Kaatz, P. Edward French, and Hazel Prentiss-Cooper, "City Council Conflict as a Cause of Psychological Burnout and Voluntary Turnover Among City Managers," *State and Local Government Review* 31 (Fall 1999): 162–72.

52. Rob Gurwitt, "Are City Councils a Relic of the Past?" *Governing* 16 (April 2003): 20–24.

53. Alan Ehrenhalt, "Boldness Without Bluster," *Governing* 14 (December 2000): 8.

54. J.M. Ferris, "The Role of the Nonprofit Sector in a Self-Governing Society," *Voluntas* 9 (1998): 137–51.

55. Richard C. Hula and Cynthia Jackson-Elmoore, "Governing Nonprofits and Local Political Processes," *Urban Affairs Review* 36 (January 2001): 324–58.

56. National Civic League, "All-America City Awards Announced," www.ncl.org/aac/2007/(October 12, 2007).

57. Katherine Barrett and Richard Greene, "Grading the Cities," *Governing* 13 (February 2000): 22–91.

58. Josh Goodman, "Out of the Blue," *Governing* 20 (October 2007): 40.

59. Michael Bloomberg, as quoted in "Observer," *Governing* 19 (July 2006): 18.

CHAPTER 12 TAXING AND SPENDING PP. 269–300

1. Chris Christoff, "State Budget Talks to Resume at 1 p.m." *Detroit Free Press* (September 28, 2007); Chris Christoff, "Lawmakers Reach Budget Deal," *Detroit Free Press* (October 31, 2007).

2. Data obtained from U.S. Bureau of the Census (www.census.gov) and Governing's State and Local Sourcebook (http://sourcebook.governing.com/topicmain.jsp#19).

3. Ivan Sciupac, "Federal Estate Tax Repeal Would Affect States," www.stateline.org (March 16, 2001).

4. U.S Bureau of the Census, October 2007, www.census.gov.

5. Robert Tannenwald and Jonathan Cowan, "Fiscal Capacity, Fiscal Need, and Fiscal Comfort Among U.S. States: New Evidence," *Publius: The Journal of Federalism* 27 (Summer 1997): 113–25.

6. Mark Schneider, "Local Budgets and the Maximization of Local Property Wealth in the System of Suburban Government," *Journal of Politics* 49 (November 1987): 1114.

7. Thomas R. Dye and Richard C. Feiock, "State Income Tax Adoption and Economic Growth," *Social Science Quarterly* 76 (September 1995): 648–54.

8. *The Book of the States,* vol. 36 (Lexington, KY: Council of State Governments, 2004): 339.

9. Neal R. Peirce, "Service Tax May Rise Again," *Public Administration Times* 11 (August 12, 1988): 2.

10. *Quill v. North Dakota*, 504 U.S. 298 (1992).

11. Powell, "Internet Taxation and U.S. Intergovernmental Relations,"

12. Declan McCullough and Anne Broache, "Days Numbered for Tax-free Net Sales," CNET News.com (May 14, 2007).

13. www.taxfoundation.org/sri30.pdf (January 12, 2005).

14. www.taxfoundation.org (April 8, 2005).

15. Council of State Governments, 2004: 345–349.

16. www.apfc.org/Alaska/dividendprgrm.cfm (September 30, 2007).

17. John L. Mikesell, "Lotteries in State Revenue Systems: Gauging a Popular Revenue Source After 35 Years," *State and Local Government Review* 33 (Spring 2001): 86–100.

18. Ibid.; see also Donald E. Miller and Patrick A. Pierce, "Lotteries for Education: Windfall or Hoax?" *State and Local Government Review* 29 (Winter 1997): 43–52.

19. Elizabeth A. Freund and Irwin L. Morris, "The Lottery and Income Inequality in the States," *Social Science Quarterly* 86 (2005): 996–1012.

20. Patrick A. Pierce and Donald E. Miller, *Gambling Politics* (Washington, D.C.: Congressional Quarterly Press, 2004).

21. Timothy Egan, "They Give but They Also Take: Voters Muddle States' Finance," *New York Times* (March 2, 2001), 1, 4.

22. Mark A. Glaser and W. Bartley Hildreth, "A Profile of Discontinuity Between Citizen Demand and Willingness to Pay Taxes: Comprehensive Planning for Park and Recreation Investment," *Public Budgeting and Finance* 16 (Winter 1996): 97.

23. Daniel R. Mullins and Bruce A. Wallin, "Tax and Expenditure Limitations: Introduction and Overview," *Public Budgeting and Finance* 24 (Winter 2004): 2–15.

24. James C. Clingermayer and B. Dan Wood, "Disentangling Patterns of State Debt Financing," *American Political Science Review* 89 (March 1995): 108–20; Daniel E. O'Toole and Brian Stipak, "Coping with State Tax and Expenditure Limitation: The Oregon Experience," State and Local Government Review 30 (Winter 1998): 9–16.

25. Alan Greenblatt, "Paradise Insolvement," *Governing* (November 2005): 41–46.

26. Alan Sokolow, "The Changing Property Tax and State–Local Relations," *Publius: The Journal of Federalism* 28 (Winter 1998): 165–87.

27. Rob Gurwitt, "The Job of Rudy Giuliani," *Governing* 8 (June 1995): 23–27.

28. "Losing Control," *New York Times* (November 13, 2001), 1–2.

29. Katherine Barrett and Richard Greene, "The $3 trillion Challenge," *Governing* (October 2007): 28.

30. David Brunori, *State Tax Policy: A Political Perspective* (Washington, D.C.: The Urban Institute, 2001).

31. Christopher G. Reddick, "Assessing Local Government Revenue Forecasting Techniques," *International Journal of Public Administration* 27 nos. 8 and 9 (2004): 597–615.

32. Ibid.

33. John E. Petersen, "Don't Forget Your Umbrella," Governing 11 (October 1998): 70.

34. Sallie Hofmeister, "Fund Head Resigns in California" and "Many Questions, But Too Late," *New York Times* (December 6, 1994), D1, D2.

35. Richard Florida, *The Rise of the Creative Class* (New York: Basic Books, 2002).

36. Matthew J. Burbank, Charles H. Heying, and Greg Andranovich, "Antigrowth Politics or Piecemeal Resistance? *Urban Affairs Review* 35 (January 2000): 334–57.

INDEX